Machine Translation: A View from the Lexicon

Machine Translation: A View from the Lexicon

Bonnie Jean Dorr

The MIT Press
Cambridge, Massachusetts
London, England

This book was typeset with Donald E. Knuth's TeX and Leslie Lamport's LaTeX and printed and bound in the United States of America.

Library of Congress Cataloging-in-Publication Data

Dorr, Bonnie Jean.
  Machine translation : a view from the lexicon / Bonnie Jean Dorr.
      p.   cm. — (Artificial intelligence)
  Includes bibliographical references and index.
  ISBN 0-262-04138-3
  1. Machine translating.   2. Lexicology—Data processing.   3. Spanish language—Translating   into   English.   I. Title.   II. Series: Artificial intelligence (Cambridge, Mass.)
P308.D67 1993
418'.02'0285—dc20   92-35158
                                                                CIP

For Bruce and Carissa.

Contents

II LEXICAL-SEMANTIC COMPONENT

III APPLICATION OF THE MODEL

Series Foreword

Artificial intelligence is the study of intelligence using the ideas and methods of computation. Unfortunately a definition of intelligence seems impossible at the moment because intelligence appears to be an amalgam of so many information-processing and information-representation abilities.

Of course psychology, philosophy, linguistics, and related disciplines offer various perspectives and methodologies for studying intelligence. For the most part, however, the theories proposed in these fields are too incomplete and too vaguely stated to be realized in computational terms. Something more is needed, even though valuable ideas, relationships, and constraints can be gleaned from traditional studies of what are, after all, impressive existence proofs that intelligence is in fact possible.

Artificial intelligence offers a new perspective and a new methodology. Its central goal is to make computers intelligent, both to make them more useful and to understand the principles that make intelligence possible. That intelligent computers will be extremely useful is obvious. The more profound point is that artificial intelligence aims to understand intelligence using the ideas and methods of computation, thus offering a radically new and different basis for theory formation. Most of the people doing work in artificial intelligence believe that these theories will apply to any intelligent information processor, whether biological or solid state.

There are side effects that deserve attention, too. Any program that will successfully model even a small part of intelligence will be inherently massive and complex. Consequently artificial intelligence continually confronts the limits of computer-science technology. The problems encountered have been hard enough and interesting enough to seduce artificial intelligence people into working on them with enthusiasm. It is natural, then, that there has been a steady flow of ideas from artificial intelligence to computer science, and the flow shows no signs of abating.

The purpose of this series in artificial intelligence is to provide people in many areas, both professionals and students, with timely, detailed information about what is happening on the frontiers in research centers all over the world.

J. Michael Brady
Daniel G. Bobrow
Randall Davis

Preface

Machine translation has been a particularly difficult problem in the area of natural language processing for over four decades. Early approaches to translation failed in part because interaction effects of complex phenomena made translation appear to be unmanageable. Later approaches to the problem have achieved varying degrees of success. (See Hutchins (1986), King (1987), Maxwell *et al.* (1988), Nirenburg (1987), Nirenburg *et al.* (1992), Slocum (1988), and Hutchins and Somers (1992) for cogent reviews of this area.) This book describes an alternative approach to machine translation that provides a general solution to the specific subproblem of cross-linguistic distinctions (or *divergences*). The approach has been implemented in an interlingual system called UNI-TRAN that translates English, Spanish, and German on the basis of a lexical-semantic representation.[1]

The primary objective of this book is to demonstrate the validity of the theoretical underpinnings of the system by showing that the interlingual representation lends itself readily to a solution to cross-linguistic divergences without recourse to language-specific rules. In particular, this study aims to demonstrate that a lexical-semantic framework provides the basis for a systematic mapping between the interlingua and the syntactic structure. The approach supports the view that each lexical-semantic divergence may be classified into one of a small number of types (approximately seven). (This classification excludes distinctions that are characterized by properties pertaining to knowledge outside of lexical-semantics *e.g.*, properties associated with entries in the lexicon that are not based on purely syntactic information, idiomatic usage, aspectual knowledge, discourse knowledge, domain knowledge, or world knowledge.) Because lexical-semantic divergences are so carefully delimited into this manageable (*i.e.*, small) classification, one need only specify a single translation mapping that is parameterized by means of lexical switches, each corresponding to a different divergence type.

The interlingual representation adopted is an extended version of *lexical conceptual structure* (see Jackendoff (1983, 1990), Hale and Keyser (1986a,b, 1989), and Hale and Laughren (1983)), which is suitable to the task of translating between divergent structures for two reasons: (1) it provides an *abstraction* of language-independent properties from

---

[1]The name UNITRAN stands for UNIversal TRANslator, that is, the system serves as the basis for translation across a variety of languages, not just two languages or a family of languages.

structural idiosyncrasies; and (2) it is *compositional* in nature. The lexical-semantic approach addresses the divergence problem by using a linguistically grounded mapping that has access to parameter settings in the lexicon. A key result of the current investigation is that it has demonstrated that translation divergences have formal correlates that fall out from the lexical conceptual structure.

The contributions of the present study are twofold. In the area of linguistics, this study has defined the notion of divergence, classified a small set of cross-linguistic variations relevant to translation using this notion, provided a systematic solution to the divergence problem by means of parameterization, and implemented this solution in a model that serves as a testbed for linguistic theories of syntax and lexical-semantics. In the area of computer science and artificial intelligence, this study has produced a new processing design in which the parser and generator operate in tandem with linguistic constraints, applied constraint-based techniques to the problem of analyzing and synthesizing of language, designed automatic grammar construction techniques to simplify the extension of the system to new languages, formalized the operations required for translation, provided an extensible and portable design through the use of parameterization, and eliminated the need for detailed transfer rules through the use of an interlingual design.

More specifically, the main contributions of the present study are the following:

- The development of a uniform processor that uses the same syntactic and lexical-semantic processing modules for each language.

- The use of a single underlying language-independent form (the interlingua) that accommodates all three languages: English, Spanish, or German.

- The use of a single, systematic translation mapping that relates the lexical-semantic structure to the syntactic structure for all three languages.

- The classification of syntactic divergences into linguistically motivated categories that are handled uniformly through syntactic parameterization.

- The classification of lexical-semantic divergences into a small number of categories that are accommodated uniformly by a single, parameterized translation mapping. Surprisingly, many seemingly distinct lexical-semantic phenomena fall into one of seven divergence categories.

- The formalization of the notion of divergence and the translation mapping that solves the divergence problem. This contribution is important because it provides the basis for proving that the seven divergence categories are all that are needed to handle a wide range of lexical-semantic phenomena.

- The use of compositionality to derive the interlingua in such a way as to accommodate the effects of several (recursively) interacting divergence types.

Chapter 1 provides the motivation behind the framework including a description of the architectural design of the system, an introduction to the notion of parameterization, a discussion about the divergence problem, a comparison to alternative approaches, and a brief description of the basis for the interlingual representation. Following the introduction, the book is organized into three parts.

Part I begins with a description of the syntactic component of the system. Chapter 2 describes the syntactic processor that is parameterized in such a way as to account for syntactic divergence types cross-linguistically. The design of this processor is described and the solution to syntactic divergences is illustrated by means of detailed examples. Chapter 3 describes the morphological processor that is based on a two-level scheme by Kimmo Koskenniemi (see Kartunnen and Wittenburg (1983, pp. 163–278)). Although the morphological processor is not a central focus of this study, it has nonetheless been included here for two reasons: (1) important extensions have been made that allow it to be more uniformly applicable than the original Kimmo specification thus lending itself to a cross-linguistic model of translation; and (2) the output forms of the morphological component (*i.e.*, the root forms and feature values) are used later by the syntactic and lexical-semantic components thus making morphology a critical part of the overall processing design. Part I is fairly self-contained, but is included for completeness. Those readers who are not familiar with Government and Binding theory or two-level morphological processing may want to skip to part II.

Part II concerns the lexical-semantic component of the system. Just as the syntactic component is parameterized to accommodate syntactic divergences, this section describes how parameterization of the lexicon accommodates lexical-semantic divergences. A number of relevant issues will be examined. Chapter 4 discusses the problem of defining primitives, issues of interlinguality, cross-linguistic coverage of the system, the structure of the interlingua, the organization of the lexicon, and extensions to the framework proposed by Jackendoff. In addition, this chapter informally defines the mapping between the syntactic structure and the interlingua and shows how the syntactic operation of thematic role assignment relates to the lexical-semantic operation that constructs the interlingual representation. Chapter 5 examines the resolution of lexical-semantic divergences through parameterization of the interlingua and focuses on refining the systematic mapping between the interlingua and the syntactic representation. Chapter 6 describes the inverse of the process described in chapter 4, *i.e.*, it describes the process of generation from the interlingual representation and discusses such issues as lexical selection and syntactic realization. Finally, chapter 7 provides a more formal presentation of the divergence problem and the mechanisms required for the solution. In so doing, this chapter formally carries out the task of demonstrating the systematicity of the translation mapping and provides justification for the claim that translations divergences are delimited in such a way that only a handful of parameters are required for the solution to the divergence problem.

Part III discusses the application of the model described in the preceding chapters. Chapter 8 provides actual examples of translation, discusses the coverage of the system, and outlines some of the limitations of the system, especially with respect to the use of the system on a complicated (free-text) example. Chapter 9 presents a description of current research on the extension of the model to include aspectual information and also proposes a model of lexical acquisition that makes use of featural information that relates lexical conceptual structure to aspectual information. Finally, chapter 10 discusses the conclusions, limitations, and future work.

Acknowledgments

This book represents a major revision of my 1990 doctoral dissertation, *Lexical Conceptual Structure and Machine Translation*. However, the structure of this revised version does not follow that of the original document, and much of the content has been replaced with more recent findings and additional detailed analyses. Abbreviated versions of parts of this work have appeared in *Machine Translation* and *Artificial Intelligence* and in proceedings of conferences and meetings such as *Conference of the Association for Computational Linguistics*, *Conference of the American Association of Artificial Intelligence*, *Conference of the Cognitive Science Society*, *MIT Cognitive Science Parsing Seminar*, *International Joint Conference of Artificial Intelligence Workshop on Lexical Acquisition*, *International Conference on Theoretical and Methodological Issues in Machine Translation of Natural Languages*, *Association for Computational Linguistics Workshop on Lexical Semantics and Knowledge Representation*, *IRIT Seminar on Computational Lexical Semantics*, *International Conference on Computational Linguistics*, and *AAAI Symposium Series* as well as in edited volumes by Winston and Shellard (1990), Berwick *et al.* (1991), Zernik (1991), Pustejovsky and Bergler (1992), and Saint-Dizier and Viegas (1993). (For complete references, see Dorr (1987a–1987c, 1988, 1989, 1990a–1990d, 1991a–1991c, 1992a–1992e, 1993a–1993b).)

The research reported here never would have been realized without the aid of Bob Berwick, my thesis advisor, who offered infinite support, introduced me to a new perspective on Natural Language Processing, and guided me with enthusiasm and encouragement.

A special thanks goes to those who thoroughly reviewed, and offered comments on, preliminary versions of this work: Bruce Dawson, Joel Hoffman, Paola Merlo, Patrick Saint-Dizier, Clare Voss, and Amy Weinberg. I am forever in their debt for helping to shape my ideas on the relevant issues and to organize my thoughts into a more coherent and comprehensible presentation. All errors are, of course, the fault of the author, not theirs.

Many people have contributed to this effort, in one form or another, perhaps without even realizing it. I would like to take this opportunity to thank the following people: Irma Amenero, Peter Andreae, Ed Barton, Sam Bayer, Scott Bennett, Jack Benoit, Bob Berwick, David Braunegg, Michael Brent, Dan Brotsky, John Burger, Vilma Cabrera, Jaime Carbonell, Noam Chomsky, Gary Coen, Nelson Correa, Larry

Davis, Bruce Dawson, Sue Felshin, Klaudia Dussa-Zieger, Terry Gaaster-
land, Eric Grimson, Ken Hale, Joachim Heel, Uli Heid, Jim Hendler,
Graeme Hirst, Joel Hoffman, Saadia Husain, Bill Idsardi, Ray Jackend-
off, Paul Jacobs, Pam Jordan, Mike Kashket, Mark Kantrowitz, Boris
Katz, Jay Keyser, Gudrun Klinker, Ki Lee, Wendy Lehnert, Beth Levin,
Jeremy Lindop, Jorge Lobo, Tomás Lozano-Pérez, Carl de Marcken,
Paola Merlo, Jack Minker, Sathya Narayanan, Sergei Nirenburg, James
Pustejovsky, Louiqa Raschid, Jim Reggia, Eric Ristad, Jose Luis Robles,
Christian Rohrer, Lukas Rücker, Tom Russ, Patrick Saint-Dizier, Mar-
wan Shaban, Jeffrey Siskind, Noyuri Soderland, Stephen Soderland, Ed
Stabler, Brian Subirana, Tanveer Syeda, Mark Villain, Clare Voss, Amy
Weinberg, Yorick Wilks, Linda Wills, Patrick Winston, George Yaeger,
and Uri Zernik. I would also like to thank all of the anonymous reviewers
who so carefully reviewed articles written about various pieces of this
research. Terry Ehling also deserves a thank you for putting up with
my numerous requests for extensions along the way, and for seeing the
book through to production.

I would like to thank my family members for their love and support:
Florence Dawson, Vernon Dawson, Dick Dorr, Jo Dorr, Sandy Dorr,
and Tina Dorr. And also to the Clifton and Kasulis families. This book
carries with it the memory of four family members, all of whom left us
in one difficult year, 1990: Charlie Dorr, Jeffrey Gates, Margaret Hugo,
and Ernestine Nimtz; and also of Faustina Hall, who left us in 1988.

A special thanks goes to Bruce for putting up with me during the two
years it took me to complete this document, as well as for seeing me
through the preceding years of graduate study that formed the foundation for the research reported herein. And a doubly special thanks to
Carissa for providing her company during the typing of my dissertation
prior to her 0th birthday, and for keeping me energized subsequently, so
that I was finally able to tie together all of the assorted pieces into this
one single document.

Support for this research has been provided in part by NSF Grant
DCR-85552543 at MIT and by NSF Grant IRI-9120788 at the University
of Maryland. The resources for pulling the pieces of this text and figures
together were provided by the Institute for Advanced Computer Studies
at the University of Maryland.

Machine Translation: A View from the Lexicon

1 Introduction

The task of designing a machine translation system is difficult because, in order to achieve a desirable degree of accuracy, such a system must capture *language-independent* information while still systematically processing many types of *language-specific* phenomena in each of the individual languages. For example, it is conceivable that a system would translate a Spanish sentence incorrectly on the basis of knowledge that would successfully translate English sentences. Consider the following Spanish sentence:

(1) Qué golpeó Juan
     'What hit John'
     (What did John hit)

If the translator were to use its knowledge of English syntax in this example, it would understand the meaning of (1) to be *what hit John* (*i.e.*, the *agent* and *patient* roles would be reversed). Thus, the translator critically relies on language-specific knowledge (*e.g.*, the linear ordering permitted by the language), but it also must know about certain language-independent information (*e.g.*, the roles that are introduced by the *hit* action) so that it can assign the appropriate interpretation regardless of how the particular languages structurally realize the sentence.

One could argue that word order is not an issue in (1) but rather that, in Spanish, the erroneous interpretation (*i.e.*, *what hit John*) is not obtainable because such an interpretation would require the insertion of the preposition *a*:

(2) Qué golpeó a Juan
     'What hit (to) John'
     (What hit John)

The insertion of the word *a* is a lexical requirement (with syntactic ramifications) for animate objects in Spanish. However, this lexical requirement does not hold in other languages with similar word order (*e.g.*, Italian). Moreover, it is still possible to demonstrate that word order is an independent factor that distinguishes Spanish from English in such cases. Consider a Spanish double-object construction:

(3) Qué dio Juan a María
     'What gave John to Mary'
     (What did John give to Mary)

This example illustrates that, in the Spanish interrogative form, the main verb precedes its subject whereas, in the English interrogative form, the main verb follows its subject. Note that it is not possible to construct a double-object case analogous to (2) in which the *a* is inserted:

(4)   * Qué dio a Juan a María
        'What gave (to) John to Mary'
        (What gave John to Mary)

In this example, the Spanish sentence is syntactically ill-formed and, at best, semantically odd. Thus, two types of language-specific knowledge required by the system are selectional restrictions for individual lexical items (*e.g.*, that *golpear* forces animate objects to be preceded by *a*) and word order (*e.g.*, that Spanish forces the main verb to precede the subject in interrogative sentences).

Given that both language-independent and language-specific knowledge are required to fulfill the translation task, one approach to machine translation is to assume that it is possible to convert the surface sentence into an internal representation (*i.e.*, an *interlingua*) that is common to more than one language. Distinctions across languages would then be captured by means of a parameterized mapping between this form and the syntactic structure. The interlingua would encode language-independent information (*e.g.*, that *María* is the recipient of the "giving" action in sentence (3)) while the parameterized mapping would account for language-specific idiosyncrasies (*e.g.*, that the recipient must be realized as the object of the preposition *a*).

This is the approach adopted in UNITRAN. The primary features that make this approach interlingual are that it relies on a language-independent underlying form and also that it makes use of a single, parameterized mapping between this representation and the syntactic structure for all three languages. The underlying form that is used in UNITRAN is based on *lexical conceptual structure* (henceforth, LCS) (see Jackendoff (1983, 1990)). Parameterization of the translation mapping is achieved at two different processing levels, syntactic and lexical-semantic; the former concerns the shape of the surface form and the latter concerns the properties of lexical items.

Within this framework, universal principles are parameterized so that they capture language-specific information. For example, there is a universal principle that requires each event to have a conceptual subject. Whether or not this conceptual subject is syntactically realized is a language-specific consideration that determines the setting of a parameter of variation associated with this principle: the *null subject* parameter. This parameter is set to *yes* for Spanish (also, Italian, Hebrew, *etc.*) but *no* for English and German (also French, Warlpiri, *etc.*). The setting of the null subject parameter allows the system to handle missing subjects in Spanish while still disallowing missing subjects in English and German (except for the imperative form).

It should be emphasized here that it is not the intent of the present study to give a definitive explanation for why Spanish or other languages are the way they are (*e.g.*, why some languages allow missing subjects and others do not), but rather to describe how the current translation system uses the linguistically-motivated notion of *parameter* to account for cross-linguistic distinctions in a principled, systematic fashion. While this study discusses the effects that can be achieved by setting parameters one way or another, it does not address the issue of whether such parameters are a part of the human language processor — an issue which is entirely outside of the scope of this endeavor (but see, *e.g.*, Borer and Wexler (1987), Hyams (1987), Wexler and Manzini (1987), Roeper and Weissenborn (1990), and Fodor (1990)). Nonetheless, the approach adopted here is consistent with the framework of those who do address the issue, most notably Williams (1987, p. viii):

(5)   "The parameterized model has no rule writing system. Rather, the rules of grammar (or the 'principles,' as it is now fashionable to call universal rules) are specified as a part of the innate. The rules, however, are slightly 'under-specified' — that is, certain 'parameters' are left unspecified, to be filled in by the child according to the language he is exposed to."

There are descriptive advantages to using parameters, such as the complete characterization of phenomena pertaining to word order and null subjects as described above. These advantages translate into computational advantages in that they provide a concise means for specifying the grammar. From an engineering point of view, this is beneficial because it makes the system easy to design and extend.

The next section provides the motivation for the architectural design of the UNITRAN system. Section 1.2 describes the technique of pa-

rameterization used in the current model. Section 1.3 discusses certain
classes of machine translation problems that are addressed by the present
approach. Section 1.4 examines some alternative approaches to solving
this problem. Finally, section 1.5 discusses the interlingual representation that is used in UNITRAN and compares it to the representation of
earlier approaches.

1.1   Architecture of a Principle-Based Approach

The UNITRAN system takes on interlingual design based on a
principles-and-parameters approach in the spirit of the proposal of Barton (1984) and later adopted in work by Abney (1989), Berwick and
Fong (1990), Coen (1991), Dorr (1990c), Frank (1990), Johnson (1989),
Kashket (1991), Marcus (1980), Merlo (1992), Sharp (1985), Wehrli
(1992), and Weinberg (1988), among others. Within the context of machine translation, the use of parameterized principles permits the system
to operate without recourse to *ad hoc* stipulations found in pattern-
matching approaches (*i.e.*, *direct* translators) or rule-based approaches
(*i.e.*, *transfer* translators). For the purposes of comparison to, and motivation for, the current interlingual design, we will discuss some of the
characteristics of these two competing approaches.

The primary characteristic of the direct approach to translation is
that it is designed to translate out of one specific language into another.
Systems that adopt this approach generally consist of one large mono-
lithic program with highly language-specific word-for-word replacement
routines and *ad hoc* transformations that are performed after lexical
substitution. Transfer translation, on the other hand, maps the source-
language sentence into a machine-readable form corresponding to the
source language; this form is then mapped into a machine-readable form
for the target-language, from which the target-language text is generated. Thus, the underlying representation of the surface sentence differs
depending on the language that it is intended to represent. In contrast
to the one-stage direct approach, the transfer approach is a three-stage
process: a third module called the transfer module maps one language-
specific representation into another. The direct and transfer approaches
are illustrated, respectively, in figures 1.1 and 1.2.   Note that the direct approach uses n^2 direct translation modules and that the transfer

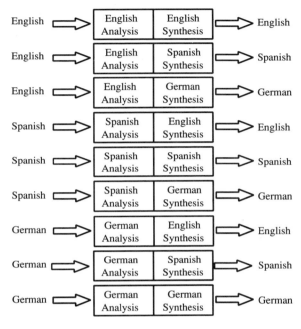

Figure 1.1
The direct approach to translation is a one-stage process with highly
language-specific word-for-word replacement routines and *ad hoc* substitutions. In
this approach there are n^2 direct processors, where n is the number of languages.

approach uses n^2 transfer modules, n analysis components, and n synthesis components (where n is the number of languages in the translation system).[1]

---

[1] If the designer excludes the case in which a language translates into itself, the direct approach would require $n(n-1)$ direct translation modules and the transfer approach would require $n(n-1)$ transfer modules. Such an exclusion would clearly be reasonable, particularly in the case of the direct translation which, by definition, applies an identity mapping in order to translate a language into itself.

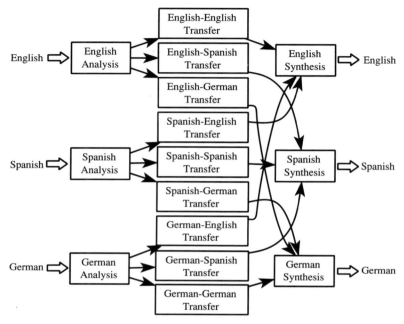

Figure 1.2
The transfer approach to translation is a three-stage process that maps the
source-language sentence into a language-specific machine-readable form which is
then "transferred" into a machine-readable form for the target-language; this form
is used to generated the target-language sentence. In this approach there are n
analyzers, n^2 transfer processors, and n synthesizers, where n is the number of
languages.

As an example of how these approaches would handle the types of
phenomena that are addressed in the current approach, consider the
following:[2]

(6)   S: Me gusta María[3]
            'Mary pleases me'
            (I like Mary)

---

[2]Throughout this (and subsequent) chapters, the abbreviations D, E, F, G, P,
and S will be used to stand for Dutch, English, French, German, Portuguese, and
Spanish, respectively.

[3]This sentence illustrates an inversion effect that is characteristic of Spanish and

In general, the direct and transfer approaches would achieve the translation from English to Spanish by means of rules of the following form, respectively:

(7) (i) **Direct Approach:**
         X LIKE Y $\Rightarrow$ Y GUSTAR X

     (ii) **Transfer Approach:**[4]
         gustar(SUBJ(ARG1:NP),OBJ1(ARG2:PREP)) $\Rightarrow$
         like(SUBJ(ARG2:NP),OBJ1(ARG1:NP))

On one hand, such rules encode certain types of syntactic information that cannot be ignored (*i.e.*, that there is a subject/object reversal and that the category of the second argument is different in each language).[5] On the other hand, specifying the information in this way is tedious because it requires such mappings to be constructed for each source-language/target-language pair. This shortcoming has been noted by a number of researchers (see, *e.g.*, Bennett *et al.* (1986)).

In contrast to the direct and transfer approaches, the *interlingual* approach to machine translation is a two-stage process that maps the source-language sentence into a language-independent representation

---

other Romance languages. The uninverted form is also legal, *i.e.*, *María me gusta*. In fact, there are many legal variations of this sentence, depending on whether the the clitic *me* is doubled with its pronominal counterpart *mí* and/or whether other inversion patterns are used:

   (i)   Me gusta María
   (ii)   María me gusta
   (ii)   Me gusta María a mí
   (iv)   María me gusta a mí
   (v)   A mí me gusta María
   (vi)   A mí María me gusta

Certain of these are more acceptable to native speakers than others, but native speakers generally agree that all of these are grammatical. It is important to realize that these syntactic alternations do not, in any way, degrade the effectiveness of the lexical-semantic translation routines that are used to resolve thematic distinctions such as that of example (6). Because these alternations are purely syntactic, they are processed by modules that are independent from those modules that handle thematic distinctions (and other lexical-semantic distinctions). In cases where more than one syntactic realization is acceptable, all possibilities are parsed/generated (*i.e.*, no preference strategy is currently used to choose between these cases). We will, for now, continue to show one syntactic realization for the examples given here, even in cases where more than one is possible.

[4]Rule (7)(ii) includes a preposition (PREP) for the verb *gustar* even though no such constituent is included in sentence (6). This constituent refers to the indirect object *me* which is optionally associated with a prepositional phrase *a mí*.

[5]Throughout this and subsequent examples, we will use the more general term *object* to refer to either the direct or indirect object, unless it becomes necessary to distinguish specifically between these two types. In the current example, the object of *gustar*, *me*, is actually the *indirect* object as evidenced by the fact that it cannot be passivized in Spanish (*i.e.*, one cannot produce a sentence equivalent to *I was pleased by Mary* using the Spanish verb *gustar*).

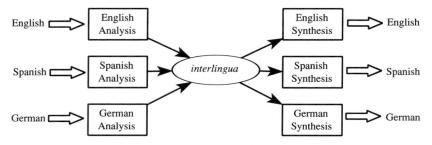

Figure 1.3
The traditional interlingual approach to translation is a two-stage process that
maps the source-language sentence into a language-independent representation from
which the target-language sentence is generated. In this approach there are n
analysis components and n synthesis components.

from which the target-language sentence is generated. There are no
transfer rules or *ad hoc* transformations. Instead, the syntactic and
lexical-semantic translation routines map the interlingua systematically
to the surface structure and *vice versa*. Traditionally, the interlingual
approach consists of n analysis components and n synthesis components,
which is clearly an improvement over the transfer approach (assuming
the mapping to the interlingua is not too complicated). An example
of such a system is the Spanish-English translation system developed
by Sharp (1985). Figure 1.3 illustrates the basic design of the system.
Note that there are no transfer components and that the interlingua is
assumed to be a form common to the three languages. [6]

One problem with this incarnation of the interlingual approach is that
the designer of the system must supply an analyzer (or parser) for each
source language and a synthesizer (or generator) for each target language. The approach taken for UNITRAN is slightly different from
that of Sharp's system in that the same parser and generator are used
for all languages. The system is still *interlingual*, by definition (*i.e.*,

---

[6]In reality Sharp's system was not a true interlingual system in that it required
transformations between the syntactic *D-structures* of the source and target languages. These transformations were, in effect, the *transfer rules* of the system.
However, the approach adopted by Sharp does not preclude the possibility of using a
deeper level of representation as the interlingua. This is, in fact, the approach taken
in the UNITRAN system, except that UNITRAN takes this idea one step further by
collapsing all analysis components into a single analyzer and all synthesis components
into a single synthesizer. This point will be discussed shortly.

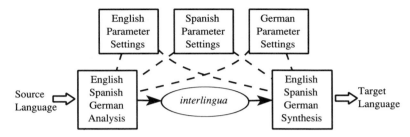

Figure 1.4
The current interlingual approach to translation is similar to the traditional
approach in that it uses a language-independent representation. However, in this
approach there is one analyzer and one synthesizer. Language-specific information
is factored out in terms of parameter settings, and the translation mapping
operates uniformly across all languages.

the source language is mapped into a form that is independent of any
language), but it more closely approximates a true universal approach
since there is a set of general principles that apply across all languages,
while language-specific characteristics are specified separately by means
of parameter settings.

Figure 1.4 illustrates the design of an alternative interlingual model
that will be the focus of the current discussion. In this design, the parser
and generator are programmable in the sense that all principles of the
system are associated with parameters that may be set one way or another in order to accommodate a new language. Thus, the programmer
need not supply a source language parser or a target language generator
when adding a new language; these are already part of the translation
system. The only requirement is that the built-in parser and generator
be *programmed* (via parameter settings) to process the source and target
languages.[7]

---

[7]It should be pointed out that other interlingual systems (*e.g.*, that of the KBMT
project reported by Nirenburg *et al.* (1992)) could also be perceived to have an architecture similar to that of figure 1.4 in that they provide only one source-language
analyzer and one target-language synthesizer. However, such systems differ from
UNITRAN in that they generally require the designer to construct a grammar of
syntactic rules for each language. The current approach not only provides a single
analyzer/synthesizer, but it is designed so that languages may be added to the system without hand-construction of language-specific grammars for each source and
target language. As we will see in chapter 2, the grammar is produced as a result of
precompilation of the syntactic parameter settings; thus, the designer never has to
think up, or even look at, the encoded grammars of the languages processed by the

The current approach strives to provide an interlingua that is not so
completely different from the syntactic structure that information encoded in rules such as (7) could not, somehow, be retrievable. On the
other hand, this approach represents a shift away from the use of a
"shallow" interlingua such as that of Sharp (1985). The new design has
achieved a middle ground between representations that depart radically
from their corresponding syntactic structures and those that are too
language specific to allow a principled translation mapping to be constructed. Thus, the system accommodates cross-linguistic distinctions
without losing the systematic relation between the interlingua and the
surface form. The primary mechanism that has allowed the system to
achieve this middle ground is the use of parameterization, which we will
examine below in section 1.2.

Before turning to a discussion of issues relevant to the current framework, we should briefly mention that the architectural basis of the system
is only one of many axes along which one might compare machine translation systems. Another important axis of comparison that deserves
mention here is the computational paradigm of the system. Figure 1.5
enumerates some of the more recent classes of machine translation systems that researchers are currently investigating.[8]

A detailed discussion about each of these frameworks is outside of
the scope of the current study, but see the references given in the figure as well as Dorr *et al.* (1993) for a comprehensive survey of these,

---

system.

[8]This list is, by no means, exhaustive. It is intended to cover most of the approaches that have been covered in recent years, a large number of which were reported recently in the proceedings of the *Conference of the Association for Computational Linguistics*, the *International Conference on Theoretical and Methodological
Issues in Machine Translation of Natural Languages*, and the *International Conference on Computational Linguistics*.

There may be some disagreement about the boundaries of this classification. For
example, the S&BMT approach has been viewed as a CBMT approach (see, *e.g.*,
Whitelock (1991, 1992)) in that the translation process is taken to be a collection
and resolution of sets of constraints. It has also been viewed as a lexical-based
approach (see *e.g.*, Beaven (1992a,b)) in that a bilingual lexicon is used to put into
correspondence pairs of monolingual lexical entries.

Another point is that many of the translation approaches fall under more than one
category given that there are cases in which techniques from several categories have
been combined. An example of such a case is an approach by Grishman and Kosaka
(1992) which proposes to combine techniques used by EBMT SBMT, and RBMT.

[9]It should be pointed out that LBMT has also been used as an acronym for
linguistic-based machine translation, which is a more general term that refers to
approaches that belong to any category outside of EBMT, NBMT, or SBMT. It is
used in a more specific sense here, *i.e.*, it refers to those linguistic-based systems that
are driven primarily by the lexicon.

Constraint-Based MT (CBMT): Arnold and Sadler (1992), Eberle *et al.* (1992), Sadler and Arnold (1992), Whitelock (1991, 1992), Kaplan *et al.* (1989)

Dialogue-Based MT (DBMT): Boitet (1989), Jones and Tsujii (1990), Saito and Tomita (1986), Somers *et al.* (1990), Somers (1992), Tsujii and Nagao (1988)

Example- (or Case-/Memory-) Based MT (EBMT): Furuse and Iida (1992), Grishman and Kosaka (1992), McLean (1992), Nagao (1984), Nomiyama (1991, 1992), Sato, and Nagao (1990), Somers (1992), Sumita (1990), Maruyama and Watanabe (1992), Okumura *et al.* (1992)

Knowledge-Based MT (KBMT): Carbonell and Tomita (1987), Mitamura *et al.* (1991), Nagao (1990), Nirenburg *et al.* (1992)

Lexical-Based MT (LBMT):[9] Abeillé *et al.* (1990), Beaven (1992a,b), Bläser *et al.* (1992), Dorr (1989, 1990a,b,c, 1991c, 1992a,e, 1993a), Farwell and Wilks (1991), Farwell *et al.* (1992), Sanfilippo *et al.* (1992), Tsujii and Fujita (1991), Trujillo (1992), Voss (forthcoming), Wilks *et al.* (1990)

Neural Net- (or Connectionist-) Based MT (NBMT): Ishikawa and Sugimura (1992), McLean (1992)

Principle-Based MT (PBMT): Dorr (1987a,b,c, 1990d, 1991b, 1992c), Sigurd (1988), Sigurd and Eeg-Olofsson (1991), Wehrli (1992)

Rule-Based MT (RBMT): Appelo (1986), Arnold *et al.* (1988), Arnold and Sadler (1990), Arnold and des Tombe (1987), Danlos and Samvelian (1992), Fujii *et al.* (1990), Grishman and Kosaka (1992), Kaplan *et al.* (1989), Landsbergen *et al.* (1989), McCord (1989), van Noord *et al.* (1990), Okumura *et al.* (1992), Thurmair (1990)

Shake and Bake MT (S&BMT): Beaven (1992a,b), Brew (1992), Whitelock (1991, 1992)

Statistics- (or Corpus-) Based MT (SBMT): Brown *et al.* (1988a,b), Brown (1990), Brown *et al.* (1992), Doi and Muraki (1992), Grishman and Kosaka (1992), Su and Chang (1992)

Figure 1.5
The computational paradigm is another axis of comparison between machine translation systems. The UNITRAN system falls into the PBMT and LBMT categories.

Abeillé et al. (1990)	LBMT
Appelo (1986)	RBMT
Arnold and Sadler (1990)	RBMT
Arnold et al. (1988)	RBMT
Arnold and Sadler (1992)	CBMT
Arnold and des Tombe (1987)	RBMT
Beaven (1992a,b)	LBMT, S&BMT
Bläser et al. (1992)	LBMT
Boitet (1989)	DBMT
Brew (1992)	S&BMT
Brown et al. (1988a,b)	SBMT
Brown (1990)	SBMT
Brown et al. (1992)	SBMT
Carbonell and Tomita (1987)	KBMT
Danlos and Samvelian (1992)	RBMT
Doi and Muraki (1992)	SBMT
Dorr (1987a,b,c, 1990d, 1991b, 1992c)	PBMT
Dorr (1989, 1990a,b,c, 1991c, 1992c,e, 1993a)	LBMT
Eberle et al. (1992)	CBMT
Farwell et al. (1992)	LBMT
Farwell and Wilks (1991)	LBMT
Fujii et al. (1990)	RBMT
Furuse and Iida (1992)	EBMT
Grishman and Kosaka (1992)	EBMT, RBMT, SBMT
Ishikawa and Sugimura (1992)	NBMT
Jones and Tsujii (1990)	DBMT
Kaplan et al. (1989)	CBMT, RBMT
Landsbergen et al. (1989)	RBMT
Maruyama and Watanabe (1992)	EBMT
McCord (1989)	RBMT
McLean (1992)	EBMT, NBMT
Mitamura et al. (1991)	KBMT
Nagao (1984)	EBMT
Nagao (1990)	KBMT
Nirenburg et al. (1992)	KBMT
Nomiyama (1991, 1992)	EBMT, SBMT
van Noord et al. (1990)	RBMT
Okumura et al. (1992)	EBMT, RBMT
Sadler and Arnold (1992)	CBMT
Saito and Tomita (1986)	DBMT
Sanfilippo et al. (1992)	LBMT
Sato, and Nagao (1990)	EBMT
Sharp (1985)	PBMT
Sigurd (1988)	PBMT
Sigurd and Eeg-Olofsson (1991)	PBMT
Somers et al. (1990)	DBMT
Somers (1992)	DBMT, EBMT
Su and Chang (1992)	SBMT
Sumita (1990)	EBMT
Thurmair (1990)	RBMT
Trujillo (1992)	LBMT
Tsujii and Fujita (1991)	LBMT
Tsujii and Nagao (1988)	DBMT
Voss, forthcoming	LBMT
Wehrli (1992)	PBMT
Wilks et al. (1990)	LBMT
Whitelock (1991, 1992)	CBMT, S&BMT

Figure 1.6
The computational paradigm, indexed by author, reveals that researchers frequently span more than one category.

and other, approaches. For the purposes of the present discussion, it is sufficient to say that UNITRAN falls into two categories: PBMT (*i.e.*, it relies on principles and parameters at both the syntactic and lexical-semantic levels) and LBMT (*i.e.*, the classes of problems that are solved are dependent on information that is available in the lexicon). For convenience, a "reverse index" of the approaches shown in figure 1.5 are listed (in alphabetical order) in figure 1.6.

1.2   Parameterization of the Model

The parameter-setting approach is desirable from a number of different perspectives. First, it allows language-specific knowledge to be represented independently from the knowledge included in the syntactic principles and the interlingual representation. Second, it allows the descriptions of natural grammars to be simplified: the interaction of only a few parameter settings account for a wide range of linguistic phenomena that are generally characterized by construction-specific rules in other machine translation approaches. Third, the parameter-setting approach allows a machine translation system to be easily modified and augmented: one simply selects the appropriate parameter settings and supplies the appropriate lexicon for the languages to be translated. A fourth advantage is that cross-linguistic variation is accounted for uniformly in the parameter-setting approach: the same parser and generator can be used for each language, and language-specific idiosyncrasies are ironed out through access to the parameter settings during processing. Finally, the parameter-setting approach allows for a more constrained theory of processing: the parameter settings are used in conjunction with principles that determine well-formedness and act as filters of erroneous constructions during the translation.

Setting a syntactic parameter of the UNITRAN system is done through a simple menu operation. Figure 1.7 shows how this is done for the null subject parameter. Because null subject languages have the property that subjects must invert into post-verbal position in interrogative sentences, this parameter accounts for the word order variation in example (1). The setting for Spanish forces the system to interpret *Juan* as the subject of the Spanish sentence even though it would be interpreted as the object in the structurally equivalent English sentence.

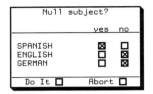

Figure 1.7
Setting the null subject parameter in UNITRAN is done through a simple menu
operation.

So far, the current discussion has focused on syntactic parameterization. A central claim of this study is that, not only should the syntactic component of a machine translation system be parameterized,
but other components of a machine translation system would also benefit from parameterization. In particular, the lexical-semantic component should be constructed in such a way as to allow principles of the
lexicon to be parameterized. Thus, UNITRAN uses two levels of processing, syntactic and lexical-semantic, both of which operate on the
basis of language-independent knowledge that is parameterized to encode language-specific information (see figure 1.8). This approach allows
surface-level distinctions to be factored out of the interlingua and cross-
linguistic generalizations to be captured at the level of lexical-semantic
structure. The separation of these two types of knowledge provides a
solid engineering basis that allows constraints to be applied at different
levels of representation.

Within the syntactic level of processing, the language-independent
and language-specific information are supplied, respectively, by the principles and parameters of *Government Binding* theory (henceforth, GB)
(see Chomsky (1981, 1982, 1986a, 1986b)). We have already seen an
example of such a parameter in figure 1.7. Within the lexical-semantic
level of processing, the language-independent and language-specific information are supplied by a systematic translation mapping and LCS
parameters in the lexicon for each language, respectively. The interface
between the syntactic and semantic levels allows the source-language
structure to be mapped systematically to the interlingua, and it allows
the target-language structure to be realized systematically from lexical
items derived from the interlingua. This work represents a shift away
from complex, language-specific syntactic translation without entirely

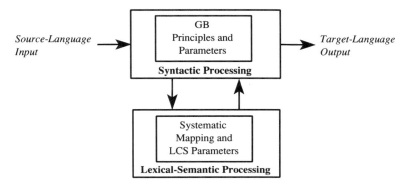

Figure 1.8
The UNITRAN system consists of two processing levels, syntactic and
lexical-semantic, both of which are designed to operate on language-independent
knowledge that is parameterized to encode language-specific information.

abandoning syntax. Furthermore, the work moves toward a model that
employs a well-defined lexical conceptual representation without requiring a "deep" semantic conceptualization.

To get a better idea of the type of parameterization that is required
at the lexical-semantic level, consider the following translation example:

(8)   E: I stabbed John ⇔
        S: Yo le di puñaladas a Juan
           'I gave knife-wounds to John'

This example illustrates a type of distinction (henceforth called *divergence* as presented by Dorr (1990a)) that arises in machine translation:
the source-language predicate, *stab*, is mapped to more than one target-
language word, *dar puñaladas*. This divergence type is lexical-semantic
rather than syntactic in that there is a word selection variation between the source language and the target language. Such divergences
are accounted for by lexical-semantic parameterization, which specifies
precisely how individual lexical items are combined with other lexical
items. This type of parameterization will be discussed in more detail in
chapters 5 and 7.

Figure 1.9 shows a snapshot of the input/output of UNITRAN for this
example (in the English-to-Spanish direction). The panes that show the
source and target syntactic trees represent the output of the syntactic

component. The pane that shows the LCS represents the output of the lexical-semantic component. The entire translation process proceeds as follows:

1. The input is typed as shown in the English Input pane. This source-language input is supplied to the parser in the syntactic component.

2. The parser takes the source-language input and produces the corresponding structure shown in the Source Syntactic Tree pane.

3. This structure is passed to the lexical-semantic component, which then produces the composed interlingual form shown in the LCS pane.

4. This composed form is then mapped to a target-language syntactic tree as shown in the Target Syntactic Tree pane.

5. The final output is obtained by reading off the leaves of the tree as shown in the Spanish Output pane. (There may be other results as well, but only one at a time may be displayed.)

We will examine the parameters that are required for lexical-semantic processing of such cases in chapters 5 and 7.

The use of parameterization in both the syntactic and lexical-semantic components allows the system to deal systematically with syntactic distinctions (*e.g.*, null subject variation) and lexical-semantic distinctions (*e.g.*, word selection variation) that often bog down other machine translation systems. Furthermore, the parameterization approach is suitable to the task of translating between divergent structures for two reasons: (1) it provides an *abstraction* of language-independent properties from structural idiosyncrasies; and (2) it lends itself to an approach that is *compositional* in nature. That is, there are two sources of parameterized information, syntactic (which provides the specific surface ordering and realization) and lexical-semantic (which provides an underlying representation), both of which are used compositionally to construct an appropriate lexical-semantic representation (*i.e.*, the interlingua) from which the target-language structure is produced.

By relying on *abstraction* and *compositionality* to drive the translation process, the system is able to produce a translation that is not a literal word-for-word replacement of the source-language sentence. For example, in (8) the interaction of syntax and lexical-semantics allows the

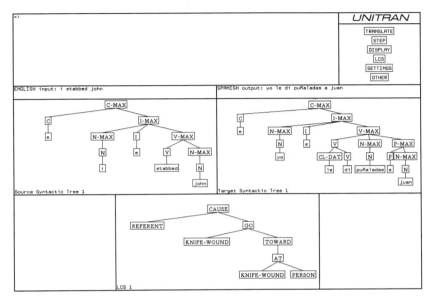

Figure 1.9
This snapshot of the I/O of UNITRAN shows the translation of the English
sentence *I stabbed John* into the Spanish sentence *Yo le di puñaladas a Juan*. The
panes that show the source and target syntactic trees represent the output of the
syntactic component. The pane that shows the LCS represents the output of the
lexical-semantic component.

system to lexically select the appropriate target-language terms (e.g., *dar*
and *puñaladas*) and to combine them in such a way as to provide the
meaning corresponding to the word *stab* while also adhering to syntactic requirements (*e.g.*, Verb-Noun-Preposition structure in Spanish) and
word order (*e.g.*, verb precedes objects in Spanish).

Figure 1.10 shows the input/output of different levels of on-line processing (including morphological) for example (8). The details of the
representations shown here will be described further in chapters 3–7,
with particular emphasis on the syntactic and lexical-semantic levels of
processing.[10]

Examples (1)–(8) illustrate certain classes of problems that arise in

---

[10]In addition to the on-line processing modules shown here, there is also an off-line
precompilation module that produces the grammars used by the syntactic component.
This will be discussed in chapter 2.

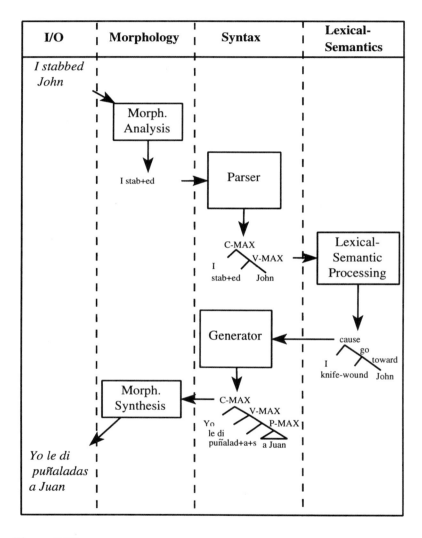

Figure 1.10
The modular design of UNITRAN allows different types of decisions to be made by different processing components.

Divergence Type	Translation Example
Constituent Order	E: I have seen him ⇕ G: Ich habe ihn gesehen (I have him seen)
Preposition Stranding	E: What store did John go to ⇕ S: * Cuál tienda fue Juan a (What store did John go to)
Long Distance Movement	E: * Who did you wonder 　　whether went to school ⇕ S: Quién contemplabas tú que fue a la escuela (Who did you wonder whether went to school)
Null Subject	E: I saw the book ⇕ S: Vi el libro (Saw the book)
Dative	E: I gave the book to him ⇕ G: Ich gab ihm das Buch (I gave him the book)

Figure 1.11
Syntactic translation divergences are accounted for by means of syntactic parameterization.

machine translation. We now turn to a more detailed discussion of the divergence problem addressed by the current translation model.

1.3   Machine Translation Divergences

A translation divergence arises when the natural translation of one language into another results in a very different form than that of the original. The UNITRAN system addresses the syntactic and lexical-semantic divergence types shown, respectively, in figures 1.11 and 1.12. In chapter 2 we will discuss the syntactic divergences of figure 1.11 (as well as other syntactic divergences). In this section, we will focus primarily on the divergences of figure 1.12. The difference between these two types of divergences is that the former category is characterized by syntactic properties associated with each language (*i.e.*, properties that are *independent* of the actual lexical items that are used) whereas the latter category is characterized by properties of that are entirely lexically determined. A key result of the current investigation is that it has

Divergence Type	Translation Example
Conflational	E: I stabbed John ⇕ S: Yo le di puñaladas a Juan 'I gave knife-wounds to John'
Structural	E: John entered the house ⇕ S: Juan entró en la casa 'I saw to John'
Thematic	E: I like Mary ⇕ S: Me gusta María 'Mary pleases me'
Categorial	E: I am hungry ⇕ G: Ich habe Hunger 'I have hunger'
Demotional	E: I like to eat ⇕ G: Ich esse gern 'I eat likingly'
Promotional	E: John usually goes home ⇕ G: Juan suele ir a casa 'John tends to go (to) home'
Lexical	E: John broke into the room ⇕ S: Juan forzó la entrada al cuarto 'John forced entry to the room'

Figure 1.12
Lexical-semantic translation divergences are accounted for by means of
parameterization of the lexicon.

demonstrated that lexical-semantic divergences have formal correlates
that fall out from the LCS representation. (This point will be fleshed
out in chapter 7.)

Consider the first divergence example of figure 1.12, which was given
above in (8), *i.e.*, *conflational* divergence. Conflation is the lexical incorporation of necessary components of meaning (or arguments) of a given
action. Here, English uses the single word *stab* for the two Spanish words
dar (*give*) and *puñaladas* (*knife-wounds*). The *knife-wounds* component
of meaning is not overtly realized in English, but is considered to be *conflated* into the main verb. By contrast, this component of meaning is
not conflated in Spanish, but is overtly realized on the surface. Such an
example is translated naturally by the compositional approach, which
readily lends itself to the specification of arguments that may or may
not be realized on the surface.

To further clarify the class of problems handled by the current approach, we will describe the rest of the lexical-semantic divergence types shown in figure 1.12. The second divergence type is *structural*: the verbal object is realized as a noun phrase (*the house*) in English and as a prepositional phrase (*en la casa*) in Spanish. The third divergence type is *thematic*: the theme is realized as the verbal object (*Mary*) in English but as the subject (*María*) of the main verb in Spanish. The fourth divergence type is *categorial*: the predicate is adjectival (*hungry*) in English but nominal (*Hunger*) in German. The fifth divergence type, *demotional*, is one of two *head swapping* divergence types: the word *like* is realized as a main verb in English but as an adverbial modifier (*gern*) in German. The sixth divergence type, *promotional*, is the second *head swapping* divergence type: the modifier (*usually*) is realized as an adverbial phrase in English but as the main verb *soler* in Spanish. [11] Finally, the seventh divergence type is a *lexical* divergence: the main verb is *break* in English but a different verb *forzar* (literally *force*) in Spanish.

Although researchers have only recently begun to systematically classify divergence types, the notion of translation divergences is not a new one in the machine translation community. For example, a number of researchers working on the Eurotra project (discussed below) have sought to solve divergent source-to-target translations, although the divergences were named differently and were resolved by construction-specific transfer rules. A comprehensive survey of divergence examples is presented by Barnett *et al.* (1991a,b), Dorr (1990a,c), Kameyama *et al.* (1991), Kinoshita *et al.* (1992), Lindop and Tsujii (1991), Tsujii and Fujita (1991), Beaven (1992a, 1992b), and Whitelock (1992) and related discussion can be found, for example, in work by Melby (1986) and Nirenburg and Nirenburg (1988). The term that is often used for divergence is "complex lexical transfer," but this term is a misnomer because divergences are a class of problems inherent in machine translation itself, not just in the transfer (or interlingual) approaches.

Note that, although the divergence effects are described here (and in subsequent chapters) by means of terms such as "thematic role reversal," this is not to say that such surface effects are achieved through the use

---

[11] The distinction between demotional and promotional divergences is not obvious at first glance. In both examples in figure 1.12, the translation mapping associates a main verb with an adverbial satellite, or *vice versa*. The justification for distinguishing between these two *head swapping* cases is given in chapter 7.

of explicit reversal rules. This is the heart of the distinction between transfer approaches (*e.g.*, the GETA system discussed below) and the current approach. Transfer approaches generally address the divergence problem by providing transfer rules between source and target structures (*e.g.*, rule (7)(ii) above). It is well known by AI and MT researchers that such an approach is problematic due to the sheer quantity of rules that would be required to have a successful system with broad coverage. We will return to this point shortly.

1.4 Alternative Approaches

One might argue that several of the examples from figure 1.12 could be translated using the direct translation approach with little loss of information. For example, if we choose English to be the target language, we could directly translate the three of the examples from figure 1.12 as follows:

(9)   S: Yo le di puñaladas a Juan $\Rightarrow$ E: I inflicted knife wounds on John

(10)   S: Me gusta María $\Rightarrow$ E: Mary pleases me

(11)   G: Ich esse gern $\Rightarrow$ E: I eat enjoyably

The problem with taking such an approach is that it is not general enough to handle a wide range of cases. For example, if we translate the word *gern* directly to the word *enjoyably* as in case (11), we will run into problems when we try to translate *gern* in other contexts. As it turns out, the adverb *gern* may be used in conjunction with *haben* to mean *like*: *Ich habe Marie gern* ('I like Mary'). The literal translation, *I have Mary enjoyably*, is not only stylistically unattractive, but it is not a valid translation for this sentence. Another problem with the direct-mapping approach is that it is not bidirectional in the general case. Thus, even if we did take (9), (10), and (11) as the desired translations, we would not be able to apply the same direct mapping in the reverse direction (*i.e.*, translating from the more appropriate English version to Spanish and German). For example, the same mapping could not be used to translate *stab* and *like* into Spanish and German. It is clear that a uniform method for bidirectional translation is required.

The direct approach to translation has been largely discounted as an alternative to the interlingual approach. However, there have been a number of arguments for the more commonly used transfer approach as an alternative to the interlingual approach. (See, *e.g.*, Arnold and Sadler (1990), Boitet (1988), and Vauquois and Boitet (1985).) Paradoxically these anti-interlingual arguments are based precisely on the same types of examples that have motivated the current research (*e.g.*, those sentences that exhibit the types of divergences shown above). The assumption of previous approaches is that it would be too difficult to design an interlingual representation that includes enough information to accommodate complex divergences. This study provides argues to the contrary, adopting the view that complex divergences are precisely what necessitates the use of an interlingual representation because the interlingual approach allows surface syntactic distinctions to be represented at a level that is independent from that of the underlying "meaning" of the source and target sentences. Factoring out these surface-level distinctions allows cross-linguistic generalizations to be captured at the level of lexical-semantic structure.

Some examples of the types of translations that are used to justify the use of a transfer approach are:[12]

(12) **Demotional divergence:**
      E: John likes to kiss Mary ⇔
      G: Johann kußt Marie gern[13]
      'John kisses Mary likingly'

(13) **Promotional divergence:**
      E: John has almost finished the book ⇔
      F: Jean a failli finir le livre[14]
      'John has missed to finish the book'

---

[12]These examples are taken from Arnold *et al.* (1988) and Arnold and Sadler (1990). The divergence types are specified using the terminology of the present author, not that of the authors from whom these (and later) examples are taken.

[13]The example given by Arnold *et al.* (1988) is actually a translation from the Dutch equivalent of the German sentence (*i.e.*, *Jan kust Marie graag*), but the construction is entirely analogous.

[14]This example is an adapted version of one taken from Arnold and Sadler (1990): *Jean a manqué de finir le livre.* Judgments as to the naturalness and acceptability of this sentence differ among native French speakers; the verb *manquer* does not convey the "almost" meaning for all speakers. Thus, the more acceptable version that uses *faillir* is given here. In any case, the concept of promotion is valid, regardless of which main verb is used.

(14) **Conflational divergence:**
       E: They run into the room ⇔
       F: Ils entrent dans la salle en courant[15]
       'They enter the room in running'

The implicit assumption rejected by the current approach is that it would
be impossible to design an interlingual system that supports a systematic
mapping between the source and target languages in cases such as (12),
(13), and (14). As we will see, these types of divergences are precisely
the ones that are handled by the UNITRAN system.

For the purposes of comparison, we will briefly discuss the approach
taken by four different systems for such examples: (1) MiMo (Arnold
et al. (1988), Arnold and Sadler (1990), van Noord *et al.* (1989), van
Noord *et al.* (1990), and Sadler *et al.* (1990)); (2) GETA/ARIANE (Vauquois and Boitet (1985), and Boitet (1987)); (3) LMT (McCord (1989));
and (4) METAL (Alonso (1990) and Thurmair (1990)). Other systems
that have attempted to deal with these (and other) divergence types are
TAUM (Colmerauer *et al.* (1971)), LFG-MT (Kaplan *et al.* (1989)), and
LTAG (Abeillé *et al.* (1990)). We will not discuss these approaches here,
but will return to specific examples of these systems when we examine
the divergence problem in more detail in chapter 7.

The MiMo system developed from an effort that had its beginnings
within the Eurotra framework. (For cogent descriptions of the Eurotra
project, see, *e.g.*, Arnold and des Tombe (1987), Copeland *et al.* (1991),
and Johnson *et al.* (1985).) Whereas the 'mainstream' Eurotra work
stops short of describing how translation divergences are handled, the
MiMo project has extended the Eurotra formalism to handle a wide
range of divergence classes. MiMo is a structural transfer approach
that addresses the solution to divergence cases such as (12), (13), and
(14) above. To achieve the translation mapping in these examples, the
transfer approach requires the existence of transfer entries. In particular,

---

[15]Again, this is an adapted version of a sentence taken from Arnold and Sadler
(1990); the original form of the sentence did not include the preposition *dans* which
forced the sentence to have a questionable status among native French speakers.
Thus, the more acceptable version that uses *dans* is given here. In any case, the
concept of conflation is valid with, or without, the preposition since the lexical items
of interest in this phenomenon are *entrer* and *en courant*.

the verb *like* must be related to the adverb *gern* by means of a transfer entry of the form:

(15)   r!((cat = S).[mod = GERN]) ⇔
       LIKE((cat = S).[r!arg1])

This rule indicates that the word *gern* would be realized as an adverbial modifier in German, whereas the English counterpart would be realized as a main verb that takes a sentential argument.

As for (13) and (14), the required transfer rules are (16) and (17), respectively:

(16)   r!([1!arg1],[2!arg2][mod = ALMOST]) ⇔
       FAILLIR([1!arg1],[!arg2=r![2!arg2]])

(17)   ENTRER([1!arg2],[mod = EN[!arg1=COURIR]]) ⇔
       RUN([mod=INTO[1!arg2]])

Rule (16) ensures that the French main verb *faillir* (in (13)) is translated as an English adverbial *almost* in English. (The r! variable is bound to *finir* in French and *finish* in English.) Rule (17) maps the compound French construction *entrer en courant* (in (14)) into the simple English construction *run into*.

We need not dwell on the well-known problem that such transfer entries are required for each source-language/target-language pair of the system, including pairs that exhibit less complicated divergences such as in the *like-gustar* case of example (6) (as well as pairs for which there is no divergence at all). Suffice it to say that specifying transfer mappings for all of the lexical items of each source-language/target-language pair is very tedious work. There are, however, other problems with the transfer approach that are worth mentioning here. One problem is that much of the information that is, or could be, lexically stored (*e.g.*, the argument structure of the word *entrer*) is included in the transfer rules as well. The use of transfer rules results in a severe proliferation of redundancy on a per-language basis. For example, *faillir* is not the only verb that gives rise to the type of construction shown in (13); in fact, Arnold and Sadler (1990) present a similar verb, *venir* (which translates to the adverbial *just*) that is precisely analogous to the verb *faillir*. Thus, rules analogous to (16) must be constructed for *venir*, differing

only in that *venir* is used in place of *faillir* and *just* in place of *almost*. [16]
The multiplicative effect of all of these combinations wreaks havoc with
the number of transfer rules that are required on a per-language basis.

Another problem with the transfer approach is that it misses a number
of cross-linguistic generalizations. For example, not only do constructions such as (12), (13) and (14) arise *within* a single language, but such
constructions exist *across* languages as well. The root of the problem
with the MiMo approach is that it does not use a canonical representation that would factor out this redundancy. As we will see shortly,
the UNITRAN system takes advantage of such a representation to map
between languages in a more systematic and uniform fashion.

Another translation system that has attempted to handle divergences
such as the thematic divergence in example (6) is that of the Groupe
d'Etudes pour la Traduction Automatique (GETA) at the University
of Grenoble. This group developed a multilingual (Russian-French,
German-French) system called ARIANE-78. (Comprehensive descriptions can be found in work by Boitet (1978), Chauché (1975), Vauquois
(1977) and more recently in work by Vauquois and Boitet (1985), and
Boitet (1987).) GETA/ARIANE is based on dependency-tree representations that include a certain amount of surface information. The approach accommodates divergence examples by providing transfer rules
between source and target dependency-tree structures.

Consider the following example:

(18)   **Thematic divergence:**
         F: Cette musique plaît aux jeunes gens ⇒
             'This music pleases (to) young people'
         E: Young people like this music

This example illustrates a subject-object interchange analogous to that
of the *like-gustar* example given earlier. The dependency tree for the
source-language sentence is shown in figure 1.13. [17] This tree represents
the logico-semantic relation of *plaire* to its two arguments, the subject
(ARG1 = *cette musique*) and the object (ARG2 = *aux jeunes gens*).

Given that the GETA/ARIANE framework uses transfer rules to map

---

[16] In addition, unlike *faillir*, the verb *venir* requires the particle *de* to be inserted:
Jean vient de tomber (John just fell).

[17] This dependency tree is taken from Hutchins (1986, p. 242).

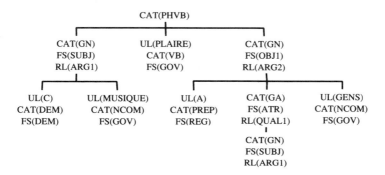

Figure 1.13
The GETA Transfer Representation for *Cette musique plaît aux jeunes gens* is a
dependency tree that represents the relation of *plaire* to its subject and object.

between dependency structures, this example would be translated by a
rule of the following form:

(19)   plaire(SUBJ(ARG1:GN),OBJ1(ARG2:PREP,GN)) ⇔
       like(SUBJ(ARG2:GN),OBJ1(ARG1:GN))

This tree-transduction approach suffers from the same proliferation of
redundancy that is apparent in the MiMo system.
     Another example of a machine translation system that attempts to
solve such divergences is the LMT system (McCord (1989)), a logic-
based (English-German) machine translator. This system is based on
a modular logical grammar formalism that is an extension of the *definite clause grammar* (DCG) formalism of Pereira *et al.* (1980). McCord
specifically addresses the problem of thematic divergence in the following
translation example:

(20)   **Thematic divergence:**
       E: I like the car ⇒
       G: Mir gefällt der Wagen
          'To me pleases the car'

Here, the subject of the English sentence is *I*, whereas the subject of
the German sentence is *der Wagen*. The solution offered by the LMT
approach is to provide a "transfer entry" that interchanges the abstract

case of the subject and object positions (and thus changes the form of the main verb):

(21)   gverb(like(dat:*,nom:X),ge+fall,*:X)

This transfer entry would presumably match a portion of the English analysis tree that looks like the following:

(22)   like(W:I,Z:car)

The result is that the bindings W=dat and Z=nom are obtained. These bindings determine the case of the arguments in the German translation; thus, the word *I* is realized lexically as *mir* and the word *car* is realized lexically as *der Wagen*.

While rules of this type do not preclude the possibility of generating more than one possible word order in German, the peculiar nature of the LMT approach imposes artificial restrictions on the possible form of target-language sentences. In particular, the system is designed so that it maps English syntactic structures into German syntactic structures of the same "shape"; then the generator applies transformations to the "English-like" structures to arrive at the appropriate German word order. A side effect of this approach is that a sentence such as *Mir gefällt der Wagen* is generated with an object-initial ordering, even though the sentence is arguably more preferable with a subject-initial ordering (*i.e.*, *Der Wagen gefällt mir*). It is not clear how the subject-initial version of this sentence would be generated since this would require that the system be capable of realizing the pronoun *mir* in a syntactically different position from that of the corresponding English pronoun *I*. The approach does not separate language-independent information (*e.g.*, that both *like* and *gefallen* are represented as the same conceptual state) from language-dependent information (*e.g.*, syntactic ordering considerations); thus, it fails to produce sentences in which arguments are not in their "English-like" canonical positions.

A more fundamental problem with this approach is that it does not attempt to tie this particular type of divergence to the rest of the space of divergence possibilities. Thus, it cannot translate a conceptually similar sentence *Ich fahre das Wagen gern* (*I like to drive the car*) by the same mechanism that it uses to translate (20). That is, *gern* would require a transfer entry distinct from that of *gefallen*, even though these lexical items arguably have a similar conceptual structure.

A major shortcoming of LMT is that there is no language-independent mapping that derives the surface structure; thus, lexical entries must specifically encode information about syntactic structure. In particular, a transfer entry must be constructed for every source-target lexical pair (*i.e.*, surface syntactic decisions are, in a sense, performed off-line). In contrast, the LCS approach separates syntactic information from lexical-semantic information. Because a canonical representation is provided for lexical items, there is no need to use construction-specific transfer entries for each source-target pair. Instead, the system uses a general source-to-target mapping that allows construction-specific syntactic information to be abstracted away from the conceptual representation; thus, (on-line) syntactic decisions are made independently of conceptual decisions, and translation divergences are uniformly handled without reference to purely syntactic properties (such as word order).

Another system that attempts to resolve thematic divergences is the METAL system (English-German, German-English). (See Thurmair (1990) for a description of the handling of translation divergences.) METAL differs from other transfer approaches in that it has recently become known as a "semantic transfer" system: it has been designed to accommodate the METAL,Interface Representation (MIR) (a representation that approaches language-independence); case frames and other semantic information are thus used as the point of transfer.

A specification of the transfer rules used in METAL is presented by Alonso (1990). Given that case frames are used as the point of transfer, thematic divergences are easily accommodated in this scheme by means of rules of the following form:

(23)   like V $\Rightarrow$ gustar V
       NP ([ROLE SUBJ]) $\Rightarrow$ NP ([ROLE IOBJ])
       NP ([ROLE DOBJ]) $\Rightarrow$ NP ([ROLE SUBJ])

This rule accounts for the thematic divergence of example (6) by realizing the subject *I* as the indirect object *me* and the direct object *Mary* as the subject *María*.

While this solution is suitable for local divergences such as simple subject-object reversal, it is well known that case-frame based transfer does not readily accommodate more complicated divergences:

(24)   **Demotional divergence:**
       E: He likes reading
       G: Er liest gern ⇔
          'He reads likingly'

This example is specifically identified by Thurmair (1990) as a problem for lexical transfer within the case-frame approach adopted by METAL. Unlike the METAL system, the current framework accommodates examples of this type using the same mapping that is used to resolve thematic divergences.

1.5   The Interlingua

In order to adopt an interlingual approach to machine translation, one must construct a language-independent representation that lends itself readily to the specification of a systematic mapping that operates uniformly across all languages. To meet this objective, one needs a clear characterization of the entire range of divergences that could possibly arise in machine translation. Such a characterization can emerge only from a serious cross-linguistic investigation into the adequacy of different lexical representations for natural language. Recent work (see Dorr (1992a,b,c,e) has provided an appropriate representation in terms of a lexical conceptual structure based on work by Jackendoff (1983, 1990).[18] This representation abstracts away from syntax just far enough to enable language independent encoding, while retaining enough structure to be sensitive to the requirements for language translation and, in particular, the resolution of divergences such as those shown in figure 1.12.

The approach described here is an alternative to interlingual solutions that have been criticized in the past. For example, Bennett *et al.* (1986,

---

[18]Others who have studied this representation are Hale and Keyser (1986a,b, 1989), Hale and Laughren (1983), Levin and Rappaport (1986), and Zubizaretta (1982, 1987). For alternative (lexical-)semantic and case representations, see, *e.g.*, Fillmore (1968), Gruber (1965), Schank (1972, 1973, 1975), and Wilks (1973).

p. 86) criticizes two possible approaches to an interlingual system: (1) using a canonical syntactic structure (because of the degree of language specificity); and (2) defining an interlingua that is specifically geared toward the languages in the system (because of the difficulty of adding a new language). The solution described here does not fall into either of these two categories. Rather, it appeals to a different notion of interlingua that excludes language-specific syntactic properties and includes language-independent lexical-semantic properties.

The field of machine translation has (almost from the beginning) been concerned with the use of a "deep semantic representation" and with looking for "universals" for translation. One of the biggest objections to the use of an interlingual representation is that it relies on defining a set of primitives (to represent the information to be translated) which allow the mapping to and from the languages in question. Because it is generally difficult to define such a set, many researchers have abandoned this model. (See, *e.g.*, Vauquois and Boitet (1985).) However recently, there has been a resurgence of interest in the area of lexical representation and organization (with special reference to verbs) that has initiated an ongoing effort to delimit the classes of lexical knowledge required to process natural language. (See, *e.g.*, Grimshaw (1990), Hale and Keyser (1986a,b, 1989), Hale and Laughren (1983), Jackendoff (1983, 1990), Levin and Rappaport (1986), Levin (1985, in press), Pustejovsky (1987, 1988, 1989, 1990, 1991), Rappaport *et al.* (1987), Rappaport and Levin (1988), Olsen (1991), and Zubizarreta (1982 1987).) As a result of this effort, it has become increasingly more feasible to isolate the components of meaning common to verbs participating in particular classes. These components of meaning can then be used to determine the lexical representation of verbs across languages.

The representation used in UNITRAN (which is by no means exhaustive) is based a version of the LCS proposed by Jackendoff that is adapted to take into account recent theories of the lexicon. This representation has been adapted to the UNITRAN machine translation model in that it is associated with an algorithm for recursive composition and decomposition of the interlingual form, and it is linked systematically to the syntactic structure, both during parsing as well as during generation. The advantage to using the LCS representation is that it is easy to parameterize it so that cross-linguistic divergences are accommodated without losing the systematic relation between the interlingual represen-

tation and the syntactic structure. Moreover, the representation lends
itself readily to the specification of a systematic mapping that operates
uniformly across all languages.

The LCS approach views semantic representation as a subset
of conceptual structure, *i.e.*, the language of mental representation.
Jackendoff's approach includes *types* such as Event and State, which
are specialized into *primitives* such as GO, STAY, BE, GO-EXT, and
ORIENT. As an example of how the primitive GO is used to represent
sentence semantics, consider the following sentence:

(25) (i)   The ball rolled toward Beth.

      (ii)   [$_{\text{Event}}$ GO ([$_{\text{Thing}}$ BALL],
                      [$_{\text{Path}}$ TOWARD
                              ([$_{\text{Position}}$ AT ([$_{\text{Thing}}$ BALL], [$_{\text{Thing}}$ BETH])])])]

Note that this representation differs from a "deeper" representation (*e.g.*,
the conceptual dependency representation described below) in that it retains enough structure to support a systematic mapping to the syntactic
structure of the surface form.

A crucial point concerning the LCS representation is that, although
it appears to be somewhat "English-like," it is only superficially so by
virtue of the labels of the primitives (*e.g.*, GO, TO, *etc.*) that are used
in the representation. These primitives were chosen on the basis of an
extensive cross-linguistic investigation, though they may be labeled and
used in a fashion that appears to be modeled after a particular language.
A detailed discussion about the primitives and the well-formedness conditions on their combination are presented in chapter 4.

Alternative machine translation approaches that have used an interlingua based on "deeper" knowledge representations are presented by
Wilks (1973), Vauquois (1975) (CETA),[19] and more recently by Carbonell and Tomita (1987) and Nirenburg *et al.* (1992) (KBMT), Nirenburg *et al.* (1987) (TRANSLATOR), Muraki (1987) (PIVOT), Uchida
(1989) (ATLAS), among others. We will not survey all of the different
ways that one can construct an interlingua here. However, given that
the LCS representation has been commonly compared to the *conceptual
dependency* (CD) representation, a brief comparison is presented.

---

[19]Although the CETA system has been classified as interlingual here it should
be pointed out that there have been a number of persuasive arguments against this
classification due to the fact that the lexicon used in the CETA system had a bilingual
transfer-like mechanism (see, *e.g.*, Hutchins (1986) and Nirenburg *et al.* (1992)).

Figure 1.14
The CD Representation for *I like Mary* or *Mary pleases me* is a causality relation
that relates the state of being pleased to something Mary does.

Early AI approaches to translation used the CD representation as the
basis for interlingual machine translation. (See, *e.g.*, Schank (1972, 1973,
1975), Schank and Abelson (1977), and Lytinen and Schank (1982).)
These approaches were similar to that of UNITRAN in that they relied
on a compositional representation based on a small set of primitives.
However, a well-known problem with the traditional CD-based approach
is that it provides a target-language paraphrase of the source-language
sentence rather than a target-language translation of the source-language
sentence; it is now widely accepted that this approach is not adequate
for machine translation. The paraphrased output is a symptom of a
more serious problem, *i.e.*, that CD-based systems lack a canonical mapping from the interlingual representation to the syntactic structure. For
example, there is no uniform mechanism for handling even the simplest divergences such as the subject-object reversal in example (6).
Figure 1.14 shows the CD representation for this example.[20] The reason
that this representation does not lend itself readily to the specification
of a uniform mechanism for handling subject-object reversal (and other
divergence types) is that there is no systematic relationship between the
conceptual arguments of the representation and the corresponding syntactic positions in which these arguments are realized. For example, it
would be difficult to imagine a principled mapping that would realize
the conceptual entity *Mary* as the syntactic object in English, but as
the syntactic subject in Spanish.

Of course, the same argument could be used to shoot down the LCS
approach, which adopts the following representation as the interlingua

---

[20]See Schank (1972, 1973, 1975) for a description of the notation and additional
examples.

for the *like-gustar* example:

(26) [$_{\text{State}}$ BE$_{\text{Ident}}$
               ([$_{\text{Thing}}$ I],
               [$_{\text{Position}}$ AT$_{\text{Ident}}$ ([$_{\text{Thing}}$ I], [$_{\text{Thing}}$ MARY])],
               [$_{\text{Manner}}$ LIKINGLY])]

The difference is that the mapping between this representation and the
syntactic structure is systematically defined (as we will see in Part II of
this book) such that the syntax of the two representations approaches an
isomorphism. For example, the logical subject (which, in this example,
is the conceptual token [$_{\text{Thing}}$ I]) is mapped into the syntactic subject
position in the canonical case. This mapping may be overridden, in
cases of divergences, through the use of lexical parameter settings. In
the present example, the distinction between the English and Spanish
realizations of this sentence is captured by means of lexical parameterization that will be described in chapters 5 and 7. We will see how the
use of lexical parameterization provides the means for the use of a systematic mapping that applies cross-linguistically, while still accounting
for cases such as this subject-object reversal example.

One might argue that the same sort of parameterization could be used
in the CD approach as well. The problem is that the CD representation, in general, is so entirely different from the corresponding syntactic
structure in any given language that it would be impossible to devise a
principled mapping between the interlingua and the surface form. Consider the representations for *Mary died* and *John killed Mary* shown in
figure 1.15. One might wonder why the corresponding syntactic structures do not reflect these radically complex semantic structures for the
causative and non-causative forms. The realization of the syntactic subject, which would be *Mary* in the case of *die* and *John* in the case of
kill, illustrates the difficulty in constructing a principled mapping between the interlingua and the syntactic structure. Perhaps it could be
argued that a plausible mapping would be one that relates the highest
left-most conceptual constituent to the syntactic subject position. This
would work for the current example, but not for one such as *I believe
that John is a fool*, which has the conceptualization shown in figure 1.16.
Note that John is the highest left-most conceptual constituent in this
representation, but the subject of the sentence is *I*.

An additional difference worth mentioning is that the CD approach

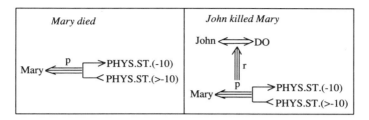

Figure 1.15
The CD representation for *Mary died* indicates that Mary changed into a "very bad physical state" (*i.e.*, dead). The CD representation for *John killed Mary* indicates that John caused this state to come about.

John
$\Uparrow$ $\Longleftrightarrow$ LOC(M)
fool $\Uparrow$ POSS-BY
            I

Figure 1.16
The CD Representation *I believe John is a fool* indicates that the conceptualization *John is a fool* is located in the memory of *I*.

does not provide a principled relationship between well-known syntactic alternations, most notably the causative alternation. Causative forms are represented as a function over two events in CD notation as shown in the representation for *John killed Mary* in figure 1.15. It might be argued that adding "John $\stackrel{P}{\Longleftrightarrow}$ DO" to the state-change portion of the CD provides a principled method of deriving the causative form of the action. However, this method does not carry over to other causative forms such as *John threw the ball from the roof* derived from the non-causative form *The ball fell from the roof* (see figure 1.17). Here, the non-causative and causative forms are distinguished by means of the specification of the agent: the non-causative form includes an unspecified agent (designated by '*'), whereas the causative form fills this position with an overt agent.

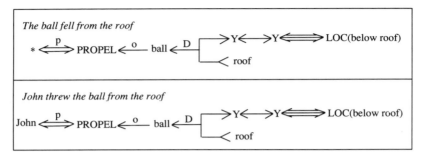

Figure 1.17
The CD representation for *The ball fell from the roof* indicates that the ball was propelled by some unknown agent (∗) from the roof level to a location below roof level. The CD representation for *John threw the ball from the roof* indicates that John caused this action to come about.

In the UNITRAN system, the causative and non-causative forms are systematically related by means of the CAUSE primitive:

(27) (i) Mary died
       [Event GOIdent
           ([Thing Mary],
           [Position TOWARDIdent
               ([Position ATIdent ([Thing Mary], [Property DEAD])])])]

      (ii) John killed Mary
       [Event CAUSE
           ([Thing John],
           [Event GOIdent
               ([Thing Mary],
               [Position TOWARDIdent
                   ([Position ATIdent ([Thing Mary], [Property DEAD])])])])][21]

---

[21] It might be argued that this representation is subject to the objections raised by Fodor (1970) regarding the inadequacy of deriving *kill* from *cause to die* (*e.g.*, one can cause someone to die on Tuesday by shooting him on Monday, but one cannot kill someone on Tuesday by shooting him on Monday). Jackendoff discusses this problem, but does not specifically address it in his approach. Rather, Jackendoff proposes that the primary task of defining be assigned to "typicality conditions" (*e.g.*, that the verb *climb* usually incorporates the notion of *up* or that *X causing Y to die* usually implies *that X killed Y*) not necessary and sufficient conditions. That is, Jackendoff is concerned with what structure the meaning has, not whether all the details of the causal relationships are precisely conveyed. The dependence on necessary and sufficient conditions, he argues, is characteristic of exhaustive decomposition approaches such as that of Schank (1972, 1973, 1975) and also that of generative semanticists (*e.g.*, Lakoff (1971)), whose goals diverge significantly from those of Jackendoff. The LCS approach relies on a non-exhaustive decompositional paradigm that provides a

(28) (i)   The ball fell from the roof
      [$_{\text{Event}}$ GO$_{\text{Loc}}$
          ([$_{\text{Thing}}$ BALL],
          [$_{\text{Position}}$ FROM$_{\text{Loc}}$
              ([$_{\text{Position}}$ AT$_{\text{Loc}}$ ([$_{\text{Thing}}$ BALL], [$_{\text{Location}}$ ROOF])])])]

      (ii)   John threw the ball from the roof
      [$_{\text{Event}}$ CAUSE
          ([$_{\text{Thing}}$ John],
          [$_{\text{Event}}$ GO$_{\text{Loc}}$
              ([$_{\text{Thing}}$ BALL],
              [$_{\text{Position}}$ FROM$_{\text{Loc}}$
                  ([$_{\text{Position}}$ AT$_{\text{Loc}}$ ([$_{\text{Thing}}$ BALL], [$_{\text{Location}}$ ROOF])])])])]

Note that, unlike the CD representation, both (27) and (28) follow the same principle of causative formation. Furthermore, the syntactic structure of the causative and non-causative forms reflects the structure of the corresponding conceptual forms. In particular, the logical subject, which consistently appears in the highest/left-most position of the LCS, maps directly to the syntactic subject position. Thus, a systematic mapping between the LCS and the syntactic structure is readily available.

If we dig a bit deeper into the reasons behind the difficulty of using the CD representation as an interlingua, we find that the fundamental problem is that the CD framework subscribes to the notion that every imaginable component of meaning must be captured in a single representational formalism. Indeed, the CD formalism is one of the most thoroughly developed representations ever devised in the history of the field of AI. Clearly there are elements of meaning available in the CD representation that are not available in the LCS representation, e.g., information concerning short-term and long-term memory. Nonetheless, such an approach pays a high price for incorporating "deeper" knowledge in a single representation without preserving structurally defined lexical-semantic information. The most notable drawback, as we have seen, is the lack of systematicity in the relation between the representation and the surface form. This point has often been ignored by AI researchers that have compared the LCS framework to that of early AI

---

systematic relation between the structure of meaning and the structure of language on the surface; unlike alternative decompositional approaches, it does not attempt to provide an exhaustive decomposition of word meaning into a finite set of semantic/conceptual primitives that define a finite collection of necessary and sufficient conditions. We will return to this point again in chapter 4.

researchers, although it has been given (a very brief) acknowledgment in a recent review of Jackendoff (1990) by Wilks (1992, p. 96):

(29)   "But Jackendoff seems to have done a lot more work on [AI and CL codings] and particularly on the explicit relationship of the lexical codings to related syntactic structures, which was often left implicit in the structure of the parser in the early CL work I referred to [by Schank (1975), Schank and Riesbeck (1981), and Wilks (1973)]."[22]

The current approach attempts to achieve a middle ground between representations that encode too much information and those that encode too little. In particular, the interlingua includes those aspects of lexical knowledge related to lexical-semantic properties of words (*e.g.*, argument structure of verbs) but does not include "deeper" notions of meaning such as aspectual, contextual, domain, and world knowledge. While these "deeper" notions are indisputably necessary for a general solution to machine translation, previous approaches that have employed deep semantic representations say very little about how to construct a single, cross-linguistically applicable mapping between the syntactic structure and the interlingua. Furthermore, the types of divergences that are addressed here do not require deeper notions of knowledge, but rather knowledge about general lexical-semantic properties that hold across languages. Clearly, the techniques used in deeper knowledge approaches (*e.g.*, KBMT by Carbonell and Tomita (1987) and Nirenburg *et al.* (1992)) are necessary for filling other gaps in the translation process, most notably the process of lexical selection, which generally requires more than just argument-structure information for disambiguation of nouns and attachment of modifiers.

The current approach strives to fill what I truly believe to be a serious gap in many existing approaches to machine translation, namely that of

---

[22]This remark was virtually the only positive comment given in the entire book review, and no elaboration was given on this point. Regarding the rest of the review, I may not be so quick to agree on his point that the framework has resulted in no serious computer program; I believe this to be a matter of opinion. (I imagine that many other researchers might disagree as well, *e.g.*, Palmer and Polguère (1992), Siskind (1992), White (1992), among others.) Nonetheless, to Wilks' credit, many of the points made in the review were justified, most notably the discussion regarding the lack of comment about the relation between Jackendoff's linguistic framework and the frameworks of both early and contemporary AI/CL researchers. (Regarding this point, however, the reader is referred to the response by Jackendoff (1992).) It is my sincere hope that this point has been addressed by the discussion in the current chapter, as well as by additional discussion interleaved with relevant sections in later chapters.

providing systematic linking rules between the lexical representation and the syntactic structure. The LCS-based framework is intended to be a supplement to, not a substitute for, models that employ knowledge-based techniques. It is expected that a fully interlingual translation system would require knowledge-based techniques to operate in tandem with the techniques described here.

To sum up, this book will examine a number of issues concerning the lexical-semantic framework adopted in UNITRAN. The primary focus will be on the accommodation of distinctions across languages through the interaction of the lexical-semantic representation with the technique of parameter setting. A critical component of this research is the provision of a catalog of cross-linguistic divergence types that involve both syntactic properties (*e.g.*, word ordering) and lexical-semantic properties (*e.g.*, selectional requirements of lexical items). This catalog was the basis for a number of decisions that were made during the design and construction of UNITRAN including the definition of primitives, structure of the interlingua, organization of the lexicon, and definition of a parameterized mapping between the syntax and lexical semantics.

I SYNTACTIC COMPONENT

2 Syntactic Processing

This chapter describes the syntactic processing involved in the translation of a source-language sentence to a target-language sentence. An overview of the design of the syntactic processor will be presented in the next section. Following the overview, the remainder of this chapter will discuss the implementation of the principles of *Government Binding* (GB) theory. In particular, we will focus on the parameterization of these principles and we will examine the English, Spanish, and German phenomena that are handled by parameterization.

2.1 Overview of the Design of the Syntactic Processor

Figure 2.1 shows a diagram of the UNITRAN syntactic processing component. Note that the example shown here was given in example (8) of chapter 1.[1] The parser of this component provides a source-language syntactic structure to the lexical-semantic processor, and, after lexical-semantic,processing is completed, the generator of this component provides a target-language syntactic structure. In terms of figure 1.10, the syntactic processor is executed after morphological analysis and then again prior to morphological synthesis (after returning from lexical-semantic,processing).

Both the parser and generator of the syntactic component have access to the syntactic principles of GB theory.[2] These principles, which act as constraints (*i.e.*, filters) on the syntactic structures produced by the parser and the generator, operate on the basis of parameter settings that supply certain language-specific information; the parameters enable the system to account for syntactic divergences such as those given previously in figure 1.11, repeated here as figure 2.2.

Structure-building operations applied by the parser and generator are defined independently from operations associated with GB constraints. These two types of operations are related in a co-routine design in the spirit of Dorr (1987a,b,c). We will briefly discuss the mechanism used for

---

[1] The syntactic structures shown here include morphologically parsed words at leaf nodes (*e.g.*, *stab+ed* instead of *stabbed*), which more closely reflects the actual representations that are used by the system. However, this parsed format will generally be used for illustrational purposes (*i.e.*, in most cases, syntactic structures will include the surface forms of words).

[2] For the reader who is interested in exploring the theory in more detail, the recent and comprehensive publication by Haegeman (1991) describes GB theory in more detail than is presented here.

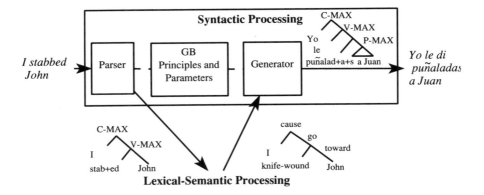

Figure 2.1
The syntactic processing component is designed so that the parser and generator
both operate on the basis of the same principles and parameters of
government-binding theory.

parsing a source-language sentence. The algorithm used for generating
a target-language structure within the current framework is discussed in
detail in chapter 6.

Figure 2.3 illustrates the parsing stage of translation. During the
parse of a source-language sentence, there is a back-and-forth flow between the structure building component and the constraint module, yet
the operations defined in each component are independently defined.
The modularization of these operations allows for uniform processing:
both the parser and generator apply the same constraints (in the same
order) *after* a skeletal phrase structure has been built, even though the
mechanism for building the structure is not necessarily the same during
parsing and generation.

The Earley Structure Builder constructs skeletal phrase structures
using a modified version of a system built by de Marcken (1989) based
on the Earley algorithm (Earley (1970)). The resulting representations
are underspecified in that they do not include information about agreement, abstract case, thematic roles, argument structure, *etc.* The GB
Constraint Module enforces well-formedness conditions (agreement filters, case filters, *etc.*) on the structures passed to it, and adds missing
information (argument structure, thematic roles, *etc.*) not available to

Divergence Type	Translation Example
Constituent Order	E: I have seen him ⇕ G: Ich habe ihn gesehen (I have him seen)
Preposition Stranding	E: What store did John go to ⇕ S: * Cuál tienda fue Juan a (What store did John go to)
Long Distance Movement	E: * Who did you wonder whether went to school ⇕ S: Quién contemplabas tú que fue a la escuela (Who did you wonder whether went to school)
Null Subject	E: I saw the book ⇕ S: Vi el libro (Saw the book)
Dative	E: I gave the book to him ⇕ G: Ich gab ihm das Buch (I gave him the book)

Figure 2.2
Syntactic translation divergences are accounted for by means of syntactic parameterization.

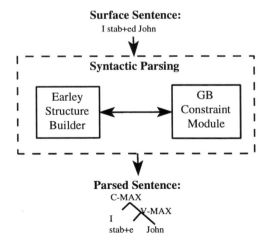

Figure 2.3
Structure-building operations are executed independently from, but in tandem with, operations applied by the constraint module.

the structure building component. Note that the model assumes that a syntactic structure will initially be assigned to a sentence, and that this structure may be eliminated or modified according to principles of GB. This design is consistent with several studies that indicate that the human language processor initially assigns a (possibly ambiguous or underspecified) structural analysis to a sentence, leaving lexical and semantic decisions for subsequent processing.

As described in Dorr (1987a,b,c), the modifications that have been made to the original Earley implementation concern the use of a set of precompiled templates which will be described in section 2.3. In addition, the system has been modified in that it delays the *scan* operation (*i.e.*, traversing a word of input) until a *subcategorization* check has been made. Subcategorization refers to selection by a verb. For example, the subcategorization frame for *put* indicates that this verb selects two arguments, one that is a noun phrase (the theme), and another that is a prepositional phrase (the location) as in the sentence *I put the car in the garage*. The use of a subcategorization check greatly increases the efficiency of the system by allowing the parser to determine whether a particular rule is applicable in a given context. For example, if the current word were *put*, then during the scan operation, the rule V-MAX $\Rightarrow$ • V N-MAX P-MAX would be allowed to apply because it passes the subcategorization test (thus allowing sentences such as *put the book on the table*). On the other hand, the rule V-MAX $\Rightarrow$ • V P-MAX would not be allowed to apply because it does not pass the subcategorization test (thus disallowing sentence such as **put on the table*).[3] These rules are derived on the basis of information associated with the LCS for the word *put* as described in chapter 4.

The algorithm for parsing a source-language sentence is conceptually simple. Essentially, the words of the input, $w_i \ldots w_n$, are read left to right. As the Earley parser scans a word w_i, a set of word-level constraints are applied. An example of such a constraint is the subcategorization test mentioned above. Similarly, as the Earley parser predicts (*i.e.*, builds) and completes (*i.e.*, attaches) a phrase, a set of phrase-level constraints are applied. An example of such a constraint is one that determines whether all constituents of a phrase have been assigned

---

[3]The $\overline{\mathrm{X}}$ symbols used in these rules is described below in section 2.3. The dot (•) notation is used by the Earley algorithm to indicate that the symbol immediately to the right is predicted to be the category of the next input word.

thematic roles appropriately. Additional details about the algorithm are presented in Dorr (1987c).

In the example of figure 2.1, the syntactic constraints reduce the number of source-language structures produced by the parser to one. The reduced set of parses then gets shipped off to the lexical-semantic component. Upon return from this component, the generator takes over to syntactically realize the conceptual structure (*i.e.*, the LCS pivot form) for the target-language sentence. At this point there are (once again) a number of syntactic structures to choose from. The same syntactic constraints (with the target-language parameter settings) are applied again, this time to the target-language structures, and the invalid possibilities are weeded out. Finally, the winning target language structure is returned.[4]

2.2   Implementation of the GB Modules

The GB principles and parameters of the syntactic component are organized into modules whose constraints are applied in the following order: (1) $\overline{\text{X}}$, (2) Bounding, (3) Case, (4) Trace, (5) Binding, and (6) θ. The $\overline{\text{X}}$ module builds a phrase-structure representation from a set of precompiled templates. Then the parameterized principles of the five remaining modules are applied as constraints to the phrase-structure representation. In addition, there is another module called the Government module, which is not mentioned as one of the steps above because it is an

---

[4]There are actually additional translations for this example (*e.g.*, *Yo le apuñalé a Juan*), although only one surface tree is shown here. In general, the system returns all possibilities when there is more than once choice for the translation. It also returns more than one result in the case of ambiguity: if there were a prepositional-phrase attachment ambiguity as in *John saw the man with the telescope* (the telescope may be associated either with the act of seeing, or with the man), two source-language syntactic trees would be returned, two LCS's would be composed, and, if the target language did not have a single (ambiguous) way of stating the two concepts, two target-language syntactic trees would be returned. Without context, this is the best that can be expected from a parser or a generator. Because UNITRAN does not attempt to apply any sort of disambiguation strategy, it may return multiple structures, both during parsing and during generation. We will return to the issue of disambiguation in chapter 4.

integral part of all the steps (except 1). Thus, we can visualize the order
of constraint application as follows:

(30)   1. $\overline{\text{X}}$
        2. Bounding ⎫
        3. Case   ⎪
        4. Trace   ⎬ Government
        5. Binding   ⎪
        6. θ ⎭

Figure 2.4 summarizes the parameters used by the constraint modules
of the syntactic component. Each of these will be discussed, in turn,
in sections 2.3–2.9. Appendix A summarizes the divergence examples
with respect to these linguistic modules and parameters described in
this chapter.

One point to note about these parameters is that their domain of
accessibility is restricted. The $\overline{\text{X}}$ parameters plus a handful of other
parameters are only accessed *off-line i.e.*, during the precompilation of
a set of phrase-structure templates (as discussed below). The automatic
precompilation of parameter settings related to phrase structure allows
languages to be added without hand-construction of language-specific
grammars for each source and target languages. (See fn. 7 of chapter 1.)
The rest of the parameters are accessed during *on-line* processing.

The decision to automatically compile a small number of parameters
into the phrase-structure templates prior to on-line processing is based
on empirical determination that this tends to result in more efficient
parsing and generation than if we leave out this information. This is because we are more likely to build the correct structure in the first place
if we start with a more constrained phrase-structure representation. An
alternative approach is to use *only* the $\overline{\text{X}}$ principles and parameters to
build unconstrained phrase-structure templates, and to apply all other
principles as constraints on-line; however, in this approach, the remaining constraints have the burden of cleaning up an exponentially large
mess that the syntactic processors have built through the invalid instantiation of wholly unconstrained templates. Another alternative is to pre-
compile *all* of the GB principles and parameters, building an enormous
library of fully specified phrase-structure templates (as in traditional
grammar-based approaches such as GPSG). This approach is even more
costly: the system would have an inordinately large search space during

GB Module	GB Parameter	Purpose	Restrictions	Example
X̄	Basic Categories	Provides head categories	precompilation	E,S,G: V is head of V-MAX
	Constituent Order	Determines order of head wrt specs & comps	precompilation	E,S: V precedes object
	Base Specifiers	Determines allowable specifiers	precompilation	E,S,G: N-MAX is spec of I
	Base Adjuncts	Determines allowable adjuncts	precompilation	E: A is left-min adjunct of N
	Affix Removal	Specifies separable affix categories	precompilation	G: P and ADV are separable prefixes
Gov't	Proper Governors	Determines distribution of lexical heads wrt to traces	on-line	S: no preposition stranding allowed
Bounding	Moved Specifiers	Determines movable specifiers	precompilation	E,S,G: ADV may move to specifier of I
	Moved Adjuncts	Determines movable adjuncts	precompilation	E,S,G: ADV may adjoin left-max of V
	Bounding Nodes	Constrains distance between trace and antecedent	on-line	S: movement beyond I-MAX allowed
Case	Type of Gov't	Specifies structural case ass't conditions	on-line	S: P required before clitic-doubled object
	Case Properties	Specifies lexical case ass't conditions	on-line	E: *believe* takes inf clause w/ subject
Trace	Traces	Determines trace categories	precompilation	E,S,G: V is a trace category
	Empties	Specifies category and pos'n of non-overt elements	precompilation	E,S,G: N-MAX in specifier of I
	Empty Funct'l Elts	Specifies comp structure of empty funct'l elements	precompilation	E,S,G: C selects I-MAX
	Null Subject	Specifies whether subject is optional	on-line	S: null subject is allowed
	Chain Conditions	Specifies whether empty head can be a governor	on-line	S: empty head may be a governor
Binding	Governing Category	Determines domain of binding	on-line	E,S,G: anaphor must have local anteced.
θ	Clitics	Specifies categories for clitic elts	precompilation	S: dat and acc clitic pronouns allowed
	Clitic Doubling	Determines whether clitic doubling is allowed	on-line	S: clitic doubling allowed
	Nom-Drop	Determines conditions for θ-role assignment of pleonastics	on-line	E: no empty pleonastics allowed

Figure 2.4
The parameters used by the syntactic component are defined in seven independent modules.

each step of parsing or generation since the number of structures grows exponentially as each word is projected and positioned into the working structure.

It has been argued that a parser or generator is ideally specified if there is an optimal balance between those constraints that are compiled off-line in the phrase-structure component and those that are applied on-line after the structure has been built. The question of balance between off-line precompilation and on-line processing in the context of parsing has been investigated recently by a number of researchers including Berwick and Fong (1990) Dorr (1990c), Fong (1991), and Merlo (1992). Although the optimal balance may not be present in the model described here, this newer arrangement has at least been found to be more beneficial than that of an earlier version of the system (see *e.g.*, Dorr (1987a,b,c)) in which the phrase-structure rules were wholly unconstrained, and also that of the traditional GPSG approach of Gazdar *et al.* (1985), in which the phrase-structure rules have all the grammatical constraints encoded into them.[5] For alternative approaches to parsing within the GB framework, see, for example, Abney (1989) Fong (1991), Coen (1991), Frank (1990), Johnson (1989), Kashket (1991), Marcus (1980), Merlo (1992), Sharp (1985), Wehrli (1992), and Weinberg (1988).

We will now discuss each of the GB modules, in detail, focusing on how the syntactic divergences of figure 2.2 (as well as others) are accounted for by the parameter-setting approach.

2.3 Principles and Parameters of the $\overline{\text{X}}$ Module

The $\overline{\text{X}}$ constraint module of the syntactic component provides the phrase-structure representation of sentences. Figure 2.5 shows the structure of a $\overline{\text{X}}$ phrase.[6] The fundamental principle of the $\overline{\text{X}}$ module is that each phrase of a sentence has a *maximal projection*, X-MAX, for a *head* of category X, where X is determined by a parameter of $\overline{\text{X}}$-Theory called *basic categories*. In addition to the head X, the X-MAX projection potentially contains *complements* $\text{Z-MAX}_1 \ldots \text{Z-MAX}_n$ (*e.g.*, the objects

---

[5] For more on the complexity of GPSG, see Ristad (1986).

[6] This is a revised version of the $\overline{\text{X}}$-Theory presented by Chomsky (1986b). Note that the configuration shown in figure 2.5 corresponds to the spec-initial/head-initial case (*i.e.*, the word order for English). As we will see shortly, there are three other possible configurations.

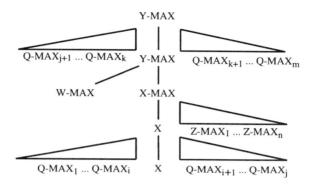

Figure 2.5
The $\overline{\text{X}}$ phrase-structure template is "fit" onto the phrase structure of each language by providing the appropriate settings for the parameters of the $\overline{\text{X}}$ module.

of a verb) and *minimal adjuncts* $Q\text{-MAX}_1 \ldots Q\text{-MAX}_j$ (*e.g.*, adverbial modifiers of a verb). A phrase may be projected one level higher, (*i.e.*, to the Y-MAX level shown in figure 2.5), under which would be attached the *specifier* W-MAX and *maximal adjuncts* $Q\text{-MAX}_{j+1} \ldots Q\text{-MAX}_m$.[7] The specifier and complements are ordered according to the *constituent order* and *base specifiers* parameters, and the adjuncts (both minimal and maximal) are positioned according to the *base adjuncts* and *affix removal* parameters.

An example that makes this description more concrete is the following sentence:

(31)   Yesterday John saw Mary's older sister in her car

Here, there are three specifier phrases: the noun phrase *John* is in the specifier position of projection of the verb phrase headed by *saw*; the noun phrase *Mary's* is in the specifier position of the noun phrase headed by *sister*; and the noun phrase *her* is in the specifier position of the noun phrase headed by *car*. There are also three adjoined phrases: the adverbial phrase *yesterday* is adjoined maximally to the left of the top-level clause, the adjectival phrase *older* is adjoined minimally to the left of the noun *sister*, and the prepositional phrase headed by *in* is adjoined

---

[7] In many phrase types, *e.g.*, noun phrases, Y is the same category as X.

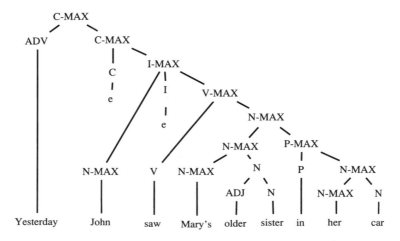

Figure 2.6
The instantiation of the $\overline{\mathrm{X}}$ phrase-structure representation for *Yesterday John saw Mary's older sister in her car* illustrates the structural positioning of specifiers (*e.g., John*), complements (*e.g., her car*), minimal adjuncts (*e.g., older*), and maximal adjuncts (*e.g., Mary's*).

maximally to the right of the noun phrase headed by *sister*. In addition, there are two complement phrases: the noun phrase headed by *sister* is in the complement position of the verb phrase headed by *saw*, and the noun phrase headed by *car* is in complement position of the prepositional phrase headed by *in*. Figure 2.6 illustrates the instantiation of the $\overline{\mathrm{X}}$ representation for this example.

Given the general $\overline{\mathrm{X}}$ phrase-structure representation of figure 2.5, we can now "fit" this template onto the phrase structure of each language by providing the appropriate settings for the parameters of the $\overline{\mathrm{X}}$ module. We will examine what these parameter settings are for English, Spanish, and German, and we will look at some examples of how these settings account for certain syntactic divergences among the three languages.

2.3.1 $\overline{\mathrm{X}}$ Parameter Settings

Figure 2.7 shows the English, Spanish, and German settings for the $\overline{\mathrm{X}}$ module. These parameter settings are used for building phrasal projec-

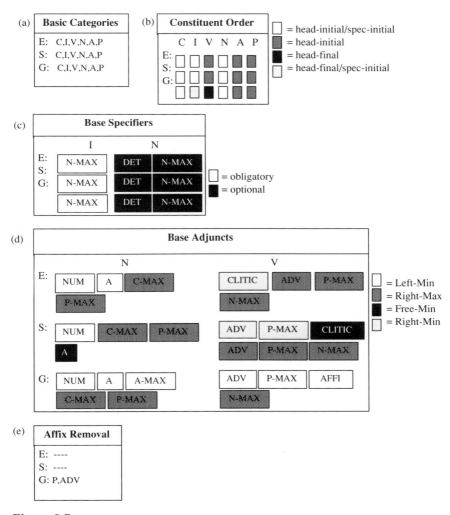

Figure 2.7
The parameter settings for the $\overline{\text{X}}$ module are used for off-line precompilation.

tions. We will discuss the effect of each of these parameter settings in turn.

The choices for the head X of a phrase X-MAX are determined by the *basic categories* parameter (see figure 2.7(a)). The common setting for English, Spanish, and German is not universal across languages; thus, this parameter has been made available in anticipation of adding other languages. For example, it has been argued that Japanese has no functional categories (*e.g.*, determiners such as *the*) by Chomsky (1987), and that Warlpiri has no adjectives (*e.g.*, modifiers such as *good*) by Nash (1980). In the case of English, Spanish, and German, this parameter has the same value {C, I, V, N, A, P}, where C, I, V, N, A, and P are Complementizer, Inflection, Verb, Noun, Adjective, and Preposition, respectively.[8]

The *constituent order* parameter (see figure 2.7(b)) accounts for the word-order distinctions for English, Spanish, and German on a per-category basis.[9] The setting of the constituent order parameter determines where the specifier and complement (*i.e.*, the W-MAX and Z-MAX's in figure 2.5) of a phrase will be positioned. For example, in a language like English, the complement of a verb (*i.e.*, the verbal object) is positioned *after* the verb, and the specifier of the verb (*i.e.*, the subject) is positioned *before* the verb; thus, English is considered to be head-initial/spec-initial with respect to verbs.

As it turns out, the configuration shown in figure 2.5 corresponds to the spec-initial/head-initial case (*i.e.*, the word order for English and Spanish). The constituent order parameter also accommodates the three phrase-structure configurations shown in figure 2.8.

Unlike English and Spanish, German is assumed to be a subject-object-verb language, which means that verb phrases and inflectional

---

[8]The C(omplementizer) category corresponds to relative pronouns such as *that* in *the man that I saw*. The I(nflectional) category corresponds to modals such as *would* in *I would eat cake*. The term "Inflection" refers to *verbal* inflection, not other types of inflection (*e.g.*, noun declension in German). Thus, I is considered to be a projection of V. Both C and I are often empty as they are in figure 2.6.

[9]The head-initial and head-final settings are used in degenerate cases where no specifier is available (*i.e.*, phrases headed by verbs, adjectives, and prepositions in English, Spanish, and German). Note that two configurations are missing, *i.e.*, head-initial/spec-final and head-final/spec-final. Such cases do arise in natural language (*e.g.*, Greek has a spec-final setting for the I category). However, since none of the three languages fits into these categories, these parameter settings do not appear in figure 2.7(b).

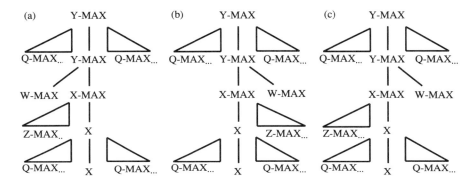

Figure 2.8
Three additional constituent orders are available to the $\overline{\text{X}}$ module:
head-final/spec-initial, head-initial/spec-final, and head-final/spec-final.

phrases follow the head-final/spec-initial template of figure 2.8(a). [10] It is
also assumed to adhere to the verb-second requirement in matrix clauses
(see Safir (1985)). The verb-second requirement forces the specifier of C
to be non-empty (usually the subject moves here) and the final tensed
verb to move into the head of C (for matrix clauses only). Thus, the
typical syntactic structure of a matrix clause in German is as shown in
figure 2.9. By contrast, the corresponding syntactic structure for English and Spanish is as shown in figure 2.10. Thus, for the sentence *I
have seen him*, we have the following contrasting argument structures:

(32) **Constituent Order divergence:**

> E: [C-MAX [I-MAX [N-MAX I]
>> [V-MAX [V have] [V-MAX [V seen] [N-MAX him]]]]]]
>
> S: [C-MAX [I-MAX [N-MAX Yo]
>> [V-MAX lo [V he] [V-MAX [V visto]]]]]]
>
> G: [C-MAX Ich$_i$ habe$_j$
>> [I-MAX [N-MAX t$_i$]
>>> [V-MAX [V-MAX [N-MAX ihn] [V gesehen]] [V t$_j$]]]]]

The constituent order parameter (in particular, the setting for I and V)
accounts for these distinctions by forcing verb phrases and inflectional

---

[10]The German verb phrase is a degenerate case of this template (*i.e.*, it is a head-
final phrase without a specifier) since verb phrases do not locally include a specifier.

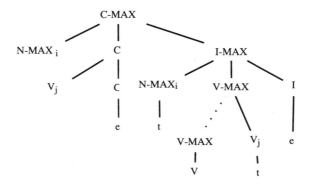

Figure 2.9
The canonical phrase structure template corresponding to a German matrix clause
positions the verb in second position. Thus, there is a trace corresponding to the
fronted verb as well as the fronted subject.

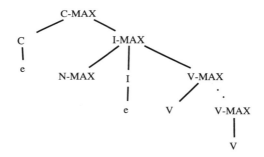

Figure 2.10
The canonical phrase structure template corresponding to an English or Spanish
matrix clause uses subject-verb-object positioning.

phrases to be head-final in German, whereas these phrases are forced to
be head-initial in English and Spanish.

The *base specifiers* parameter (see figure 2.7(c)) is necessary for determining the type of specifier that is allowed for each basic category, and
whether that specifier is obligatory or optional. There are two types of
specifiers: ones that are base-generated and ones that are moved. The
base-generated specifiers are included in the $\overline{X}$ module; the moved specifiers are included in the Bounding module. In terms of the template of
figure 2.5, the base specifiers fill the W-MAX position.

The base specifiers are allowed to be either optional or obligatory as determined by this parameter setting. The setting for I corresponds to subject position; in all three languages, the subject position is obligatory (even though it may be filled with an empty element such as *pro* or PRO). The setting for N corresponds to determiner constructions (*e.g.*, *the book*) and possessive constructions (*e.g.*, *my book*).

As in the case of specifiers, there are two types of adjuncts: base-generated and moved. The *base adjuncts* parameter (see figure 2.7(d)) specifies those adjuncts that are base generated (*i.e.*, they are included in the $\overline{\text{X}}$ module); the moved adjuncts are included in the Bounding module (to be discussed in section 2.3.2). The base adjuncts parameter specifies the position (left, right or free) and level (minimal or maximal) of each adjunct with respect to the category to which it is adjoined. In terms of the template of figure 2.5, the base adjuncts fill the Q-MAX positions.

From the parameter settings shown for English, Spanish, and German, we are able to account for the syntactic divergences associated with different types of adjunct structures. For example, English, Spanish, and German differ with respect to the possible positions where an adjective may be attached under a noun phrase. In English and German, an adjective may only be placed to the left of the head noun, whereas in Spanish it may be placed on either side:

(33) **Adjunction divergence:**
      E: the [$_A$ large] book
          $*$ the book [$_A$ large]^{11}
      S: el [$_A$ gran] libro^{12}
          el libro [$_A$ grande]
      G: das [$_A$ große] Buch
          $*$ das Buch [$_A$ groß]

In addition to bare adjective adjunction, in German an entire adjecti-val phrase (A-MAX) may be placed to the left of the head noun, whereas

---

[11] The '$*$' symbol indicates an ungrammatical construction.

[12] There is often a slight distinction in meaning depending on the side on which the adjective appears. In the case of *grande*, appearing on the left (as *gran*) corresponds to the meaning "great," whereas, appearing on the right corresponds to the meaning "large."

in English and Spanish, the same construction is not allowed:

(34) **Adjunction divergence:**
    E: * the [A-MAX lying ?on the table] book
    S: * el [A-MAX puesto en la mesa] libro
    G: das [A-MAX auf dem Tisch liegende] Buch

Another adjunct construction that diverges across English, Spanish, and German is adverbial and prepositional phrase adjunction with respect to a verb phrase. In English, an adverb or prepositional phrase may occur on the right side of the verb, but at the maximal level only (*i.e.*, not between the verb and its object). On the other hand, in Spanish, an adverb or prepositional phrase may occur on the right side of the verb, both at the maximal level and also between the verb and its object. In German, an adverb or prepositional phrase can occur between the verb and its object (on the left side), but it cannot adjoin maximally on the right. The following examples illustrate these distinctions:

(35) **Adjunction divergence:**
    E: John has eaten breakfast [ADV frequently]
       * John has eaten [ADV frequently] breakfast
       John has eaten breakfast [P-MAX in the morning]
       * John has eaten [P-MAX in the morning] breakfast
    S: Juan ha comido el desayuno [ADV frecuentamente]
       Juan ha comido [ADV frecuentamente] el desayuno
       Juan ha comido el desayuno [P-MAX en la mañana]
       Juan ha comido [P-MAX en la mañana] el desayuno
    G: * Johann hat Frühstück gegessen [ADV oft]
       ? Johann hat Frühstück [ADV oft] gegessen[13]
       * Johann hat Frühstück gegessen [P-MAX im Zimmer]
       Johann hat Frühstück [P-MAX im Zimmer] gegessen

The *affix removal* parameter (see figure 2.7(e)) is particularly relevant to languages in which an affix may be separated from its associated verb. In German, the affix removal parameter accounts for the case where an affix is left behind by a verb that has moved to a verb-second position. This happens in the German sentence *Johann brach ins Zimmer hinein,*

---

[13]The sentence *Johann hat Frühstück oft gegessen* is not acceptable to all native German speakers. The '?' symbol indicates that the construction is generally considered to be grammatical, but slightly awkward.

which means *John broke into the room*. Here, the affix-verb *hinein-brechen* has been separated into the two pieces: the verb *brach* and the adverb *hinein*. The affix removal parameter specifies the type of affixes that are allowed to be separated from the root form. Affix forms may only adjoin to categories specified by the base adjuncts parameter.

2.3.2 Other Parameters Used for Structure-Building

In addition to the parameters of the $\overline{\text{X}}$ module, a small set of parameters from other GB modules are used for the construction of the phrase structures of the form shown in figure 2.5. Although these parameters are not associated with the principles of $\overline{\text{X}}$ theory, they are discussed in this section since they are used at the same time as the $\overline{\text{X}}$ parameters to fill in additional phrase-structure information. These parameter settings are accessed (together with the $\overline{\text{X}}$ parameter settings) *off-line* for precompilation of additional phrase-structure templates. The templates are then used by the parser and generator to build the syntactic structure for each language. The majority of the other non-$\overline{\text{X}}$ parameter settings are accessed on-line *after* the phrase structure has been built; these parameters are associated with the GB constraints that rule out syntactically invalid phrase structures during processing. We will discuss these on-line constraints in sections 2.4– 2.9. The non-$\overline{\text{X}}$ principles and parameters that are precompiled into the phrase-structure templates are shown in figure 2.11. We will discuss the effect of each of these parameter settings in turn.

The Trace module (to be described in section 2.7) includes three parameters that are used for precompilation: *traces*, *empties*, and *empty functional elements*. The *traces* parameter specifies the categories that are allowed to appear in an empty sentence position that is related to an overt element elsewhere in the sentence (*e.g.*, t_i in *What$_i$ did he see t$_i$*). The *empties* parameter specifies the category and position of non-overt elements (*e.g.*, PRO$_i$ in *I$_i$ want PRO$_i$ to go home*, or *pro* in *pro tengo hambre*). The *empty functional elements* parameter specifies the complement structure of potentially empty elements such as C and I (see fn. 8 earlier in this chapter). The settings for each of these three parameters is the same for English, Spanish, and German as shown in figure 2.11(a)–(c).

The reason for using these parameter settings for precompilation is that they provide information that would otherwise be unavailable given

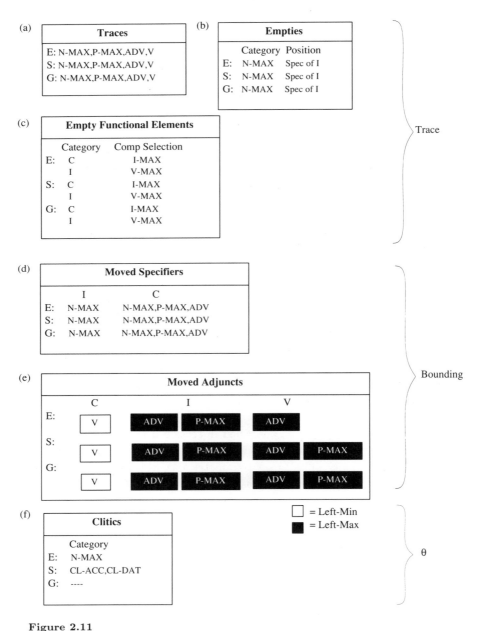

Figure 2.11
Certain of the parameter settings from the Trace, Bounding, and θ modules are used for off-line precompilation.

that the head element is allowed to be non-lexical (*i.e.*, empty) in all three cases. In order to build a phrase that conforms to the representation shown in figure 2.5, a maximal category must be projected from the empty head, and, in the case of a functional element, the complement must be generated in its appropriate position. The phrase-structure templates that are generated from these parameter settings for English, Spanish, and German are shown in figure 2.12. Note that even though the settings of the trace parameters are the same for all three languages, the phrase-structure templates are not all exactly the same due to an interaction with other parameter settings such as the *null subject* parameter and the *constituent order* parameter. For example, the empty functional elements parameter setting for English, Spanish, and German specifies that the category is potentially lexically empty and that, by default, it selects a V-MAX as a complement. However, the position of the V-MAX complement with respect to the head I varies depending on the setting of the constituent order parameter; thus, the empty functional elements template for German differs from that of both English and Spanish in that the empty head I occurs to the right of the V-MAX complement.

The Bounding module (to be described in section 2.5) includes two parameters that are accessed during precompilation: *moved specifiers* and *moved adjuncts*. These are analogous to the *base specifiers* and *base adjuncts* parameters described in the last section except that they refer to positions that are *derived* (via movement) rather than base generated. In terms of the template of figure 2.5, the moved specifiers fill the W-MAX position and the moved adjuncts fill the Q-MAX positions. The settings for these two parameters are shown in figure 2.11 (d) and (e).

The moved specifiers parameter has a similar specification to that of the base specifiers except that they are always optional. The settings are the same for English, Spanish, and German; thus, the same specifier movement constructions appear in all three languages:

(36) **Movement divergence:**
  E: $[_{\text{N-MAX}}$ John$]_i$ seems $[_{\text{N-MAX}}$ t$]_i$ to like Mary
  $[_{\text{N-MAX}}$ Who$]_i$ $[_{\text{N-MAX}}$ t$]_i$ gave the book to John?
  $[_{\text{P-MAX}}$ To whom$]_i$ did you give the book $[_{\text{P-MAX}}$ t$]_i$?
  $[_{\text{ADV}}$ When$]_i$ did you give the book to John $[_{\text{ADV}}$ t$]_i$?

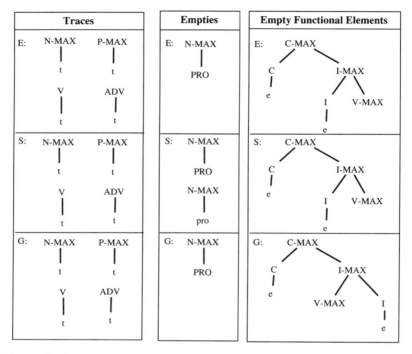

Figure 2.12
Phrase-structure templates are precompiled from three different trace parameters.

S: [N-MAX María]ᵢ le parece [N-MAX t]ᵢ gustar a Juan

¿[N-MAX Quién]ᵢ [N-MAX t]ᵢ le dio el libro a Juan?

¿[P-MAX A quién]ᵢ le diste el libro [P-MAX t]ᵢ?

¿[ADV Cuándo]ᵢ le diste el libro a Juan [ADV t]ᵢ?

G: [N-MAX Johann]ᵢ scheint [N-MAX t]ᵢ Marie gern zu haben

[N-MAX Wer]ᵢ gab [N-MAX t]ᵢ Johann das Buch?

[P-MAX Wem]ᵢ gabst du [P-MAX t]ᵢ das Buch?[14]

[ADV Wann]ᵢ gabst du Johann das Buch [ADV t]ᵢ?

From the settings of the moved adjuncts parameter, we are able to account for the syntactic divergences associated with different types of moved adjuncts. For example, in English, only an adverb can adjoin

---

[14]The German pronoun *wem* is analyzed as a prepositional phrase when it has the dative case inflection.

to the left of a verb phrase whereas, in Spanish and German, both an
adverb and a prepositional phrase can adjoin to the left of a verb phrase:

(37) **Movement divergence:**
    E: John [$_{ADV}$ frequently]$_i$ has eaten breakfast [$_{ADV}$ t]$_i$
     * John [$_{P\text{-}MAX}$ in the room]$_i$ has eaten breakfast [$_{P\text{-}MAX}$ t]$_i$
    S: Juan [$_{ADV}$ frecuentamente]$_i$ ha comido el desayuno [$_{ADV}$ t]$_i$
     Juan [$_{P\text{-}MAX}$ en el cuarto]$_i$ ha comido el desayuno [$_{P\text{-}MAX}$ t]$_i$
    G: Johann hat [$_{ADV}$ oft]$_i$ Frühstück [$_{ADV}$ t]$_i$ gegessen
     Johann hat [$_{P\text{-}MAX}$ im Zimmer]$_i$ Frühstück [$_{P\text{-}MAX}$ t]$_i$ gegessen

The final parameter that is accessed during precompilation is the
clitics parameter, which is included in the θ module (to be described
in section 2.9). This parameter is used for specifying the category (*i.e.*,
N-MAX, CL-ACC, *etc.*) of clitic elements. A *clitic* is a phonologically
"weak" element (*i.e.*, it never bears stress) that depends on a phonologically "strong" element. An example of a clitic is a pronominal constituent that is associated with a verbal object such as the word *le* in
the following:[15]

(38) S: Yo le$_i$ di el libro a Juan$_i$
    'I (him) gave the book to John'

Here, the pronoun clitic *le* refers to the noun phrase *Juan*.

The settings for the clitics parameter are shown in figure 2.11(f). Note
that English has a clitic category. This is not the conventional setting
for GB theory, but it is the setting for this implementation given that
certain English argument constructions seem to act like the clitic argument constructions of Spanish. For example, in English, the dative
alternation allows the sentence *I gave the book to him* to be restated as
I gave him the book. In the dative alternation *him* is treated as a clitic,
just as the pronoun *le* is treated as a clitic in the equivalent Spanish
sentence *Yo le di el libro (a él)*.[16] The German setting for this param-

---

[15]There are also other types of clitics that are not discussed here. For example,
French has locative and partitive clitics such as "y" and "en."

[16]Technically, dative pronouns cannot be considered clitics since it is always possible to stress a dative, but never a clitic. However, the syntactic properties are
similar enough to allow both of these to be handled by the same phrase-structure
mechanism.

eter is *none* since there is no equivalent dative/non-dative construction
in German. Thus, German differs from its English counterpart:[17]

(39) **Dative divergence:**
      E: I gave him the book
         I gave the book to him
      G: Ich gab ihm das Buch
         * Ich gab zu ihm das Buch

Using the above-described precompiled off-line templates together
with the other on-line GB constraints, the syntactic component is able to
build a phrase-structure from the source-language sentence (in the case
of parsing) or from the interlingual form (in the case of generation).
Once this structure has been built, it is possible to apply the remaining
constraints from the Government, Bounding, Case, Trace, Binding, and
θ modules as described in the next six subsections.

Before we look at these additional constraint modules, it is important
to understand that both the off-line precompilation stage and on-line
constraint application of the syntactic component are used for generation
as well as parsing. That is, the phrase structure shown in figure 2.5 is
used not only during analysis of the source-language sentence, but also
during synthesis of the target-language sentence. Then the rest of the
GB constraints are applied to this phrase-structure in the same order
in both directions (*i.e.*, the order given earlier in (30)). The parameter
settings accessed during on-line processing are shown in figure 2.13. We
will discuss each of these in the following six sections.

2.4   Principles and Parameters of the Government Module

Government Theory is a central notion to the Bounding, Case, Trace,
Binding, and θ modules. A familiar example of the government principle
in English is that a verb governs its object.[18] Several Spanish-English

---

[17]This is not to say that there is no German sentence corresponding to *I gave the
book to him*, just that the meaning of such a sentence would be of a different nature.
In particular, the sentence *Ich gab das Buch zu ihm* is grammatical, but is highly
marked for emphasis on *zu ihm* ('to him') as if to say *I did not give her that book, I
gave the book TO HIM*.

[18]See Dorr (1987c) for a more formal definition of the government principle.

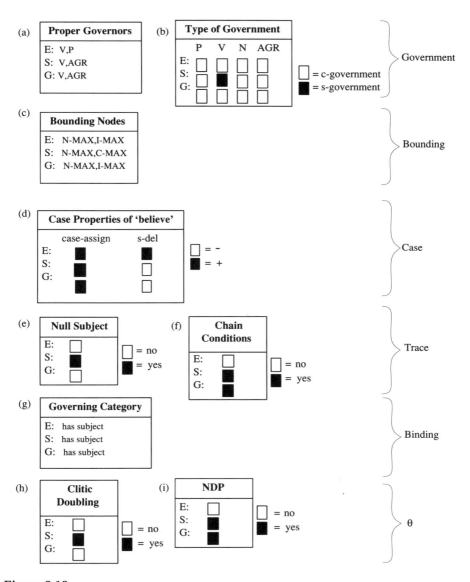

Figure 2.13
Parameter Settings from the Government, Bounding, Case, Trace, Binding, and θ modules are used for on-line processing.

divergences reveal *type of government* as a possible parameter of variation. These divergences show up during application of constraints by the Case module as we will see in section 2.6.

An additional parameter associated with the Government module is the *proper governors* parameter (see figure 2.13(a)). The choice of proper governor accounts for preposition-stranding distinctions in the three languages:

(40) **Preposition-Stranding divergence:**
    E: [$_{\text{N-MAX}}$ What store]$_i$ did John go to t$_i$?
    S: * [$_{\text{N-MAX}}$ Cuál tienda]$_i$ fue Juan a t$_i$?
    G: * [$_{\text{N-MAX}}$ Welchem Geschäft]$_i$ geht Johann zu t$_i$?

The English sentence is valid because the preposition *to* is a proper governor for the trace; by contrast, the Spanish and German sentences are ruled out since a preposition cannot be a proper governor.

The choice of proper governor also accounts for null-subject phenomena:

(41) **Null Subject divergence:**
    E: I know that there was dancing
        * I know that was dancing
    G: Ich weiß, daß getanzt wurde
        'I know that (there) was dancing'
    S: Yo sé que había un baile
        'I know that (there) was dancing'

The Spanish and German sentences are valid because AGR is a proper governor for the empty subject position; by contrast, the English sentence is ruled out since AGR cannot be a proper governor.[19]

2.5   Principles and Parameters of the Bounding Module

The Bounding module is concerned with the distance between pairs of co-referring elements (*e.g.*, trace-antecedent pairs). The fundamental principle of the Bounding module is that the distance between co-referring elements is not allowed to be more than one bounding node

---

[19] AGR is the part of the Inflection node that contains agreement features such as tense and number. Proper government will be discussed in more detail in section 2.7. Note that the English sentence in 2.4 is also ruled out because the null subject parameter of the Trace module disallows an empty subject.

apart, where the choice of *bounding nodes* is allowed to vary across languages as shown in figure 2.13(c). This restriction is called the *Subjacency Constraint*.

There are two tasks delegated to the Bounding module: trace linking and move-α. These tasks are actually inverses of each other. Trace linking, when applied to a parse structure, associates surface positions with base positions. On the other hand, move-α, which is applied to a generated structure, associates base positions with surface positions.[20] During both tasks, the bounding nodes parameter prohibits the base position and surface position from being "too far apart" (a maximum of one bounding node may be crossed).

The bounding nodes parameter setting accounts for a syntactic divergence between Spanish and English (and German). For example, because I-MAX is a bounding node for English (and German) but not for Spanish, the following divergent constructions are accounted for:

(42) **Long Distance Movement divergence:**
      E: * Who$_i$ did you wonder whether t$_i$ went to school?[21]
      S: ¿Quién$_i$ contemplabas tú que t$_i$ fue a la escuela?
      G: * Wer frage ich mich, ob schon nach Schule gegangen ist?

The reason the English and German are ruled out is that the word *who* has moved beyond two I-MAX nodes into the specifier position of C in the matrix clause. This violation of the Subjacency Constraint is discovered during trace linking (see figure 2.14(a)).[22] By contrast, the corresponding Spanish sentence *is* well-formed: since I-MAX is not a bounding node in Spanish, the coindexation is taken to be valid (see figure 2.14(b)).

The difference between the trace-linking and move-α procedures is that trace-linking will always be executed once a parse structure is de-

---

[20]The constituent α is intended to be any syntactic constituent in the phrase-structure representation.

[21]If *who* is spoken emphatically, this sentence can almost be understood as an echo question corresponding to the statement *I wondered whether John went to school*.

[22]This sentence structure also violates the empty category principle (to be discussed in section 2.7): the trace t$_i$ is not properly governed. Because the Subjacency Constraint is obviated by the empty category principle in many cases, it might be argued that this constraint should be eliminated. Although the incorporation of the Subjacency Constraint leads to a certain amount of redundancy, it is used in UNITRAN for reasons of implementational efficiency: the Bounding module is executed long before the Trace module is executed, thus ruling out a large number of syntactic structures as early as possible.

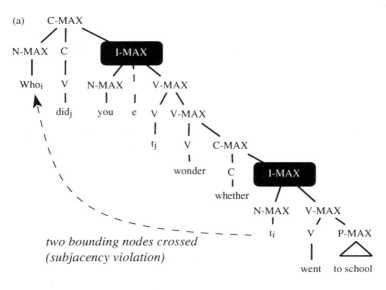

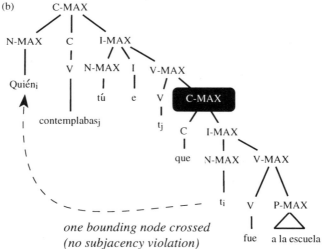

Figure 2.14 .
Trace linking, which is applied to a source-language structure, associates surface positions with base positions. If these two positions are "too far away," the Subjacency Constraint is violated and the structure is considered to be ungrammatical.

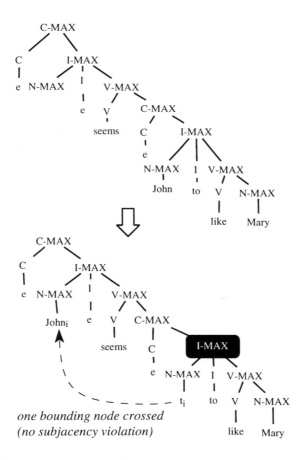

Figure 2.15
Move-α, which is applied during the generation of a target-language structure,
generally moves a constituent (in this case *John*) to a case-marked position.

rived, whereas move-α will operate only on an if-needed basis. An example where move-α is needed is when a noun phrase cannot get case in base position as in the sentence *seems John to like Mary*, which might be generated initially from an LCS. This sentence would be ruled out since *John* does not receive case; however, the move-α procedure ensures that *John* receives case by moving it into subject position of the verb *seems* as shown in figure 2.15. Note that the coindexation of *John* with its trace crosses only one bounding node; thus, there is no violation of the Subjacency Constraint.

2.6 Principles and Parameters of the Case Module

The Case module is in charge of ensuring that all noun phrases are properly assigned abstract case (*e.g.*, nominative, objective, *etc.*). The notion of government is relevant to case assignment since an element assigns case only if it is a governing case-assigner.

The fundamental principles of the Case module are summarized as follows:

1. Objective case is assigned to the object governed by transitive V.
2. Oblique case is assigned to the object governed by transitive P.
3. Possessive case is assigned to the object governed by transitive N.
4. Nominative case is assigned to the subject governed by AGR.[23]
5. Case Filter: Any sentence that contains a non-case-marked noun phrase (except PRO) is ill-formed.[24]

The *type of government* parameter (see figure 2.13(b)) determines the definition of government for these principles. C-government is the familiar notion of government in which a lexical item governs its phrasal siblings. S-government, on the other hand, is defined with respect to a strict subcategorization feature: it provides a unique pairing of c-governed elements of a verb to the subcategorization features of that verb. Thus, all c-governed elements that have a unique position in the subcategorization frame of the verb are s-governed. This distinction accounts for the ungrammaticality of:

---

[23] AGR must carry the +*tns* feature which corresponds to a tensed verb (*e.g.*, *eats*) as opposed to an infinitival verb (*e.g.*, *to eat*).

[24] In addition, any sentence that contains a case-assigned PRO is ill-formed. However, this is not stated as part of the Case Filter since government (hence, case assignment) of PRO will be ruled out by the Trace module; this is discussed in the next section.

Case Properties		
case-assign	s-del	Examples
eaten: □	□	*Was eaten breakfast Breakfast$_i$ was eaten t$_i$
seem: □	■	*Seems John to eat breakfast John$_i$ seems t$_i$ to eat breakfast
believe: ■	■	John believes Bill to eat breakfast *John$_i$ believes PRO$_i$ to eat breakfast
expect: ■	▦	John expects Bill to eat breakfast John$_i$ expects PRO$_i$ to eat breakfast
try: ■	□	*John tries Bill to eat breakfast John$_i$ tries PRO$_i$ to eat breakfast

□ = -
■ = +
▦ = +/-

Figure 2.16
The interaction of case assignment properties accounts for the varied distribution of different lexical items.

(43)   S: * Lo vimos Guille
       'We saw Guille'

and the grammaticality of:

(44)   S: Lo vimos a Guille[25]
       'We saw (to) Guille'

In (43) the accusative clitic *lo* absorbs s-government, and *Guille* remains ungoverned since its subcategorization position is already filled with *lo*; thus, *Guille* does not receive case and the sentence violates the Case Filter. On the other hand, in (44) the preposition *a* assigns objective case. Thus, even though *Guille* is not s-governed by *vimos*, it receives case from the preposition *a* and the sentence passes the Case Filter.

In addition to the *type of government* parameter, case assignment also relies on certain lexical properties that are allowed to vary from language to language. In particular, case assignment requires the assigner to have the property +*case-assign*. While most lexical items are case assigners, certain lexical items are non-case assigners such as passives (*e.g.*, *eaten*) and certain predicates (*e.g.*, *seems*). Another lexical property that case

---

[25] As noted by Jaeggli (1981), animate objects (*e.g.*, *Guille*) are associated with a clitic pronoun (*e.g.*, *lo*) only in certain dialects such as that of the River Plate area of South America.

assignment uses is the *s-del* feature. Verbs that have the +*s-del* feature
have an *exceptional* case-marking property: they are allowed to assign
case to a noun phrase dominated by the clause that is governed by the
verb. The *case-assign* feature interacts with the *s-del* feature in such
a way as to provide the appropriate distribution for a variety of lexical
items as shown in figure 2.16.[26]

The *case-assign* and *s-del* properties figure into parametric variations
across lexical items for different languages. For example, the verb *believe*
has different syntactic distributions for English, on the one hand, and
Spanis 1 and German on the other:

(45) **Lexical Case divergence:**
       E: John believes Bill ate breakfast
          John believes Bill to have eaten breakfast
          John believes he is happy
          * John$_i$ believes PRO$_i$ to be happy
       S: Juan cree que Bill se comió el desayuno
          * Juan cree Bill comerse el desayuno
          Juan cree que está contento
          Juan$_i$ cree PRO$_i$ estar contento
       G: Johann glaubt, daß Bill Frühstück ißt
          * Johann glaubt Bill Frühstück zu essen
          Johann glaubt, daß er glücklich ist
          Johann glaubt, glücklich zu sein

These syntactic divergences are accounted for by the *case-assign* and
s-del feature settings shown in figure 2.13(d).[27]

2.7   Principles and Parameters of the Trace Module

After case has been assigned, the Trace module applies the *empty category* principle (ECP) which checks for proper government of empty
elements. Simply stated, the ECP is applied to all empty noun phrases
as follows:

---

[26]The ± setting of the *s-del* feature indicates that the verb optionally has the
s-deletion property; the effect is that the verb is allowed to take an infinitival complement with or without a subject.

[27]In the cases where an empty subject PRO occurs, the sentences are ultimately
ruled out by the Trace module, as described in the next section.

ECP:

If an empty noun phrase is PRO, then it cannot be governed; else it must be *properly governed*.

where *proper government* is defined as follows:

Proper Government:

X properly governs Y if X *c-governs* Y or X is an antecedent of Y.

The ECP rules out sentences such as *$John_i$ believes PRO_i to be happy* (where PRO is governed by the +*s-del* verb *believes*) and *$Juan$ cree pro estar contento* (where the null subject is not properly governed by the −*s-del* verb *cree*).

The ECP is parameterized by means of the *null subject* parameter (see figure 2.13(e)) and the *chain conditions* parameter (see figure 2.13(f)). As discussed in chapter 1, the null subject parameter accounts for the null subject distinction between Spanish, on the one hand, and English and German on the other:

(46) **Null Subject divergence:**
    S: Yo vi el libro
       Vi el libro
    E: I saw the book
       * Saw the book
    G: Ich sah das Buch
       * Sah das Buch

In addition, null subject languages have the property that subjects can freely invert into post-verbal position as illustrated in (6), repeated here as (47):

(47) S: Me gusta María
       'Mary pleases me'
       (I like Mary)

The way the null subject parameter figures into the ECP is that in Spanish, an empty element in subject position is allowed to be *pro* in Spanish (hence, it must be properly governed), but not in English and German.

The second parameter of the Trace module, chain conditions, is necessary for allowing an empty head to be a proper governor for certain languages. (This parameter is based on work by Torrego (1984).) The reason this parameter is important is that it accounts for the verb movement distinction between English, on the one hand, and Spanish and German on the other:

(48)   **Verb Movement divergence:**

   E: * What$_j$ saw$_i$ John t_i t_j

   S: Qué$_j$ vio$_i$ Juan t_i t_j

   G: Was$_j$ sah$_i$ Johann t_j t_i

In all three of these sentences, a verb has been fronted leaving behind a trace t_i. This trace must properly govern the object trace t_j left behind by fronted noun phrase in order for the ECP to be satisfied. In the case of Spanish and German, however, the chain conditions parameter is set to *yes*; thus, the verb trace is a proper governor for the object trace, and the ECP is satisfied. In the case of English, no proper governor is available for the object trace since the setting of the chain conditions parameter is *no*; thus, the English sentence is ruled out by the ECP.[28]

2.8   Principles and Parameters of the Binding Module

The Binding module is the final module applied before thematic roles are assigned. This module is concerned with coreference relations among noun phrases, and it is dependent on the *governing category* parameter (see figure 2.13(g)). The setting of this parameter specifies that a governing category for a syntactic constituent is (roughly) the nearest dominating clause that has a subject. This parameter happens to have the same setting for English, Spanish, and German, but see Dorr (1987c) for a description of other settings of this parameter (*e.g.*, for Icelandic) based on work by Wexler and Manzini (1987). The way this parameter figures into the principles of the Binding module is that it places a locality condition on the Binding relations. The (slightly modified) principles of the Binding module are summarized as follows:[29]

---

[28]In effect, this parameter distinguishes between those languages that require an auxiliary verb for *wh*-object questions and those that do not require one.

[29]The full set of Binding Conditions are:

   (A)   An anaphor must be *bound* in its *governing category*
   (B)   A pronoun must be *free* in its *governing category*
   (C)   A lexical NP must be *free*

1. Anaphors and *NP*-traces must be bound in their governing category.
2. Pleonastics cannot be bound in their governing category.[30]
3. *Wh*-traces must be bound by an element outside of their governing category.

These three conditions correspond to (49), (50), and (51), respectively:

(49) (i)   E: John$_i$ likes himself$_i$

     (ii)   E: John$_i$ seems t_i to like Mary

(50) (i)   E: There$_i$ are men$_i$ in the room

     (ii)   S: pro$_i$ me gusta María$_i$

(51) E: What$_i$ does John like t_i

In (49)(ii), and (51), the coindexation has already been set up by the trace-linking routines of the Bounding module, and the Binding module need only check that the traces are bound to their antecedents. In (49)(i), (50)(i), and (50)(ii), the coindexation has not yet been set up, so the Binding module must first link the relevant constituents through coindexation before checking the Binding Conditions.

Once all coreference information has been determined for the syntactic tree, the θ module assigns the appropriate thematic roles.

2.9   Principles and Parameters of the θ Module

The θ module provides the interface between the syntactic component and the lexical-semantic component. In particular, the assignment of *thematic roles* (henceforth θ-roles) after parsing leads into the construction of the interlingual form. In addition, the assignment of θ-roles takes place after generation of the syntactic structure in order to ensure that the generated arguments match the roles that are assigned by the predicate that selects them.

UNITRAN uses a version of these conditions that is concerned only with associating empty categories (and overt anaphors) with their potential antecedents: in place of Condition (A), only anaphors (such as *himself*) and *NP*-traces will be considered; in place of Condition (B), only empty pronouns (*i.e.*, pleonastics) will be considered; and in place of Condition (C), only *Wh*-traces will be considered. Each of these types of elements is required to be bound in an appropriate way.

[30] A pleonastic is a syntactic constituent that has no semantic content (*e.g.*, the word *it* in the sentence *it is raining*). Frequently, pleonastics are linked to some other constituent that carries the appropriate semantic content. Two examples of such cases handled by the current model are coindexed null-content pronouns (*e.g.*, the word *there* in *there$_i$ are men$_i$ in the room*) or coindexed null subjects (*e.g.*, the empty *pro* subject in *pro$_i$ me gusta María$_i$*).

The fundamental principle of the θ module is the θ-*Criterion* which states that a lexical head must assign θ-roles in a unique one-to-one correspondence with the argument positions specified in the lexical entry for the head. Because lexical entries contain lexical-semantic information, the assignment of θ-roles is not strictly based on syntactic information, as it is in the traditional theory of GB. In particular, θ-role assignment is not based on atomic symbols such as *agent* and *theme*, but on positions in lexical conceptual structures such as Thing and Path. This will become clearer when we look at the lexical-semantic principles and parameters in chapter 5.

The θ module relies almost entirely on information supplied in the lexical entries of the source- and target-language words. Prior to the application of the θ-Criterion, θ-roles are assigned by verbs to their subcategorized arguments. Two parameters are accessed during this process: the *clitic doubling* parameter (based on work by Jaeggli (1981)) and the *nom-drop paradigm* (NDP) parameter (based on work by Safir (1985)). The settings of these parameters are shown in figure 2.13 (h) and (i) for English, Spanish, and German.

The clitic doubling parameter is accessed during θ-role assignment to ensure that θ-roles are transmitted properly in certain constructions. An example in which θ-role transmission is required is the case of clitic doubling as in (44), repeated here as (52):

(52)   S: Lo vimos a Guille
          'We saw (to) Guille'

In (52), the clitic *lo* actually stands for a noun phrase (*Guille*) that does not yet have a θ-role. The θ module imposes a θ-role transmission rule that supplies a θ-role to the object noun phrase:

(53) $[_{\text{CL}} +case_i +\theta_j]$ ... $[_{\text{N-MAX}} +case_i] \Rightarrow$
          $[_{\text{CL}} +case_i +\theta_j]$ ... $[_{\text{N-MAX}} +case_i +\theta_j]$

Note that in order for this transmission rule to trigger, the clitic and noun phrase must have the same case. If a clitic is not present, a θ-role is assigned in the usual fashion (*i.e.*, from the verb that subcategorizes for the NP). Thus, for languages that allow clitics, clitic doubling must be available as a parameter of variation to the θ module.

The NDP parameter is checked during θ-role assignment in order to determine whether an unassigned position is legal. An argument cannot be left unassigned unless it is a pleonastic.[31] If the element is a pleonastic, it is allowed to be unassigned under three conditions as illustrated in the following examples:

(54) **Pleonastic Divergence:**
E: It is raining
S: Está lloviendo
'(it) is raining'
G: Ich weiß, daß *pro* getanzt wurde
'I know that (there) was dancing'

The first condition is that the NDP is set to *no* and the element is an overt subject *i.e.*, the word *it* in the English sentence. The second condition is that the NDP parameter is set to *yes* and the language is a null subject language as in the Spanish sentence. The third condition is that the NDP parameter is set to *yes*, the language is *not* a null subject language, but the language allows empty constituents to occur as the subject of embedded clauses as in the German example.

Note that this third condition correctly rules out cases, in German, where the empty subject is *not* embedded as in:

(55) G: * *pro* getanzt wurde
'(there) was dancing'

Once θ-roles assignment is complete, the θ-Criterion is applied to ensure that all arguments are assigned roles that match the requirements of the θ-assigning verbs that select them. If the structure passes the θ-Criterion, then the lexical-semantic component of the system constructs the interlingual form using θ-roles as the basis of instantiation of the underlying LCS representations. Chapter 4 describes this instantiation process in more detail.

This chapter has described how parameterization of the syntactic processing component is used to resolve syntactic divergences. In chapter 5, we will see how parameterization is used to resolve a number of divergences *outside* the realm of syntax.

---

[31]See fn. 30 for a definition and examples of pleonastics.

3 Morphological Processing

This chapter takes a very brief detour away from the theme of processing machine translation divergences in order to examine the morphological processing component of UNITRAN. While this component is not central to the focus of this study, it is discussed here to bridge the mysterious gap between the actual input/output of the system and the syntactic and lexical-semantic representations described in other chapters. In addition, the description given here presents some important extensions that have been made to the model proposed by Kimmo Koskenniemi (see Karttunen and Wittenburg (1983)) which is still considered to be state-of-the-art by many natural language researchers (see, *e.g.*, Barton (1986a,b), Barton *et al.* (1987), Karttunen *et al.* (1992), Ritchie (1992), among others).

The next section describes the extensions that have been made to the two-level Kimmo approach to analysis and generation. Section 3.2 describes the format of the information provided in the morphological lexicon. Section 3.3 presents some examples of morphological analysis and generation. Section 3.4 discusses the featural interface between the Kimmo system and the syntactic processing component.

3.1 Extensions to Morphological Analyzer/Generator

As described in Karttunen and Wittenburg (1983), the Kimmo system is a two-level model of analysis and synthesis. Figure 3.1 shows the organization of the model. The fundamental idea behind this design is that the model is reversible: the same grammar description and lexicon are used both for analysis and for generation. The grammar, or morphological rules, are represented as finite-state transducers. The rules implemented for English, Spanish, and German are shown in appendix B.

As it turns out, the organization shown in figure 3.1 is not entirely accurate. In particular, the lexicon is not accessed at all during generation; instead, a word (*e.g.*, *tries*) is generated from its root (*e.g.*, *try*) and endings (*e.g.*, *+s*) solely on the basis of the morphological rules. In addition, the features (*e.g.*, [v sg p3 pres indic]) are returned by the analyzer, but they are not allowed as input to the generator.[1] A more accurate picture of the Kimmo system would be that of figure 3.2.

---

[1] A description of the features that are used in the definitions and examples of this chapter is provided in section 3.4.

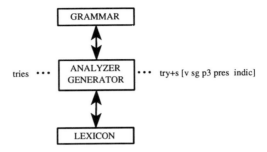

Figure 3.1
The organization of Kimmo as depicted in Karttunen and Wittenburg (1983)
illustrates that the model is reversible.

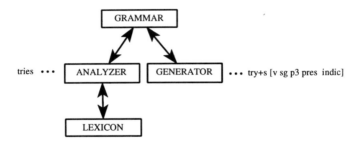

Figure 3.2
The actual organization of Kimmo does not include access to the lexicon during
generation.

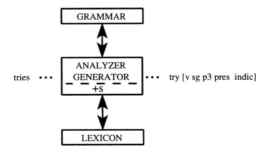

Figure 3.3
The modified organization of Kimmo in UNITRAN includes access to the lexicon
during generation.

The UNITRAN implementation by Dorr (1987c) sought to remedy this asymmetry by tacking a feature-to-affix module onto the generator, thus allowing features (*e.g.*, [v sg p3 pres indic]) to be mapped to an affix form (*e.g.*, +*s*). However, this augmentation to Kimmo made it difficult to maintain the morphology of each language: rules of the form [v sg p3 pres indic]⇒+*s* were required for every feature-affix pair that was in the recognizer lexicon (which is frequently updated).

The root of the problem with the Kimmo system is that the lexicon is not accessed during generation. An undesirable consequence of this deficiency is that generation is more cumbersome than analysis. This problem has been addressed recently by Karttunen *et al.* (1992) who have adopted an approach similar to the one implemented by Dorr (1990c) described herein. In particular, the current approach adopts two principles given by Karttunen *et al.* (p. 142):

1. Inflected forms of the same word are mapped to the same canonical dictionary form.

2. Morphological categories are represented as part of the lexical form.

In terms of the current solution, the first of these two principles corresponds to the "root word" form and the second of these two principles corresponds to the feature lists (*e.g.*, [p1 sg] for the first person singular), both of which are defined in Dorr (1990c) and discussed below.

The solution consists of the provision of a format that is suitable for use both by the generator and by the analyzer. In the lexicon, every entry consists of a root word, a list of features, and a list of continuation specifications.[2] This lexicon is compiled out to the form used by the Kimmo analyzer, and it is also used (uncompiled) by the generator. The modified version of the morphological component is shown in figure 3.3.

Note that the form returned by the analyzer, and input to the generator, includes the root form (*try*) and its associated features ([v sg p3 pres indic]); it does not include any affixes (+*s*) that have been discovered during processing. However, during the processing, any affixes that are discovered are used as an intermediate part of the calculation. In a sense, the processor internally applies rules of the form [v sg p3 pres indic]⇒+*s* without requiring that the affix +*s* be passed in (as input)

---

[2]A continuation specification consists of a root form (such as *try*) and a continuation class (such as *IV1). A continuation class refers to a set of suffixes (such as +*s*, +*ing*, etc.) that are applicable to a root form.

or out (as output); the grammar and lexicon together provide the basis
for extracting the affix form.

3.2 Root Words, Continuation Classes, and Endings

The morphological lexicon of the Kimmo framework makes use of three
types of information: (1) root word entries; (2) continuation classes;
and (3) endings. A root word entry is specified by means of the DEF-
MORPH-ROOT macro:

(56)   (DEF-MORPH-ROOT *language root features*
              (*string-root$_1$ continuation-class$_1$ features$_1$*)
              (*string-root$_2$ continuation-class$_2$ features$_2$*)
                  ⋮
              (*string-root$_n$ continuation-class$_n$ features$_n$*))

For example, the entry for the Spanish word *ver* (to see) would be specified as follows:

(57)   (DEF-MORPH-ROOT SPANISH VER [v]
              ("v" *ER-IRREG-6 NIL)
              ("ve" *ER-IRREG-7 NIL)
              ("visto" NIL [perf -tns])
              ("visto" NIL [pass -tns]))

Note that the root form is the canonical dictionary form that is specified
for all inflected forms of the verb, regardless of whether they are regular
or irregular. Thus, the irregular forms *vi* (I saw), *veo* (I see), and *visto*
(seen) are all classified under the single morphological root VER. Using
this single root form provides a mechanism for "keying in" on particular
lexical items during processing by other modules. For example, the root
form VER is used as an index into the LCS dictionary, which will be
described in the next chapter.

Continuation classes are prefixed with a '*', by convention, and are resolved into endings by means of alternations, which are defined by the DEF-MORPH-ALTERNATIONS macro:

(58) (DEF-MORPH-ALTERNATIONS *language*
        (*continuation-class$_1$* = *endings$_{11}$* *endings$_{12}$* ...)
        (*continuation-class$_2$* = *endings$_{21}$* *endings$_{22}$* ...)
        $\vdots$

        (*continuation-class$_m$* = *endings$_{m1}$* *endings$_{m2}$* ...))

A portion of the alternations for Spanish is shown in (59):

(59) (DEF-MORPH-ALTERNATIONS SPANISH
        (*AR-INF = AR-INF)
        (*ER-INF = ER-INF)
        (*IR-INF = IR-INF)
        (*ER-IRREG-6 = ER-IR-PRET-X-P1-P3-SG
                        ER-IR-PRET-P1-P3-SG-IRREG ...)
        (*ER-IRREG-7 = ER-IR-IMP ER-IR-SUBJ-PRES ...)
        $\vdots$

(NIL =))

As an example of how a continuation class is resolved, consider the continuation classes *ER-IRREG-6 and *ER-IRREG-7. These classes include a number of morphological endings such as ER-IR-PRET-X-P1-P3-SG (*i.e.*, the preterit past tense endings excluding first and third person singular) ER-IR-PRET-P1-P3-SG-IRREG (*i.e.*, the irregular past tense endings for first and third person singular), and ER-IR-IMP (*i.e.*, the imperfect tense). These identifiers act as indices into classes of endings that get fleshed out by means of the DEF-MORPH-ENDINGS macro, which has the following format:

(60) (DEF-MORPH-ENDINGS *language ending*
        (*string-ending$_1$* *continuation-class$_1$* *features$_1$*)
        (*string-ending$_2$* *continuation-class$_2$* *features$_2$*)
        $\vdots$

        (*string-ending$_p$* *continuation-class$_p$* *features$_p$*))

Language	Number of Roots	Number of Endings	Upper Bound
English	305	34	10370
Spanish	273	99	27027
German	297	125	37125

Figure 3.4
The number of morphological roots and endings multiplies out to an upper bound
on the number of possible surface forms.

The definitions for the identifiers mentioned above are specified as follows:

(61)   (DEF-MORPH-ENDINGS SPANISH ER-IR-PRET-X-P1-P3-SG
            ("+iste" NIL [past indic p2 sg])
            ("+imos" NIL [past indic p1 pl])
            ("+ieron" NIL [past indic p3 pl]))

       (DEF-MORPH-ENDINGS SPANISH ER-IR-PRET-P1-P3-SG-IRREG
            ("+io" NIL [past indic p3 sg])
            ("+i" NIL [past indic p1 sg]))

       (DEF-MORPH-ENDINGS SPANISH ER-IR-IMP
            ("+ía" NIL [past indic p1 sg])
            ("+ías" NIL [past indic p2 sg])
            ("+ía" NIL [past indic p3 sg])
            ("+íamos" NIL [past indic p1 pl])
            ("+ían" NIL [past indic p3 pl]))

The number of root words and endings in the morphological lexicon for
each language is shown in figure 3.4. An upper bound on the number
of morphological forms that can be recognized/generated for each of
these languages is also included in the figure. This bound is calculated
by multiplying the number of roots by the number of endings; thus,
it is likely to be much higher than the actual number of forms that are
recognized/generated due to the fact that the endings are not applicable
to every root form in the lexicon.

(a)   ANALYZING: "vi"
      "v" Root = VER [v]
         *ER-IRREG-6 →
            ER-INF → NIL (fail)
            ER-IR-PRET-X-P1-P3-SG → NIL (fail)
            ER-IR-PRET-P1-P3-SG-IRREG → "+i" [past indic p1 sg]
      "ve" Root = VER [v]
         *ER-IRREG-7 →
            ER-IR-IMP → NIL (fail)
            ER-IR-SUBJ-PRES → NIL (fail)
      "visto" Root = VER [v] → NIL (fail)
     RESULTS:
      "v+i" Root = VER [v past indic p1 sg]
(b)   ANALYZING: "veía"
      "v" Root = VER [v]
         *ER-IRREG-6 →
            ER-INF → NIL (fail)
            ER-IR-PRET-X-P1-P3-SG → NIL (fail)
            ER-IR-PRET-P1-P3-SG-IRREG → NIL (fail)
      "ve" Root = VER [v]
         *ER-IRREG-7 →
            ER-IR-IMP → "+ía"
             [past indic p1 sg]
             [past indic p3 sg]
            ER-IR-SUBJ-PRES → NIL (fail)
      "visto" Root = VER [v] → NIL (fail)
     RESULTS:
      "ve+ía" Root = VER [v, past, indic, p1, sg]
      "ve+ía" Root = VER [v, past, indic, p3, sg]

Figure 3.5
Morphological analysis of both *vi* and *veía* determines that the root is VER with features [v past indic v1 sg].

Morph_Gen (R, F)

1. Find the morphological root word R′ in the lexicon that matches R and whose features F′ match F; if none, fail.

2. Collect all strings S = {S₁, S₂, ..., Sₙ} in the entry for for R′ whose features match F; if none, fail.

3. For each $S_i \in$ S:

   3.1 Collect S_i into temporary variable T.

   3.2 If S_i has no continuation class, then:

      3.2.1 Apply the Kimmo generator to the strings in T (*e.g.*, {"try", "+s"} → "tries"), collecting into final result FR.

      3.2.2 Set T to { }.

      3.2.3 Go to step 3.

   3.3 Let C be the continuation class associated with S_i.

   3.4 Resolve C to the corresponding list of entries S′ = {S₁, S₂, ..., S$_k$} whose features F″ match F; if none, then set T to { } and go to step 3.

   3.5 Apply step 3 recursively on each of the continuation strings in S′ (*i.e.*, treat S′ as S).³

4. Return final result FR.

Figure 3.6
The algorithm for generating a target-language string uses a canonical root form R and a set of features F as indices into the lexicon.

3.3 Examples of Analysis and Generation

The new format of morphological entries allows the morphological processor to analyze the forms *vi* and *veía* (two past tense forms of the verb *see*) using the morphological root, alternations, and endings in (57), (59), (61), above. The algorithm for analyzing these forms is basically the same as that of Karttunen and Wittenburg (1983). The results are derived as shown in figures 3.5(a) and (b).

Note that there are two analyses for the verb *veía*: the first-person

---

³The astute reader might notice that there is a bug in this algorithm concerning the use of the variable T, namely that it is incorrectly set to { } by steps 3.2.2 and 3.4 on recursive re-entry to the main loop (step 3). In the actual Lisp implementation, this variable reuse problem does not arise since the loop is implemented as a recursive procedure and each recursive call has its own copy of the variable T.

singular (*yo veía*) and the third-person singular (*ella veía*). Also, note that both *vi* and *veía* have the same first-person singular features. This is due to the fact that there are two past tenses (preterit and imperfect) in Spanish. The preterit *vi* provides the meaning 'saw at one moment in time,' whereas the imperfect *veía* provides the meaning 'saw over a period of time.'[4]

Using the same morphological format in the opposite direction, the system relies on a modified version of the Kimmo generation algorithm to derive a surface form from a set of features. The algorithm for the modified procedure is shown in figure 3.6. The input to the **Morph_Gen** procedure consists of the root form R (*e.g.*, VER) and the feature complex F (*e.g.*, [v past p1 sg indic]). The root word R and features F are values determined by means of lexical selection from an underlying LCS representation as described in chapter 6. The output consists of all strings whose associated features match F. All possible answers are kept in parallel (in the variable FR). Using this algorithm, the forms *veía* and *vi* are generated from R = *ver* and F = [v past p1 sg indic] as shown in figure 3.7.

In addition to the new algorithm described above, the derivation of the target-language string requires the use of a matching procedure that determines whether the features in F are compatible with those of the string S that is currently being processed. Because it is possible for the features of F to be compatible with more than one final result, a "best match" procedure is invoked after generation by the above algorithm is complete. The string that is chosen is the one that matches the features of F in the most *specific* way possible. For example, if R is *ver* and F is [past indic cond], then there will be a choice between the strings *veía*, the past tense of *see*, and *vería*, the past tense conditional of *see*. The processor would choose *vería* since it matches F more specifically: in addition to a match between tense (past) and mood (indic), the aspectual feature (cond) matches. In the case where two strings are equally matched, both choices are returned. This is the case in the above example: both *veía* and *vi* are equally compatible with the features [v past p1 sg indic].

The morphological analyzer and generator described in this section

---

[4]These aspectual nuances of meaning are not handled at the morphological level of processing, but see chapter 9 for a discussion of an extension to the model that includes aspectual information.

R = VER
F = [v past p1 sg indic]
R' = VER
F' = [v]
Match.
S = {"v", "ve"}
   S_1 = {"v"
   T ← {"v"}
   C ← *ER-IRREG-6 =
      (ER-IR-PRET-X-P1-P3-SG, ER-IR-PRET-P1-P3-SG-IRREG, ...)
   S' = {"+i"}
     S_1 = "+i"
     F'' = [past indic p1 sg]
     Match.
     T ← {"v" "+i"}
     C = NIL
     FR ← {"vi"}
   S_2 = "ve"
   T ← {"ve"}
   C ← *ER-IRREG-7 = (ER-IR-IMP, ER-IR-SUBJ-PRES, ...)
   S' = {"+ía"}
     S_1 = "+ía"
     F'' = [past indic p1 sg]
     Match.
     T ← {"v" "+i"}
     C = NIL
     FR ← {"vi", "veía"}
Final Result (FR): {"vi", "veía"}

Figure 3.7
Morphological Generation derives two target-language forms, *vi* and *veía*, from the root VER and features [v past indic p1 sg].

allow UNITRAN to analyze a string of source-language words into feature complexes used for parsing and also to generate a string of target-
language words from roots and features derived from LCS operations
to be described in the next chapter. In terms of figure 1.10, the morphological processor is executed upon reading the source input (prior
to entering the syntactic parser) and again upon returning the target
output (after invoking the syntactic generator). We now turn to a more
detailed discussion about the relation of the morphological information
to syntactic processing.

3.4   Interface to Syntax

The morphological component interfaces with the syntactic component
by means of features. Figure 3.8 describes some of the features that are
used in the Kimmo lexicons for English, Spanish, and German. This
is not an exhaustive list, but see Dorr (1987c, 1990c) for additional
features.

Two examples of the use of features by the syntactic component are (1)
the application of feature-percolation routines and (2) the application of
feature-matching routines. Feature percolation ensures that features of
phrasal heads are copied onto their dominating maximal projections and
also that functional heads receive features from the maximal projections
that they select. Figure 3.9 shows an example of feature percolation on
the parsed sentence *John likes Mary*. Note that the features of the verb
likes [v p3 sg pres indic] are percolated up to the maximal level V-MAX,
then up to the functional head I, then further up to the maximal level
I-MAX, then again up to the functional head C, and finally up to the
maximal level C-MAX.

Feature matching enforces agreement between a maximal projection
X-MAX and a phrasal constituent Y that occur in the configuration
shown in figure 3.10 under the following circumstances:

  1. Y is a specifier of X-MAX.
      Example: *los* in *los libros* (the books)
  2. Y is a predicate (+pred) complement of X-MAX.
      Example: *rojos* in *los libros son rojos* (the books are red)
  3. Y is a predicate (+pred) adjunct of X-MAX.
      Example: *rojos* in *libros rojos* (red books)

Thus, in figure 3.9, the specifier *John* must agree with the maximal pro-

Feature	Description	Example
p1	first person	go
p2	second person	go
p3	third person	goes
sg	singular number	man
pl	plural number	men
masc	masculine gender	him
fem	feminine gender	her
neut	neuter gender	it
obj	objective case	me
nom	nominative case	I
poss	possessive case	my
pronoun	pronominal noun	he
anaphor	anaphoric noun	himself
pleonastic	pleonastic element	it
inf	infinitive tense	go
perf	perfect tense	gone
prog	progressive tense	going
past	past tense	went
pass	passive	gone
pres	present tense	go
-tns	untensed	seen
fut	future tense	will (go)
cond	conditional aspect	would (go)
indic	indicative mood	goes
+pred	predicate (adjective)	red

Figure 3.8
The features produced through morphological analysis by the Kimmo program are
used as input to the syntactic component. These same features are also used as
input to Kimmo during morphological synthesis.

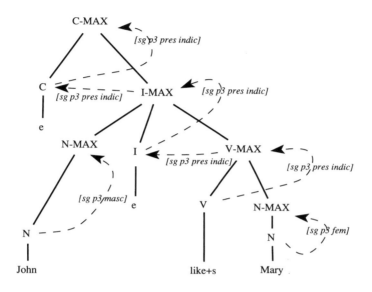

Figure 3.9
Feature Percolation for *John likes Mary* copies features of phrasal heads onto their dominating maximal projections (*e.g.*, the features [sg p3 pres indic] are percolated from the verb *likes* up to the maximal projection V-MAX) and from maximal projections up to functional heads that select them (*e.g.*, the features [sg p3 pres indic] are percolated from the maximal projection V-MAX up to the functional head I).

Figure 3.10
Feature matching enforces agreement between a maximal projection X-MAX and a phrasal constituent Y, where Y is either a specifier, a predicate complement, or a predicate adjunct of X-MAX.

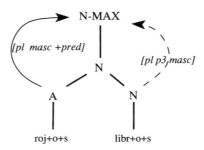

Figure 3.11
Feature percolation and matching for *rojos libros* enforces agreement between the
number (pl) and gender (masc) features of the predicate adjective and those of the
head noun.

jection I-MAX. Because both the specifier and the maximal projection
are associated with [p3, sg] features, the feature-matching procedure
succeeds for this example.

The feature-matching procedure is particularly useful in the context
of generation due to the fact that the lexical-selection procedure does
not have the capability of choosing the appropriate morphological form
of a particular root word. For example, during the translation of the
phrase *red books* into Spanish, the lexical-selection procedure chooses
the root word *roj* as the translation of the word *red*. The morphological
generator realizes this word in four ways (*rojo*, *roja*, *rojos*, and *rojas*),
but when feature-percolation is applied, only the masculine plural form
rojos passes the test due to the fact that *libros* is a masculine plural
noun. Figure 3.11 shows how the feature-percolation (dotted lines) and
feature-matching (solid lines) operations proceed for this example.

In the next three chapters, we return to the theme of processing machine translation divergences through parameterization. In particular,
the next part of this book demonstrates how a linguistically grounded
mapping makes use of parameter settings in the lexicon to resolve lexical-
semantic divergences.

II LEXICAL-SEMANTIC COMPONENT

4 The Interlingual Representation

A key part of the research for UNITRAN was the development of the interlingual representation and its associated lexical-semantic processing modules. This chapter demonstrates how the lexical-semantic framework of UNITRAN provides a useful foundation for representing meaning in an interlingual representation that includes, among other things, the participants in the activities or states described by verbs.

In order to adopt an interlingual approach to machine translation, one must construct a language-independent representation that lends itself readily to the specification of a systematic mapping that operates uniformly across all languages. To meet this objective, one needs a clear characterization of the entire range of divergences that could possibly arise in machine translation. This characterization can emerge only from a serious cross-linguistic investigation into the adequacy of different lexical representations for natural language. Such a representation has been constructed for use in the UNITRAN system *i.e.*, the *lexical conceptual structure* (henceforth, LCS) as formulated by Jackendoff (1983, 1990) and further studied by Hale and Keyser (1986a,b, 1989), Hale and Laughren (1983), Levin and Rappaport (1986), and Zubizaretta (1982, 1987). This representation is suitable to the task of translating between divergent structures for two reasons: (1) it provides an *abstraction* of language-independent properties from structural idiosyncrasies; and (2) it is *compositional* in nature.

Many machine translation systems operate on the basis of non-compositional representations that are specifically tailored to each of the source and target languages. We have seen some examples of direct and transfer approaches that map between lexical entries without accounting for cases in which the arguments themselves have a special compositional status that needs to be considered during the translation mapping (see, for example, (7) in chapter 1). Using a compositional approach allows one to define a recursive translation mapping that treats arguments of verbs as compositional units in their own right. Thus, the properties of the verb coupled with the properties of the verb's arguments are considered during each step of the translation process.

The approach taken here is to use a single compositional representation for all three languages, Spanish, English, or German, and to factor out language-specific information by means of parametric markers in the lexicon. The advantage to using the LCS as an interlingual representation is that source-to-target transfer rules are not required. Instead, the

system maps between the LCS and the surface syntactic form by means
of a generalized linking routine that is grounded in linguistic theory.

Two central claims are made here: (1) the current representation addresses the divergence problem cross-linguistically without recourse to
language-specific rules; and (2) the lexical-semantic framework provides
the basis for a systematic mapping between the interlingua and the syntactic structure. We will focus both on the representation itself as well as
how the representation is used during translation. Thus, we will discuss
the theoretical basis and cross-linguistic applicability of the interlingual
representation and we will also describe how the lexical-semantic composition process maps the source language into this representation.

The next section presents the primitive building blocks of the interlingual representation and addresses the issue of linguistic generalization.
Section 4.2 defines the structure of the lexical-semantic interlingua. Section 4.3 describes the extensions that have been made to the version of
LCS proposed by Jackendoff. Section 4.4 presents the organization of
the lexicon, demonstrating the use of the LCS in lexical entries and the
definition of LCS classes. Section 4.5 defines the relation of the interlingua to the syntactic structure. Section 4.6 describes the process of LCS
composition (*i.e.*, the construction of the interlingual representation),
presenting an example in detail. Finally, the issue of adequacy of the
LCS as an interlingua is discussed in section 4.7.

4.1   Primitive Building Blocks of the Interlingua

The field of machine translation has (almost from the beginning) been
concerned with the use of a "deep semantic representation" and with
looking for "universals" for translation. One of the biggest objections
to the use of an interlingual representation is that it requires the system designer to define a set of primitives (to represent the information
to be translated) which allows the mapping to and from the languages
in question. Because it is generally difficult to define such a set, many
researchers have abandoned this model. (See, *e.g.*, Vauquois and Boitet
(1985).) However, recently, there has been a resurgence of interest in the
area of lexical representation and organization (with special reference to
verbs) that has initiated an ongoing effort to delimit the classes of lexical
knowledge required to process natural language. (See, *e.g.*, Grimshaw

(1990), Hale and Laughren (1983), Hale and Keyser (1986a,b, 1989), Jackendoff (1983, 1990), Levin and Rappaport (1986), Levin (1985, in press), Pustejovsky (1987, 1988, 1989, 1990, 1991), Rappaport *et al.* (1987), Rappaport and Levin (1988), Olsen (1991), and Zubizarreta (1982, 1987).) As a result of this effort, it has become increasingly more feasible to isolate the components of meaning common to verbs participating in particular classes. These components of meaning can then be used to determine the lexical representation of verbs across languages.

In defining a set of primitives for an interlingua, one must abide by a number of general restrictions such as those proposed by Wilks (1987): *finitude, comprehensiveness, independence, noncircularity*, and *primitiveness*. While the LCS scheme has been designed to fulfill these requirements, it has also been designed to fulfill an additional requirement which is considered to be central to the current approach:

(62)   **Linguistic Generalization:** The primitives should be defined so that their combination captures both conceptual and syntactic generalities of actions or entities that might otherwise be represented differently.

That is, each action (*e.g.*, GO) and entity (*e.g.*, PERSON) must be associated with a representation that is both conceptually plausible and systematically related to a syntactic structure. The choice of one representation over another, then, depends on the degree to which the representation captures conceptual and syntactic generalities. The LCS approach fulfills this requirement by imposing certain constraints on the way the primitives may be combined in the conceptual structure and realized in the syntactic structure. We will return to this point shortly.

As discussed in chapter 1, the LCS approach views semantic representation as a subset of conceptual structure and includes *types* such as Event and State, which are specialized into *primitives* such as GO, STAY, BE, GO-EXT, and ORIENT. We have already seen how the GO primitive is used to represent sentence semantics in example (25) of chapter 1, repeated here as (63):

(63)   (i)   The ball rolled toward Beth.

     (ii)   [Event GO ([Thing BALL],
                       [Path TOWARD
                            ([Position AT ([Thing BALL], [Thing BETH])])])]

This representation illustrates one dimension (*i.e.*, the *spatial* dimension) of Jackendoff's representation. Another dimension is the *causal* dimension, which includes the primitives CAUSE and LET. These primitives take a Thing and an Event as arguments. Thus, we could embed the structure shown in (63)(ii) within a causative construction:

(64) (i)   John rolled the ball toward Beth.

      (ii)   [$_{\text{Event}}$ CAUSE
                ([$_{\text{Thing}}$ JOHN],
                 [$_{\text{Event}}$ GO ([$_{\text{Thing}}$ BALL],
                    [$_{\text{Path}}$ TOWARD
                       ([$_{\text{Position}}$ AT ([$_{\text{Thing}}$ BALL], [$_{\text{Thing}}$ BETH])])])])]

Jackendoff includes a third dimension by introducing the notion of *field*. This dimension extends the semantic coverage of spatially oriented primitives to other domains such as Possessional, Temporal, Identificational, Circumstantial, and Existential.[1] For example, the primitive GO$_{\text{Poss}}$ refers to a GO event in the Possessional field as in the following sentence:

(65) (i)   Beth received the doll.

      (ii)   [$_{\text{Event}}$ GO$_{\text{Poss}}$
                ([$_{\text{Thing}}$ DOLL],
                 [$_{\text{Path}}$ TO$_{\text{Poss}}$
                    ([$_{\text{Position}}$ AT$_{\text{Poss}}$ ([$_{\text{Thing}}$ DOLL], [$_{\text{Thing}}$ BETH])])])]

To further illustrate the notion of field, the GO primitive can be used in the Temporal and Identificational fields:

(66) (i)   The meeting went from 2:00 to 4:00.

      (ii)   [$_{\text{Event}}$ GO$_{\text{Temp}}$
                ([$_{\text{Thing}}$ MEETING],
                 [$_{\text{Path}}$ FROM$_{\text{Temp}}$
                    ([$_{\text{Position}}$ AT$_{\text{Temp}}$ ([$_{\text{Thing}}$ MEETING], [$_{\text{Time}}$ 2:00])])]
                 [$_{\text{Path}}$ TO$_{\text{Temp}}$
                    ([$_{\text{Position}}$ AT$_{\text{Temp}}$ ([$_{\text{Thing}}$ MEETING], [$_{\text{Time}}$ 4:00])])])]

---

[1] The label Loc has been adopted to distinguish the spatial field (which would apply to examples (63) and (64)) from the non-spatial fields. Note that the spatial field is used to denote the primitives that fall in the spatial dimension. Jackendoff argues that spatial primitives are more fundamental to those of other domains (*e.g.*, Possessional); in particular, all primitives from other domains pattern after those in the spatial domain with respect to argument-structure constraints (to be discussed shortly). Thus, spatial primitives have their own special status as an independent dimension.

(67) (i)   The frog turned into a prince.

    (ii)   [$_\text{Event}$ GO$_\text{Ident}$
         ([$_\text{Thing}$ FROG],
         [$_\text{Path}$ TO$_\text{Ident}$
             ([$_\text{Position}$ AT$_\text{Ident}$ ([$_\text{Thing}$ FROG], [$_\text{Thing}$ PRINCE])])])]

As these examples illustrate, there are also other primitives that are included in the LCS framework. In particular, the Position and Path types are used to include primitives such as AT and TO.[2] Furthermore, the Thing, Location, Time, Manner, and Property types are used. Figure 4.1 shows a subset of the types and primitives that are currently used in the LCS scheme.[3] Some examples of the types of sentences that are represented using the LCS framework are shown in figure 4.2 with their corresponding primitive-field combinations.[4] (Additional types and primitives will be presented in section 4.3.)

A crucial point concerning the LCS representation is that, although it appears to be somewhat "English-like," it is only superficially so by virtue of the labels of the primitives (*e.g.*, GO, TO, *etc.*) that are used in the representation. These primitives were chosen on the basis of an extensive cross-linguistic investigation, though they may be labeled and used in a fashion that appears to be modeled after a particular language.

An additional point about the representation is that a large percentage of primitives fall under the Manner category, which may appear to be peculiar at first glance. Because Jackendoff says very little about the function of the Manner type in his description of conceptual structure,

---

[2]The Position type corresponds to the Place type used by Jackendoff (1983). An extension that has been made to the Position type is that it is a two-place predicate rather than a one-place predicate. For example, in (66)(ii), the MEETING argument appears both internally and externally to the AT$_\text{Temp}$ node. This is due to the observation that primitives such as AT, IN, ON, *etc.* are actually relations between two arguments (*e.g.*, the representation for *the book is on the table* incorporates the relation ON(BOOK,TABLE) as part of its meaning). The use of the two-place predicate also allows for additional type-checking when the LCS representation for a word (*e.g.*, *on*) is composed with the LCS representation for another word (*e.g.*, *put*) in order to derive the underlying representation for the entire concept (*e.g.*, *put the book on the table*). Both argument positions must be checked for a match before the composition can take place. In the case of *put the book on the table*, the two arguments associated with the predicate ON are: a movable Thing and a locative Thing, respectively. It cannot be the case that one of these arguments is, for example, a State or an Event. (The LCS composition process will be discussed in section 4.6.)

[3]Note that primitives have not been included for *John, Beth, I, me, it, etc.* In actuality, proper names are represented by the PERSON primitive and referring expressions (*e.g.*, pronouns) are represented by the REFERENT primitive. For notational convenience, the examples and figures will continue to use the more informative labels in place of these primitives.

[4]The example sentences were taken from Siskind (1989), with minor modifications.

Type	Primitives
Event	CAUSE, LET, GO, STAY
State	BE, GO-EXT, ORIENT
Position	AT, IN, ON
Path	TO, FROM, TOWARD, AWAY-FROM, VIA
Thing	BOOK, PERSON, REFERENT, KNIFE-WOUND, KNIFE, SHARP-OBJECT, WOUND, FOOT, CURRENCY, PAINT, FLUID, ROOM, SURFACE, WALL, HOUSE, BALL, DOLL, MEETING, FROG
Property	TIRED, HUNGRY, PLEASED, BROKEN, ASLEEP, DEAD, STRETCHED, HAPPY, RED, HOT, FAR, BIG, EASY, CERTAIN
Location	HERE, THERE, LEFT, RIGHT, UP, DOWN
Time	TODAY, SATURDAY, 2:00, 4:00
Manner	FORCEFULLY, LIKINGLY, WELL, QUICKLY, DANCINGLY, SEEMINGLY, HAPPILY, LOVINGLY, PLEASINGLY, GIFT-INGLY, UPWARD, DOWNWARD, WITHIN, HABITUALLY

Figure 4.1
LCS primitives are divided into a handful of types. A subset of the types and primitives used by UNITRAN is shown here.

Type	Primitive-Field	Example
Event	GO_{Poss}	Beth received the doll.
	GO_{Ident}	Elise became a mother.
	GO_{Temp}	The meeting went from 2:00 to 4:00.
	GO_{Loc}	We moved the statue from the park to the zoo.
	GO_{Circ}	John started shipping goods to California.
	GO_{Exist}	John built a house.
	$STAY_{Poss}$	Amy kept the doll.
	$STAY_{Ident}$	The coach remained a jerk.
	$STAY_{Temp}$	We kept the meeting at noon.
	$STAY_{Loc}$	We kept the statue in the park.
	$STAY_{Circ}$	John kept shipping goods to California.
	$STAY_{Exist}$	The situation persisted.
State	BE_{Poss}	The doll belongs to Beth.
	BE_{Ident}	Elise is a pianist.
	BE_{Temp}	The meeting is at noon.
	BE_{Loc}	The statue is in the park.
	BE_{Circ}	John is shipping goods to California.
	BE_{Exist}	Descartes exists.
	$GO\text{-}EXT_{Ident}$	Our clients range from psychiatrists to psychopaths.
	$GO\text{-}EXT_{Temp}$	The meeting lasted from noon to night.
	$GO\text{-}EXT_{Loc}$	The road went from Boston to Albany.
	$ORIENT_{Loc}$	The sign points to Philadelphia.
	$ORIENT_{Circ}$	John intended to ship goods to California.

Figure 4.2
A number of different types of sentences are represented using the Event and State primitives of the LCS framework.

the approach taken here is to use the Manner component to distinguish between verbs that fall within the same linguistic class when no other distinguishing features are available. Additional discussion about this point is given in section 4.3.

Returning to the issue of linguistic generalization as defined in (62), a set of constraints is imposed on the way the primitives may be combined in the conceptual structure and realized in the syntactic structure. These constraints are available along the three dimensions illustrated in examples (63)–(67). The *spatial* dimension, which includes the basic set of primitive building blocks, GO, STAY, BE, ORIENT, and GO-EXT, must adhere to the following constraints on argument structure:

(68) (i)

Events		
Primitive	**Argument 1**	**Argument 2**
GO	Thing	Path
STAY	Thing	Position

(ii)

States		
Primitive	**Argument 1**	**Argument 2**
BE	Thing	Position
ORIENT	Thing	Path
GO-EXT	Thing	Path

The second dimension, the *causal* dimension, must adhere to the following constraints on argument structure:[5]

(69)

Primitive	**Argument 1**	**Argument 2**
CAUSE	{ Thing / Event }	{ Event / State }
LET	{ Thing / Event }	{ Event / State }

---

[5] The {} notation denotes choice. For example, the first argument of the CAUSE primitive may either be a Thing or an Event.

Finally, the *field* dimension imposes the following constraints:

(70)

Field	Argument 1	Argument 2[6]
Locational	$\left\{\begin{array}{l}\text{Thing}\\\text{Event}\end{array}\right\}$	Location
Possessional	Thing	Thing
Temporal	$\left\{\begin{array}{l}\text{Event}\\\text{State}\end{array}\right\}$	Time
Identificational	Thing	$\left\{\begin{array}{l}\text{Thing}\\\text{Property}\end{array}\right\}$
Circumstantial	Thing	$\left\{\begin{array}{l}\text{Event}\\\text{State}\end{array}\right\}$
Existential	Thing	EXIST

A crucial point concerning the linguistic generalization proposed in (62) is that it requires the rules for combining primitives to have a direct correspondence to the syntactic structure. This is precisely the nature of the lexical-semantic constraints shown in (68)–(70). One might think of these constraints as a means of specifying argument-selection restrictions that are imposed on the lexical-semantic representation, but that also have their corresponding syntactic reflexes in the surface sentence. For example, the ORIENT primitive selects a Thing and a Path as in the following lexical conceptual structure:

(71) $[_{\text{State}}$ ORIENT$_{\text{Loc}}$
        $([_{\text{Thing}}$ SIGN],
          $[_{\text{Path}}$ TOWARD$_{\text{Loc}}$
            $([_{\text{Position}}$ AT$_{\text{Loc}}$ $([_{\text{Thing}}$ SIGN], $[_{\text{Location}}$ BOSTON])])])]$

These conceptual constituents are then realized in the syntactic structure, respectively, as a noun phrase subject and a prepositional phrase object:

(72) $[_{\text{C-MAX}}$ $[_{\text{I-MAX}}$ $[_{\text{N-MAX}}$ The sign]
        $[_{\text{V-MAX}}$ points
          $[_{\text{P-MAX}}$ toward $[_{\text{N-MAX}}$ Boston]]]]]$

Thus, the constraints support the linguistic generalization requirement in (62) by allowing the primitives to be combined in such a way as to

---

[6]Technically, the second argument for each of these fields is a Path or a Position. For the purposes of the current description, the column under "Argument 2" refers to the lowest leaf node embedded inside of the second argument.

capture both conceptual and syntactic generalities. In the next section we will see that the constraints are consistent with a systematic correspondence between syntactic structure and lexical-semantic structure.

Clearly, such an approach could not hope to distinguish among all possible meanings of every lexical item. However, the intent of the current scheme is to provide a linguistically motivated approach to handling translation divergences, not to describe the deep semantic content of lexical items. While the primitives proposed in the current approach have been defined specifically for the task of resolving translation divergences, there is clearly additional information that would be required for solving other pieces of the translation problem. In the spirit of Wilks (1987), the current approach adopts the view that there may be other representational *levels*, with their own primitive definitions, that might be superimposed on top of the current framework to handle other types of problems (*e.g.*, distinguishing between verbs like *donate* and *give*, which occur in the same lexical-semantic class of possessional transfer).

One could argue against this approach on the grounds that the LCS representation has been constructed in such a way that is biased toward the particular translation problem to be solved. That is, the choice of lexical-semantic primitives and their allowable combinations appear to rely heavily on linguistic knowledge about the nature of translation divergences. However, it is not clear that developing the interlingua on the basis of this knowledge is a drawback to the approach. It is much more worthwhile to construct a representation on the basis of a carefully studied, and finitely specified, classification system than on the basis of vague intuitions about the nature of what a word means in a particular language. Furthermore, since the divergence types addressed by this approach (*i.e.*, the classification given in figure 1.12) are expected to cover all potential source-language/target-language distinctions based on properties of lexical items, it is considered an advantage to use this classification as the basis for the representation. Since the range of divergence possibilities has been carefully delimited, it is feasible to use the classification to isolate components of verb meaning for the construction of an appropriate interlingua.

An additional argument for constructing the lexical-semantic representation based on a study of cross-linguistic divergences is that it is consistent with the philosophy behind well-grounded lexical-semantic theories such as *meaning-text theory* (MTT) by Mel'čuk and Polguère

(1987, p. 266); that is, rather than postulating a set of semantic primitives *a priori*, the intention is to discover them by means of a "painstaking process of semantic decomposition applied to thousands of actual lexical items." Given that recent research has made it increasingly more feasible to isolate components of verb meaning, this approach to the construction of an interlingual representation is no longer impractical. Note that this is in direct contrast to other approaches that employ primitives that are chosen *a priori* such as the conceptual dependency approach by Schank (1972, 1973, 1975) and Schank and Abelson (1977), for which there has never been a cross-linguistic investigation into the applicability of the primitives.

4.2   Structure of the Interlingua

Now that we have examined the primitive units of the interlingua, we turn to a definition of the structure of the interlingua itself. The interlingua is defined primarily on the basis of *domination* relations in the LCS. Unlike the syntactic structure, *linear ordering* is not as critical as hierarchical structure in preserving the meaning of the LCS. However, certain positioning conventions are retained in order to preserve uniformity during the mapping between the interlingua and the syntactic structure.

There are potentially three types of lexical-semantic tokens that may be associated with a logical head in an LCS. The first is the *logical subject*. There is only one such argument, and it is always the highest/leftmost argument of an LCS. The second type of lexical-semantic token is the *logical argument*; there may be any number of these, all occurring to the right of the logical subject. Finally, there are any number of (optional) *logical modifiers*, which are ordered, by convention, to the right of logical arguments. Thus, the overall structure is defined as follows:

(73) $[_{T(X')}$ X'

$\qquad ([_{T(W')}$ W'],

$\qquad [_{T(Z'_1)}$ Z'$_1$], ..., $[_{T(Z'_n)}$ Z'$_n$]

$\qquad [_{T(Q'_1)}$ Q'$_1$], ..., $[_{T(Q'_m)}$ Q'$_m$])]

where X' is the logical head, W' is the logical subject, Z'$_1$, ..., Z'$_n$ are the

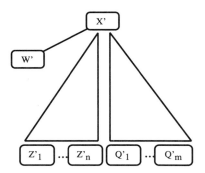

Figure 4.3
The formal structure of the interlingua defines canonical positions for the logical head, logical subject, logical arguments, and logical modifiers.

logical arguments, Q'_1, ..., Q'_m are the logical modifiers, and $T(\phi)$ is the LCS type corresponding to the primitive ϕ. The tree-like representation corresponding to this structure is shown in figure 4.3.[7]

As mentioned in the last section, a set of constraints is imposed on the structure of the interlingua so that there is a systematic correspondence between this representation and the syntactic structure. This correspondence is shown in figure 4.4 and is defined as follows:

(74) [Y-MAX

     Q-MAX_{j+1} ... Q-MAX_k

     [Y-MAX

      W-MAX

      [X-MAX [X Q-MAX_1 ... Q-MAX_i X Q-MAX_{i+1} ... Q-MAX_j]

      Z-MAX_1 ... Z-MAX_n]]

     Q-MAX_{k+1} ... Q-MAX_m]

   corresponds to

---

[7]For ease of illustration, this diagram shows the primitive-field without the type. We will retain this convention throughout the book. In addition, the ordering given in the syntactic tree is the one used for English and Spanish. In actuality, the syntactic component determines the appropriate syntactic ordering from the setting of the constituent order parameter discussed in chapter 2. For the purposes of illustration, we will use this ordering throughout the rest of the book.

$$[_{T(X')} \; X'$$
$$([_{T(W')} \; W'],$$
$$[_{T(Z'_1)} \; Z'_1], \; \ldots, \; [_{T(Z'_n)} \; Z'_n],$$
$$[_{T(Q'_1)} \; Q'_1], \; \ldots, \; [_{T(Q'_m)} \; Q'_m])]$$

where:

1. X is the *head* of the X-MAX phrase.

2. W-MAX is the *external argument* (or subject) of X.

3. $Z\text{-MAX}_1 \ldots Z\text{-MAX}_n$ are the *internal arguments* (or objects) of X.[8]

4. $Q\text{-MAX}_1 \ldots Q\text{-MAX}_j$ are the *minimal adjuncts* of X and $Q\text{-MAX}_{j+1}$ $\ldots Q\text{-MAX}_m$ are the *maximal adjuncts* of X.

5. X' and $T(X')$ are, respectively, the primitive-field and type corresponding to the syntactic constituent X. (X' is the *logical head*.)

6. W' and $T(W')$ are, respectively, the primitive-field and type corresponding to the syntactic constituent W-MAX. (W' is the *logical subject*.)

7. $Z'_1, \ldots, Z'_n$ and $T(Z'_1), \ldots, T(Z'_n)$ are, respectively, the primitive-fields and types corresponding to the syntactic constituents $Z\text{-MAX}_1$ $\ldots Z\text{-MAX}_n$. ($Z'_1, \ldots, Z'_n$ are the *logical arguments*.)

8. $Q'_1, \ldots, Q'_m$ and $T(Q'_1), \ldots, T(Q'_m)$ are, respectively, the primitive-fields and types corresponding to the syntactic constituents $Q\text{-MAX}_1 \ldots Q\text{-MAX}_m$. ($Q'_1, \ldots, Q'_m$ are the *logical modifiers*.)

As we will discuss in section 4.5, this correspondence is used as the basis of the mapping between the interlingua and the syntactic structure.

An example of such a correspondence would be:

(75) $[_{\text{C-MAX}} \; [_{\text{I-MAX}} \; [_{\text{N-MAX}} \; \text{John}] \; [_{\text{V-MAX}} \; \text{went} \; [_{\text{P-MAX}} \; \text{to} \; [_{\text{N-MAX}} \; \text{school}]]]]]$
corresponds tó
$[_{\text{Event}} \; \text{GO}_{\text{Loc}}$
$\quad ([_{\text{Thing}} \; \text{John}],$
$\quad [_{\text{Path}} \; \text{TO}_{\text{Loc}} \; ([_{\text{Position}} \; \text{AT}_{\text{Loc}} \; ([_{\text{Thing}} \; \text{John}], \; [_{\text{Location}} \; \text{school}])])])]$

---

[8]The term *complement* was used in chapter 2 to mean the same thing as *internal argument*; the two terms will be used interchangeably throughout this, and subsequent, chapters.

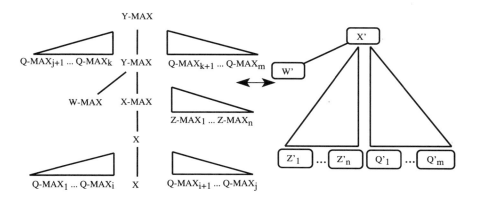

Figure 4.4
The structure of the LCS lends itself to a systematic specification of the
correspondence between syntactic structure and lexical-semantic structure.

This example relates to (74) as follows:

1. X corresponds to the verb *went*.

2. X' corresponds to GO_{Loc}.

3. $T(X')$ corresponds to Event.

4. W' corresponds to John.

5. $T(W')$ corresponds to Thing.

6. Z' corresponds to TO_{Loc}.

7. $T(Z')$ corresponds to Path.

The tree-like structures corresponding to (75) are shown in figure 4.5.

We turn now to a discussion of the use of the LCS as an interlingual
representation. Consider the *stab* example presented in (8) of chapter 1,
repeated for convenience here:

(76)   E: I stabbed John $\Leftrightarrow$
       S: Yo le di puñaladas a Juan
          'I gave knife-wounds to John'

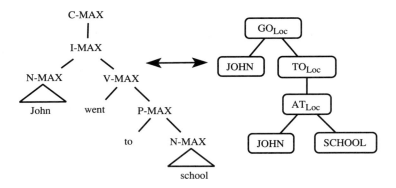

Figure 4.5
An example of the syntactic/lexical-semantic correspondence for the sentence *John
went to school* demonstrates that there is a systematic relationship between the two
structures.

The LCS representation for this event would be the following:

(77) [$_{Event}$ CAUSE
          ([$_{Thing}$ I],
          [$_{Event}$ GO$_{Poss}$
             ([$_{Thing}$ KNIFE-WOUND],[9]
             [$_{Path}$ TOWARD$_{Poss}$
                ([$_{Position}$ AT$_{Poss}$ ([$_{Thing}$ KNIFE-WOUND], [$_{Thing}$ John])])])])]

The tree-like representation corresponding to this structure is shown in
figure 4.6.

---

[9]It should be pointed out that the KNIFE-WOUND argument included in this
conceptual representation is intended to be more generic than its name implies. (Perhaps it would be better to name it STAB-WOUND.) The representation is not only
applicable to the case in which the wound is inflicted by a knife, but could correspond to a number of possible surface realizations including *he stabbed the robber*,
*he stabbed the robber with a knife, he stabbed the robber with a poker, he stabbed
the robber with scissors, etc.* Note that this representation is only a first approximation for the stabbing event given that one can *give* "puñaladas" in Spanish, but one
cannot then *have* "puñaladas" when the action is complete. A possible solution to
this problem would be to represent *stab* as an act of swinging a sharp instrument
into someone, rather than as an act that causes the person to have a stab-wound.
Such possibilities are not addressed here since the focus of this study is not on the
details of the concepts behind the primitives used in the representation, but on the
use of the representation as a compositional means of translating from one language
to another.

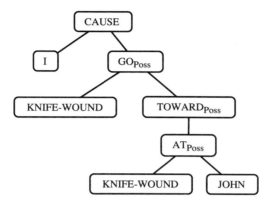

Figure 4.6
The tree-like representation corresponding to the LCS for *I stabbed John* and *Yo le di puñaladas a Juan* illustrates the compositional nature of the interlingua.

There are two properties of this representation that enable the system to derive an appropriate interlingual representation for the event described in (76) even though the source and target sentences are not structurally equivalent. The first is that the LCS representation provides an *abstraction* of language-independent properties from structural idiosyncrasies. For example, the recipient of the stabbing action is associated with a single, canonical representation in the interlingua regardless of how it is syntactically realized on the surface. In the case of English, the recipient (*John*) is realized as an object of the main verb, whereas in the case of Spanish, the recipient (*Juan*) is realized as an object of the preposition *a*. The second property is that the LCS representation is *compositional* in nature. Through a process called lexical-semantic composition (to be described in section 4.6), the implicit KNIFE-WOUND argument associated with the word *stab* is made available for realization as the word *puñaladas* in Spanish, even though the argument does not appear overtly in the English sentence.

The interlingua is designed specifically so that the mapping between the syntactic structure and conceptual structure can be performed systematically by a single, general *linking routine* based on the correspondence shown in (74). This mapping relies heavily on the thematic roles assigned by the syntactic component as described in chapter 2. In particular, the mapping cannot take place until all θ-roles are assigned. The θ-roles represent positions in the lexical entries that are associated with the words of the input sentence. Thus, LCS composition is essentially a unification process that is guided by the pointers left behind by θ-role assignment. We will return to the relation between θ-role assignment and lexical-semantic composition in section 4.5.1.

It should be pointed out that notions similar to thematic roles are already widely used in many machine translation systems, although they have been variously called proto-roles, deep cases, thematic relations, or semantic roles (see Dowty (1991), Fillmore (1968), Gruber (1965), and Ostler (1979), among others). For example, a simple verb of motion such as *push* has a very similar semantic-role labeling in Fillmore's framework as it does in Jackendoff's thematic-role framework:

		Mary	pushed the	ball	into the	bucket
(78)	F:	*agent*		*object*		*goal*
	J:	*agent*		*theme*		*goal*

However, for verbs of affect such as *break*, thematic roles differ from the traditional notion of semantic roles:

			Mary	broke the	glass	with a	hammer
(79)	(i)	F:	*agent*		*object*		*instrument*
		J:	*agent*		*goal*		*theme*

			Mary	broke the	glass	against the	wall
	(ii)	F:	*agent*		*object*		*location*
		J:	*agent*		*theme*		*location*

In the traditional framework of semantic roles, the labeling is relevant to the causal dimension; thus, the glass is recognized as the affected object (*i.e.*, it undergoes a change of state), and it bears the same role in both (79)(i) and (79)(ii). In contrast, the thematic-role approach of the LCS framework (and also of older approaches, most notably Schank (1972, 1973, 1975)) is concerned with the notion of motion/location, not causality.[10] Thus, there is no way to determine that the glass is the affected object within this framework; instead, the object that undergoes

---

[10]Schank's framework clearly uses causality but the notions of motion and location figure more prominently in the theory. This is evident in the choice of primitives (four of which are transfers) and in the types of arguments they take (most primitives are associated with a source and goal, analogous to the handling of primitives of motion).

positional change is identified (as the theme) and the notion of affected object is ignored.

The motivation for emphasizing the motion/location dimension is that similar syntactic behavior is exhibited for verbs within, but not across, the motion and location verb classes. However, as pointed out by Levin (1985), a complete analysis of an event needs to take both the causal dimension and the motion/location dimension into account. For example, the notion of instrument that figures prominently in the causally oriented approach has no special place in a system of thematic roles (although it may be derived from the fact that a theme takes on a special meaning when it co-occurs with a goal). Clearly, this is an omission that cannot be dismissed. On the other hand, the causally oriented approach does not strive to provide a system of verb classification that captures syntactic/semantic generalizations such as that of the thematic-role framework.

Given these observations, the lexical representation used in UNITRAN seeks to strike a balance between the causal and motion/location dimensions by using a dual representation of sentences; the LCS framework of Jackendoff has been modified to allow fields such as *identificational* (change of state) to co-occur with other fields such as *instrumental* (object causing the state change). This allows an affected object to be identified (*i.e.*, it is the object that undergoes the state change) as well as the instrument (*i.e.*, it is the object that affects the state change), without ignoring the syntactic/semantic generalizations that can be derived from the structure of the LCS in which these two objects occur. In this way, the thematic-role approach differs from traditional semantic-role approaches that are widely used in many machine translation systems; in particular, it provides the foundation for a uniform mapping between the interlingua and the syntactic structure, even for syntactically divergent source- and target-language structures. The extension of the representation to include the instrumental field is discussed further in the next section.

Note that this approach differs from more recent views on the relation of thematic roles to the surface structure. For example, Dowty (1991) assumes a monostratal theory of compositional semantics in which thematic roles are defined prototypically (hence the label *proto-roles*) and are lexicalized directly in their appropriate surface-structure positions (*i.e.*, subject, direct object, and oblique object). Dowty defines only

two roles, *proto-agent* and *proto-patient*, each of which is characterized
by a list of entailments such as the "volitional involvement in the state
or event" associated with the *proto-agent* role.

Unlike the current approach, Dowty's notion of lexicalization is not a
mapping between two different levels of representation, but a constraint
on how verbs and their associated arguments are realized on the surface. There is no notion of syntactic D-structure (*i.e.*, the underlying
syntactic representation); rather, arguments are positioned in the surface structure according to conditions associated with the corresponding
proto-roles. For example, the proto-agent argument, if present, is always
lexicalized as the subject.

In some ways, Dowty's approach is entirely compatible with the current approach in that it proposes a systematic relation between thematic
roles and their corresponding realizations on the surface. In addition,
the list of entailments that are used to characterize the different roles
would be useful in the current framework for additional type checking
during the assignment of θ-roles. Moreover, Dowty's discussion about
"nonstandard lexicalizations" provides support for a theory of lexical
parameters such as those proposed in the current framework (to be discussed in chapter 5). An example of a nonstandard lexicalization is that
of the verb *receive* which realizes the proto-agent (*i.e.*, *Mary* in *John
received the book from Mary*) as an oblique argument rather than as a
subject. Fortunately, as Dowty himself comments, "such exceptions are
few in number, so the selection principle is not an absolute rule but
is nevertheless a strong tendency" (1991, p. 581). No solution is given
for such cases; thus, the current approach fills a critical gap in Dowty's
theory by proposing lexical parameters (in this case, :INT and :EXT)
which are used as overrides in cases such as *receive*.

While compatible in many ways, Dowty's approach, nonetheless, differs from the current approach in that it uses a monostratal representation (the surface structure) which is directly linked up with thematic
roles. In contrast, the current approach uses two GB levels of representation, D-structure and S-structure, with the D-structure acting as the
output representation for the linking procedure, and the S-structure acting as the output for syntactic movement rules of the type discussed in
chapter 2. Thus, the representation that is linked up with thematic roles
is the D-structure — not the S-structure — and the positioning of arguments in the S-structure is then dependent on syntactic requirements

(*e.g.*, case assignment) — not on thematic role assignments. Dowty's approach also differs from the current one in that it focuses primarily on English and does not address the problems inherent in translating between languages (*e.g.*, the divergences addressed in the current research), nor does it imply that the proto-roles are to be taken as components of an interlingual representation. Finally, unlike the current approach, Dowty's framework does not provide a mechanism for handling non-arguments (*i.e.*, adjuncts such as *with a knife*).

Before considering the extensions that have been made to the original LCS framework, let us turn to a discussion about the implications of using the LCS as an interlingua. Those who are familiar with other proposals for representing word meaning might object to the use of the LCS as an interlingua because of its incompatibility with standard lexical-semantic paradigms which generally use representations that are more language-specific in nature.

An example of a related approach that does not view lexical-semantics as the basis of an interlingua is that of Hale and Keyser (1989). This approach focuses on issues concerning the lexical-semantics of specific types of verbs within a *particular* language. It proposes that verbs such as *shelve* (*e.g.*, *shelve the books*), *carpet* (*e.g.*, *carpet the floor*), *mine* (*e.g.*, *mine the gold*), *etc.* that incorporate a thematic role directly into the verb are defined by means of a language-specific Lexical Relational Structure (LRS) of the form shown in figure 4.7.[11] That is, a lexical item that incorporates a thematic argument is formed by successive cyclic movement of the lowest NP (*e.g.*, *shelf* in the case of the verb *shelve*) through the preposition and verb of the inner VP, arriving at the matrix verb. For example, the LRS that is derived by this process for the verb *shelve* is shown in figure 4.8(a). The D-structure VP projection of this LRS is derived by "reduction of superfluous structure" as shown in figure 4.8(b).

The viewpoint adopted by Hale and Keyser is similar to that of the Generative Semantics framework (see, for example, Lakoff (1971)) in that the notion of "possible lexical item" is constrained by certain principles of grammar that also determine the well-formedness of syntactic

---

[11]The parenthetical NPs are variable positions that will be filled in by the subject and object. The unfilled verb and prepositions are intended to be abstract (empty) members of their categories. The two constants in this representation are the lexical item and the NP that has been vacated (t_i).

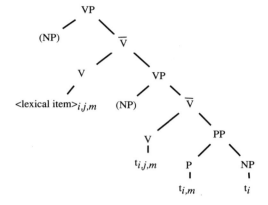

Figure 4.7
The Lexical Relational Structure (LRS) for the verb *shelve* accommodates argument incorporation by means of successive cyclic movement of the lowest NP *shelf*.

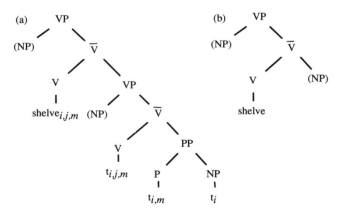

Figure 4.8
The D-structure VP Projection for verb *shelve* is derived from the LRS representation.

structures. For example, the structure of figure 4.8(a) is deemed to be grammatical because no known principle of grammar is violated. The process of incorporation is taken to be a head-movement variant of the syntactic rule move-α discussed in chapter 2, and its successive cyclic application is subject to an analog of the subjacency condition, namely the requirement that no barriers intervene between any trace and its proper governor.

Clearly it would not be appropriate to use the LRS as an interlingua because the operations applied to the LRS are specific to the lexical item of a particular language. The LCS representation, by contrast, is a suitable representation for an interlingua because lexical-specific transformations are not used, nor is the LCS representation subject to the same constraints of syntactic theory. Perhaps the LCS representation could be thought of as the *input* to the process by which incorporation is achieved. In fact, the categories V, N, A, and P of the LRS representation are not intended to be syntactic categories; they are intended to be abstract categories that are determined by canonical realization of the semantic constructs <event>, <entity>, <state>, and <interrelation>. In terms of LCS types, these constructs are analogous to Event, Thing, Property, and Path/Place, respectively. Thus, there is a correspondence between the LCS representation and the LRS representation shown in figure 4.8(a) and then a correspondence between the LRS representation and the D-structure of figure 4.8(b). The entire derivation from LCS to D-structure is shown in figure 4.9.[12] The LRS, then, is viewed as the language-specific analog of the LCS.

The advantage to using the LCS representation as an interlingua is that it is easy to parameterize so that it accommodates cross-linguistic divergences without losing the systematic relation between lexical-semantic structure and the syntactic structure. Moreover, the representation lends itself readily to the specification of a systematic mapping that operates uniformly across all languages. Thus, the LCS is a crucial component of the machine translation model; it serves as a pivot, not only between the syntactic structures of the source and target languages,

---

[12]The $*$ marker will be defined in section 4.4.1. The :CONFLATED marker, which will be defined in the next chapter, indicates that this position will be mapped to a constant in the LRS representation. Note that all LCS variables map to corresponding variables in the LRS representation.

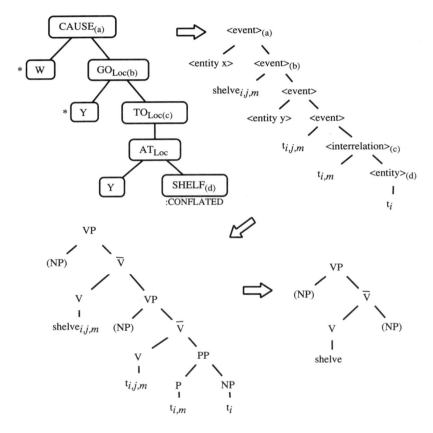

Figure 4.9
A possible view of the LCS is that it is the *input* to the process by which
incorporation is achieved. Thus, there is a mapping from the LCS to D-structure
via the LRS for the verb *shelve*.

but also potentially between the source and target lexical items at a lower
level (if the LRS view is adopted).

One more point worth mentioning here is that it could easily be argued that this approach (as well as that of Hale and Keyser) would
be subject to the same objections raised by Fodor (1970) regarding the
inadequacy of deriving *kill* from *cause to die* as in the representation
assumed by McCawley (1968). (See fn. 21 in chapter 1 for our initial
discussion about this point.) However, there are some significant differences between the approach that Fodor was criticizing and that of
contemporary lexical-semanticists. First, the framework of early generative semanticists is intended to provide an exhaustive decomposition of
word meaning into a finite set of semantic/conceptual primitives that define a finite collection of necessary and sufficient conditions; by contrast,
the framework of contemporary lexical semanticists pursues a different
goal, namely that of providing a systematic relation between the structure of meaning and the structure of language on the surface. While the
current approach is clearly decompositional, it is does not claim to be
exhaustively decompositional. Thus, it does not attempt to convey all
the details of the causal relationships involved in the meaning of a word.
Jackendoff takes this one step further by proposing that the primary
task of defining be assigned to "typicality conditions" (*e.g.*, that the
verb *climb* usually incorporates the notion of *up* or that *X causing Y to
die* usually implies *that X killed Y*) not necessary and sufficient conditions. That is, Jackendoff is concerned with what structure the meaning
has, not whether all the details of the causal relationships are precisely
conveyed. The dependence on necessary and sufficient conditions, he
argues, is characteristic of exhaustive decomposition approaches such as
that of Schank (1972, 1973, 1975) and also that of generative semanticists (*e.g.*, Lakoff (1971)), whose goals diverge significantly from those
of Jackendoff.

Another difference between contemporary lexical-semantic frameworks
and those of earlier researchers is that the latter presupposes, for example, that *kill* is derived from a "deep structure" syntactic representation
of *cause to die* as shown in figure 4.10. Neither Hale and Keyser nor
Jackendoff adopt such an approach to representing meaning. In the
case of Hale and Keyser, the verbs derived by incorporation are lexical
items that are themselves input *to* the D-structure representation (they
are not derived *from* the D-structure representation). This is where

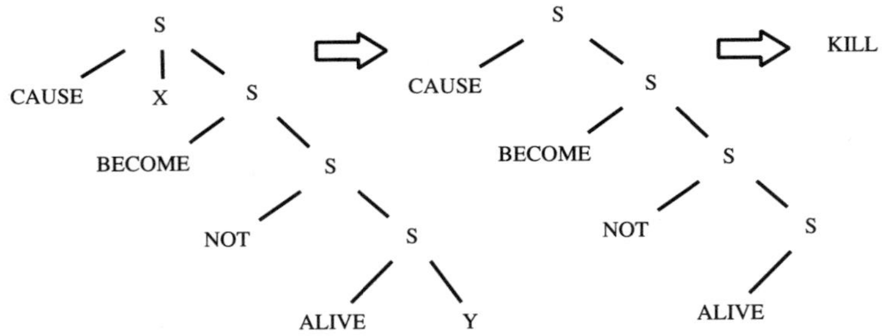

Figure 4.10
McCawley (1968) proposes that the word *kill* is derived from a "deep structure"
syntactic representation of *cause to die*.

the LRS representation diverges from the generative semantics framework. Jackendoff's framework also diverges from the generative semantics framework for the same reason, namely that the LCS representation
is not derived from a D-structure representation, but is constructed on
the basis of properties of lexical items and their potential realizations in
the surface syntactic structure.

Now that we have examined the structure of the LCS as an interlingual
representation, we will discuss some of the extensions that have been
made to the original framework proposed by Jackendoff.

4.3   Extensions to Jackendoff's LCS Framework

The primary extension to Jackendoff's original framework is the association of the representation with an algorithm for recursive composition
and decomposition of the interlingual form. The algorithm is defined
on the basis of a systematic linking of the LCS to the syntactic structure, both during parsing as well as during generation (*i.e.*, the mapping
shown in figure 4.4). The most critical mechanism that brings about this
linking is the * marker, one of several lexical-semantic parameters discussed in section 4.4 and in subsequent chapters.

As we saw in the last section, the use of the LCS as an interlingua for
more than one language is generally considered to be nonstandard, and
in fact, is a possibility that is not even discussed by Jackendoff himself.

Because the lexicon has been parameterized to account for lexical-semantic divergences, this possibility has been realized in the UNITRAN system with a minimal amount of engineering. One of the reasons that the latest version of the LCS framework by Jackendoff (1990) is not well-suited to an interlingual specification of more than one language is that it retains the language-specific syntactic and semantic subcategorization information in the frame of each lexical entry rather than deriving syntactic properties via linking rules. Other proposals have been made for using a lexical-semantic representation that does not retain syntactic information in lexical entries (see, *e.g.*, Pinker (1989), Rappaport and Levin (1988), and White (1992)), but so far, most approaches have concentrated on representing English and have not entertained the possibility of parameterizing the representation for use as an interlingua.

We will temporarily defer the discussion about the parameterization of the framework until section 4.4.1 and subsequent chapters. We turn now to a discussion about the primitives that have been added to the framework beyond those shown in figure 4.1. In particular, the primitives CAUSE-EXCHANGE, DO, EAT, SEE, HEAR, FEEL, SEARCH, UP, DOWN, ACROSS, and ALONG have been added. In addition to new primitives, the fields Perceptional, Intentional, and Instrumental have been added to the original framework. We will see that the addition of these new primitives and fields has induced further extensions to the Manner type. In addition, the ORIENT primitive has been extended to include the Identificational and Temporal fields. Also, a new type called Intensifier has been added. Finally, a number of primitives corresponding to question words have been added. All of these extensions came about as a result of an in-depth investigation of translation divergences. In order to demonstrate the effectiveness of the current approach, a number of verbs needed to be added that were not adequately characterized by Jackendoff's primitives. Thus, the original framework needed to be augmented. We will briefly sketch the general intuition behind these extensions.

The CAUSE-EXCHANGE primitive has been added to include verbs such as *buy* and *sell*. This primitive is a shorthand notation for the CAUSE primitive coupled with a subordinating function called EXCH as presented by Jackendoff (1990). The representation distinguishes between *buy* and *sell* by using a different causative agent (*i.e.*, logical subject) in each case:

(80) (i)   John sold the book to Mary

      (ii)   [Event CAUSE-EXCHANGE
                 ([Thing JOHN],
                 [Event GOPoss
                     ([Thing BOOK],
                     [Path FROMPoss
                         ([Position ATPoss ([Thing BOOK], [Thing JOHN])])]
                     [Path TOPoss
                         ([Position ATPoss ([Thing BOOK], [Thing MARY])])])],
                 [Event GOPoss
                     ([Thing MONEY],
                     [Path FROMPoss
                         ([Position ATPoss ([Thing MONEY], [Thing MARY])])],
                     [Path TOPoss
                         ([Position ATPoss ([Thing MONEY], [Thing JOHN])])])])]

(81) (i)   Mary bought the book from John

      (ii)   [Event CAUSE-EXCHANGE
                 ([Thing MARY],
                 [Event GOPoss
                     ([Thing BOOK],
                     [Path FROMPoss
                         ([Position ATPoss ([Thing BOOK], [Thing JOHN])])]
                     [Path TOPoss
                         ([Position ATPoss ([Thing BOOK], [Thing MARY])])])],
                 [Event GOPoss
                     ([Thing MONEY],
                     [Path FROMPoss
                         ([Position ATPoss ([Thing MONEY], [Thing MARY])])],
                     [Path TOPoss
                         ([Position ATPoss ([Thing MONEY], [Thing JOHN])])])])]

The primitive DO has been added to cover the English, Spanish, and German verbs *do*, *hacer*, and *tun*, respectively. Thus, the representation for *John did the wash* is:

(82) [Event DO ([Thing John], [Event WASH ([Thing John], [Thing Y])])][13]

It might be argued that the verb *do* should not be represented at the level of conceptual structure. That is, instead of using the representation

---

[13]Note that the logical Thing argument is left uninstantiated since the object of the washing action is not stated.

in (82) for the sentence *John did the wash*, we could simply represent this sentence in the same way that we would represent *John washed*:

(83) $[_{\text{Event}}$ WASH $([_{\text{Thing}}$ John$], [_{\text{Thing}}$ Y$])]$

However, without the DO primitive, these two sentences would be translated interchangeably, which would not be appropriate in all contexts. Furthermore, without such a primitive there would be no way of representing a sentence in which the main action is not stated, such as *John did it*. Finally, the DO primitive is completely analogous to the CAUSE and LET primitives which are independently motivated by Jackendoff (1983). To the extent that these primitives can be justified in an interlingual system, so too can the DO primitive. This primitive is analogous to CAUSE and LET in three ways: (1) it does not have a field dimension; (2) it takes the same number and type of arguments (*i.e.*, a Thing and an Event or State); and (3) it is optionally realizable on the surface depending on the requirements of the language. Regarding this final point, note that the same types of cross-linguistic realization alternatives are available for CAUSE and DO:

(84) (i)   S: John forzó la entrada al cuarto   (CAUSE realized as *forzar*)
             E: John broke into the room   (CAUSE not realized)

      (ii) E: John did the wash yesterday   (DO realized as *do*)
             S: Juan lavaba ayer   (DO not realized)

Another primitive that has been added to the system is EAT because no such action was included in the original Jackendoff framework.[14] The EAT primitive does not have a field dimension given that no field seems to apply (with the possible exception of the Locational field). Thus, it is assumed that this primitive already has its field incorporated into it. This incorporated field, whatever it is called, is likely to be the same

---

[14]Note that this primitive might be better formulated as the more general INGEST primitive (as in that of Schank (1972, 1973, 1975)) where the ingested object is FOOD (for *eat*), FLUID (for *drink*), SMOKE (for *smoke*), *etc.*, but it has been left as the more specific formulation in the current implementation.

one that DRINK and SMOKE use. (Note that these primitives are more
specific than those that can be moved around from field to field, such
as GO and BE.) An example of the use of the EAT primitive is the
following:

(85) (i)   John ate beans

     (ii)   [Event EAT ([Thing JOHN], [Thing BEANS])]

The Perceptional field has been created in order to accommodate verbs
such as *see*, *hear*, and *feel*.[15] However, unlike other Perceptional verbs
(to be described next), these verbs are characterized by the new primitives SEE, HEAR, and FEEL. The reason these new primitives are
adopted instead of using the BE primitive (*e.g.*, BE_{Perc} SEEINGLY)
is that these verbs are considered to be events, not states. A syntactic
test, attributed to Dowty (1979), that teases apart events and states is
the progressive construction:

(86) (i)   I was hearing the sirens as we danced. (event)

     (ii)   * I was wanting him to talk softly as we danced. (state)

This Perceptional field is also used with the primitive BE to represent
verbs such as *believe*, *know*, *want*, *etc.*, *i.e.*, it is used to characterize
verbs of *mental* perception as well as *visual*, *aural*, and *tactile* perception. When the BE primitive is used in the Perceptional field, it
is generally used in conjunction with a manner component such as BE-
LIEVINGLY, KNOWINGLY, WANTINGLY, *etc.* in order to distinguish
between the different types of perceived notions. (The manner component will be discussed shortly.) The Perceptional field has also been
shown to be useful for paths: $TOWARD_{Perc}$ (*e.g.*, *look toward*), AWAY-
$FROM_{Perc}$ (*e.g.*, *look away from*), $ABOUT_{Perc}$ (*e.g.*, *know about*), and
IN_{Perc} (*e.g.*, *believe in*). An example of the use of BE in the Perceptional
field is the following:

(87) (i)   John believes in unicorns

     (ii)   [Event BE_{Perc}
       ([Thing JOHN],
       [Path IN_{Perc}
         ([Position AT_{Perc} ([Thing JOHN], [Thing UNICORNS])])]
       [Manner BELIEVINGLY])]

---

[15]There are surely others (*e.g.*, *smell*, *taste*, *etc.*) that can be added to this set.

Instead of using a Perceptional field, Jackendoff represents mental notions by means of the Rep operator which provides a referential reading of something that might occur in someone's mind. Thus, sentence (87)(i) might be represented as:

(88)   [_State_ BE ([_Rep_ UNICORN], [_Position_ IN ([_Location_ JOHN'S MIND])])]

There are two problems with using this representation. The first is that it relies on an operator that exists at a meta-level above the conceptual representation (*i.e.*, the Rep operator). If this meta-level were used in UNITRAN, another tier of lexical-semantic processing would be required for translation since the conceptual representation currently adopted is intended to be mapped uniformly to the syntactic structure. (We will see this in section 4.5.) The additional tier would greatly complicate the mapping between the interlingua and the syntactic structure. The second problem, as acknowledged by Jackendoff, is that this representation does not differentiate the thematic analyses of *believe*, *imagine*, *remember*, and so forth.

In the simplified representation used by UNITRAN, these notions are differentiated by means of a manner component.[16] This representation has the advantage that it is mapped to the syntactic structure uniformly by the same mapping that is used for non-mental verbs.

Another new primitive, SEARCH, has been added to represent the notion of *searching* or *looking for* something. This primitive is used only in the Possessional field and is generally used in conjunction with the new position primitive, FOR:[17]

(89)   (i)   John searched / looked for the book

        (ii)   [_Event_ SEARCH_Poss_
                  ([_Thing_ JOHN],
                  [_Path_ FOR_Poss_ ([_Thing_ JOHN], [_Thing_ BOOK])])]

---

[16]The differentiation of mental states is also a problem in Schank's system (see Schank (1972, 1973, 1975)) which relies on the same primitive (MTRANS) for a number of different verbs such as *want*, *know*, *think*, *believe*, *etc.* Later versions of Schank's model (*e.g.*, Rieger (1975)) extended the framework to include primitives such as WANT. In effect, this is a close approximation to the solution adopted here.

[17]An alternative to defining the new SEARCH primitive is to define *search* and *look for* as a causative form of the GO_Poss_ primitive:

The new paths UP, DOWN, and ALONG have been added to the system in order to handle sentences such as the following:

(90) (i)   John went up/down the stairs (UP$_{Loc}$/DOWN$_{Loc}$)

(ii)   John walked along the river (ALONG$_{Loc}$)

Note that these paths are used only in the Locational field.[18]

Another modification that has been made to the primitives is the use of the ORIENT primitive in the identificational and temporal fields to account for the following cases:

(91) (i)   The book costs $10.00 (ORIENT$_{Ident}$)

(ii)   John aims to start at 2:00 (ORIENT$_{Temp}$)

In addition to new primitives, two more fields have been added to the system: Instrumental and Intentional. The Instrumental field is used to represent various types of instrumental modifiers (as we will see below in the lexical entry for *stab*). The primitives that are used in this field, FOR, WITH, and CO, are also new:

(92) (i)   John bought the book for $5.00 (FOR$_{Instr}$)

(ii)   John stabbed Mary with a knife (WITH$_{Instr}$)

(iii) John walked with Mary (CO$_{Instr}$)

The Intentional field is used for cases where an action is done for the purpose of something or for the benefit of someone. The two primitives used in this field are FOR and AT:

(93) (i)   John signed the book for Mary (FOR$_{Intent}$)

(ii)   John ate because he was hungry (FOR$_{Intent}$)

(iii) John turned the light on so that he could see (FOR$_{Intent}$)

(iv) The book cost me $10.00 (AT$_{Intent}$)

[Event CAUSE
  ([Thing W],
  [Event GO$_{Poss}$
    ([Thing W], [Path TOWARD$_{Poss}$ ([Position AT$_{Poss}$ ([Thing W], [Thing Z])])])])
  [Manner SEARCHINGLY])]

The SEARCH primitive can be thought of as an abbreviation for this longer expression.

[18]It might also be possible to use these paths in other fields such as the Perceptional field *e.g., John looked up* (UP$_{Perc}$).

The justification for adding these fields is that there are a number of conjunctions and particles (such as *so that*, *because*, *for*, *with*, *etc.*) that must be made distinguishable in order for the system to make the appropriate lexical selection during generation. For example, the word *for* (FOR_{Poss}), not *because* (FOR_{Intent}), is used to represent the modifier phrase *for John* in the sentence *John bought the book for Mary*.

Another extension to the Jackendoff framework is the augmentation of the Manner type to include a wide range of primitives. While the LCS framework currently provides a means for distinguishing between verbs *across* LCS classes, it does not yet provide a principled account of constraints *within* LCS classes. Verbs within a particular class are frequently distinguishable by some feature corresponding to Manner (*e.g.*, *walk vs. run*), yet Jackendoff says very little about the function of the Manner type in his description of conceptual structure. In fact, he claims that "it is not the business of conceptual structure" to encode different Manner types since conceptual structure is designed "to encode primarily an appropriate argument structure ..."; the lexicon, then, must be linked to "a more detailed spatial structure encoding" in order to distinguish between verbs in a particular verb class (*e.g.*, *wriggle* and *wiggle*) (see Jackendoff (1990, p. 88)). Although I whole-heartedly agree with this view, we are left with the question of what is meant by a "detailed spatial structure encoding," *i.e.*, how such a representation would be constructed and how it interacts with the conceptual structure. Moreover, this approach does not address the problem of representing the Manner type in other categories outside of the spatial domain (*e.g.*, *like vs. love* or *repossess vs. steal*).

The current solution has been to use the Manner component to distinguish between two verbs that fall within the same linguistic class when no other distinguishing features are available. A side effect of this solution is that the representation appears to be too specific in certain cases. While Manner primitives are no more specific than many other open-ended primitives (*e.g.*, HOUSE, ASLEEP, 9:00, HERE, *etc.*), one could conceive of a worst case scenario in which the number of Manner primitives grows linearly with respect to the number of verbs that are added to each verb class. It could even be argued that the work of categorizing predicates such as *believe* and *want* into the BE_{Perc} class is wasted since the use of BELIEVINGLY and WANTINGLY is equivalent to categorizing the predicates into two distinct classes (*i.e.*, we could just use primitives called BELIEVE and WANT and get rid of the BE_{Perc} primitive).

These concerns have recently been addressed by Siskind (1992) who argues that the Manner component of certain types of verbs can be broken down into primitives of a different type. For example, Siskind is able to differentiate among such spatial verbs as *turn*, *spin*, *revolve*, and *rotate* simply by using the GO_{Loc} primitive with a Manner component that is defined in terms of physical notions such as "orientation at the end of the action with respect to the starting point." (The formal mechanism for capturing this physical notion is not discussed here.) It is expected that the same principle carries over to non-spatial classes of predicates such as *believe* and *want*. Clearly this is an area that requires further investigation, but while there are still a number of open questions, the current solution has proven to be sufficient for addressing the problem of translation divergences. That is, Manner components such as BELIEVINGLY and WANTINGLY can be taken to be "macros" that may be expanded into some form of primitive notion analogous to the physical descriptions used in Siskind's work.

Note that there are a number of alternatives for representing the Manner component. For example, the Manner component might be represented by means of feature values (*i.e.*, ±believe, ±want, *etc.*) that are independent from the lexical representation. A number of researchers have taken a feature-setting approach to distinguish among verbs that belong to the same lexical class. (See, *e.g.*, Bennett *et al.* (1990).) The reason for adopting the approach described here is that the Manner component often shows up in the surface syntactic structures of different languages (*e.g.*, German *gern* corresponds to LIKINGLY, French *a la nage* corresponds to SWIMMINGLY, *etc.*). In order to provide a uniform mapping between LCS representations and their surface realizations, we need a lexical place holder for Manner components as well as argument components. Although these lexical tokens are not "reusable" in the sense of the more general tokens (GO, BE, TO, AT, *etc.*), it is expected that these tokens may ultimately be decomposed into primitives that *are* reusable at a different level of representation (as discussed above). In any case, these tokens are necessary to support the general scheme of LCS composition and decomposition of surface structures that include a corresponding Manner component of meaning. The mapping between the LCS representation and the surface syntactic structure is

set up so that it is easy to determine whether the Manner component is
suppressed or overtly realized in the surface sentence.[19]

One final comment in defense of the "macro" version of the Manner component is that it does avoid some of the well-known problems of extreme decomposition. (For a detailed discussion, see *e.g.*, Sproat (1985).) One such problem is the potential for deep recursion that is inherent in the CD framework of Schank. As noted by Schank himself (1973, p. 201), this is particularly a problem with instrumentality:

(94)   "If every ACT requires an instrumental case which itself contains an
       ACT, it should be obvious that we can never finish diagramming a
       given conceptualization. For [the] sentence [John ate the ice cream with
       a spoon], for example, we might have 'John ingested the ice cream by
       transing the ice cream on a spoon to his mouth, by transing the spoon
       to the ice cream, by grasping the spoon, by moving his hand to the
       spoon, by moving his hand muscles, by thinking about moving his hand
       muscles,' and so on ... These instrumental actions are not really needed
       and are rarely actively thought about ... but we shall retain the ability
       to retrieve these instruments should we find this necessary."

While the current approach does not pretend to solve the problem of representing the deep meaning of the Manner component, it does at least avoid the infinite recursion problem by leaving out the detailed mechanics underlying the modifying action (*e.g.*, that SWIMMINGLY involves certain leg and arm motions that rely on moving certain muscles, *etc.*).

In addition to new fields and primitives, the system also has a new type, Intensifier, that currently allows Properties, Manners, and Intensifiers themselves to be intensified. The intensifier is placed in the Identificational field for modifying properties and the Instrumental field for modifying manners:

(95)   (i)   John was very happy

       (ii) $[_{\text{State}} \text{BE}_{\text{Ident}}$
               $([_{\text{Thing}} \text{JOHN}],$
               $[_{\text{Position}} \text{AT}_{\text{Ident}}$
               $([_{\text{Thing}} \text{JOHN}],$
               $[_{\text{Property}} \text{HAPPY} ([_{\text{Intensifier}} \text{VERY}_{\text{Ident}}])])])]$

---

[19]The mechanism that determines whether the Manner component is suppressed or realized in the surface structure is described in chapter 5.

(96) (i)   John ate very happily

      (ii) $[_{\text{Event}}$ EAT
                 $([_{\text{Thing}}$ JOHN$]$,
                 $[_{\text{Thing}}$ FOOD$]$,
                 $[_{\text{Manner}}$ HAPPILY $([_{\text{Intensifier}}$ VERY$_{\text{Instr}}])])]$

(97) (i)   John was so very happy

      (ii) $[_{\text{State}}$ BE$_{\text{Ident}}$
                 $([_{\text{Thing}}$ JOHN$]$,
                 $[_{\text{Position}}$ AT$_{\text{Ident}}$
                    $([\text{ctype:Thing JOHN}]$,
                    $[_{\text{Property}}$ HAPPY
                       $([_{\text{Intensifier}}$ SO$_{\text{Ident}}$ $([_{\text{Intensifier}}$ VERY$_{\text{Ident}}])])])])]$

(98) (i)   John ate so very happily

      (ii) $[_{\text{Event}}$ EAT
                 $([_{\text{Thing}}$ JOHN$]$,
                 $[_{\text{Thing}}$ FOOD$]$,
                 $[_{\text{Manner}}$ HAPPILY
                    $([_{\text{Intensifier}}$ SO$_{\text{Instr}}$ $([_{\text{Intensifier}}$ VERY$_{\text{Instr}}])])])]$

A final augmentation to the set of primitives is the addition of the
capability to handle question words referring to Intensifiers, Manners,
Things, Locations, Times, Properties, and Purposes.[20] The relevant
primitives are: WH-INTENSIFIER (*e.g.*, *how*), WH-MANNER (*e.g.*,
how), WH-THING (*e.g.*, *what*), WH-LOCATION (*e.g.*, *where*), WH-
TIME (*e.g.*, *when*), WH-PROPERTY (*e.g.*, *how*), and WH-PURPOSE
(*e.g.*, *why*). For example, the WH-THING primitive would be used as
follows:

(99) (i)   What did John eat

      (ii) $[_{\text{Event}}$ EAT $([_{\text{Thing}}$ JOHN$]$, $[_{\text{Thing}}$ WH-THING$])]$

To sum up, the primitive/field combinations that have been added
to the system are shown in figure 4.11 along with relevant examples.[21]
The full extended set of primitives is shown in figure 4.12. There are

---

[20] The Purpose type is not included in Jackendoff's description of the model; in the
current model, the Purpose is intended to be the reference object of the Intentional
field, just as the Location is considered to be the reference object of the Locational
field.

[21] This list is by no means exhaustive. In particular, the primitives corresponding
to Manners, Things, Locations, Times, Properties, and Purposes are too numerous
to list here given that these categories are intended to be open-ended. Note that
open-ended categories correspond precisely to those primitives that do not have field
specifications, *i.e.*, the taking primitives that do not take any arguments.

Type	Primitive-Field	Example
	CAUSE-EXCHANGE	John sold the book to Mary
	DO	John did the wash
	EAT	John ate breakfast
	SEE_{Perc}	John saw the rain
Event	$HEAR_{Perc}$	John heard the rain
	$FEEL_{Perc}$	John felt the rain
	$SEARCH_{Poss}$	John looked for the book
	$ORIENT_{Ident}$	The book costs $10.00
	$ORIENT_{Temp}$	John aims to start at 2:00
State	BE_{Perc}	John believed Mary
	$TOWARD_{Perc}$	John looked toward the sun
	$AWAY\text{-}FROM_{Perc}$	John looked away from the sun
	$ABOUT_{Perc}$	John knew about Mary
Path	IN_{Perc}	John believed in Mary
	UP_{Loc}	John went up the stairs
	$DOWN_{Loc}$	John went down the stairs
	$ALONG_{Loc}$	John walked along the river
	FOR_{Instr}	John bought the book for $5.00
	$WITH_{Instr}$	John stabbed Mary with a knife
Position	CO_{Instr}	John walked with Mary
	FOR_{Intent}	John signed the book for Mary
	AT_{Intent}	The book cost me $10.00
	FOR_{Poss}	John bought the book for Mary
	$VERY_{Ident}$	John was very happy
	$VERY_{Instr}$	John ate very happily
Intensifier	SO_{Ident}	John was so happy
	SO_{Instr}	John ate so happily
	$WH\text{-}INTENSIFIER_{Ident}$	How happy was John
	$WH\text{-}INTENSIFIER_{Instr}$	How happily did John eat
	BELIEVINGLY	John believed Mary
	WANTINGLY	John wanted Mary
Manner	KNOWINGLY	John knew Mary
	READINGLY	John read the book
	WRITINGLY	John wrote the book
	WH-MANNER	How did John write the book
Thing	WH-THING	What did John eat
Location	WH-LOCATION	Where did John go
Time	WH-TIME	When did John write the book
Property	WH-PROPERTY	How did John feel
Purpose	WH-PURPOSE	Why did John write the book

Figure 4.11
The extended set of fields and primitives includes types from the following
categories: Events, States, Paths, Positions, Intensifiers, Manners, Things, Times,
Locations, Properties, and Purposes.

Type	Primitive
Event	CAUSE, LET, GO, STAY, CAUSE-EXCHANGE, DO, EAT, SEE, HEAR, FEEL, SEARCH
State	BE, GO-EXT, ORIENT
Path	TO, FROM, TOWARD, AWAY-FROM, VIA, ABOUT, IN, UP, DOWN, ALONG
Position	AT, IN, ON, WITH, CO, FOR
Intensifier	VERY, SO, WH-INTENSIFIER
Manner	BELIEVINGLY, WANTINGLY, KNOWINGLY, READ-INGLY, WRITINGLY, HAPPILY, WH-MANNER
Thing	BOOK, PERSON, REFERENT, KNIFE-WOUND, WH-THING
Location	HERE, THERE, LEFT, RIGHT, UP, DOWN, WH-LOCATION
Time	TODAY, SATURDAY, 2:00, 4:00, WH-TIME
Property	TIRED, HUNGRY, PLEASED, BROKEN, ASLEEP, DEAD, HAPPY, WH-PROPERTY
Purpose	WH-PURPOSE

Figure 4.12
The extended set of primitives includes 33 primitives multiplied out into 9 fields, not including the more open-ended types (*i.e.*, Manners, Things, Locations, Times, Properties, and Purposes).

33 primitives multiplied out into 9 fields, not including the more open-ended types (*i.e.*, Manners, Things, Locations, Times, Properties, and Purposes). Although the system currently uses a small set of lexical-semantic primitives, the set is quite adequate for defining a wide variety of words due to the compositional nature of LCS's.

In attempting to cover a wide range of phenomena, a subset of the linguistic classes from Levin (1985, in press) has been implemented using this extended LCS framework. The implemented classes are summarized in figure 4.13 with examples of verbs given in English. It is expected that this verb classification scheme will need further refinement as more properties of verbs are identified. A more detailed listing of the types of sentences handled by the extended set of primitives is given in appendix C.

4.4 Organization of the Lexicon

We have just seen how the LCS representation is used as the basis of the interlingua. We now turn to the use of the LCS in lexical entries.

Class of Verb	Examples
position	be, remain, ...
change of position	fall, throw, drop, change, move, slide, float, roll, fly, bounce, move, drop, turn, rotate, shift, ...
directed motion	enter, break into, bring, carry, remove, come, go, leave, arrive, descend, ascend, put, raise, lower, ...
motion with manner	sail, walk, stroll, jog, march, gallop, jump, float, dance, run, skip, ...
exchange	buy, sell, trade, ...
physical state	be, remain, keep, leave, ...
change of physical state	open, close, melt, redden, soften, break, crack, freeze, harden, dry, whiten, grow, change, become, ...
orientation	point, aim, face, ...
existence	exist, build, grow, shape, make, whittle, spin, carve, weave, bake, fashion, create, appear, disappear, reappear, persist, ...
circumstance	be, start, stop, continue, keep, exempt, ...
range	go, last, extend, intend, aim, range, ...
change of ownership	give, take, receive, relinquish, borrow, lend, loan, steal, ...
ownership	belong, remain, keep, own, ...
ingestion	eat, drink, smoke, gobble, munch, sip, ...
psychological state	like, fear, admire, detest, despise, enjoy, esteem, hate, honor, love please, scare, amuse, astonish, bore, surprise, stun, terrify, thrill, ...
perception and communication	see, hear, smell, feel, look, watch, listen, learn, sniff, show, tell, talk, speak, shout, whisper, scream, ...
mental process	know, learn, ...
cost	cost, charge, ...
load/spray	smear, load, cram, spray, stuff, pile, stack, splash, ...
contact/effect	cut, stab, crush, smash, pierce, bite, shoot, spear, ...

Figure 4.13
A subset of the linguistic classes from Levin (1985, in press) has been implemented using the extended LCS framework.

4.4.1 Lexical Entries

We shall distinguish between the use of the LCS as an interlingua from
the use of the LCS in lexical entries by using the term CLCS (*composed
LCS*) for the former and the term RLCS (*root word* LCS) for the latter.

Each language processed by the system requires a dictionary of RLCS
entries. An RLCS has two levels of description: the first is the language-
independent LCS representation of the lexical word (which conforms
to (73) above) and the second is the language-specific parametric specification that guides the syntactic realization of the word and its arguments. Consider the RLCS entry for the English verb *stab*:

(100) [$_{\text{Event}}$ CAUSE
     ([$_{\text{Thing}}$ * W],
     [$_{\text{Event}}$ GO$_{\text{Poss}}$
       ([$_{\text{Thing}}$ KNIFE-WOUND],
       [$_{\text{Path}}$ TOWARD$_{\text{Poss}}$
         ([$_{\text{Position}}$ AT$_{\text{Poss}}$ ([$_{\text{Thing}}$ KNIFE-WOUND], [$_{\text{Thing}}$ * Z])])])],
     [WITH$_{\text{Instr}}$ * ([$_{\text{Event}}$ *HEAD*], [$_{\text{Thing}}$ U SHARP-OBJECT])])]

The first level of description specifies the language-independent meaning
which, in this case, roughly corresponds to "thing W causes thing Z to
possess a knife-wound by means of a sharp object U." Note that the
SHARP-OBJECT modifier is included in the definition even though this
constituent does not show up in the CLCS in (77).[22] Because modifiers
are considered to be optional constituents, they may be omitted from
the interlingua. Thus, the same RLCS may be used to build different
CLCS representations. In particular, the RLCS provides flexibility in
representing the source and target language sentences, which may or
may not include certain modifiers. This means it would be possible to
generate either *he stabbed the robber*, or *he stabbed the robber with a
knife (scissors, poker, etc.)* from this single lexical entry.

The second level of description in the RLCS is imposed by means of
the "*" (pronounced "star") notation (and other potential markers not
present in this example), which is used to specify the language-specific
correspondence between LCS arguments and the syntactic structure.

---

[22]The variable U refers to a locally introduced modifier. The *HEAD* symbol is a
place-holder that points to the root (CAUSE) of the overall *stab* event (*i.e.*, the *stab*
event is performed with a sharp object).

Figure 4.14 illustrates the use of the * notation for the English and Spanish entries corresponding to the *stab* event in example (76) given earlier. In section 4.5, we will see how the * marker acts as a parameter of variation that allows the system to accommodate this divergence example during the lexical-semantic composition process.

4.4.2 LCS Classes

Lexical entries are organized into *LCS classes*. These classes are not identical to the linguistic classes that are typically studied by researchers of the lexicon (*e.g.*, the classes shown in figure 4.13). Each LCS class is based, not on syntactic distribution and alternation constraints, but on a template that conforms to the well-formedness constraints shown in (68)–(70). Thus, each LCS class may include verbs from more than one linguistic class, and conversely, each linguistic class may include verbs from more than one LCS class. For example, the verb *give* (from the linguistic class of change of ownership) and the verb *stab* (from the linguistic class of contact/effect) are in the same LCS class associated with the GO_{Poss} primitive. Conversely, the linguistic class *directed motion* includes verbs associated with the GO_{Loc} primitive (*e.g.*, *enter*) and verbs associated with the GO_{Poss} primitive (*e.g.*, *receive*).

All lexical items belonging to an LCS class are grouped together in the dictionary according to a particular LCS template. For example, the lexical entries defined within the GO_{Poss} class are shown in figure 4.15. (For brevity, a small subset of the verbs from this class is shown.) In this example, L is the LCS template and the words defined in this class are grouped into different path types by means of the path pointer P. The two path types shown here are $TOWARD_{Poss}$ (*e.g.*, *go*, *receive*, *stab*, *cut*, *give*, *repossess*, *obtain*, and *accept*) and $AWAY\text{-}FROM_{Poss}$ (*e.g.*, *lose*, *relinquish*, and *surrender*). Note that each lexical entry includes the surface realization information (specified by means of the "* =" notation).[23] The use of this information is discussed in section 4.5.

In addition to specifying the LCS and path templates, L and P, the LCS class specifies a causative template, C, and a permissive template, T. These templates may be used compositionally with the LCS template L to form more complex LCS constructions. For example, the

---

[23]In addition to the * marker, the lexicon also makes use of the :INT and :EXT markers (*e.g.*, in the lexical entry for *receive*) which will be discussed in chapter 5.

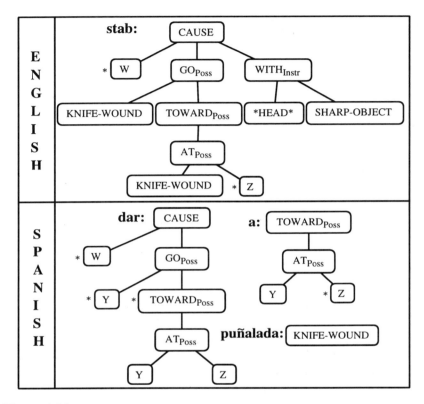

Figure 4.14
The English and Spanish lexical entries for *stab* event demonstrate the utility of the
∗ marker for pinpointing language-specific distinctions.

representation for the words *go* and *receive* has a causative form that
corresponds to the words *stab*, *cut*, *give*, *repossess*, and *obtain* and a
permissive form that corresponds to the word *accept*. Causative and
permissive entries specify coreference information about the logical subject (*i.e.*, the variable W in the current example). For example, in the
case of *give*, the logical subject is not coreferential with any other arguments (as in *I gave John the gift*). In contrast, *repossess* requires the
logical subject to be coreferential with the recipient Z since the subject
of the event is also the recipient of the possessional transfer (as in *I*

L = GO$_{Poss}$ Template: [$_{Event}$ GO$_{Poss}$ ([$_{Thing}$ Y], [$_{Path}$ P])]
C = Causative Template: [$_{Event}$ CAUSE ([$_{Thing}$ W], [$_{Event}$ L])]
T = Permissive Template: [$_{Event}$ LET ([$_{Thing}$ W], [$_{Event}$ L])]

P = Path Template: [$_{Path}$ TOWARD$_{Poss}$ ([$_{Position}$ AT$_{Poss}$ ([$_{Thing}$ Y], [$_{Thing}$ Z])])]	
Root Word:	*go* (* = [$_{Thing}$ Z]; * = [$_{Path}$ P])
	receive (* = [$_{Thing}$:INT Y]; * = [$_{Thing}$:EXT Z])
Causative:	*stab* (W $\neq$ U,Y,Z; Y = KNIFE-WOUND; * = [$_{Thing}$ W]; * = [$_{Thing}$ Z];
	Modifier:
	[WITH$_{Instr}$ * ([$_{Event}$ *HEAD*], [$_{Thing}$ U SHARP-OBJECT])])
	cut (W = U, or W $\neq$ U,Y,Z; Y = KNIFE-WOUND;
	* = [$_{Thing}$ W]; * = [$_{Thing}$ Z];
	Modifier:
	[WITH$_{Instr}$ * ([$_{Event}$ *HEAD*], [$_{Thing}$ U SHARP-OBJECT])])
	give (W $\neq$ Y,Z; * = [$_{Thing}$ W];
	* = [$_{Thing}$ Z]; * = [$_{Path}$ P] or [$_{Thing}$ Z])[24]
	repossess (W = Z; * = [$_{Thing}$ W]; * = [$_{Thing}$ Y])
	obtain (W = Z; * = [$_{Thing}$ W]; * = [$_{Thing}$ Z])
Permissive:	*accept* (W = Z; * = [$_{Thing}$ W]; * = [$_{Thing}$ Z])

P = Path Template:	
[$_{Path}$ AWAY-FROM$_{Poss}$ ([$_{Position}$ AT$_{Poss}$ ([$_{Thing}$ Y], [$_{Thing}$ Z])])]	
Root Word:	*lose* (* = [$_{Thing}$ Y]; * = [$_{Thing}$ Z])
Permissive:	*relinquish* (W = Z; * = [$_{Thing}$ W]; * = [$_{Thing}$ Y])
	surrender (W = Z; * = [$_{Thing}$ W]; * = [$_{Thing}$ Y])

Figure 4.15
The lexical entries for English verbs in the GO$_{Poss}$ LCS class are characterized by
an LCS template L and a path pointer P. The two path types shown here are
TOWARD$_{Poss}$ (*e.g.*, *go*, *receive*, *stab*, *cut*, *give*, *repossess*, *obtain*, and *accept*) and
AWAY-FROM$_{Poss}$ (*e.g.*, *lose*, *relinquish*, and *surrender*).

repossessed John's car).[25] Note that, in the case of *stab* and *cut*, the
subject is non-coreferential (*I stabbed/cut John*), but in the case of *cut*,
the subject may also be coreferential with the instrument (*the knife cut
John*).[26] For illustrative purposes, figure 4.16 shows some examples of
causative trees implicitly represented by the specification given in the
GO$_{Poss}$ LCS class. For reasons of readability, we will continue to use the

---

[24]The disjoint * specification used in the entry for *give* allows the verb to be realized
both in the dative (*e.g.*, *I gave him the book*) and in the non-dative (*e.g.*, *I gave the
book to him*). The special use of the * notation will be discussed in section 4.7.

[25]The LCS representation used for the word *repossess* might also be used for the
word *steal*. In order to distinguish between these, the entry for *steal* would require
an additional modifier, STEALINGLY.

[26]Note that the coreference here refers to the values of the arguments as defined
in the lexical entry. It does not refer to cases of Binding coreference in the surface
structure (*i.e.*, coindexation of instantiated arguments). In particular, the lexical
entries do not rule out cases such as *I stabbed myself* where the subject and object
become coindexed during syntactic processing.

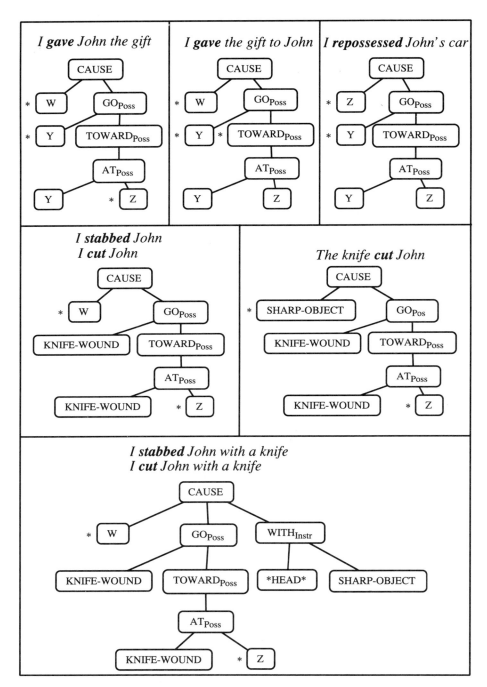

Figure 4.16
A number of different causative trees are implicitly represented by GO_{Poss} class.

tree-like representations rather than the LCS template format used for lexical entries.

Optional modifiers are not included in the lexical entries (except for illustrative purposes in chapter 5) unless they provide immutable information that is idiosyncratic to a particular verb (such as the SHARP-OBJECT modifier included in *cut* and *stab* entries). In general, modifiers are available through an inheritance mechanism based on the following field specifications:

(101) (i)   **Events and States:** Inherit modifiers from the Intentional, Instrumental, Temporal, and Locational Fields.

(ii)   **Things:** Inherit modifiers from the Identificational, Possessional, Temporal, and Locational Fields.

For example, the verb *stab* is an Event; thus, it automatically inherits optional modifiers in the Intentional field (*e.g., I stabbed John for Harry*), Instrumental field (*e.g., I stabbed John with a knife*), Temporal field (*e.g., I stabbed John at 9:00*), and Locational field (*e.g., I stabbed John in the street*). Note that the use of LCS fields rather than LCS types provides a more flexible means of specifying LCS modifiers. For example, the noun *book* may be modified by a number of different types in the possessional field including Position (*e.g., the book of John's*), State (*e.g., John's book*), Event (*e.g., the book that John owns*), etc.

The system of LCS classes and modifier inheritance offers a number of benefits. First, arguments and modifiers need not be stated for every word in the dictionary because lexical entries automatically inherit arguments from the LCS template and modifiers from the field specifications shown in (101). This eliminates proliferation of redundancy across lexical entries. Second, the LCS classes allow causative and permissive forms to specify their idiosyncratic argument information by means of coreference and other types of argument indexation. Thus, words with related meanings may be grouped together despite different argument specifications; this avoids having to define these words independently in unrelated lexical entries. Finally, the LCS classes allow syntactically distinct lexical items to be defined in the same class if they have the same word sense. For example, the deverbalized noun *entrance* is defined in the same LCS class (GO_{Loc}) as its verbal counterpart *enter* even though these two words are not of the same syntactic category.

4.5   Mapping Between the Interlingua and the Syntactic Structure

This section discusses the parameterized linking routine, the canonical syntactic realization function, and the Control relations in the LCS, all of which serve to relate the interlingual representation to the syntactic structure.

4.5.1   Parameterization of the Linking Routine

In order to relate source- and target-language structures to an interlingual form, lexical entries must specify certain language-specific syntactic information. This is the nature of the second level of lexical description alluded to in section 4.4.1. The most critical mechanism that is used by this level is the * marker, which is required for every explicitly realized argument and modifier in the lexical entries for each language. [27] This marker acts as parameter of the lexicon that specifies the LCS positions that correspond to syntactic realizations in a particular language.

Earlier in figure 4.14, we saw that the * notation is used in the English and Spanish lexical entries for the *stab* event. Note that the * marker makes two crucial language-specific distinctions: (1) the TOWARD$_{Poss}$ portion of the RLCS is *-marked for *dar* but not for *stab*; and (2) the KNIFE-WOUND argument is not *-marked for *stab* whereas the corresponding Y position is *-marked for *dar*. These parametric distinctions force the representation for the word *dar* to be combined with the representations of other words such that the composite representation is equivalent to the single lexical structure specified in the entry for *stab*. In particular, the TOWARD$_{Poss}$ portion of the lexical entry for *stab* is forced to unify with the lexical entry for the word *a*, and the Y position must be filled in with the LCS for *puñalada*. Note that the lexical entry for *a* also has its own * marker, which must be filled in recursively by means of the same mechanism.

The * marker is used in conjunction with a *generalized linking routine* ($\mathcal{GLR}$) based on the correspondence given earlier in (74) and illustrated in figure 4.4. This routine defines the mapping between the syntactic

---

[27]There are also other lexical markers that are discussed in the next chapter.

structure and the lexical-semantic structure and is specified as follows:

(102) **Generalized Linking Routine:**

    a.   Relate the syntactic head X to the logical subject position X′.

    b.   Relate the syntactically external position W to the logical subject position W′.

    c.   Relate the syntactically internal positions $Z_1, \ldots, Z_n$ to the logical argument positions $Z'_1, \ldots, Z'_n$.

    d.   Relate the syntactic adjunct positions $Q_1, \ldots, Q_m$ to the logical modifier positions $Q'_1, \ldots, Q'_m$.

This routine is used in both directions, *i.e.* composition of the interlingua and decomposition of the interlingua. We will defer discussion about the second direction until chapter 6 and will focus primarily on the first direction for the remainder of this chapter.

The ∗ marker plays an important role in the implementation of the general linking routine. In particular, the θ-roles that are assigned during syntactic processing correspond to ∗-marked positions in the lexical entries of the words in the sentence. Consider the translation example (76) given above and repeated here as (103):

(103) E: I stabbed John ⇔
    S: Yo le di puñaladas a Juan
       'I gave knife-wounds to John'

If we examine the entries given in figure 4.14, we see that only two θ-roles are assigned in the case of *stab* since only two positions are ∗-marked, namely the agent $[_{\text{Thing}} * W]$ and the recipient $[_{\text{Thing}} * Z]$.[28] In contrast, the entry for *dar* indicates that three θ-roles are assigned, namely, the agent $[_{\text{Thing}} * W]$, the theme $[_{\text{Thing}} * Y]$, and the recipient $[_{\text{Path}} * \text{TOWARD}_{\text{Poss}} \ldots]$. Since $[_{\text{Path}} * \text{TOWARD}_{\text{Poss}} \ldots]$ is non-atomic, it must unify with the LCS of some other lexical entry (*i.e.*, the entry for the word *a*) which potentially has its own θ-role to assign (*i.e.*, $[_{\text{Thing}} * Z]$).

The result of θ-role assignment for both the source- and target-language structures corresponding to this example is shown in figure 4.17.

---

[28]The modifier WITH$_{\text{Instr}}$ is also ∗-marked, but it does not correspond to an obligatory θ-role.

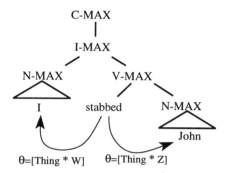

English θ-assigned structure

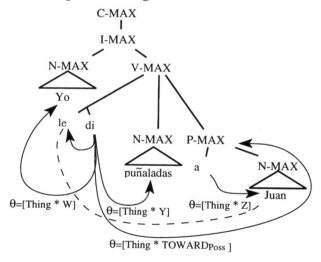

Spanish θ-assigned structure

Figure 4.17
θ-role assignment acts as an interface between the syntactic component and the
lexical-semantic component. θ-roles correspond to ∗-marked positions in lexical
entries. Such positions are instantiated during the lexical-semantic composition
process that produces the interlingua. (The dotted line in the Spanish tree
corresponds to the coindexation of the clitic *le* with the object noun phrase *Juan*.)

LCS Type	Syntactic Category
EVENT	V
STATE	V
THING	N
PROPERTY	A
PATH	P
POSITION	P
LOCATION	ADV
TIME	ADV
MANNER	ADV
INTENSIFIER	ADV
PURPOSE	ADV

Figure 4.18
The $\mathcal{CSR}$ associates an LCS type with a syntactic category.

Note that the Spanish case is slightly more complicated, not only because more θ-roles are assigned, but also because the clitic *le* transmits a θ-role to its corresponding object NP. (See rule (52) in chapter 2.) This transmitted role must be checked for a match against the role assigned by the preposition *a*. Because both *le* and *Juan* bear the same θ-role, these constituents are then considered to be coreferential; thus, the discussion in the next section does not mention the handling of the clitic *le* since this is subsumed by the handling of the NP *Juan*.

4.5.2 Canonical Syntactic Realization

In addition to the $\mathcal{GLR}$ given above in (102), the interlingua is related to the syntactic structure by means of a function called *canonical syntactic realization* ($\mathcal{CSR}$) which associates an LCS type (*e.g.*, Thing) with a syntactic category (*e.g.*, N-MAX) as shown in figure 4.18.

The $\mathcal{CSR}$ is used for building representations that are later used for parsing and generation. Recall (from chapter 2) that a small number of parameters are precompiled into phrase-structure templates prior to on-line processing. Part of this precompilation process involves the construction of *lexical expansion structures*, that is, head-complement structures based on subcategorization requirements of lexical entries corresponding to phrasal heads. These structures are particularly useful for subcategorization checking during the *scan* operation as described in chapter 2.

The way lexical expansion structures are constructed is through precompilation of information specified in the entries associated with LCS classes described in the last section. Once all the LCS classes are defined, these structures are compiled out in advance of running the system. For example, the lexical entry for the word *put* defined in the GO_{Loc} LCS class has the following expanded representation:

(104) [$_{\text{Event}}$ CAUSE
    ([$_{\text{Thing}}$ * W],
    [$_{\text{Event}}$ GO_{Loc}
       ([$_{\text{Thing}}$ * Y],
       [$_{\text{Path}}$ * $\text{TOWARD}_{\text{Loc}}$
          ([$_{\text{Position}}$ IN_{Loc} ([$_{\text{Thing}}$ Y], [$_{\text{Thing}}$ Z])])])])]

During precompilation of lexical expansion structures, the $\mathcal{CSR}$ operates on lexical entries of this sort and automatically stores the structural information along with the word in the lexicon. The driving mechanism for this process, not surprisingly, is the * marker since it points to the RLCS positions that have a corresponding syntactic realization on the surface. Only those *-marked positions relevant to the derivation of a lexical expansion structure (*i.e.*, logical arguments) are used during this process. In the current example, the $\mathcal{CSR}$ maps Y (which is a Thing) to a noun phrase (N-MAX) and it maps $\text{TOWARD}_{\text{Loc}}$ (which is a Path) to a prepositional phrase (P-MAX); thus, the precompilation procedure produces a lexical expansion structure corresponding to the context-free rule V-MAX $\Rightarrow$ • V N-MAX P-MAX.[29] During parsing, the context-free rule is used directly by the Earley Structure Builder described in chapter 2. During generation, the corresponding lexical expansion structure is used instead. The lexical expansion structure associated with *put* is shown in figure 4.19(a).

A crucial point concerning the categorial realization of RLCS constituents is that this process could not be done in isolation of other parametrically specified information. In particular, the construction of head-complement structures relies heavily on the phrase-structure templates produced from the empty functional elements parameter in many

---

[29]The dot (•) notation is used by the Earley parser. (See related discussion in fn. 3 of chapter 1.)

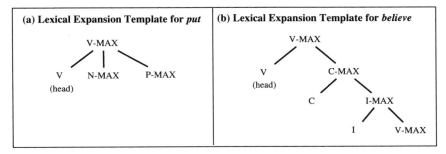

Figure 4.19
During precompilation of lexical expansion structures, the $\mathcal{CSR}$ operates on lexical entries and automatically stores the structural templates along with the word in the lexicon.

cases. An example of such a case is the head-complement structure for the verb *believe*. The RLCS for this word is:

(105) [Event BEPerc
         ([Thing * W],
         [Path INPerc
              ([Position ATPerc ([Thing W], [Event * E])])],
         [Manner BELIEVINGLY])]

Note that the logical argument E is an Event, which means that this constituent is projected as a V-MAX by the $\mathcal{CSR}$. This forces the pre-compiler to construct a lexical expansion structure corresponding to a rule of the form V-MAX $\Rightarrow$ • V V-MAX. This rule is not appropriate for the verb *believe*; rather, the desired rule is V-MAX $\Rightarrow$ • V C-MAX, *i.e.*, the verb *believe* subcategorizes for a clausal complement, not a verb-phrase complement. The solution is to implement the $\mathcal{CSR}$ so that it relies not only on the canonical realization specifications shown in fig-ure 4.18, but also on the phrase-structure templates generated from the setting of the empty functional elements parameter given in figure 2.12. The full projection is a result of the combination of these two pieces of information. Thus, the lexical expansion precompiler correctly produces a rule with a C-MAX complement that is used by the parser. The cor-responding lexical expansion structure used by the generator is shown

in figure 4.19(b).[30] Note that the same type of projection is required
for the outermost syntactic clause since there is no subcategorizing head
to trigger a lexical expansion template. This projection is performed
automatically during processing of the highest syntactic head.

4.5.3   Control Relations in the LCS

Another aspect of the relation between the interlingua and the syntactic
structure is the use of Control relations. Control specifies coreference
properties of certain syntactic constituents such as empty subjects of
embedded clauses (*e.g.*, *John$_i$ wanted PRO$_i$ to go home*). In standard
GB theory, this type of coreference information is generally considered
to be part of the syntactic processing component. In the current model,
Control information is specified as a part of the LCS representation and
is accessed during lexical-semantic processing. The decision to implement Control at the level of LCS is primarily due to the need to include
coreferring LCS variables in the definition of lexical items. [31]

In the current model, there are two types of Control relations: one that
is internal to a lexical definition, and one that is referentially dependent
on arguments that are filled in during lexical-semantic composition. We
have already seen an example of the first type of Control relation in
the entry for the word *cut* in the GO$_{Poss}$ LCS class of figure 4.15. The
expanded representation for this lexical entry is:

---

[30]The functional heads in the expansion template for the verb *believe* are left
uninstantiated to allow for the possibility of lexical items to fill these positions (*e.g.*,
the word *that* under C or the word *would* under I). If no such lexical items are
available during generation of the target-language structure, these positions are filled
with the empty marker *e*.

[31]Nonetheless, Control relations interact with other processes that are considered
to be part of the syntactic component, most notably Binding Conditions. One could
argue that it would be erroneous to prohibit access to Control information during
syntactic processing if this were the only place that Binding constraints were applied.
For example, a sentence such as *John wants PRO to kill him* could potentially receive
an invalid interpretation in such a model: the word *him* could be bound to *John* by
the syntactic component (since there is no Binding violation), and then PRO could
be bound to *John* (since *want* is a subject-control verb) by the lexical-semantic
component, thus leading to the invalid interpretation *$*$John$_i$ wants PRO$_i$ to kill
him$_i$*. (I am indebted to Amy Weinberg (personal communication) for pointing this
out to me.) So it appears that Binding and Control constraints interact in such
a way that they both need to be represented at the same level. There are three
possible solutions to this: (1) represent both at the syntactic level; (2) represent
both at lexical-semantic level; and (3) represent both at some other independent
level. Because of the heavy interaction of Binding and Control information with lexical-semantic processing, the ideal level of representation would presumably be at the
lexical-semantic level, although the implementation described here does not capture
this modified organization. We leave this possibility open to future augmentations
of the current model.

(106) [Event CAUSE
        ([Thing * W],
         [Event GO_Poss
           ([Thing KNIFE-WOUND],
            [Path TOWARD_Poss
              ([Position AT_Poss ([Thing KNIFE-WOUND], [Thing * Z])])])],
         [WITH_Instr * ([Event *HEAD*], [Thing U SHARP-OBJECT])])]

This definition allows the logical subject W to control the instrument U
as in the sentence *the knife cut John* or it allows W to be independent
of any reference to other variables in the definition as in the sentence *I
cut John with a knife*. The way these Control possibilities are spelled
out is by means of the variable coreference specification (W = U, or W
$\neq$ U,Y,Z) shown in figure 4.15. The control distinction is more clearly
illustrated in figure 4.16, which shows W to be a non-control argument
(in the first two cases, the fourth case, and the last case), a control
argument for Z (in the third case), and a control argument for U =
SHARP-OBJECT (in the fifth case). Note that this type of Control is
resolved when a word is defined, not during the translation process.

The second type of Control relation is resolved during lexical-semantic
composition, thus accounting for the sentences of figure 4.20. This type
of Control concerns the reference of the empty subject position, designated as PRO. (The PRO element will have subject control or arbitrary
control, depending on the lexical item.) The Control relation is specified
in the lexicon by using the marker *LOWER-SUBJECT* in cases where
a predicate requires the logical subject to corefer with the subject of an
embedded clause. This type of Control is illustrated in the entry for the
word *want*, which controls the subject of an embedded clause (if it is
PRO):

(107) [Event BE_Perc
        ([Thing * *LOWER-SUBJECT* W],
         [Path IN_Perc
           ([Position AT_Perc ([Thing *LOWER-SUBJECT* W], [Event * E])])]
         [Manner WANTINGLY])][32]

---

[32]Note that this language-particular encoding occurs only in the entries of the
lexicon; it does not show up in the interlingual form derived from the lexical entries.
Such an encoding is expected to be non-controversial since, in most schools of thought,
it is considered acceptable to indicate Control and other lexically specific information
in the lexicon on a per-language basis.

Lexical Item	Control	Example
believe	——	*John believes PRO to eat dinner
		John believes Bill to eat dinner
expect	subject	John$_i$ expects PRO$_i$ to eat dinner
		John expects Bill to eat dinner
like	subject	John$_i$ likes PRO$_i$ to eat dinner
		John likes Bill to eat dinner
try	subject	John$_i$ tries PRO$_i$ to eat dinner
		*John tries Bill to eat dinner
want	subject	John$_i$ wants PRO$_i$ to eat dinner
		John wants Bill to eat dinner
easy	arbitrary	*John$_i$ is easy t$_i$ to please
		John$_i$ is easy PRO$_j$ to please t$_i$
eager	subject	*John$_i$ is eager t$_i$ to please
		John$_i$ is eager PRO$_i$ to please

Figure 4.20
Control properties accounts for the varied distribution of different lexical items.

Here, W is associated with the *LOWER-SUBJECT* marker, thus enabling it to corefer with the subject of the embedded clause that fills the variable E during lexical-semantic composition.

Note that the lexical entry for *believe* given above in (105) does not include any such a marker. The distinction between these two definitions allows *want* and *believe* to behave differently with respect to their surface realizations:

(108) John$_i$ wants PRO$_i$ to eat breakfast

(109)* John$_i$ believes PRO$_i$ to eat breakfast

If PRO does not fill the subject position of the embedded clause, the *LOWER-SUBJECT* marker will be ignored. Thus, we are still able to interpret the following:

(110) John believes Bill to eat breakfast.

(111) John wants Bill to eat breakfast.

We now turn to a discussion about how the syntax-LCS relation described in this section is used during the process of lexical-semantic composition.

4.6 Lexical-Semantic Composition

Lexical-semantic composition (henceforth LCS composition) is the first of two processes performed by the lexical-semantic component shown in figure 1.8.[33] This process constructs the interlingual representation by recursively filling the arguments of a predicate into their θ-assigned (*i.e.*, *-marked) LCS positions. We will first discuss the algorithm used for this process and will then turn to a detailed example.

4.6.1 Algorithm for LCS Composition

The algorithm for LCS composition relies on the output produced by the parser of the syntactic component. In particular, LCS composition cannot take place until all θ-roles are assigned.[34] The θ-roles represent positions in lexical entries associated with the words of the input sentence. Thus, LCS composition is essentially a unification process that is guided by the pointers left behind by θ-role assignment.

We will first introduce the algorithm for LCS composition and then illustrate how this procedure works for our translation example (103). Figure 4.21 shows the top-level LCS-composition procedure called **Compose_LCS**. This procedure takes a syntactic tree whose top phrasal node is X-MAX and finds the RLCS associated with the lexical item X (steps 1 and 2). It then extracts the arguments and adjuncts of X-MAX, if there are any (steps 3–5), and recursively passes these to the same procedure after extracting the assigned θ-roles (steps 6.a and 6.b). The result of the recursive call is unified with the current RLCS (step 6.c). Finally, the procedure returns the CLCS (*i.e.*, the RLCS for X instantiated with its arguments) corresponding to the head of the top phrasal node (step 7).

Step 6 requires further elaboration. First, step 6.a extracts the θ-roles that were assigned during syntactic processing by virtue of the general linking routine and the position of the * marker in the RLCS. Next, step 6.b calls the procedure, recursively, in order to construct the CLCS representations for the logical subject, arguments, and modifiers. This step ensures that the procedure will be called exactly once for each syn-

---

[33] The second of the two LCS processes will be discussed in chapter 6.

[34] θ-role assignment does not change the structure of the parse tree output of the syntactic component, but it does add information that is required for composition of the interlingual representation.

Compose_LCS (X-MAX)

1. Let X = head of X-MAX.

2. Let X′ = RLCS corresponding to head X.

3. Let W = external argument of X-MAX

4. Let $Z_1, \ldots, Z_n$ = internal arguments of X-MAX

5. Let $Q_1, \ldots, Q_m$ = adjuncts of X-MAX

6. For i ∈ {W,$Z_1, \ldots, Z_n$,$Q_1, \ldots, Q_m$}

   6.a Extract the θ-role i′ associated with i. (This is the *-marked position in X′ that corresponds to i according to linking routine (102).)

   6.b Let L = **Compose_LCS** (i).

   6.c Unify L with position i′ in X′.

7. Return X′.

Figure 4.21
The algorithm for LCS composition takes a syntactic tree and composes the interlingua on the basis of θ-role assignment information.

tactic head appearing in the source-language structure. Finally, step 6.c fills the *-marked positions with the CLCS representations constructed by step 6.b, thus producing a new CLCS. Note that this final step is a "pseudo-unification" step in the sense that the *-marked position may be instantiated directly, if the position constitutes a leaf node of the RLCS, or indirectly (through unification), if the position constitutes a non-leaf node of the RLCS.

4.6.2 LCS Composition for Stab-Dar Example

Now that the algorithm for LCS Composition has been presented, we will see how it applies to the translation example (103). We will defer discussion about generation of the target-language sentence for this example until chapter 6 and will focus instead on showing how the algorithm of figure 4.21 produces the same CLCS (*i.e.*, the interlingua) for both of these sentences. The intent here is to demonstrate the adequacy of the representation and the accompanying procedure for both sentences of this example.

In the case of the English sentence, the parser in the syntactic component of UNITRAN supplies the source-language syntactic tree shown

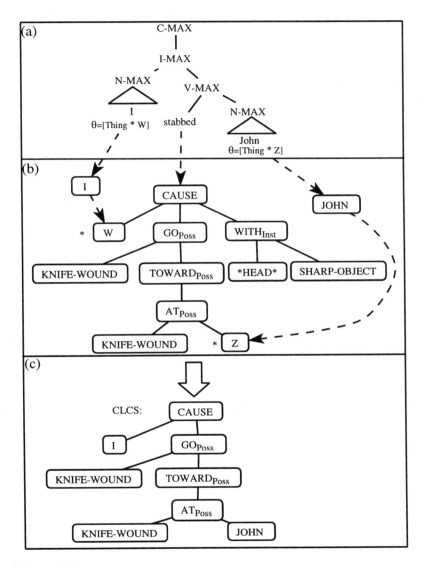

Figure 4.22
The LCS composition for *I stabbed John* is a straightforward argument-filling process driven by θ-role assignment.

in figure 4.22(a). When this tree is passed to the LCS component, the
RLCS's corresponding to the words *I*, *stab*, and *John* are selected as
shown in figure 4.22(b). Finally, a single CLCS is composed from these
RLCS's as shown in figure 4.22(c).

The trace of this process is shown in figure 4.23.[35],[36] The key point
to note about this trace is that the two *-marked positions in the
RLCS for *stab* are instantiated on the fourth and fifth entries to the
Compose_LCS routine. This difference is due to the position of the *
specification in the RLCS for *stab*. Recall that step 6.a of the algorithm
selects an RLCS position by appealing to the $\mathcal{GLR}$ in conjunction with
the *-marker. Since there are only two *-marked positions ($[_{\text{Thing}} * \text{W}]$
and $[_{\text{Thing}} * \text{Z}]$), these are the only ones that are instantiated during the
unification step 6.c; the first is instantiated as $[_{\text{Thing}} \text{I}]$ and the second is
instantiated as $[_{\text{Thing}} \text{JOHN}]$.

The instantiation step differs crucially from the analogous step in the
composition of the interlingua for the Spanish sentence. Figure 4.24(a)
shows the syntactic tree for the Spanish case. This tree is passed to the
LCS component which selects the RLCS's corresponding to the words
Yo, *dar*, *puñaladas*, *a*, and *Juan* as shown in figure 4.24(b). A single
CLCS is then composed from these RLCS's as shown in figure 4.24(c).

The trace of this process is shown in figure 4.25.[37] There are two
differences between the English and Spanish composition processes. The
first is that, because an additional θ-role is assigned in Spanish (*i.e.*, to
the word *puñaladas*), there is an additional invocation of the procedure
(*i.e.*, the fifth entry). This invocation results in the instantiation of the
$[_{\text{Thing}} \text{KNIFE-WOUND}]$ constituent which fills the $[_{\text{Thing}} * \text{Y}]$ position
of the RLCS corresponding to *dar*. Thus, the different positioning of
the * accounts for the fact that the Spanish verb *dar* must explicitly

---

[35]The first two calls to **Compose_LCS** do little more than "peel off" a level of
maximal projection. This is because both the C-MAX and the I-MAX phrases contain an *empty* head (*i.e.*, a head with no lexical content). Such phrases are considered
to be projections of their internal argument, which means they inherit their result
from the structure produced by the recursive call on their internal argument.

[36]Note that the WITH$_{\text{Instr}}$ modifier that appears in the RLCS is not included in the
final CLCS since it is an uninstantiated optional modifier. (See relevant discussion
in section 4.4.1).

[37]The clitic pronoun *le* is handled by an independent process of θ-role transmission (see rule (52) of chapter 2) that allows both *le* and *Juan* to bear the same
θ-role. These constituents are then considered to be coreferential; thus, the current
description only shows the handling of *Juan*, not *le*.

1. Entering **Compose_LCS**:
   [$_{\text{C-MAX}}$ [$_{\text{I-MAX}}$ [$_{\text{N-MAX}}$ I] [$_{\text{V-MAX}}$ stabbed [$_{\text{N-MAX}}$ John]]]]
   X = empty (projection of I-MAX)
   Z_1 = [$_{\text{I-MAX}}$ [$_{\text{N-MAX}}$ I] [$_{\text{V-MAX}}$ stabbed [$_{\text{N-MAX}}$ John]]]

   2. Entering **Compose_LCS**:
   [$_{\text{I-MAX}}$ [$_{\text{N-MAX}}$ I] [$_{\text{V-MAX}}$ stabbed [$_{\text{N-MAX}}$ John]]]
   X = empty (projection of V-MAX)
   Z_1 = [$_{\text{V-MAX}}$ stabbed [$_{\text{N-MAX}}$ John]]

     3. Entering **Compose_LCS**: [$_{\text{V-MAX}}$ stabbed [$_{\text{N-MAX}}$ John]]
   X = stab
   X′ = [$_{\text{Event}}$ CAUSE ([$_{\text{Thing}}$ * W],
         [$_{\text{Event}}$ GO$_{\text{Poss}}$ ([$_{\text{Thing}}$ KNIFE-WOUND],
          [$_{\text{Path}}$ TOWARD$_{\text{Poss}}$
           ([$_{\text{Position}}$ AT$_{\text{Poss}}$ ([$_{\text{Thing}}$ KNIFE-WOUND], [$_{\text{Thing}}$ * Z])])])],
         [WITH$_{\text{Instr}}$ ([$_{\text{Event}}$ *HEAD*], [$_{\text{Thing}}$ U SHARP-OBJECT])])]
   W = [$_{\text{N-MAX}}$ I]
   Z_1 = [$_{\text{N-MAX}}$ John]
   i′ = [$_{\text{Thing}}$ * W]

      4. Entering **Compose_LCS**: [$_{\text{N-MAX}}$ I]
   X = I
   X′ = [$_{\text{Thing}}$ I]

      4. Exiting **Compose_LCS**: L = [$_{\text{Thing}}$ I]
   X′ = [$_{\text{Event}}$ CAUSE ([$_{\text{Thing}}$ I],
         [$_{\text{Event}}$ GO$_{\text{Poss}}$ ([$_{\text{Thing}}$ KNIFE-WOUND],
          [$_{\text{Path}}$ TOWARD$_{\text{Poss}}$
           ([$_{\text{Position}}$ AT$_{\text{Poss}}$ ([$_{\text{Thing}}$ KNIFE-WOUND], [$_{\text{Thing}}$ * Z])])])],
         [WITH$_{\text{Instr}}$ ([$_{\text{Event}}$ *HEAD*], [$_{\text{Thing}}$ U SHARP-OBJECT])])]
   i′ = [$_{\text{Thing}}$ * Z]

      5. Entering **Compose_LCS**: [$_{\text{N-MAX}}$ John]
   X = John
   X′ = [$_{\text{Thing}}$ JOHN]

      5. Exiting **Compose_LCS**: L = [$_{\text{Thing}}$ JOHN]
   X′ = [$_{\text{Event}}$ CAUSE ([$_{\text{Thing}}$ I],
         [$_{\text{Event}}$ GO$_{\text{Poss}}$ ([$_{\text{Thing}}$ KNIFE-WOUND],
          [$_{\text{Path}}$ TOWARD$_{\text{Poss}}$
           ([$_{\text{Position}}$ AT$_{\text{Poss}}$ ([$_{\text{Thing}}$ KNIFE-WOUND], [$_{\text{Thing}}$ JOHN])])])],
         [WITH$_{\text{Instr}}$ ([$_{\text{Event}}$ *HEAD*], [$_{\text{Thing}}$ U SHARP-OBJECT])])]

     3. Exiting **Compose_LCS**:
   L = X′ = [$_{\text{Event}}$ CAUSE ([$_{\text{Thing}}$ I],
         [$_{\text{Event}}$ GO$_{\text{Poss}}$ ([$_{\text{Thing}}$ KNIFE-WOUND],
          [$_{\text{Path}}$ TOWARD$_{\text{Poss}}$
           ([$_{\text{Position}}$ AT$_{\text{Poss}}$ ([$_{\text{Thing}}$ KNIFE-WOUND], [$_{\text{Thing}}$ JOHN])])])])]

   2. Exiting **Compose_LCS**:
   L = X′ = [$_{\text{Event}}$ CAUSE ([$_{\text{Thing}}$ I],
       [$_{\text{Event}}$ GO$_{\text{Poss}}$ ([$_{\text{Thing}}$ KNIFE-WOUND],
        [$_{\text{Path}}$ TOWARD$_{\text{Poss}}$
         ([$_{\text{Position}}$ AT$_{\text{Poss}}$ ([$_{\text{Thing}}$ KNIFE-WOUND], [$_{\text{Thing}}$ JOHN])])])])]

1. Exiting **Compose_LCS**:
   L = X′ = [$_{\text{Event}}$ CAUSE ([$_{\text{Thing}}$ I],
      [$_{\text{Event}}$ GO$_{\text{Poss}}$ ([$_{\text{Thing}}$ KNIFE-WOUND],
       [$_{\text{Path}}$ TOWARD$_{\text{Poss}}$
        ([$_{\text{Position}}$ AT$_{\text{Poss}}$ ([$_{\text{Thing}}$ KNIFE-WOUND], [$_{\text{Thing}}$ JOHN])])])])]

Figure 4.23
The LCS composition process for the English sentence *I stabbed John* consists of five entries to the **Compose_LCS** procedure.

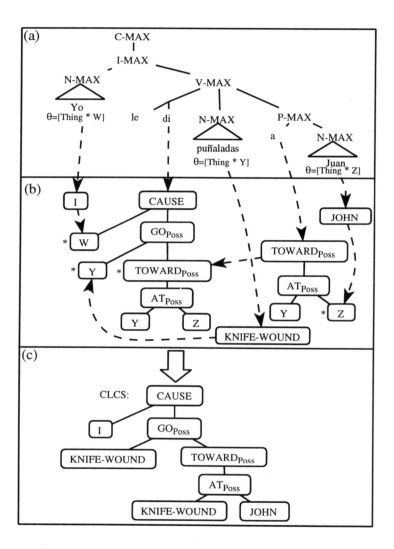

Figure 4.24
The LCS composition for *Yo le di puñaladas a Juan* requires recursive unification
of θ-assigned arguments.

realize the $[_{\text{Thing}}$ KNIFE-WOUND] argument as *puñaladas*, whereas no corresponding syntactic constituent is required for the English verb *stab*.

The second difference is that, in the Spanish case, the sixth entry to the procedure (which is analogous to the fifth entry in the English case) calls the **Compose_LCS** procedure recursively (*i.e.*, the seven$_{.}$h entry). This is because the $*$ marker is positioned at the level of $[_{\text{Path}}$ $*$ TOWARD$_{\text{Poss}}$ ...], not at the level of $[_{\text{Thing}}$ Z], in the lexical entry for *dar*. The recursive entry allows the RLCS corresponding to the word *a* to be unified with the matching portion of the *stab* RLCS. Note that the *a* RLCS has its own $*$-marked $[_{\text{Thing}}$ $*$ Z] that is unified with $[_{\text{Thing}}$ JOHN] after exiting the sixth invocation. Thus, the positioning of the $*$ marker accounts for the fact that the Spanish verb *dar* must realize the recipient of the action inside of a prepositional phrase, whereas the recipient of the English verb *dar* is realized directly as a noun phrase.

We have just seen how two divergences, conflational (*i.e.*, the suppression/realization of an argument and structural (*i.e.*, the noun-phrase/prepositional-phrase distinction) are handled by means of an *abstraction* of language-independent properties (*e.g.*, the use of general representational constituents such as $[_{\text{Path}}$ TOWARD$_{\text{Poss}}$ ...]) from language-specific idiosyncrasies (*e.g.*, the position of the $*$ marker with respect to such constituents). Furthermore, we have seen that the *compositional* nature of the LCS representation allows these divergences to be handled by means of a recursive process that operates on each subcomponent of the representation first before combining them together by means of unification. In the next section we will examine a number of issues concerning the adequacy of the LCS as an interlingua.

4.7   Adequacy of the Interlingua

The LCS is suited to the description of information concerning verbs and their arguments as well as possible syntactic realizations of such constituents. However, there are clearly components of meaning that are not definable in terms of the LCS representation. Consider the two verbs *fight* and *follow*. One might consider both of these verbs to be in the Locational class, which up until this point, have been the easiest to describe in the current framework. However, there are components of meaning for these two verbs that may exist at a level that is distinct from

1. Entering **Compose_LCS**:
   $[_{\text{C-MAX}}\ [_{\text{I-MAX}}\ [_{\text{N-MAX}}\ \text{Yo}]\ [_{\text{V-MAX}}\ \text{le di}\ [_{\text{N-MAX}}\ \text{puñaladas}]\ [_{\text{P-MAX}}\ \text{a}\ [_{\text{N-MAX}}\ \text{Juan}]]]]]$
   $X = $ empty (projection of I-MAX)
   $Z_1 = [_{\text{I-MAX}}\ [_{\text{N-MAX}}\ \text{Yo}]\ [_{\text{V-MAX}}\ \text{le di}\ [_{\text{N-MAX}}\ \text{puñaladas}]\ [_{\text{P-MAX}}\ \text{a}\ [_{\text{N-MAX}}\ \text{Juan}]]]]$

   2. Entering **Compose_LCS**:
      $[_{\text{I-MAX}}\ [_{\text{N-MAX}}\ \text{Yo}]\ [_{\text{V-MAX}}\ \text{le di}\ [_{\text{N-MAX}}\ \text{puñaladas}]\ [_{\text{P-MAX}}\ \text{a}\ [_{\text{N-MAX}}\ \text{Juan}]]]]$
      $X = $ empty (projection of V-MAX)
      $Z_1 = [_{\text{V-MAX}}\ \text{le di}\ [_{\text{N-MAX}}\ \text{puñaladas}]\ [_{\text{P-MAX}}\ \text{a}\ [_{\text{N-MAX}}\ \text{Juan}]]]$

      3. Entering **Compose_LCS**:
         $[_{\text{V-MAX}}\ \text{le di}\ [_{\text{N-MAX}}\ \text{puñaladas}]\ [_{\text{P-MAX}}\ \text{a}\ [_{\text{N-MAX}}\ \text{Juan}]]]$
         $X = \text{dar}$
         $X' = [_{\text{Event}}\ \text{CAUSE}\ ([_{\text{Thing}}\ *\ \text{W}],$
         $\qquad\qquad [_{\text{Event}}\ \text{GO}_{\text{Poss}}\ ([_{\text{Thing}}\ *\ \text{Y}],$
         $\qquad\qquad [_{\text{Path}}\ *\ \text{TOWARD}_{\text{Poss}}\ ([_{\text{Position}}\ \text{AT}_{\text{Poss}}\ ([_{\text{Thing}}\ \text{Y}],\ [_{\text{Thing}}\ \text{Z}])]])])]$
         $W = [_{\text{N-MAX}}\ \text{Yo}],\ Z_1 = [_{\text{N-MAX}}\ \text{puñaladas}],\ Z_2 = [_{\text{P-MAX}}\ \text{a}\ [_{\text{N-MAX}}\ \text{Juan}]]$
         $i' = [_{\text{Thing}}\ *\ \text{W}]$

         4. Entering **Compose_LCS**: $[_{\text{N-MAX}}\ \text{Yo}]$
            $X = \text{Yo},\ X' = [_{\text{Thing}}\ \text{I}]$

         4. Exiting **Compose_LCS**: $L = [_{\text{Thing}}\ \text{I}]$
            $X' = [_{\text{Event}}\ \text{CAUSE}\ ([_{\text{Thing}}\ \text{I}],$
            $\qquad\qquad [_{\text{Event}}\ \text{GO}_{\text{Poss}}\ ([_{\text{Thing}}\ *\ \text{Y}],$
            $\qquad\qquad [_{\text{Path}}\ *\ \text{TOWARD}_{\text{Poss}}$
            $\qquad\qquad\qquad ([_{\text{Position}}\ \text{AT}_{\text{Poss}}\ ([_{\text{Thing}}\ \text{Y}],\ [_{\text{Thing}}\ \text{Z}])]])])]$

         $i' = [_{\text{Thing}}\ *\ \text{Y}]$
         5. Entering **Compose_LCS**: $[_{\text{N-MAX}}\ \text{puñaladas}]$
            $X = \text{puñaladas},\ X' = [_{\text{Thing}}\ \text{KNIFE-WOUND}]$

         5. Exiting **Compose_LCS**: $L = [_{\text{Thing}}\ \text{KNIFE-WOUND}]$
            $X' = [_{\text{Event}}\ \text{CAUSE}\ ([_{\text{Thing}}\ \text{I}],$
            $\qquad\qquad [_{\text{Event}}\ \text{GO}_{\text{Poss}}\ ([_{\text{Thing}}\ \text{KNIFE-WOUND}],$
            $\qquad\qquad [_{\text{Path}}\ *\ \text{TOWARD}_{\text{Poss}}$
            $\qquad\qquad\qquad ([_{\text{Position}}\ \text{AT}_{\text{Poss}}\ ([_{\text{Thing}}\ \text{KNIFE-WOUND}],\ [_{\text{Thing}}\ \text{Z}])]])])]$

         $i' = [_{\text{Path}}\ *\ \text{TOWARD}_{\text{Poss}}$
         $\qquad ([_{\text{Position}}\ \text{AT}_{\text{Poss}}\ ([_{\text{Thing}}\ \text{KNIFE-WOUND}],\ [_{\text{Thing}}\ \text{Z}])])]$
         6. Entering **Compose_LCS**: $[_{\text{P-MAX}}\ \text{a}\ [_{\text{N-MAX}}\ \text{Juan}]]$
            $X = \text{a},\ X' = [_{\text{Path}}\ \text{TOWARD}_{\text{Poss}}\ ([_{\text{Position}}\ \text{AT}_{\text{Poss}}\ ([_{\text{Thing}}\ \text{Y}],\ [_{\text{Thing}}\ *\ \text{Z}])])]$
            $Z_1 = [_{\text{N-MAX}}\ \text{Juan}]$
            $i' = [_{\text{Thing}}\ *\ \text{Z}]$
            7. Entering **Compose_LCS**: $[_{\text{N-MAX}}\ \text{Juan}]$
               $X = \text{Juan},\ X' = [_{\text{Thing}}\ \text{JOHN}]$
            7. Exiting **Compose_LCS**: $L = [_{\text{Thing}}\ \text{JOHN}]$
               $X' = [_{\text{Path}}\ \text{TOWARD}_{\text{Poss}}\ ([_{\text{Position}}\ \text{AT}_{\text{Poss}}\ ([_{\text{Thing}}\ \text{Y}],\ [_{\text{Thing}}\ \text{JOHN}])])]$

         6. Exiting **Compose_LCS**:
            $L = [_{\text{Path}}\ \text{TOWARD}_{\text{Poss}}\ ([_{\text{Position}}\ \text{AT}_{\text{Poss}}\ ([_{\text{Thing}}\ \text{Y}],\ [_{\text{Thing}}\ \text{JOHN}])])]$
            $X' = [_{\text{Event}}\ \text{CAUSE}\ ([_{\text{Thing}}\ \text{I}],$
            $\qquad\qquad [_{\text{Event}}\ \text{GO}_{\text{Poss}}\ ([_{\text{Thing}}\ \text{KNIFE-WOUND}],$
            $\qquad\qquad [_{\text{Path}}\ \text{TOWARD}_{\text{Poss}}$
            $\qquad\qquad\qquad ([_{\text{Position}}\ \text{AT}_{\text{Poss}}\ ([_{\text{Thing}}\ \text{KNIFE-WOUND}],\ [_{\text{Thing}}\ \text{JOHN}])])])])]$

      3. Exiting **Compose_LCS**:
         $L = X' = [_{\text{Event}}\ \text{CAUSE}\ ([_{\text{Thing}}\ \text{I}],$
         $\qquad\qquad [_{\text{Event}}\ \text{GO}_{\text{Poss}}\ ([_{\text{Thing}}\ \text{KNIFE-WOUND}],$
         $\qquad\qquad [_{\text{Path}}\ \text{TOWARD}_{\text{Poss}}$
         $\qquad\qquad\qquad ([_{\text{Position}}\ \text{AT}_{\text{Poss}}\ ([_{\text{Thing}}\ \text{KNIFE-WOUND}],\ [_{\text{Thing}}\ \text{JOHN}])])])])]$

   2. Exiting **Compose_LCS**:
      $L = X' = [_{\text{Event}}\ \text{CAUSE}\ ([_{\text{Thing}}\ \text{I}],$
      $\qquad\qquad [_{\text{Event}}\ \text{GO}_{\text{Poss}}\ ([_{\text{Thing}}\ \text{KNIFE-WOUND}],$
      $\qquad\qquad [_{\text{Path}}\ \text{TOWARD}_{\text{Poss}}$
      $\qquad\qquad\qquad ([_{\text{Position}}\ \text{AT}_{\text{Poss}}\ ([_{\text{Thing}}\ \text{KNIFE-WOUND}],\ [_{\text{Thing}}\ \text{JOHN}])])])])]$

1. Exiting **Compose_LCS**:
   $L = X' = [_{\text{Event}}\ \text{CAUSE}\ ([_{\text{Thing}}\ \text{I}],$
   $\qquad\qquad [_{\text{Event}}\ \text{GO}_{\text{Poss}}\ ([_{\text{Thing}}\ \text{KNIFE-WOUND}],$
   $\qquad\qquad [_{\text{Path}}\ \text{TOWARD}_{\text{Poss}}$
   $\qquad\qquad\qquad ([_{\text{Position}}\ \text{AT}_{\text{Poss}}\ ([_{\text{Thing}}\ \text{KNIFE-WOUND}],\ [_{\text{Thing}}\ \text{JOHN}])])])])]$

Figure 4.25
The LCS composition process for the Spanish sentence *Yo le di puñaladas a Juan*
consists of six entries to the **Compose_LCS** procedure.

that of the LCS representation. A number of researchers, notably Miezitis (1988), have argued that the verb *fight* could be inferred from other forms of knowledge representation, such as knowledge about punching and kicking:

(112) (punch Mary John) AND (kick John Mary) → (fight Mary John)

Clearly, the LCS representation for *fight* could not be composed from the events corresponding to punching and kicking since these are not considered to be primitive activities, nor are they considered to be inherent in the lexical-semantic structure of the verb. Miezitis' system achieves the mapping in (112) by means of abstraction to the next highest level in a concept network: *punch* and *kick* are instances of *violent-action*, which is an instance of *fight* (as long as there are two participants).

Similarly, the word *follow* has components of meaning that exist at a level that is independent of the LCS representation. For example, the sentence *John follows Mary* may be derived from two ideas:

(113) (walk John) AND (walk Mary (behind John Mary))

These implicational relations are not part of the LCS representation, which serves only to capture the relation between a predicate and its arguments. While it might be possible to extend the system to handle these implications, such an extension would probably be made at a representational level that is distinct from that of the LCS.

Another verbal construction that is not addressed in the current framework is that of light verbs (see *e.g.*, Grimshaw and Mester (1988), and Grimshaw (1990)). For example, we have seen that the verb *give* currently exists in the system as a verb of possessional transfer, but this verb may also be viewed as a light verb in constructions such as "give X a kiss" or "give X a kick." In these cases, it is the direct object noun phrase, not the main verb, that supplies the information pertaining to the affected entity (*i.e.*, X). The current implementation does not handle light verbs because the notion of "affected entity" — the traditional role of Patient — is omitted from the theory of LCS. However, Jackendoff (1990) presents a considerably richer version of conceptual structure in which this notion is now included. He proposes that conceptual roles fall into two tiers, a *thematic tier* dealing with motion and location (*i.e.*, the LCS), and an *action tier* dealing with Actor-Patient relations. Light

verbs are then handled by expressing the possessional transfer portion
of the verb *give* in the thematic tier (which he claims must remain intact) while simultaneously expressing the role of the affected entity of
the nominal constituent in the action tier (*i.e.*, Beneficiary for the nominal *kiss*, Patient for the nominal *kick*, *etc.*). The design of the current
model does not preclude the possibility of superimposing this additional
level of representation on the pre-existing LCS representation. Whether
this enriched representation is general enough to serve as the foundation
for interlingual machine translation is an area that has been left open
for future investigation.

An additional extension that might be made to the current framework
is one that concerns the handling of verbal alternations such as the
locative and conative, illustrated here in (114) and (115), respectively:

(114) John smeared paint on the wall
       John smeared the wall with paint

(115) John cut the rope
       John cut at the rope

While the syntactic realization of alternating types is readily accommodated within the current framework, the semantic ramifications of these
alternations are not fully addressed. The alternating surface forms are
handled by using the * marker in such a way as to allow for more than
one surface realization of the relevant arguments. [38] For example, the
lexical entry for *smear* specifies that the argument corresponding to
paint may be realized in the "normal" object position or in an optional
modifier slot headed by $WITH_{Instr}$. In addition, this entry specifies that
the argument corresponding to *wall* may be realized as the argument of

---

[38]We have already seen a case where the * marker was used in this way to accommodate the dative alternation for the verb *give* (see figure 4.15 and fn. 24).

the directional path *on* or it may be realized without a path. The full entry is specified as follows:[39]

(116) [$_\text{Event}$ CAUSE
         ([$_\text{Thing}$ * W],
         [$_\text{Event}$ GO$_\text{Loc}$ ([$_\text{Thing}$ * Y FLUID],
                       [$_\text{Path}$ * TOWARD$_\text{Loc}$
                                     ([$_\text{Position}$ ON$_\text{Loc}$ ([$_\text{Thing}$ Y], [$_\text{Thing}$ * Z])])])],
         [WITH$_\text{Instr}$ * ([$_\text{Event}$ *HEAD*], [$_\text{Thing}$ Y])])]

The advantage to representing alternating verbs this way is that they do not require a different lexical entry for each alternation. Instead, the syntactic information that differentiates the altered and unaltered forms is specified by the * mechanism within the same entry. However, using the same representation for both forms does not allow the system to distinguish between meaning-preserving alternations and non-meaning preserving alternations. For example, meaning is preserved in cases such as the following:

(117) I entrusted him with my keys
      I entrusted my keys to him

This is not true in cases such as (115) above: in the first sentence the rope was actually cut, whereas in the second sentence the rope was not necessarily cut. Clearly, some mechanism beyond lexical semantics is required in order to capture this information. Brent (1988) proposes a theory that accounts for the difference in meaning between locative and conative alternations based on the degree of guaranteed completion for

---

[39]Note that the representation in (116) would allow an unconstrained syntactic processor to incorrectly accept or generate the following sentences:

   * John smeared paint the wall
   * John smeared the wall paint
   * John smeared with paint on the wall
   * John smeared on the wall with paint

The current approach avoids such cases by applying a set of syntactic constraints pertaining to case assignment. In the current example, all four sentences are eventually ruled out due to the requirement that *smear* obligatorily assigns case to its adjacent argument. In the first two sentences, the second of the two objects does not receive case since it is not adjacent to the verb; thus, the sentence is ruled out by the Case Filter. In the second two sentences, the verb assigns objective case to the noun phrase in the adjacent prepositional phrase, but this results in a case conflict since the preposition assigns oblique case.

Class of Verb	Examples
presentation	entrust, furnish, supply, trust, credit, ...
removal	strip, drain, clean, clear, empty, rob, shovel, ...
attaching	attach, fasten, bolt, glue, nail, staple, affix, ...
gesture	wink, shrug, yawn, ...
marking	mark, emboss, embroider, engrave, imprint, inscribe, stamp, ...

Figure 4.26
Certain verb classes are not currently implemented in UNITRAN.

given word senses. A future area of investigation would be to incorporate such a notion of "completion" into the LCS framework.

Other classes of verbs that are currently not implemented are those shown in figure 4.26.[40] Within the current set of LCS primitives, it may be possible to define certain of the classes of figure 4.26. For example, the verbs of presentation (*e.g.*, *entrust*, *furnish*, *etc.*) and removal (*e.g.*, *strip*, *drain*, *etc.*) could be defined using the already existing GO$_{Poss}$ and GO$_{Ident}$ primitives. However, other verbs may need to be defined in terms of additional primitives or different machinery altogether. For example, the notion of attachment might be captured by a new path primitive ATTACH. The GO primitive would then be used in conjunction with this new path to define verbs in this class. Another solution proposed by Jackendoff (1990) for verbs of attachment is to relate these verbs to verbs of contact (*e.g.*, *touch*, *rub*, *etc.*) by means of a hierarchy of binary features such as ±contact and ±attachment. The features are then used to annotate a conceptual representation that involves the spatial primitive GO. Both of these are reasonable solutions that have not yet been implemented in the current model.

The notion of gesture could also be defined by means of a new primitive, say, GESTURE, which would cover *wink*, *shrug*, *yawn*, *etc.* This primitive would be used in the Locational field since gestures are considered to be spatial in nature.[41] Finally, the marking class of verbs

---

[40]These are a subset of the classes presented by Levin (1985). In addition to the verb classes shown here, Levin includes an "exerting force" class of verbs: force, push, pull, haul, hoist, drag, shove, ... This class is included in the current implementation, but it is distributed across other classes since the verbs in this class are equivalent to the causative form of verbs from other classes. For example, *push* is simply the causative of a directed motion verb of GO$_{Loc}$.

[41]Using the GESTURE primitive opens up questions about other related verbs such as *cry*, *laugh*, *sob*: Should these verbs also be included in the gesture class? Should they be considered verbs of communication? Or should they exist in their own class? Jackendoff (1990) presents such verbs as instances of the new primitive

might be included within the current framework by adding the primitive MARK.[42]

Another issue concerning the adequacy of the representation is the question of whether the current framework is applicable to machine translation of non-European languages. Unlike the representation used in systems such as Eurotra (discussed in chapter 1), the LCS is intended to be more than just a "euroversal" representation (see Copeland *et al.* (1991)). An interesting example that demonstrates the potential applicability of the LCS representation to a non-European language is the translation of *I stabbed John* in Japanese:

(118) E: I stabbed John
      J: watashi ga John ni (naifu de)   kizu tsukemashita
       'I   to John (with knife) cut   attached'

The *kizu tsukemashita* portion of the Japanese is a compound construction formed from the phrase *kizu o tsukemashita* where *o* is the direct object marker. Thus, the word *kizu* is a noun that corresponds to the KNIFE-WOUND concept and the verb *tsukemashita* corresponds the possessional transfer portion of the LCS representation given earlier for the verbs *dar* and *stab*.[43] Several researchers have investigated the use of an LCS for languages such as Warlpiri (Hale and Laughren (1983)), Urdu (Husain (1989)), Greek (Olsen (1991)), Arabic (Shaban (1991)), and Chinese, Indo-European, and North American Indian (Talmy (1983, 1985)), among others. These investigations will be useful for future extensions of UNITRAN.

A final issue that must be addressed with respect to the LCS translation model is that of semantic ambiguity resolution. Whereas disambiguation strategies have been the focus of many previous semantics-based approaches (see *e.g.*, the Preference Semantics approach (Wilks (1973)), such strategies have not been the focus of the current investigation. However, there is no reason to assume that such strategies would

---

MOVE. While this primitive covers the "motion" portion of meaning, it does not the notion of "communication" that is inherent in these verbs (*e.g.*, *"More ice cream,"* *laughed the little girl*). The representation for these types of verbs has been left open to future investigation.

[42]As in the case of the alternating verbs shown in (114)–(117), the placement of the ∗ marker in two different positions would allow for alternating forms (*i.e.*, as "mark the spot with an X" *vs.* "mark an X on the spot").

[43]This example was given to me by Noyuri Soderland of the University of Massachusetts (personal correspondence).

be incompatible with the current framework. Most types of disambiguation require the use of a deeper type of knowledge that currently is not available in the LCS representation. Clearly, a fully interlingual system would require knowledge-based techniques to operate in tandem with the techniques described here in order to handle semantic ambiguity.

Two types of ambiguity that are particularly problematic for the LCS framework are lexical ambiguity and multiple modifier attachment. The first type of ambiguity arises most frequently in the context of selecting appropriate nominal and prepositional constituents for a given verb. It is clear that, at best, this type of ambiguity requires a richer knowledge-representation scheme.[44] The semantic network of nominal primitives used in the preference semantics approach by Fass (1988) is one example of such a scheme.

Two examples of lexical ambiguity are the following:

(119) John borrowed money from the bank

(120) The man in the picture was tall

In (119), a strong semantic link (or *preference*, in the terminology of Wilks) exists between the act of *borrowing money* and the nominal *bank*. If such a link were made accessible to the LCS representation, the system would be able to determine that the word *bank* corresponds to a financial institution, and not to the border of a river. Such information is critical to machine translation. For example, the Spanish translation would be *banco* in the former case and *orilla* in the latter case. The use of a rich knowledge representation coupled with a preference semantics scheme would facilitate the process of lexical selection in such cases.

In (120), the preposition *in* does not have the same *contained-in* sense that is found in sentences such as *the man in the room was tall*. Such distinctions are not made in the LCS representation, though they are

---

[44]Most likely, other types of knowledge (*e.g.*, discourse knowledge) would be needed as well. For example, in sentence (119), it would be useful to have more knowledge about the context of the borrowing event such as the fact that John had just entered a building and was in front of the teller's window. For this, a fully developed context theory would be necessary.

clearly necessary for translation. Consider the following English-French translations:

	(i)	in a photo	⇒	sur la photo
	(ii)	in the paper	⇒	dans le journal
(121)	(iii)	in Canada	⇒	au Canada
	(iv)	in Spain	⇒	en Espagne
	(v)	in a tobacco shop	⇒	chez un marchant de tabac

In order to select the appropriate preposition in French, the underlying meaning of the preposition is a critical component of the translation process. Research is currently underway (see Dorr and Voss (1993) and Voss (forthcoming)) to investigate a possible augmentation to the LCS scheme that allows for finer distinctions among spatial prepositions.

With respect to the second type of ambiguity, the LCS scheme currently uses a *preference scheme* for handling such cases.[45] However, this scheme uses syntactico-semantic knowledge, not the deeper type of knowledge that is used in other preference schemes such as that of Wilks (1973). Consider the following sentence:

(122) Mary ran in the room.

This sentence would be parsed in two different ways, one where *in the room* is parsed as an adjunct (*i.e.*, modifier) and the other where *in the room* is parsed as a complement (*i.e.*, argument). The preference scheme is set up so that it prefers argument readings over modifier readings. Thus, it rules out the modifier reading (*i.e.*, Mary was already in the room and was running around) and it prefers the argument reading instead (*i.e.*, Mary ran from outside of the room to inside of the room). This is the desired result for the current example. However, the scheme does not work in the general case. If a simple change is made to the main verb, the modifier reading tends to be preferred:

(123) Mary jumped in the room.

Most people interpret this sentence to mean that Mary was already in the room and was jumping.[46]

---

[45] No preference scheme is currently used for the second half of translation (*i.e.*, during generation). We will return to this point in chapter 6.

[46] Many people still prefer the argument reading for this sentence, which indicates that the preference scheme may be a close, though not exact, approximation to the correct scheme.

On the other hand, the scheme does rule out certain semantically unattainable cases such as the modifier reading of the analogous Spanish sentences:

(124) Juan entró al cuarto
       'John entered (to) the room'

Here, only the argument reading is possible for the prepositional phrase (*i.e.*, 'John went from outside of the room to inside of the room'); the sentence cannot be understood as meaning 'John was already in the room and he was walking around.'[47]

In other types of modifier ambiguities, the LCS scheme does not attempt to disambiguate, but it returns all possible interpretations. For example, if there were a prepositional-phrase attachment ambiguity as in *John saw the man with the telescope* (the telescope may be associated either with the act of seeing, or with the man), two source-language syntactic trees would be returned, two LCS's would be composed, and, if the target language did not have a single (ambiguous) way of stating the two concepts, two target-language syntactic trees would be returned. Without context, this is the best that can be expected from any translation system.

Despite these problematic cases, the LCS representation succeeds in filling the gap between the lexicon and syntactic structure, particularly in the context of the translation divergences presented earlier in chapter 1. Clearly, the techniques used in deeper knowledge approaches are necessary for filling other gaps, including disambiguation.

The approach presented here tries to incorporate some of the more promising syntactic and semantic aspects of existing translation systems. Although several other approaches have attempted to find a systematic relation between syntactic structure and conceptual structure, UNITRAN is unique in that it attempts to account for a number of different language-specific syntactic phenomena by a simple parametric mechanism while remaining general and uniform enough to apply a single linking routine cross-linguistically. The next chapter will discuss the use of parameterization in more detail and will introduce a number of parametric markers beyond the * marker that are used by the system.

---

[47]The preference scheme also eliminates invalid cases such as the modifier reading of *vi a Juan* ('I saw John') in which *ver* is intransitive, and *a Juan* is interpreted as some sort of modifier akin to *for the benefit of John* (*i.e.*, I saw (something) for the benefit of John).

5 Parameterization of the Interlingua

Chapter 4 examined the structure of the LCS and issues related to the use of the LCS as an interlingua. It also showed how the * marker is crucial to the success of the composition procedure in the face of certain lexical-semantic divergences. In this chapter, we will examine the resolution of other types of lexical-semantic divergences through additional parameterization of the interlingua.

Figure 5.1 shows a diagram of the UNITRAN lexical-semantic processing component. There are two stages to lexical-semantic processing: (1) composition of the LCS (*i.e.*, the CLCS) from the source-language syntactic structure; and (2) decomposition of the CLCS and realization of the target-language syntactic structure. The first of these two stages was described in the last chapter; the second will be described in the next chapter. The current chapter focuses on the systematic mapping between the CLCS and the syntax and also on the LCS parameters that are accessed by both stages.

What is important to recognize about the lexical-semantic processor is that, just as the syntactic component relies on parameterization to account for source-to-target divergences, so too does this component. In fact, the lexical-semantic component has a structure parallel to that of the syntactic component as illustrated in figure 2.1, but it differs in that the parameter settings of the lexical-semantic component are specified in the lexicon.

The types of divergences that will be addressed in this chapter are those of figure 1.12 repeated here as figure 5.2. The next section discusses the systematic mapping between the interlingua and the syntactic structure. The six subsequent sections will discuss each of the six types of lexical-semantic parameters specified in the lexicon. Finally, a detailed translation example is presented.

5.1 Systematic Mapping Between Interlingua and Syntax

The systematic mapping between the CLCS and the syntax is based on two fundamental principles. The most critical principle is the $\mathcal{GLR}$ which was defined in (102) of the last chapter. We have already seen how this routine is used in conjunction with the * marker to construct

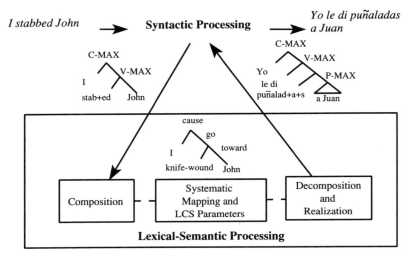

Figure 5.1
The lexical-semantic processing component is designed so that the composition and decomposition/realization processes both rely on the same systematic mapping and LCS parameters.

the interlingua during LCS composition. The second principle is the $\mathcal{CSR}$, which was also presented in the last chapter in figure 4.18.

The $\mathcal{GLR}$ and the $\mathcal{CSR}$ are the only two mapping relations defined in the system. These two principles are instrumental to the translation mapping between the source and target languages. In order to account for lexical-semantic divergences, these principles rely on parameterization of the interlingua as specified through the use of markers in lexical entries. In general, translation divergences occur when there is an exception to one (or both) of these principles in one language, but not in the other. Thus, the lexical entries have been constructed to support parametric variation that accounts for such exceptions. We have already seen the use of one such parameter, the * marker, in the previous chapter. Figure 5.3 summarizes additional parameters used in lexical entries. As we will see shortly, these parameters are used as overrides for the $\mathcal{GLR}$ and $\mathcal{CSR}$.

The use of parameters allows composition to be adjusted so that lexical-semantic divergences can be processed uniformly. The compo-

Divergence Type	Translation Example
Conflational	E: I stabbed John ⇕ S: Yo le di puñaladas a Juan 'I gave knife-wounds to John'
Structural	E: John entered the house ⇕ S: Juan entró en la casa 'I saw to John'
Thematic	E: I like Mary ⇕ S: Me gusta María 'Mary pleases me'
Categorial	E: I am hungry ⇕ G: Ich habe Hunger 'I have hunger'
Demotional	E: I like to eat ⇕ G: Ich esse gern 'I eat likingly'
Promotional	E: John usually goes home ⇕ G: Juan suele ir a casa 'John tends to go (to) home'
Lexical	E: John broke into the room ⇕ S: Juan forzó la entrada al cuarto 'John forced entry to the room'

Figure 5.2
Lexical-semantic translation divergences are accounted for by means of
parameterization of the lexicon.

sition process that is used in UNITRAN differs from that of standard
unification-based approaches in that it is a more "relaxed" notion of unification, analogous to that of Arnold *et al.* (1988), Sadler *et al.* (1990),
and Sadler and Thompson (1991). As in these approaches, the current
approach manipulates the representation by means of operations that
choose structures (and their associated positions) on the basis of lexically specified information — not on the basis of a strict grammar-driven
control mechanism. However, UNITRAN differs from these approaches
in that it uses a single underlying canonical representation (*i.e.*, the
CLCS). The use of such a representation in conjunction with the $\mathcal{GLR}$
and $\mathcal{CSR}$ obviates the need for transfer rules such as those of (15)–
(17) presented in chapter 1. Instead, only those words that *must* be
mapped in a "relaxed" way need to be associated with special lexical
information (*i.e.*, the :INT, :EXT, :PROMOTE, :DEMOTE, *, :CAT,

LCS Parameter	Purpose	Restrictions	Example
*	allows a logical subject, argument, or modifier to be syntactically realized at different levels	associated with an argument or modifier at the leaf and non-leaf levels of an LCS	used in all definitions
:INT/:EXT	allows the $\mathcal{GLR}$ to be overridden by associating a logical subject with a syntactic complement and a logical argument with a syntactic subject	associated with an LCS argument at the leaf level	used in the LCS definition for *gustar*
:CAT	allows the $\mathcal{CSR}$ to be overridden	associated with an LCS argument or modifier at the leaf level	used in the LCS definition for *tener* (when used with a condition)
:DEMOTE	allows the $\mathcal{GLR}$ to be overridden by associating a logical head with a syntactic adjunct	associated with an LCS argument of a syntactic adjunct at the leaf level	used in the LCS definition for *gern*
:PROMOTE	allows the $\mathcal{GLR}$ to be overridden by associating a logical modifier with a syntactic head	associated with an LCS complement specification of a syntactic head	used in the LCS definition for *soler*
:CONFLATED	allows for argument incorporation	associated with an argument or modifier at the leaf level	used in the LCS definition for *stab*

Figure 5.3
The parameters used by the lexical-semantic component are classified into six
different categories corresponding to the lexical-semantic divergence classification.

and :CONFLATED markers to be described below). The notion of "relaxed" compositionality is then used uniformly across all source- and target-language sentences, and special cases are handled as they arise. Thus, the mapping routines operate uniformly across all sub-structures of the CLCS without recourse to additional rules or special-case mapping routines. (This will become clearer later when we look at some concrete examples.)

We will see that this "relaxed" notion of compositionality is crucial to the success of a translation system. In particular, a purely compositional approach such as the semantic head-driven model of Shieber *et al.* (1989, 1990), the structural correspondence approach by Kaplan *et al.* (1989), and other recent work in MT (*e.g.*, van Noord *et al.* (1990) and

Zajac (1990)) does not provide a full account of the divergences investigated in the current research. On the other hand, the compositionality of UNITRAN has not been relaxed to the extent that a construction-by-construction approach is needed. (Compare to the approaches taken by MiMo, LMT, and METAL as described in chapter 1.) Finally, the parametric approach to compositionality allows the conceptual representation to be mapped systematically to the syntactic structure, in contrast to those interlingual systems that reject a systematic relation to the syntax altogether (as in the CD approach discussed in chapter 1).

We will now examine the parameters of figure 5.3 in more detail. We will discuss the translation process showing how the parameterized $\mathcal{GLR}$ and $\mathcal{CSR}$ account for a number of different types of lexical-semantic divergences.

5.2 ∗ Parameter

The ∗ parameter refers to RLCS positions that are ultimately syntactically realized on the surface. This parameter accounts for the following distinction:

(125) **Structural divergence:**
      E: John entered the house
      S: Juan entró en la casa
         'John entered (into) the house'

Here, the Spanish sentence diverges structurally from the English sentence since the noun phrase (*the house*) is realized as a prepositional phrase (*en la casa*).

The lexicon distinguishes between *enter* and *entrar* through the use of the ∗ as shown in figure 5.4. Note that an argument variable is specified for each occurrence of the ∗ marker. In the previous chapter the ∗ marker was used without an associated variable, but from this point on the variable will be specified. The reason this specification is necessary is that in cases where the ∗ marker is associated with a non-leaf node, there may be more than one variable dominated by that node. The variable specification provides a pointer to the relevant variable in such cases.[1] For example, a ∗ marker is associated with the non-leaf

---

[1] The relevant variable does not always correspond to the node that appears on the right, as we shall see in chapter 6.

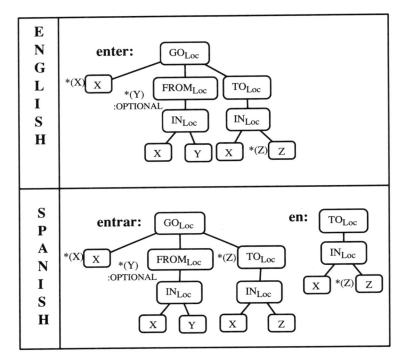

Figure 5.4
The English and Spanish RLCS entries for the *enter-entrar* example illustrate the
use of the ∗ marker.

node TO_{Loc} in the lexical entry for *entrar*. This node dominates two
variables, X and Z; the (Z) specification uniquely identifies the relevant
leaf node. This leaf node is instantiated by means of unification with
a matching representation associated with another lexical entry (in this
case the word *en*) which itself has a ∗ marker in the leaf node position
corresponding to Z.

The RLCS description for both *enter* and *entrar* provides the meaning "Thing X goes locationally from Location Y into Location Z." The
∗(Z) marker in the English RLCS for *enter* ensures that the Z argument
is filled in at the lowest level, whereas the ∗(Z) marker in the corresponding argument in the Spanish RLCS for *entrar* ensures that the Z
argument is filled in at the TO_{Loc} level. This accounts for the distinction

between the noun-phrase object *the house* and the prepositional-phrase object *en la casa* in (125). Note that an :OPTIONAL marker is associated with the $FROM_{Loc}$ argument in both definitions. We will use this marker henceforth to denote optional arguments. In the current example, this marker provides the capability of handling sentences such as *John entered the room from the hallway.*

Suppose we want to generate the Spanish sentence for this example. Figure 5.5 shows the mapping from the CLCS to the target-language syntactic tree. This portion of the mapping is performed by the decomposition and realization module of the lexical-semantic component, which chooses the appropriate Spanish root (*entrar*) and syntactically realizes the prepositional phrase object *en la casa*.[2] Since the GO_{Loc} LCS matches the RLCS entry for *entrar*, this word is chosen as the main verb. Next, the arguments of the main verb predicate must be realized. Since the TO_{Loc} argument of the RLCS for *entrar* is associated with a * marker, the procedure recursively attempts to realize this argument. The word *en* is chosen since its RLCS matches the TO_{Loc} portion of the CLCS.[3]

Next, the phrase *la casa* is realized as the complement of *en*, and the phrase *en la casa* is generated as a P-MAX. (Thus, we have accounted for the structural divergence.) Once the $\mathcal{CSR}$ projects the GO_{Loc} event as a V-MAX, the prepositional phrase is attached as the syntactic complement of *entrar*. Finally, the logical subject [$_{Thing}$ JOHN] is realized as the N-MAX *Juan*; this noun phrase is attached as the syntactic subject of *entrar*. The resulting structure is then passed to the syntactic component for constraint application, and the final output sentence, *Juan entró en la casa*, is produced.

---

[2] The lexical selection and syntactic realization processes will be described in more detail in chapter 6.

[3] During this process, the word *go* is also chosen as a match for the GO_{Loc} portion of the CLCS. Thus, the sentence *Juan fue a la casa* is generated as well. Note that the particle *a* is selected for the verb *ir* instead of the particle *en*. Because the word *a* is defined to have the same RLCS as the word *en*, the selection of *a* is possible in this context. Unfortunately, defining these two particles the same way allows for overgeneration: the system incorrectly generates the sentences *Juan fue en la casa* and *Juan entró a la casa*. Currently there is no way to rule out these sentences, but it appears that some sort of collocation test is required for these cases. (See Nirenburg and Nirenburg (1988) and Pustejovsky and Nirenburg (1987) for an approach to representing certain types of collocations.)

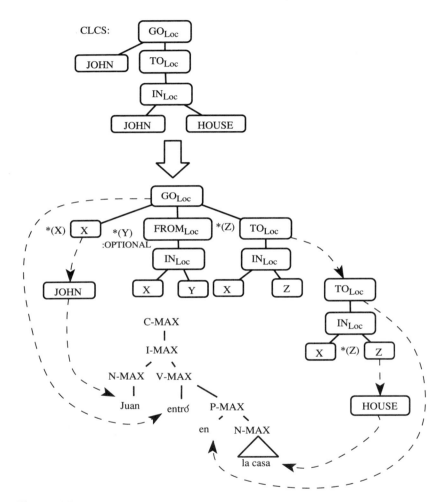

Figure 5.5
The generation of the syntactic structure for *Juan entró en la casa* illustrates how structural divergence is resolved through the use of the * marker.

5.3   :INT and :EXT Parameter

The second parameter for surface realization consists of two markers,
:INT and :EXT, that allow the $\mathcal{GLR}$ to be overridden by relating a logical
subject to a syntactic complement position and a logical argument to
the syntactic subject position. A possible effect of using these parameter
settings is that there is a subject-object reversal during translation:

(126) **Thematic divergence:**
>   E: I like Mary
>   S: Me gusta María
>   'Mary pleases me'

Here, the subject of the Spanish sentence, *María*, corresponds to the
English object *Mary*, and the object of the Spanish sentence, *me*, corresponds to the English subject *I*.

In order to account for this type of divergence, the lexicon uses the
:INT and :EXT markers in the RLCS representation associated with
the lexical entries for *gustar* as shown in figure 5.6. The RLCS description for both *gustar* and *like* provides the meaning "Thing X is in an
identificational state LIKINGLY with respect to Thing Y." Note that
the English lexical entry does not contain these markers since the $\mathcal{GLR}$
does not need to be overridden in this case; unlike the Spanish sentence,
the logical subject corresponds to the English syntactic subject, and the
logical argument corresponds to the English syntactic complement.

This subject-object reversal is illustrated more clearly in figure 5.7
which shows the entire translation mapping from English to Spanish.
The composition module of the LCS component uses the default linking-
routine positions to map the syntactic subject *I* into a logical subject
position and the syntactic object *Mary* into the logical argument position.

During the mapping to the target-language structure, the decomposition and realization module of the lexical-semantic component must
choose the appropriate Spanish root (*gustar*) and syntactically realize
its arguments. Since the BE_{Ident} CLCS matches the RLCS for *gustar*,
this word is chosen for the main verb. Next, the arguments of the main
verb must be realized. Because the :INT and :EXT markers are specified
in the RLCS for *gustar*, the linking routine places the arguments *María*
and *me* into their override positions (*i.e.*, syntactic subject and syntac-

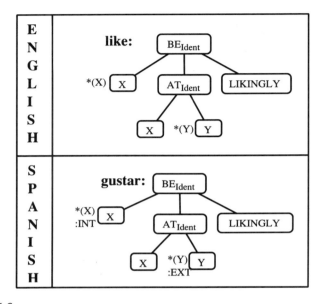

Figure 5.6
The English and Spanish RLCS entries for the *gustar-like* example illustrate the use
of the :INT and :EXT markers.

tic complement, respectively). The resulting syntactic structure is then
passed to the syntactic component for constraint application, and the
final output sentence, *Me gusta María*, is produced.[4]

5.4   :CAT Parameter

The third LCS parameter used for realization of the target language is
the :CAT marker. This provides a syntactic category for a RLCS argument. Recall that the $\mathcal{CSR}$ maps an LCS type to a syntactic category
(see figure 4.18). When this mapping is to be overridden by a lexical
entry, the language-specific marker :CAT is used.

---

[4]Note that this is the free-inversion form of the sentences. (See discussion pertaining to examples (47) and (50) in chapter 2.) The system is also able to generate
the non-inverted forms, *María me gusta* and *María me gusta a mí*. (See relevant
discussion in fn. 3 of chapter 1.) The generation of the clitic pronoun is described in
more detail in chapter 6.

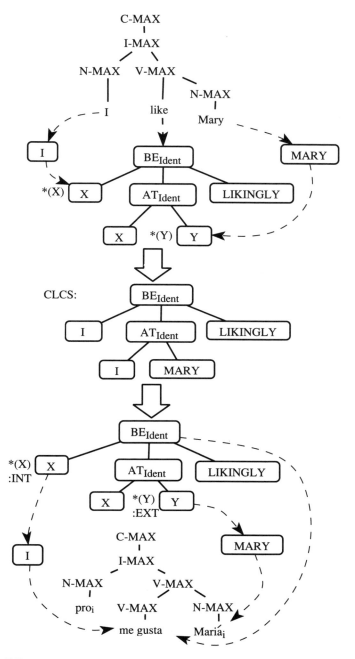

Figure 5.7
The translation of *I like Mary* as *Me gusta María* via the CLCS illustrates how the thematic divergence is resolved through the use of the :INT and :EXT markers.

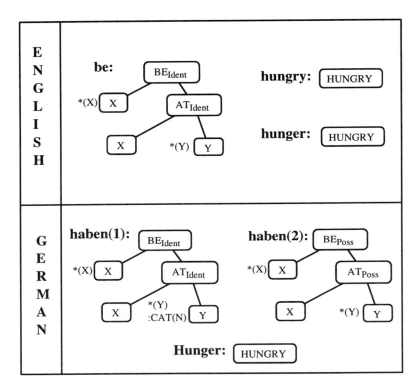

Figure 5.8
The English and German lexical entries for the *be-haben* example illustrate the use
of the :CAT marker.

This parameter accounts for distinctions such as the following:

(127) **Categorial divergence:**
    E: I am hungry
    G: Ich habe Hunger
      'I have hunger'

Here, not only are the predicates *be* and *haben* lexically distinct, but the
arguments of these two predicates are categorially divergent: in English,
the argument is an adjectival phrase, and, in German, the argument
is a noun phrase. Figure 5.8 shows the RLCS definitions used in example (127). The equivalent RLCS's for *be* and *haben*(1) provide the

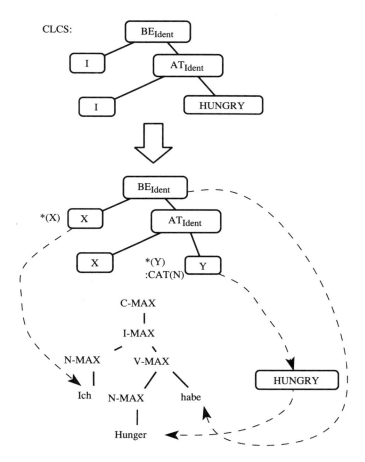

Figure 5.9
The generation of the syntactic structure for *Ich habe Hunger* from the CLCS
illustrates how categorial divergence is resolved through the use of the :CAT marker.

meaning "Thing X is in an identificational state specified by Property Y." Note that there is another RLCS for the word *haben*(2) that corresponds to a more literal translation (*have*) of the word *haben*.

Suppose we want to generate the German sentence for example (127). Figure 5.9 shows the mapping from the CLCS to the German syntactic tree for this example. During the mapping to the target-language structure, the decomposition and realization module of the lexical-semantic component must choose the appropriate German root. This choice is straightforward: *haben*(1) is chosen over *haben*(2) since the BE$_\text{Poss}$ node of *haben*(2) does not match BE$_\text{Ident}$.

For the realization of the HUNGRY argument, the system must not only choose the appropriate target-language word, but it must also choose the appropriate category that will be projected from the word. In order to account for the categorial divergence of the HUNGRY argument, the $\mathcal{CSR}$ must take the :CAT(N) override marker into consideration. Thus, this argument is realized as a noun phrase projection rather than an adjectival projection. Next, the German word *Hunger* is chosen to fill this position since it is a noun phrase that lexically matches the HUNGRY node of the CLCS.[5] The resulting structure is then passed to the syntactic component for constraint application, and the final output sentence, *Ich habe Hunger*, is produced.[6] Note that unlike the German definition of *haben*, the English definition of *be* does not include a :CAT(N) marker; this is how the argument is realized differently (*i.e.*, as A-MAX) for English.[7]

5.5 :DEMOTE Parameter

The fourth parameter used during lexical-semantic processing is the :DE-MOTE marker, which, like the :INT and :EXT markers, allows the $\mathcal{GLR}$

---

[5]Actually, there is an alternative realization of HUNGRY *hungrig* that allows *sein* ('be') to be selected as a predicate as in *Ich bin hungrig*. As long as both versions of HUNGRY are in the lexicon, both sentences are generated.

[6]The structure shown here is the base form of the surface syntactic tree.   After Move-α has applied, the structure looks like the following:
[C-MAX [N-MAX Ich]$_i$
   [C [V habe]$_j$]
   [I-MAX [N-MAX t]$_i$ [V-MAX [N-MAX Hunger] [V t]$_j$] [I *e*]]]]

[7]In particular, if we were to generate the English sentence, the nominal form *hunger* would be eliminated as a possibility since the $\mathcal{CSR}$ requires this argument to be adjectival.

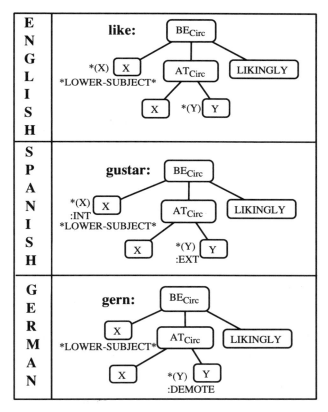

Figure 5.10
The English, Spanish, and German lexical entries for *like* illustrate three different parameterizations. In contrast to the first two entries, the German entry includes the :DEMOTE marker.

to be overridden by relating a logical head to a syntactic adjunct position (*i.e.*, the logical head is "demoted" in the syntactic structure). This parameter accounts for the following distinction: [8]

(128) **Demotional divergence:**
    E: I like to eat
    G: Ich esse gern
       'I eat likingly'

Here, the English main verb *like* corresponds to the adjunct *gern* in German, and the embedded verb *eat* corresponds to the main verb *essen* in German.

As shown in figure 5.10, the RLCS for *gern* differs from the RLCS's for *like* and *gustar* in that it associates a :DEMOTE marker with the Y argument. This marker forces the logical head of the CLCS to be mapped to a syntactic adjunct position. Note that all three of the definitions in figure 5.10 use the Circumstantial field, which means that the Y argument must be an Event (*e.g.*, *like to eat*) rather than a Thing (*e.g.*, *like Mary*). Thus, the definitions for *like* and *gustar* are slightly different from those shown in figure 5.6 (*i.e.*, these are additional lexical entries for *like* and *gustar*); however, the same parameter settings are used in both cases. [9]

Suppose we want to generate the German sentence for example (128). [10] Figure 5.11 shows the mapping from the CLCS to the German syntactic tree for this example. Here, the German main verb (*essen*) is associated with the conceptually lower (demoted) argument position Y, but it is mapped into a position that is syntactically higher than the adverb *gern*. [11] Thus, the :DEMOTE parameter accounts for the distinction between the English realization in which *like* is the main verb and the German realization in which *essen* is the main verb.

---

[8] The English sentence *I like eating* is also an acceptable translation for *Ich esse gern*. This alternative is also handled by the system and is subject to the same lexical parameterization.

[9] Note that all three of these definitions use the *LOWER-SUBJECT* marker that was described in chapter 4. The utility of this marker will become more apparent in chapter 6 when we discuss the generation of the syntactic structure from these lexical entries in more detail.

[10] The output structure is shown here in base form, not surface form. Chapter 6 describes how the realization of the surface form *Ich esse gern* is achieved.

[11] The default object being eaten is FOOD, although this argument does not appear on the surface for the current example.

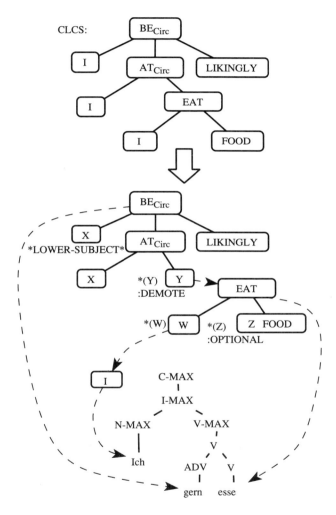

Figure 5.11
The generation of the syntactic structure for *Ich esse gern* from the CLCS
illustrates how demotional divergence is resolved through the use of the :DEMOTE
marker.

During the mapping to the target-language structure, the decomposition and realization module of the lexical-semantic component must choose the appropriate German root. Since the BE_{Circ} CLCS matches the RLCS for *gern*, this word is chosen as part of the target-language realization. However, the Event argument of the *gern* RLCS is associated with a :DEMOTE marker; thus, the system determines that the EAT node under the BE_{Circ} must be realized first. Given that the RLCS associated with the root word *essen* matches the EAT event, this word is chosen and projected into the phrase structure as the main verb. Next, the root word *gern* is attached as an adjunct to the main verb.

Finally, the syntactic subject *Ich* is generated for the verb *essen*. The resulting structure is then passed to the syntactic component for constraint application, and the final output sentence, *Ich esse gern*, is produced.

5.6   :PROMOTE Parameter

The :PROMOTE marker is the fifth parameter used during lexical-semantic processing. This marker also overrides the $\mathcal{GLR}$ by relating a logical modifier to a syntactic head position (*i.e.*, the logical modifier is "promoted" in the syntactic structure). This parameter accounts for the following distinction:

(129) **Promotional divergence:**
    E: John usually goes home
    S: Juan suele ir a casa
        'John tends to go home'

The difference between the :PROMOTE and the :DEMOTE markers is that the override takes place with respect to a head and its complement rather than a head and its adjunct.[12]

As shown in figure 5.12, the lexical entries for both *usually* and *soler* consist of the single RLCS node HABITUALLY. The difference is that, in the case of Spanish, this node is associated with a :PROMOTE marker, whereas in the case of English, no such marker is used. Suppose

---

[12]Another difference between the :PROMOTE and :DEMOTE markers is that the former is associated with the head (*i.e.*, the syntactically "higher" constituent) and the latter is associated with the adjunct (*i.e.*, the syntactically "lower" constituent). Additional justification for the distinction between these is given in chapter 7.

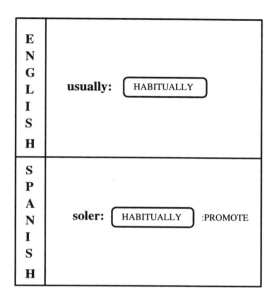

Figure 5.12
The English and Spanish RLCS entries for *usually* illustrate the use of the
:PROMOTE marker.

we want to generate the Spanish sentence of example (129). Figure 5.13
shows the mapping from the CLCS to the Spanish syntactic tree for this
example.

Here, the "higher" (promoted) GO$_{Loc}$ CLCS is realized in a "lower"
position (as *ir*) with respect to the realization of the CLCS node HA-
BITUALLY (as *soler*). Thus, the :PROMOTE parameter accounts for
the distinction between the English realization in which *go* is the main
verb and the Spanish realization in which *soler* is the main verb.

During the mapping to the target-language structure, the decomposition and realization module of the lexical-semantic component must
choose the appropriate Spanish root. Since the GO$_{Loc}$ CLCS matches
the RLCS for *ir*, this word is chosen as part of the target-language realization. However, the Manner modifier of the CLCS corresponds to
a RLCS that is associated with a :PROMOTE marker; thus, the system determines that the HABITUALLY node under the GO$_{Loc}$ must be

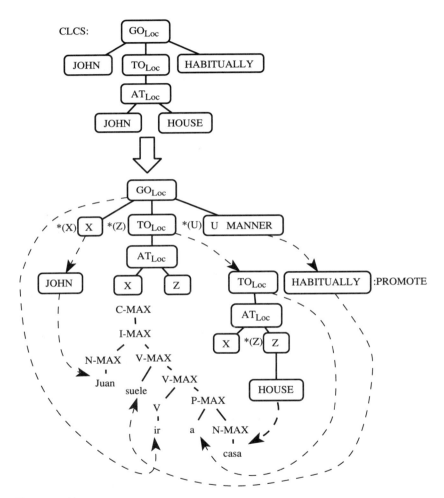

Figure 5.13
The generation of the syntactic structure for *Juan suele ir a casa* from the CLCS
illustrates how promotional divergence is resolved through the use of the
:PROMOTE marker.

realized first.[13] Given that the RLCS associated with the root word *soler* matches the HABITUALLY modifier, this word is chosen and projected into the phrase structure as the main verb. Next, the root word *ir* and its associated argument structure *a casa* are attached as the complement of the main verb.

Finally, the syntactic subject *Juan* is generated for the verb *soler*. The resulting structure is then passed to the syntactic component for constraint application, and the final output sentence, *Juan suele ir a casa*, is produced.

5.7   :CONFLATED Parameter

The sixth LCS parameter is the :CONFLATED marker. This marker is used for indicating that a particular argument need not be realized in the surface representation. This parameter accounts for the divergence example of example (8) that we saw in chapter 1 (and as examples (76) and (103) in chapter 4), repeated here:

(130) **Conflational divergence:**[14]
     E: I stabbed John
     S: Yo le di puñaladas a Juan
       'I gave knife-wounds to John'

Here, the argument that is incorporated in the English sentence is the KNIFE-WOUND argument. The *stab* construction does not realize this argument; by contrast, the Spanish construction *dar puñaladas a* explicitly realizes this argument as the word *puñalada*. (This motion-effect

---

[13]The locally introduced variable U in the definition for *ir* refers to an "inherited modifier" in the sense described in (101) of chapter 4. It has been included here for illustrative purposes only.

[14]Conflation refers to the incorporation (or suppression) of an argument. As documented by Talmy (1983, 1985), conflation of manner shows up most commonly with respect to motion. For example, English conflates manner and motion in the following:

       (i)   The boat floated on the water

On the other hand, Spanish disallows this conflation, requiring a syntactic realization for each semantic component as shown here:

       (ii)   La barca se mudaba flotando en el agua
             'The boat moved floatingly in the water'

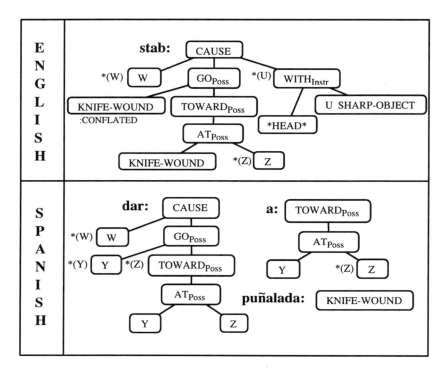

Figure 5.14
The English and Spanish RLCS entries for the *stab-dar* example illustrate the use of the :CONFLATED marker.

conflation also shows up in the *break-forzar* example, as we will see in the next section.) Figure 5.14 shows the RLCS definitions used in example (130).[15] Note that the entry for *stab* includes the :CONFLATED marker, but not the entry for *dar*.

In the last chapter we discussed the composition of the interlingua for each of the two sentences in (130). Suppose we want to generate the Spanish sentence for this example. Figure 5.15 shows the mapping from the CLCS to the Spanish syntactic tree for this example. During the mapping to the target-language structure, the decomposition and

---

[15]The variable U in the English definition refers to a locally declared variable that is associated with the WITH$_{Instr}$ modifier. This modifier is not inherited (in contrast to the definition of *ir* shown in figure 5.13); it is included to specify idiosyncratic information about the verb *stab*.

realization module of the lexical-semantic component must decompose this representation into its parts and produce a structural realization of the target-language sentence. The main verb is selected on the basis of a match between the CLCS and the RLCS for *dar*.[16] Thus, this root is selected to be the word that will be projected.

Once the appropriate target-language root word is chosen, the system must provide a syntactic tree based on the lexical entry for this root word. This is accomplished by projecting the root word up to its phrasal level, and then attaching its selected arguments according to the categorial and positioning requirements of the root word. Figure 5.15 shows how the CLCS for example (130) is disassembled into the component RLCS definitions associated with target-language words; the argument positions of these RLCS definitions map to positions in the syntactic tree (as shown).

The way the realization process operates for this example is as follows. Once *dar* is chosen as the main verb, the arguments of *dar* must be (recursively) realized. The $*$ marker is used to determine the level at which each argument will be realized. Note that, unlike the *stab* definition, the *dar* definition requires the Y argument to be overtly realized since it does not contain a :CONFLATED marker (see figure 5.14); thus, the system performs an "inverse conflation" in order to arrive at the target-language realization for this example. Because the CLCS contains the argument KNIFE-WOUND, this becomes the token that will be overtly realized for the Y variable in the Spanish RLCS. As shown in figure 5.14, the word *puñalada* is defined to be a KNIFE-WOUND, so this is the root word chosen to be the direct object of the main verb, and we have resolved the motion-effect conflational divergence. The $\mathcal{CSR}$ is then called to realize KNIFE-WOUND (which is a Thing) as a noun phrase (N-MAX).

Next, the second object of *dar* is realized. Note that this argument is realized at the level of TO_{Poss} (denoted by $*(Z)$ in figure 5.14). Since the

---

[16]In general, there may be more than one way to realize a lexical concept. If there is still more than one possibility, which occurs most frequently in situations where more than one verb describes a single concept, all possibilities are returned. In the current example, there is more than one way to realize the *stab* concept in Spanish. Specifically, the Spanish word *apuñalar* is another possible translation for the English word *stab*. This lexical item provides a more succinct way of stating the *stab* sentence: *Yo le apuñalé a Juan*. In fact, UNITRAN selects this choice as well. In the description presented here, we will only talk about one of these possibilities (*i.e.*, *dar*).

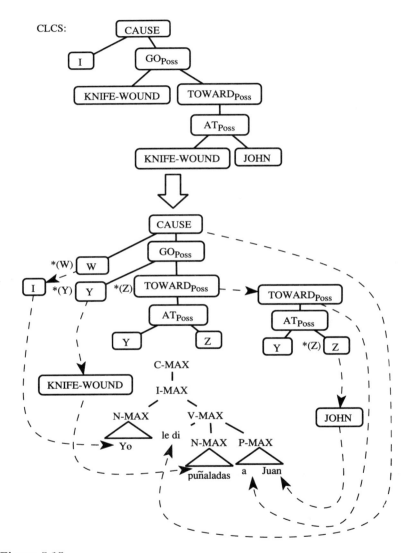

Figure 5.15
The generation of the syntactic structure for *Yo le di puñaladas a Juan* from the
CLCS illustrates how conflational divergence is resolved through the use of the
:CONFLATED marker.

lexical entry for the word *a* matches the TO$_{Poss}$ portion of the CLCS, this word is chosen as the target lexical item. A recursive call to the realization procedure is then made on the Z variable in the TO$_{Poss}$ definition. This variable, which corresponds to the [$_{Thing}$ JOHN] argument, is realized as the N-MAX *Juan*. Then the $\mathcal{CSR}$ is called on TO$_{Poss}$ (which is a Path) and the argument is realized as a prepositional phrase (P-MAX).

Once the two objects of *dar* are realized, the $\mathcal{CSR}$ is called in order to realize the CAUSE (which is an Event) as a verb phrase (V-MAX). At this point, the objects are positioned under the verb phrase as complements.

The final argument that is realized is the logical subject (the [$_{Thing}$ I] node in the CLCS). This node is realized as the first-person singular pronoun *yo*.[17] Once the $\mathcal{CSR}$ realizes this argument as a noun phrase (N-MAX), it is attached as the syntactic subject above the V-MAX, and the result is the Spanish syntactic tree shown in figure 5.15. We will return to this example again in chapter 6 when we discuss the generation process in more detail.

5.8 Detailed Translation Process for the Break-Forzar Example

Now that we have looked at the operation of the syntactic and lexical-semantic components and the principles and parameters upon which both are based, we will see how these components work in detail for the translation of the following example:

(131) **Lexical divergence:**
    E: John broke into the room
    S: Juan forzó la entrada al cuarto
       'John forced entry to the room'

This divergence type is *lexical* in that the choice of a target-language word is not a literal translation of the source-language word. However,

---

[17]Other pronouns are also chosen for the [$_{Thing}$ I] node including *me* and *mi*, both of which have the features [p1 sg]. However, the Case Filter rules out *me* (since it has inherent objective case) and *mi* (since it has inherent possessive case). The pronoun *yo* is the only one that passes the Case Filter since its inherent nominative case matches the case assigned by the verb *dar*.

lexical divergence arises only in the context of other divergence types; thus, a detailed discussion of this example will also demonstrate how other divergence types are handled. In particular, lexical divergence generally co-occurs with conflational, structural, and categorial divergences. We have already seen two examples of divergence overlap: the *be-haben* example (127) and the *stab-dar* example (130). In the current example, there is a conflational divergence (*i.e.*, the incorporation of the *entry* argument in English *vs.* the overt realization in Spanish) and a structural divergence (*i.e.*, the realization of the *room* argument as a verbal object in English *vs.* the realization as a prepositional object in Spanish). Figure 5.16 shows the RLCS definitions associated with the English and Spanish tokens in this example.

We will examine the translation of this example, from beginning to end, in the English-to-Spanish direction as illustrated in figure 5.17. The parser in the syntactic component of UNITRAN supplies a source-language syntactic tree to the LCS component of the system as shown in figure 5.17(a). This structure passes through all of the constraints of the syntactic component. In particular, the noun phrase *John* receives nominative case from AGR (since the main verb is tensed), and *room* receives objective case from *into*; thus, the Case Filter is satisfied. In addition, the θ-criterion is satisfied since these two constituents also receive θ-roles: *John* and *room* are mapped into the logical subject and logical argument positions associated with the RLCS in the lexical entry for *break*.

At this point, the syntactic component passes the source-language syntactic tree for *John broke into the room* to the LCS component, and the RLCS's corresponding to the words *John*, *broke*, *into* and *room* are composed into a single underlying representation (the interlingua). For example, the RLCS associated with the word *John* is filled into the logical subject position, and the RLCS associated with the word *room* is filled into logical argument position. Figure 5.17(b) shows the mapping from the syntactic tree to the RLCS argument positions in the definition of *break*; the result of this mapping is the CLCS as shown.

Once the interlingua has been composed, the second module of the LCS component decomposes this representation into its parts and produces a structural realization of the target-language sentence. The first task is lexical selection: the main verb is selected on the basis of a match between the interlingua and the RLCS for *forzar*. Thus, this root is se-

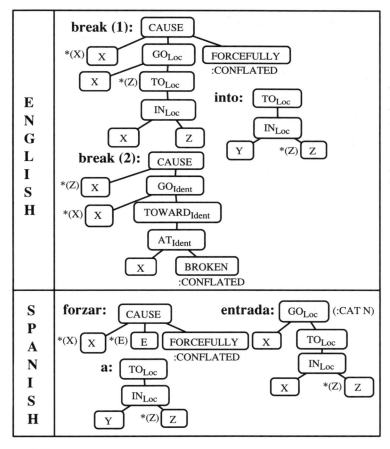

Figure 5.16
The English and Spanish RLCS entries for *forzar-break* illustrate the full
compositional potential of the LCS representation.

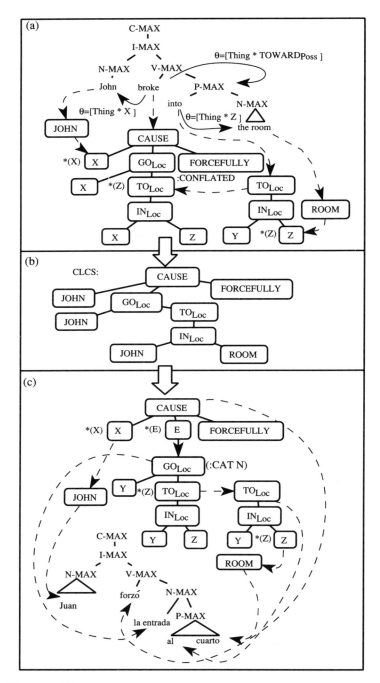

Figure 5.17
The translation of *John broke into the room* as *Juan forzó la entrada al cuarto* via
the CLCS illustrates how lexical divergence is resolved through recursive
compositionality.

lected to be the word that will be projected, and the lexical divergence has been resolved.

The next task is to produce a structural realization of the main verb and its arguments. During this process, the other two divergence types, conflational and structural, are resolved. This is accomplished by projecting the root word up to its phrasal level using the $\mathcal{CSR}$, and then attaching its selected arguments according to the categorial and positioning requirements of the root word. Figure 5.17(c) shows how the CLCS for example (131) is disassembled into the component RLCS definitions associated with target-language words; the argument positions of these RLCS definitions map to positions in the syntactic tree (as shown).

The way the realization process operates for this example is as follows. Once *forzar* is chosen as the main verb, the arguments of *forzar* must be (recursively) realized. The * marker is used to determine the level at which each argument will be realized. Note that, unlike the *break* definition, the *forzar* definition requires the E argument to be overtly realized; thus, the system performs an "inverse conflation" in order to arrive at the target-language realization for this example. Because the CLCS contains a subtree rooted at GO_{Loc}, this becomes the token that will be overtly realized for the E variable in the Spanish RLCS. The word *entrada* matches this subtree, so this is the root word chosen to be the direct object of the main verb. Thus, we have resolved the motion-effect conflational divergence mentioned earlier. Note that the $\mathcal{CSR}$ is overridden during the realization of this argument since the GO_{Loc} node in the RLCS for *entrada* has a (:CAT N) marker associated with it. The categorial setting forces the system to select the noun *entrada* (rather than the verb *entrar*, for example).

Next, the object of *forzar*, *entrada* is (recursively) realized. Because the RLCS for *entrada* contains a *(Z) marker at the non-leaf node TO_{Loc}, the word that is selected must match this portion of the tree. Thus, the word *a* is chosen as the target lexical item since it is defined as a TO_{Loc} path. When this word is syntactically realized, a recursive call is made to the realization procedure on the Z variable. This argument is realized as the N-MAX *cuarto*. Then the $\mathcal{CSR}$ is called on TO_{Loc} (which is a Path) and the argument is realized as a prepositional phrase (P-MAX), thus resolving the structural divergence mentioned earlier.

Once the object of *forzar* is realized, the $\mathcal{CSR}$ is called in order to realize the CAUSE (which is an Event) as a verb phrase (V-MAX). At this point, the object is positioned under the verb phrase as its syntactic complement.

The final argument that is realized is the logical subject corresponding to [$_{Thing}$ JOHN] in the CLCS. This node is realized as the noun *Juan*. Once the $\mathcal{CSR}$ projects this argument as a noun phrase (N-MAX), it is attached as the syntactic subject above the V-MAX, and the result is the Spanish syntactic tree.

Now that we have accounted for all three divergences during the generation of the target-language syntactic structure, the syntactic constraints are free to apply to this structure, just as they did to the source-language structure before the LCS was composed. In particular, the case module checks that the subject *Juan* and the prepositional object *cuarto* are marked for nominative and objective case, respectively. In addition, the θ module assigns θ-roles to argument positions.[18] Once it is determined that there are no constraint violations, the final output sentence, *Juan forzó la entrada al cuarto*, is produced by reading off the leaves of the syntactic tree.

To sum up, this chapter has presented what is, perhaps, the most important advance of UNITRAN: the parameterization of the interlingua. This allows the system to be designed so that only two mapping relations are required to achieve the translation from the source to the target language. We have now demonstrated the efficacy of this approach in the context of translating both syntactic and lexical-semantic divergences. The key to being able to provide a systematic mapping between languages is modularity: because the system has been partitioned into two different processing levels, there is a decoupling of the syntactic and lexical-semantic decisions that are made during the translation process. Thus, language-specific idiosyncrasies are handled without losing the systematicity of the process that produces, and generates from, the interlingual form.

---

[18] Actually, the assignment of θ-roles during generation of the target-language structure is not as productive as it is during parsing of the source-language structure. The assignment of θ-roles is used primarily for composition of the interlingua from the parsed source-language structure. No such procedure is applied to the generated target-language structure. θ-role assignment is used after generation mainly for reasons of uniformity: it produces a structure that has exactly the same status as that of the source-language structure and could, in fact, be used as input to the LCS composition routine. (This has actually been done as a test of whether "backtranslation" of the target-language structure produces the original source-language input.)

6 Generation from the Interlingua

This chapter describes the process of generating the surface form from the interlingua. This task is performed by the second stage of the lexical-semantic component, namely the stage during which the LCS is decomposed and the target-language structure is realized (see figure 5.1 of the last chapter). This stage is symmetrical to the LCS composition stage in that it relies on the ∗ parameter and also maps systematically between the interlingua and the syntactic representation; however, it is not the direct inverse of LCS composition. This is no surprise, as it is now well understood that the types of problems that must be solved during generation are not the same as those that are solved during analysis (see e.g., Goldman (1975), Hovy (1988), Jacobs (1985), McDonald (1983, 1991), McKeown (1985), Nirenburg and Nirenburg (1988), Nirenburg et al. (1988), and Pustejovsky and Nirenburg (1987)).[1] Within the context of the current model, these two processes differ in that the primary goal of LCS composition is instantiation of the concept that underlies a given structural representation, whereas during generation, the system already knows *what* the concept is and, thus, is concerned more about *how* to realize that concept.

As the generation component has not been the primary focus of the current research, it has not been designed to provide a solution to all of the problems in generation that have been well-reported by other researchers. Such problems include cohesion (Granville (1983)), selecting propositional and rhetorical goals (McKeown (1985)), selecting open-class items from "deep knowledge" (Goldman (1975), Jacobs (1985), Kittredge et al. (1988), Nirenburg and Nirenburg (1988), Nirenburg et al. (1992), among others), ordering propositions for producing coherent text (Hovy (1988)), resolving anaphora (Derr and McKeown (1984), Sondheimer et al. (1990), Werner and Nirenburg (1988)), an many others. In fact, not all of these issues (*e.g.*, selecting propositional and rhetorical

---

[1] This is not to say that a model of bidirectional processing could not be devised. For example, a number of researchers have reported success in taking a reversible-grammar approach (see, *e.g.*, Barnett et al. (1991a,b), Dymetman (1991), Estival (1990), Kay (1991), Marrafa and Saint-Dizier (1991), McDonald (1991), Neumann (1991), van Noord (1990, 1991), Strzalkowski (1991), Thompson (1991), Zajac (1991), among others). However, such models focus on reversibility of the data structures that are accessed during parsing and generation (almost invariably the grammar), not on the actual processes that use these data structures. To the extent that the processors of these models are actually reversible, the reversibility is generally restricted to syntactic parsing and generation, not deeper levels of understanding and production. Moreover, with the possible exception of Barnett et al. (1991a,b), these systems do not propose a mechanism that systematically resolves the types of translation problems addressed here.

goals) are relevant to the task of machine translation, which already has the advantage (at least from the generation point of view) that the source-language sentence and, in the current model, the conceptual analysis underlying this sentence are available at the onset of the generation process. In addition, other issues (*e.g.*, cohesiveness, coherence, and context) are more relevant to the task of generating multiple sentences, not single sentences in isolation.

Instead, the current research focuses on demonstrating the utility of the LCS-based interlingua and the associated mechanisms described in the last chapter for resolving translation divergences during generation without losing the systematic relation between the interlingua and the syntax. The tasks involved in achieving this objective have been reduced to what might be considered the standard "what" and "how" questions of generation: (1) *lexical selection*, *i.e.*, the task of deciding what target-language words accurately reflect the meaning of the corresponding source-language words; and (2) *syntactic realization*, *i.e.*, the task of determining how target-language words are mapped to their appropriate syntactic structures. In the context of the current model, the first task consists of matching the LCS-based interlingua (the CLCS) against the LCS-based entries (the RLCS) in the dictionary in order to select the appropriate word, and the second task consists of realizing the positions marked by ∗ (and other parametric markers) into the appropriate syntactic structure.

The next two sections examine the lexical selection and syntactic realization operations in more detail. Section 6.3 then describes how these operations fit together in the overall generation scheme; an example of generation to Spanish and German will be presented. Next, section 6.4 discusses the interaction of the generator with the syntactic constraints that are grounded in the linguistic framework presented in chapter 2. Finally, this chapter will conclude with a detailed illustration of the generation portion of the translation for the *stab* example of chapter 4.

6.1   Lexical Selection

Lexical selection of a target-language word involves matching the CLCS to the appropriate root word from a target-language possibility set. In general, two types of LCS nodes are taken into consideration during the matching process of lexical selection. The more general nodes (*e.g.*, BE_{Circ}, GO_{Poss}, *etc.*) are used to determine the LCS class of the target-language term; the more specific nodes (*e.g.*, LIKINGLY, LOVINGLY, *etc.*) are used for final convergence on a particular target-language term, such as *like* as opposed to *love*.

Consider the generation of the Spanish and German sentence for the *I like to eat* example given previously in chapter 5:

(132) E: I like to eat
      S: Me gusta comer (a mí)
         'To eat is pleasing to me'
      G: Ich esse gern
         'I eat likingly'

Figure 6.1 shows the CLCS and RLCS's for this example.[2] In this example, the lexical selection operation must choose a target-language word that matches the BE_{Circ} CLCS that is given as input to the generator. Initially, several target words are chosen during the lexical selection process regardless of which language is being generated:

        Spanish: gustar, parecer, ...
        German: gern, freuen, scheinen, ...

Each of the root words shown here is associated with a RLCS that matches the top node of the BE_{Circ} CLCS. However, these possibilities are pared down further once the generator determines that the LIKINGLY modifier is included in the representation. Thus, the routine selects *gustar* for Spanish and *gern* for German. Note that these two RLCS's match the CLCS even though the associated lexical parameters are set differently (*i.e.*, :INT/:EXT are used in Spanish and :DEMOTE is used in German) and they are of different categories (*i.e.*, *gustar* is a verb and *gern* is an adverb).

The matching process used by the lexical selection procedure relies on a recursive compatibility check between the CLCS and the RLCS that

---

[2]The earlier definition of figure 5.10 did not include the :CONFLATED marker because it had not been introduced yet. Note, also, that the position of the $*(X)$ in the lexical entry for *gustar* is slightly different in the current definition. The earlier definition was not entirely accurate but was presented as such for illustrational purposes. We will henceforth use the current positioning of the $*$, which allows the prepositional phrase *a mí* to be (optionally) generated for the variable X. We will see how this is achieved in section 6.3.1.

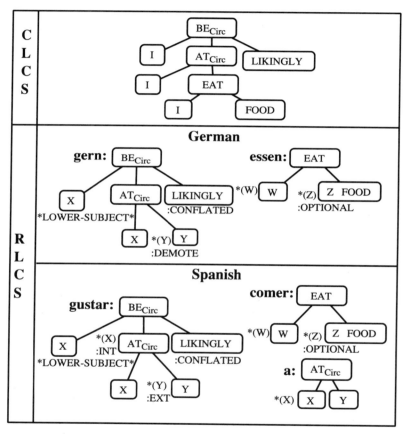

Figure 6.1
The lexical selection processes matches the Spanish and German RLCS's to the
CLCS corresponding to the sentences *me gusta comer (a mí)* and *Ich esse gern.*

is selected. This procedure checks that the primitive, type, field, and features of each RLCS node match those of the corresponding CLCS nodes. For example, the RLCS for *gern* matches the CLCS shown in figure 6.1 since it has the following representation:

(133) $[_\text{Event}\ \text{BE}_\text{Ident}$
$([_\text{Thing}\ \text{X}],$
$[_\text{Position}\ \text{AT}_\text{Ident}\ ([_\text{Thing}\ \text{X}],\ [_\text{Thing}\ \text{Y}])],$
$[_\text{Manner}\ \text{LIKINGLY}])]$

In a sense, the compatibility check is unification-like, analogous to the unification-like procedure used during LCS composition. However, the lexical selection procedure does not use a strict notion of unification to obtain the final result. To clarify this point, consider the representation for the word *be* (or *ser* in Spanish or *sein* in German):

(134) $[_\text{Event}\ \text{BE}_\text{Ident}\ ([_\text{Thing}\ \text{X}],\ [_\text{Position}\ \text{AT}_\text{Ident}\ ([_\text{Thing}\ \text{X}],\ [_\text{Thing}\ \text{Y}])])]$

A strict notion of unification would allow (134) to match any CLCS that matches (133) despite the fact that there is an unmatched modifier LIKINGLY. This is where the current approach differs from that of strict unification approaches: all "leftover" pieces *must* be matched to some other lexical item during the lexical selection process. We shall refer to this requirement as the Full Coverage Constraint:

(135) **Full Coverage Constraint:**
A RLCS R matches a CLCS C if and only if R **fully covers** C.

where R *fully covers* C under the following conditions:

(136) A RLCS R **fully covers** a CLCS C if and only if:

1. the recursive compatibility check between C and R succeeds (*i.e.*, there is no portion of R that does not match C).

2. either R completely matches C (*i.e.*, there is no portion of C that does not match R) or R matches all of C except some portion C' (*i.e.*, a subcomponent of C) which is fully covered by some other RLCS R'.

Thus, in cases where more than one lexical entry passes the compatibility check, it is the job of the lexical selection procedure to apply this constraint to determine which possibilities should be ruled out (if any). In the current example, the word *be* is ruled out later during the lexical selection process since there is no lexical item that matches the LIKINGLY portion of the CLCS. We will return to the rest of the generation process for this example in section 6.3. We now turn to a discussion of issues pertaining to the lexical selection process and we will draw a comparison between the current approach to lexical selection and that of previous generation models.

It is not always the case that the Full Coverage Constraint pares down the possibilities to one. Often times there are several different ways to satisfy this constraint, all of which are perfectly valid surface realizations for a given CLCS. In this sense, the LCS-based lexical selection process is related to those of other researchers, most notably Miezitis (1988) in that both approaches attempt to find all correct and usable matches rather than the "best" match (as in the Preference Semantics of Wilks (1973) discussed below). Neither the UNITRAN system nor the Lexical Option Generator (LOG) of Miezitis is concerned with finding a best match since (as described by Miezitis (1988, p. 20)):

"... all of the lexical units provided will be correct and usable by the process to which they are given. However, it will be up to that process to select the optimal lexical units to produce language according to its current goals and constraints."

Nevertheless, as might be predicted, the lexical selection procedure described above does not always adequately cut down the number of target-language possibilities. In particular, there are many open-ended classes of words (*e.g.*, certain nouns and adjectives) that are not distinguishable by their LCS's. This is because LCS's provide an underlying representation of predicates and their arguments; any lexical item that does not exhibit a predicate-argument relationship must be translated by other means. For most nouns (*i.e.*, proper nouns such as *John*, *Mary*, *Spain*, *etc.* and common nouns such as *boy*, *kid*, *etc.*) a direct-mapping routine is used for lexicalization to the surface form. For other open-class lexical items (*e.g.*, adjectives such as *big*, *large*, *small*, *tiny*, *etc.*) all possibilities are returned.

This open-ended approach to generation leads to several well-known problems. In particular, the question of efficiency has been raised by researchers such as Jacobs (1985) with respect to the discrimination net approach of Goldman (1975), which also returns all correct and usable

matches rather than a "best" match. Goldman's approach to verb selection in the BABEL generator is similar to that of UNITRAN in that
the target-language verbs are narrowed down according to selectional restrictions associated with argument positions. In Goldman's generator,
each primitive of the system could potentially lead to a wide range of
verbs, depending on the results of the tests in the discrimination nets.
If this range of verbs were narrowed down by defining more primitive
units, Jacobs argues, there would be a severe proliferation of primitives
due to the need to distinguish among a number of different predicates.

In response to the lexical selection problem, a number of researchers
have proposed a preference-assigning scheme. In the generation approach by Wilks (1973), a concept is realized on the basis of preference
links between the concept and other concepts.[3] For example, one meaning of the verb *play* (as in *play with friends*) would "prefer" *boy* over
man as an agent. Thus, "(PLAY PERSON (WITH FRIENDS))" would
be realized as *the boy plays with friends* if the PERSON is associated
with the feature-value pair (SEX MALE).

The DIOGENES system (see Nirenburg and Nirenburg (1988) and
Pustejovsky and Nirenburg (1987)) uses a similar scheme. The generation lexicon for this system takes the form of discrimination nets whose
non-leaves are marked with Wilks-style preference semantics information. This constrained discrimination network is used for selection of
open-class items on the basis of the context. Preferences are encoded
via meaning slots that are assigned importance values. For example, the
importance value is higher for the SEX slot than the AGE slot in the
lexical entry for *boy*:

(137) (MAKE-FRAME BOY
              . . .
          (SEX (VALUE MALE) (IMPORTANCE 10))
          (AGE (VALUE (2 15)) (IMPORTANCE 4))
              . . .
          (SYN-COLLOCATIONS-IN (VALUE BOY.SYN)))

Thus, if it is known in advance that a PERSON concept has features
(SEX MALE), then *boy* is more likely to be chosen than *girl* as a target-
language lexical item.

---

[3] A thorough description of the main principles and theoretical bases of the preference semantics approach is given in Wilks and Fass (1992).

The choice of lexical item is further constrained by context due to collocational restrictions that are associated with lexical items. For example, the lexical entry for *boy* has the values SCHOOL, PLAYGROUND, and BALLFIELD in the PLACE slot of its collocational restrictions:

(138) (MAKE-FRAME BOY.SYN
          . . .

      (PLACE (VALUE SCHOOL PLAYGROUND BALLFIELD)
      (STRENGTH 10)))

Thus, if it is known in advance that the PLACE of an event that includes a male PERSON is the playground, then *boy* is more likely to be chosen than *man*.

The disadvantage to using such collocation restrictions is that they are very tedious to construct. As a topic of future research, Nirenburg and Nirenburg (1988) suggest that the process of constructing a concept lexicon be automated. Despite the thorny problem of lexical acquisition, this investigation has illustrated the importance of constraining factors such as context and collocations in the generation process. Although contextual and collocational constraints are not implemented in the current implementation of UNITRAN, they could prove useful in future versions.

While preference assignment during lexical selection is also not currently implemented in UNITRAN, it would be easy to extend the system to use a "closest match" capability in some cases. For example, in German, the verb *schenken* (to give as a gift) has the following RLCS specification:

(139) $[_{\text{Event}}$ CAUSE
      $([_{\text{Thing}}$ X],
      $[_{\text{Event}}$ GO$_{\text{Poss}}$
          $([_{\text{Thing}}$ Y],
          $[_{\text{Path}}$ TOWARD$_{\text{Poss}}$
             $([_{\text{Position}}$ AT$_{\text{Poss}}$ $([_{\text{Thing}}$ Y], $[_{\text{Thing}}$ Z])])])],
      $[_{\text{Manner}}$ GIFTINGLY])]

There isn't a true equivalent for this form of possessional transfer in English. (The verb *present* comes fairly close, but for the purposes of this discussion, we will assume no such word exists, which might be the case in some languages.) However, the RLCS associated with the verb *give* matches "most" of the RLCS specification for *schenken* — all except for the GIFTINGLY modifier:

(140) $[_{\text{Event}}$ CAUSE
  $([_{\text{Thing}}$ X],
  $[_{\text{Event}}$ GO$_{\text{Poss}}$
   $([_{\text{Thing}}$ Y],
   $[_{\text{Path}}$ TOWARD$_{\text{Poss}}$
    $([_{\text{Position}}$ AT$_{\text{Poss}}$ $([_{\text{Thing}}$ Y], $[_{\text{Thing}}$ Z])])])])]

Perhaps *give* would be a reasonable translation for the word *schenken* and this type of "closest match" should be allowed to succeed. On the other hand, one might ask what should be done with the "leftover" pieces in such cases (*i.e.*, the unmatched tokens such as GIFTINGLY) and also how the generator decides what tokens are allowed to be left unmatched. One solution is to avoid the "closest match" approach by attempting to realize all unmatched tokens into some surface form. For example, we could realize the GIFTINGLY token as the surface form *as a gift* since *to give as a gift* is a reasonable translation for *schenken*. This is analogous to the process that would be required for certain conflational forms. For example, consider the following:

(141) **Conflational divergence:**
  E: John swam across the river
  F: John a traversé la rivière à la nage
  'John crossed the river by swimming'

The generation procedure would be required to produce the form *traverser à la nage* (literally, 'to cross by swimming') as the equivalent phrase for *swim across*. Here, the token SWIMMINGLY is realized as the surface form *à la nage* ('by swimming').[4] The matching scheme, as currently implemented, does not include such surface realizations. In order to achieve these types of realizations, we would need to superimpose a meta-level of lexical-semantics that would provide transformations between LCS's (*e.g.*, SWIMMINGLY $\Rightarrow$ BY SWIMMING, and GIFTINGLY $\Rightarrow$ AS GIFT). Because the current research has focused on providing a systematic translation mapping to resolve such divergences, it has steered clear of stipulating rules of this type. However, it is quite

---

[4]This example will be discussed again in the next chapter.

probable that such a mechanism would ultimately be necessary in order to provide a full solution to the problem.

A related question regarding lexical selection is whether the matcher should try to choose phrases that restate the source-language phrases more succinctly in the target language, and, conversely, whether the system should be allowed to restate the source-language phrases more verbosely in the target language. This comes up in cases such as the *stab* example. It turns out that there is an equally succinct way of saying *stab* in Spanish: *apuñalar*. Should this be preferred over the more verbose form *dar puñaladas*? In the reverse direction, the translation of *dar puñaladas* is the more succinct form *stab*. Should this preferred over something that is more verbose such as *inflict knife wounds*? Currently, the translator allows target-language forms to be either more succinct (*e.g.*, *dar puñaladas* ⇒ *stab*) or more verbose (*e.g.*, *stab* ⇒ *dar puñaladas*) as long as the target-language root words "cover" the CLCS (in the sense of (136) above). In all cases, if there is more than one way of matching a CLCS, multiple target-language forms will be generated (although we have only discussed one target-language form (*dar puñaladas*) in our *stab* example). As we have seen, this scheme does not always find an answer given that words such as *schenken* do not map exactly to a target-language term.

Until these issues have been resolved through further investigation, the system has been implemented so that it requires an exact match of the target-language root words to the underlying conceptual structure. Thus, while *schenken* will not match *give*, the exact match requirement does avoid certain other inappropriate cases. For example, if a partial matching were allowed, then the RLCS's in (133) and (134) above would match, and, depending on how the scheme were implemented, the LIKINGLY might be disregarded. Matching *like* to *be* or *vice versa*, however, would result in an unacceptable translation.

In the next subsection, we will see how the root words that are chosen by the lexical-selection procedure are structurally realized.

6.2 Syntactic Realization

Once an appropriate target-language RLCS is chosen as a match against a CLCS, the syntactic-realization procedure generates a syntactic phrase based on parametric information associated with the RLCS. This is accomplished by projecting the root word up to its maximal phrasal level and attaching its syntactically realized arguments according to the argument-positioning requirements of the RLCS.

A phrasal projection is initiated by calling the $\mathcal{CSR}$ function to map a RLCS type (*e.g.*, Thing) to a syntactic category (*e.g.*, N-MAX). This process is potentially overridden by the :CAT parameter described in chapter 5. Once this projection has been established, the *-marked arguments (complements, specifiers, and adjuncts) are recursively realized and are then positioned at the appropriate phrasal levels according to the $\mathcal{GLR}$. This process depends on the word order requirements of the target language (*e.g.*, head-initial *vs.* head-final) and is potentially overridden by lexical parameters associated with the root word (*i.e.*, :INT, :EXT, :PROMOTE, :DEMOTE, and :CONFLATED). The resulting phrase structure conforms to the same structural configurations assigned during parsing, namely those of figures 2.6 and 2.8. Thus, after the phrase structure is built, it is fully prepared to pass through the same constraints that are used during parsing, *i.e.*, those of the Government, Bounding, Case, Trace, Binding, and θ modules.

The next section describes how the lexical selection and syntactic realization procedures fit together in the overall generation scheme and illustrates the interaction of these procedures with the lexical parameters defined in chapter 5. The *I like to eat* example will be discussed in more detail.

6.3   Overall Generation Scheme

The main generation procedure is called **Generate_Phrase**. This procedure applies the lexical-selection and syntactic-realization operations recursively, starting at the root of the CLCS, and generates a structure by means of the steps shown in figure 6.2. Step 1 corresponds to the lexical selection operation and step 2 corresponds to the syntactic realization operation. Note that step 2 relies on the $\mathcal{CSR}$ for building a maximal projection (step 2.a) and on the $\mathcal{GLR}$ for positioning the head and satellites under the maximal projection (step 2.c). In addition, the procedure is called recursively (step 2.b) in order to build a phrase for

Generate_Phrase (CLCS-node)

1. Lexically select a word (the syntactic head) whose RLCS corresponds to the current CLCS-node by matching against entries in the target-language dictionary.

2. Syntactically realize a phrase by taking the following steps:

   2.a Project a maximal projection by calling the $\mathcal{CSR}$ on the selected RLCS.

   2.b Generate phrasal satellites by calling **Generate_Phrase** on each CLCS node that corresponds to a *-marked position in the selected RLCS.

   2.c Attach the syntactic head and phrasal satellites under the maximal projection in the positions specified by the $\mathcal{GLR}$.

3. Return the generated phrase.

Figure 6.2
Generation of a structure from a CLCS involves lexical selection (step 1) and syntactic realization (step 2). The procedure is called recursively to build a phrase for each of the *-marked children (if any) and the generated phrase is returned by step 3.

each of the *-marked children (if any) before the final syntactic phrase is constructed. Step 3 returns the generated phrase.

When **Generate_Phrase** is called initially, it is called with the top-level CLCS node and it produces a structure whose root is the clause symbol C-MAX. Each phrase under this node is recursively realized by the same routine. During this process, the generator must take into account the lexical parameters described in chapter 5. For example, the setting of the :CAT parameter is considered each time the $\mathcal{CSR}$ function is called to construct a maximal phrasal projection (*i.e.*, step 2.a of **Generate_Phrase**). If an argument has a :CAT override, this category is used instead of the default category supplied by the $\mathcal{CSR}$ function. In addition, the position of the * marker is considered each time an argument is realized as a syntactic satellite (*i.e.*, step 2.b of **Generate_Phrase**). For example, if an internal argument is to be realized, **Generate_Phrase** checks for the * marker before attempting to realize this argument. The rest of the lexical parameters, *i.e.*, :INT, :EXT, :PROMOTE, :DEMOTE, and :CONFLATED, are relevant to the step that attaches the head and satellites under the maximal projection

(*i.e.*, step 2.c of **Generate_Phrase**). The :INT and :EXT markers act
as overrides for the positioning of internal and external arguments by
the $\mathcal{GLR}$. The :PROMOTE and :DEMOTE markers act as overrides
for the positioning of heads, internal arguments, and adjuncts by the
$\mathcal{GLR}$. The :CONFLATED marker is used to suppress realization of the
arguments during realization by the $\mathcal{GLR}$.

We will now look at the generation of the Spanish and German surface
structures from the CLCS given in figure 6.1. Figure 6.3 illustrates the
entire translation process into Spanish.and German. This example will
demonstrate how the *, :INT, :EXT, and :DEMOTE markers are used
as overrides for the $\mathcal{CSR}$ and $\mathcal{GLR}$ during the generation of the surface
structure.[5] Note that all elements are generated in base position until
the constraints of the syntactic component have applied. Thus, the
output structures shown in figure 6.3 are the syntactic D-structures (*i.e.*,
the underlying syntactic representations for the corresponding surface
structures).

6.3.1   Generation of Spanish Surface Structure

Given the CLCS input shown in figure 6.3, the **Generate_Phrase** procedure must construct the appropriate syntactic structure for Spanish.
As described in section 6.1, the target-language root word *gustar* is chosen for the BE_{Circ} CLCS because its associated RLCS fully covers the
CLCS input. Once this word is selected, **Generate_Phrase** is called on
the CLCS to build a maximal phrasal projection and attach the syntactic satellites in their appropriate positions. In step 2.a, the $\mathcal{CSR}$ is used
to project the V-MAX phrase for the BE_{Circ} RLCS. This phrase is projected up to the C-MAX using the templates associated with the empty
functional elements parameter discussed in chapter 2. The internal and
external arguments must then be generated (by step 2.b) and attached
(by step 2.c). Because the :INT and :EXT markers are specified, the
$\mathcal{GLR}$ routine is overridden, and the logical subject corresponding to the
node $[_{\text{Thing}}$ I] is mapped into a syntactically internal position, while the
logical argument corresponding to the EAT node is mapped into a syntactically external position.

Since the * marker is associated with the AT_{Circ} node for the X

---

[5] We will not discuss the generation of the English surface structure for this example, since it involves a straightforward application of the $\mathcal{CSR}$ and $\mathcal{GLR}$ mappings
from the CLCS.

argument corresponding to the node [$_{\text{Thing}}$ I], the realization of this node as an internal argument involves a recursive call to the function **Generate_Phrase**.[6] The $\mathcal{CSR}$ function determines that this node is to be realized as a P-MAX, thus allowing the prepositional phrase *a mí* to be generated for the root word *gustar*.[7] This prepositional phrase is attached as an internal argument as dictated by the :INT parameter setting.[8]

Next, the function **Generate_Phrase** is called recursively to realize the EAT node. The RLCS for the word *eat* contains a ∗ marker which is associated with the logical subject position W. Normally this would entail lexical selection of a root word corresponding to the node [$_{\text{Thing}}$ I]. Note, however, that this constituent corresponds to the *LOWER-SUBJECT* marker in the lexical entry for *gustar*. This marker forces the syntactic realization procedure to produce an empty subject *i.e.*, PRO as the external argument. Thus, the syntactic phrase corresponding to the EAT node contains an empty PRO subject. This phrase is projected by the $\mathcal{CSR}$ as a C-MAX and is attached as an external argument due to the :EXT parameter setting.

The resulting structure corresponds to the sentence *comer me gusta a mí* (or *comer me gusta* if the clitic is not doubled):

(142) [$_{\text{C-MAX}}$ [$_\text{C}$ e] [$_{\text{I-MAX}}$ [$_{\text{C-MAX}}$ [$_{\text{I-MAX}}$ [$_{\text{N-MAX}}$ PRO$_i$] [$_\text{I}$ e] [$_{\text{V-MAX}}$ [$_\text{V}$ comer]]]] [$_\text{I}$ e] [$_{\text{V-MAX}}$ [$_\text{V}$ [$_{\text{CL-DAT}}$ me$_i$] [$_\text{V}$ gusta]] [$_{\text{P-MAX}}$ [$_\text{P}$ a] [$_{\text{N-MAX}}$ mí$_i$]]]]]]

Note that the inverted version *me gusta comer* has not yet been produced since the move-α procedure associated with the Bounding module has not yet been applied. In section 6.4 we will see how syntactic movement is achieved for this example.

---

[6]This is the first presentation of a case in which a logical argument appearing on the left is realized by the ∗ marker. (See fn 1 in chapter 5 for an earlier discussion relevant to this point.) The associated clitic is generated by means of an independent process that will be described in section 6.4.

[7]In addition to *mí*, a number of other first person singular pronouns are generated (*e.g.*, *yo* and *mi*); these are ruled out by Case constraints as described in section 6.4.4.

[8]The generation of the prepositional phrase is optional; this optionality is not specified explicitly, but is inherent in the setting of the clitic doubling parameter presented in chapter 2 (*i.e.*, languages that allow clitic doubling are not *forced*, but are *allowed*, to provide the doubled constituent). Thus, both forms of the sentence are generated, one with the doubled constituent, and one without the doubled constituent.

6.3.2   Generation of German Surface Structure

As in the case of Spanish, the procedure **Generate_Phrase** must determine the appropriate syntactic structure on the basis of the CLCS
input. In section 6.1, we saw that the target-language root word *gern*
was chosen for the BE$_{\text{Circ}}$ CLCS given that its associated RLCS fully
covers the CLCS input. Once this word is selected, **Generate_Phrase**
is called on the CLCS. Unlike the Spanish case, one of the ∗-marked
children under the BE$_{\text{Circ}}$ node (*i.e.*, the [$_{\text{Event}}$ Y] argument) is associated with a :DEMOTE marker. Thus, the $\mathcal{GLR}$ is not applied in the
normal fashion. Rather, the process of lexical selection is applied to
the CLCS node corresponding to the ∗-marked [$_{\text{Event}}$ Y] argument (*i.e.*,
EAT). Given that the RLCS associated with the word *essen* fully covers
the [$_{\text{Event}}$ EAT ...] portion of the CLCS, this is the word that is chosen
to be projected.[9]

Once the word *essen* is selected, the **Generate_Phrase** function is
called recursively on the EAT node. At this point the $\mathcal{GLR}$ is overridden
and the word *gern* is passed down as an adjunct associated with the
word *essen* rather than as the main verb. Inside of the recursive call,
Generate_Phrase uses the $\mathcal{CSR}$ (step 2.a) to project the EAT node
up to a V-MAX phrase. This phrase is then further projected up to C-
MAX using the templates associated with the empty functional elements
parameter discussed in chapter 2.

The internal and external arguments must then be generated (by step
2.b) and attached (by step 2.c). There are no (obligatory) internal arguments for *essen*, but there is an external argument (the [$_{\text{Thing}}$ I] node)
corresponding to the ∗-marked [$_{\text{Thing}}$ W] node in the RLCS of the word
essen. This argument is mapped into subject position according to the
$\mathcal{GLR}$. Note that if this were not a case of demotion, the subject would
be realized as PRO (as in the Spanish case) because this constituent
corresponds to a ∗LOWER-SUBJECT∗ marker in the lexical entry for
gern. However, because the word *gern* has been passed down as an adjunct, this realization is blocked, and the [$_{\text{Thing}}$ I] node is realized as the
word *Ich*. This constituent is then attached as the external argument of
essen.

---

[9]Another possible root word for EAT is *fressen*. However, this word requires an
agent that is an animal; thus, it is rejected during the matching process as soon as
it is determined that the agent is human.

At this point, the adverb *gern* that has been passed into the recursive invocation of **Generate_Phrase** is attached as an adjunct in the phrase containing *essen*. The resulting structure corresponds to the sentence *Ich gern esse*:

(143) [$_{C-MAX}$ [$_C$ e] [$_{I-MAX}$ [$_{N-MAX}$ Ich] [$_{V-MAX}$ [$_V$ [$_{ADV}$ gern] [$_V$ esse]]] [$_I$ e]]]

Here again, the generator has realized all constituents in base position. Thus, the verb-second version *Ich esse gern*, which is generated via movement of the verb into verb-second position (see figure 2.9), has not yet been produced. In section 6.4.3, we will see how the syntactic constraints enable this version to be generated.

6.4 Application of Syntactic Constraints

In figure 2.3, we saw that there are two operations applied by the syntactic component during parsing: structure building and constraint application. The generator has an analogous co-routine design in that it builds $\overline{X}$ structures (*e.g.*, the ones illustrated in figure 6.3) while also accessing a set of syntactic constraints based on GB theory. In the last section, we examined the structure-building portion of the generation task (*i.e.*, the lexical selection and syntactic realization operations as applied by the **Generate_Phrase** function). In this section we will examine the application of syntactic constraints of the GB module. In particular, we will discuss how the syntactic module incorporates functional elements (section 6.4.1), generates clitics (section 6.4.2), takes care of movement to surface positions (section 6.4.3), and applies case constraints (section 6.4.4). We will continue to discuss the example of figure 6.3 in order to show how the syntactic constraints are applied.

6.4.1 Generation of Functional Elements

The generation of purely grammatical functional elements (*i.e.*, lexical or non-lexical constituents that are not associated with a conceptual structure) is achieved by two means: (1) access to the empty functional elements parameter (see figures 2.11 and 2.12); and (2) access to backpointers from features to the root words that have been compiled into a table on a per-language basis. Figure 6.4 shows the values of this table for English, Spanish, and German.

Language	Position	Feature	Root Word
English	specifier	quantifier	THE, THIS, THAT, THESE, THOSE, A, SOME, ONE, NO, MUCH, MANY, A_LOT, SEVERAL, AN-OTHER, OTHER, EACH, ALL, EVERY, WHICH, HOW_MANY, HOW_MUCH, WHAT, ONE, TWO, THREE
	head	comp	THAT, FOR
		inf	TO
		tense	WILL
		mood	WOULD
		aspect	CAN, SHOULD, MUST, BE, HAVE, DO
Spanish	specifier	quantifier	EL, LOS, LA, EST, ES, UN, ALGUN, NINGUN, MUCH, VARI, OTR, CADA, TOD, CUÁL, CUÁNT, QUÉ, UNO, UN, DOS, TRES
	head	comp	QUE
		inf	A
		aspect	PODER, DEBER, ESTAR, HABER, SER
German	specifier	quantifier	D, EIN, KEIN, VIEL, VER-SCHIEDEN, ANDER, JED, ALL, WELCH, WIEVIEL, EIN, ZWEI, DREI
	head	comp	DAß
		inf	ZU
		tense	WERDEN
		mood	WERDEN
		aspect	KÖNNEN, SEIN, HABEN

Figure 6.4
The functional root words for English, Spanish, and German are compiled into a table. These words are purely grammatical and, thus, are not associated with a conceptual structure.

This table is compiled automatically as words are defined in the lexicon. Note that the table dictates the position in which the functional element is to be generated. For example, quantifiers such as *the, many,* and *three* are generated in specifier position, whereas complementizers and verbal elements such as *for, that,* and *be* are generated in head position. Only the root forms are included in this table. For example, the words *mucho, mucha, muchos,* and *muchas* are all morphological derivatives of the same root form MUCH that appears in the table.

The way the generator inserts functional elements is by mapping from unrealized features (*e.g.*, aspect, tense, *etc.*) to a syntactic token (using this table), and dropping an empty element *e* into any functional heads that are left over. Thus, after **Generate_Phrase** has produced a phrase, any associated functional elements are filled in before the final phrase is returned.

In general, the functional elements fall into three classes: (1) determiners (*e.g.*, the, this, *etc.*); (2) verbal elements (*e.g.*, would, have, be, *etc.*), and complementizer and infinitive markers (*e.g.*, that, for, to, *etc.*). We will examine how each of these three cases are handled during the generation half of the translation process.

Consider the following sentence:

(144) I know that John would have been eating the cake.

This sentence contains all three types of (lexical) functional elements: (1) the determiner *the*; (2) the verbal elements *would, have,* and *been*; and (3) the complementizer *that*. In addition, the sentence contains (non-lexical) functional elements I and C in the matrix clause. The CLCS for this sentence is shown in figure 6.5. Note that this CLCS is annotated with certain features that have been carried over from syntactic and morphological processing (*e.g.*, [past], which refers to past tense, and [exists], which refers to a quantifier that corresponds to an article such as *the* in English).[10] Up until now, we have not been showing the existence of such features in the interlingua; they are shown here for illustrational purposes.

In order to generate (144) from this CLCS, the syntactic realization portion of the **Generate_Phrase** procedure calls a subroutine (just prior to step 2) to find functional elements associated with the unrealized

---

[10]Refer to figure 3.8 for a list of additional features used by the system.

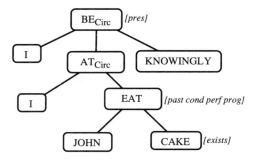

Figure 6.5
The CLCS for *I know that John would have been eating the cake* indicates that certain functional elements correspond to features, not conceptual tokens.

features. For example, when the generator attempts to syntactically realize the concept CAKE, it determines that the features [exists] cannot be realized as a part of the word *cake*. Thus, it must call the subroutine to find a functional element associated with this feature. Using the table of figure 6.4, this routine finds that the token THE matches the feature [exists].[11] Once the functional element is chosen, it is generated in specifier position of the N-MAX: [$_{\text{N-MAX}}$ [$_{\text{DET}}$ the] cake].

Next, when the syntactic realization portion of the **Generate_Phrase** procedure attempts to realize EAT, it determines that the features [cond, perf, prog, past] cannot all be realized as part of the word *eat*. Thus, it must call the subroutine that realizes functional elements in order to find functional elements associated with these features. Then it must execute a constraint propagation routine (based on selectional features) to determine the order in which these elements must occur. Using the table of figure 6.4, it finds that the root words WOULD, HAVE, and BE match the features [cond], [perf], and [prog], respectively. Then it determines that WOULD must occur first (since an I selects a V-MAX as a complement), HAVE and BE must occur next (since HAVE selects

---

[11] As we can see from figure 6.4, there are other tokens that match the feature [exists] (*i.e.*, THOSE, THESE, THAT, and THIS). Currently, there is no way to distinguish among these given that context is not part of the model. It might be possible to use additional features (such as ±deictic and ±far) to provide a finer grain of distinction for these quantifiers, but for now, the system attempts to generate all of these. (The plural forms get rejected later during the feature-matching process described in chapter 3.)

1. An empty complementizer must be licensed by a governing verb.
2. If a complementizer is not empty, the lexical complementizer is selected by the governing verb, or it is filled in by move-α.
3. Verb-second languages (*e.g.*, German) do not allow empty complementizers.
4. Non-verb-second languages (*e.g.*, English and Spanish) require that the matrix clause complementizer be empty.

Figure 6.6
Stowell (1981) proposes licensing conditions on the complementizer position.

a perfective form, and BE selects a progressive form), and EAT(ing) is the final element.[12] The tense ([past]) is then percolated up to the highest syntactic constituent. Once the functional elements have been chosen and constraint propagation has applied, the **Generate_Phrase** procedure resumes execution, and the embedded clause is generated:

(145) [c-MAX [I-MAX [N-MAX John]
            [I would]
            [V-MAX [V have]
             [V-MAX [V been]
              [V-MAX [V eating] [N-MAX [DET the] cake]]]]]]

(Note that all functional elements have been generated in head position as dictated by the table.)

Now that we have seen how determiners and verbal elements are generated as functional elements, we will look at the third case of functional element generation: complementizers. Complementizers are different from other functional heads in that they are subject to certain licensing conditions. Roughly, these conditions are as shown in figure 6.6.[13]

---

[12]Ordering the constituents on the basis of constraint propagation does not always work if only features are used. For example, the sequence *would be having eaten* could also be generated since the order of the constituents satisfies constraint propagation with respect to the features. Currently, the way this is handled is that the system requires *have* to occur before *be* in English. This is not an unreasonable requirement given that it has been argued that *have* is actually in specifier position (of the V-MAX), and *be* is in minimal adjunct position (*e.g.*, see Sharp (1985), for a modified version of the $\overline{\text{X}}$-Theory from Chomsky (1986b) in which this structural representation is used for English).

[13]I am indebted to Noam Chomsky (personal communication) for providing me with a rough statement of the licensing conditions on complementizers based on work by Stowell (1981)).

Given these constraints, it is determined that the complementizer THAT (from figure 6.4) is allowed in the embedded clause position since *know* selects it (condition 2 of figure 6.6), or it may be omitted since *know* also licenses an empty complementizer (condition 1 of figure 6.6):

(146) (i)   I know [c-MAX that John would have been eating the cake]

       (ii)   I know [c-MAX e John would have been eating the cake]

Note that if we were to generate the analogous Spanish sentence, the complementizer of the embedded clause could not be left empty since verbs do not license empty complementizers in Spanish:

(147) (i)   Yo sé [c-MAX que Juan habría estado comiendo el pastel][14]

       (ii)   * Yo sé [c-MAX e Juan habría estado comiendo el pastel]

The same is true in German:

(148) (i)   Ich weiß, [c-MAX daß Johann den Kuchen gegessen hätte][15]

       (ii)   * Ich weiß, [c-MAX e Johann den Kuchen gegessen hätte]

Now that we have discussed the generation of lexical functional elements, we will briefly look at the generation of non-lexical functional elements, in particular that of the matrix-clause complementizer position. Again, we appeal to the conditions of figure 6.6, and it is determined (by condition 3) that this position must be empty for English and Spanish:

(149) (i)   [c-MAX e I know
              [c-MAX that John would have been eating cake]]

       (ii)   * [c-MAX that I know
              [c-MAX that John would have been eating cake]]

---

[14]Note that the Spanish conditional mood and perfective aspect are merged into a single verb (*haber*) since there is no separate conditional constituent that corresponds to the word *would*.

[15]As in the case of Spanish, German merges the conditional mood and perfective aspect into a single verb (*haben*). However, as in the case of English, it is also possible to break these two components apart into the two constituents: *Ich weiß, daß Johann den Kuchen gegessen haben würde*. Currently, this second sentence is the one that is generated by the system since the details of the past subjunctive (hätte) have not yet been implemented. Note that there is no progressive verb in the German sentences; thus, the system does not attempt to generate a corresponding functional element in German. The progressive form can be expressed by means of a construction such as *dabei wäre*, which means *would be in the process of*: *Ich weiß, daß Johann dabei wäre, den Kuchen zu essen*. However, the system is currently unable to generate such a construction.

(150) (i)   [$_{\text{C-MAX}}$ e Yo sé
              [$_{\text{C-MAX}}$ que Juan habría estado comiendo el pastel]]

    (ii) * [$_{\text{C-MAX}}$ que yo sé
              [$_{\text{C-MAX}}$ que Juan habría estado comiendo el pastel]]

In the case of German, the matrix complementizer cannot be left empty (condition 4), but there is no governing verb to select a complementizer. Thus, the position must be filled by move-α (condition 2):[16]

(151) (i)   [$_{\text{C-MAX}}$ [$_{\text{N-MAX}}$ Ich]$_i$ [$_{\text{C}}$ weiß]$_j$, [$_{\text{N-MAX}}$ t]$_i$
              [$_{\text{C-MAX}}$ daß Johann den Kuchen gegessen hätte] [$_{\text{V}}$ t]$_j$]

    (ii) * [$_{\text{C-MAX}}$ e Ich
              [$_{\text{C-MAX}}$ daß Johann den Kuchen gegessen hätte] weiß]

We will see how this movement into complementizer position is accomplished in section 6.4.3.

In addition to the matrix complementizer, a functional element must also be generated as the head of I. Because the BE$_{\text{Circ}}$ node has no features (other than [past]), it is not necessary to find a lexical element to fill this position. Thus, an empty element is inserted into the head of I in the matrix clause for all three languages.

This completes the discussion of the generation of lexical and non-lexical functional elements. The final result of the **Generate_Phrase** procedure for the three languages is shown in figure 6.7. As mentioned before, there is no separate word for the conditional mood in Spanish and German, whereas English uses the word *would*. Thus, an empty functional element is generated in the head of I of the embedded clause for the Spanish and German syntactic structures.

Returning to our two examples of figure 6.3, we note that the only functional elements that are required in both cases are the empty heads [$_{\text{C}}$ e] and [$_{\text{I}}$ e] as shown in (142) and (143). The reason these elements are inserted is that there are no leftover features associated with either the BE$_{\text{Circ}}$ node or the EAT node in the CLCS. In other words, any features that are associated with the CLCS of figure 6.3 are either morphologically realized on the surface (*e.g.*, the present tense for the verbs *esse* and *gusta*) or conceptually covered by the root words that make up the surface sentence.

---

[16]Also, the subject of the sentence is required to move up in order to maintain the verb-second ordering.

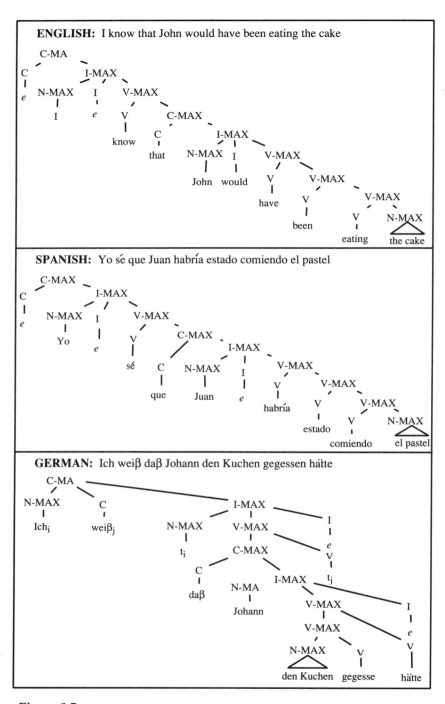

Figure 6.7
The English, Spanish, and German syntactic structures for *I know that John would have been eating* reveal different realizations of functional elements.

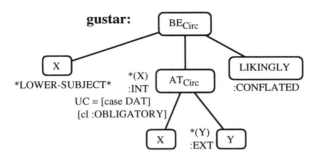

Figure 6.8
The entry for *gustar* spells out certain clitic requirements that are precompiled into
structural templates that are later used by the generator.

6.4.2   Generation of Clitics

In this section we will discuss the generation of the clitic pronoun. In
our example of figure 6.3, the clitic *me* must be generated as the object of *gustar*. This is achieved by means of access to the lexical entry
for *gustar*, which spells out certain clitic requirements. Previously, this
portion of the lexical entry was omitted; we include it here in figure 6.8
for illustrational purposes. The UC specification refers to *unconditional*
features that apply to a particular RLCS position.[17] In the case of *gustar*, this specification indicates that the X node is obligatorily associated
with a dative clitic.

As part of the process that compiles out the lexical expansion tem-

---

[17]The specification of *conditional* features is also allowed; these are specified by
the CND marker. For example, the entry for the Spanish verb *ver* (to see) associates
conditional features with the different levels of realization for the object being seen:

$$[_\text{Event} \text{ BE}_\text{Perc}$$
$$([_\text{Thing} \text{ X}],$$
$$[_\text{Path} \text{ IN}_\text{Perc}$$
$$([_\text{Position} *(\text{X}) \text{ CND} = [+\text{animate}] \text{ AT}_\text{Perc}$$
$$([_\text{Thing} \text{ X}], [_\text{Thing} *(\text{X}) \text{ CND} = [-\text{animate}] \text{ Y}])])]$$
$$[_\text{Manner} \text{ SEEINGLY}])]$$

Here, the object X has a * marker associated with AT_Perc on the condition that X
is animate; otherwise, the * marker is associated directly with X. This corresponds
to the distinction between *yo vi a Guille* and *yo vi el libro*. In the first case, the
object *Guille* is animate; thus, it must be realized as the object of the preposition
a (which matches AT_Perc). In the second case, the object *el libro* is inanimate, and
the preposition is not used.

plates described in chapter 4, the [cl :OBLIGATORY] specification forces
the precompiler to include additional information for this word:

	Compiled Argument Information: "gustar"			
	Variable	*Position*	*∗ Marker*	*Restrictions*
(152)	Y	subject	Y	
	X	object	$[_{\text{Position}} \text{AT}_{\text{Circ}} \ldots]$	
	X	clitic	$[_{\text{Position}} \text{AT}_{\text{Circ}} \ldots]$	:OBLIGATORY

This table relates each variable to a syntactic position, a ∗-marked position in the RLCS, and restrictions (if any). Each RLCS is associated
with a precompiled table that is accessed when the syntactic realization
operation is applied.

Note that the :OBLIGATORY marker is associated with the clitic
specification; this marker is generated from the [cl :OBLIGATORY]
specification in the lexical definition.[18] When the arguments of *gustar*
are realized (by the **Generate_Phrase** routine), this compiled information is taken into consideration. Thus, when the $[_{\text{Thing}} \text{I}]$ node of the
CLCS is matched with the X position of the *gustar* definition, this token
is obligatorily realized as the dative clitic *me*.[19]

This clitic generation process accounts for more complicated syntactic
phenomena such as the double-object construction of the word *dar*. For
example, there are a number of ways to generate a syntactic structure
for *Mary gave you the book* (see the CLCS in figure 6.9):

(153) (i)   María te lo dio

(ii)   María te lo dio a tí

(iii)   María te dio el libro

(iv)   María te dio el libro a tí

Sentences (153)(i)–(iv) are valid realizations for this concept, but (153)(i)
and (ii) contain "too little" information: BOOK is realized as the more
general constituent *lo*; thus, only (153)(iii) and (iv) will be generated.

---

[18]The [cl :OPTIONAL] specification is used, for example, for the English dative
alternation. Recall from chapter 2 that the dativized object is treated as a clitic. Any
verbal object that is potentially dativized will be associated with the [cl :OPTIONAL]
specification; the :OPTIONAL marker allows the object to be generated as a non-
clitic (*e.g.*, the object *him* in *I gave the book to him*) or as a clitic (*e.g.*, the object
him in *I gave him the book*).

[19]Note that X also associated with the AT_{Circ} node, thus allowing the prepositional
phrase *a mí* to be optionally generated.

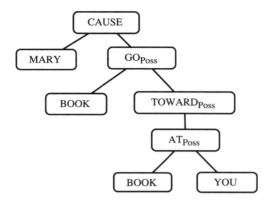

Figure 6.9
The CLCS for *Mary gave you the book* provides the basis for a number of different syntactic structures.

The generation process also produces two invalid structures:

(154) (i)   * María te lo dio el libro

　　　(ii)　* María te lo dio el libro a tí

In a sense, these structures have "too much" information: BOOK is realized both as the noun phrase *el libro* and as the more general constituent *lo*. These structures will be ruled out later by the Case module as we will see in section 6.4.4.

We will see how the clitic is generated again later when we return to the *stab* example.

6.4.3   Movement During Generation

Recall that the **Generate_Phrase** procedure generates elements in base position. In this section, we will look at how elements are moved into their surface structure positions.

The Move-α procedure of the syntactic component has the task of moving elements into their surface structure positions on an if-needed basis (see discussion in chapter 2). One case in which this occurs is when an element is moved from an uncase-marked position into a case-marked position (as in the example shown in figure 2.15, *John seems to like Mary*).

1. Interrogative sentences (in English, Spanish, and German) require that the "highest" verb be moved into the head of C-MAX.
2. *Wh*-sentences (in English, Spanish, and German) require that the *wh*-word move into the specifier of the matrix-clause C-MAX.
3. Free inversion (in Spanish) requires that the subject be moved into an adjunct position.[20]
4. Non-interrogative matrix clauses (in German) require that the subject move to the specifier of C-MAX.

Figure 6.10
An element is forced to move into a different surface structure position under a number of conditions.

There are a number of other conditions under which an element is forced into a different surface structure position (based on work by Stowell (1981), Torrego (1984), and others). These are shown in figure 6.10.

Conditions 1 and 2 of figure 6.10 allow the sentences of (155) and (156) to be generated respectively:

(155) (i) $[_V$ Does$]_i$ John t_i like to eat?

    (ii) $[_V$ Le gusta$]_i$ Juan t_i comer?

    (iii) $[_V$ Ißt$]_i$ Johann gern t_i?

(156) (i) $[_{N\text{-}MAX}$ What$]_i$ does John like to eat t_i?

    (ii) $[_{N\text{-}MAX}$ Qué$]_i$ le gusta Juan comer t_i?

    (iii) $[_{N\text{-}MAX}$ Was$]_i$ ißt Johann t_i gern?

Returning to our example of figure 6.3, condition 3 allows the free-inversion form of the Spanish sentence (142) to be generated:

(157) (i)   Me gusta comer

    (ii) $[_{C\text{-}MAX}$ $[_C$ $e]$
            $[_{I\text{-}MAX}$ $[_{C\text{-}MAX}$ $t]_i$ $[_I$ $e]$
                $[_{V\text{-}MAX}$ $[_{V\text{-}MAX}$ $[_V$ $[_{CL\text{-}DAT}$ me$_i]$ $[_V$ gusta$]]]$
                  $[_{C\text{-}MAX}$ $[_{I\text{-}MAX}$ $[_{N\text{-}MAX}$ PRO$]$ $[_I$ $e]$
                    $[_{V\text{-}MAX}$ $[_V$ comer$]]]]]]]]$

---

[20] Free inversion is tightly intertwined with the null subject parameter in that it can only occur if there is a *pro* constituent that is coindexed with the inverted subject (*e.g.*, *pro$_i$ me gusta el hombre$_i$*). This is the only movement case in which a *pro* is left behind rather than a trace. This type of construction is analogous to that of *there* sentences in English (*e.g.*, *there$_i$ is a man$_i$ in the room*). Although the generation of *there* sentences is currently not implemented it is expected that the same mechanism that is used for free inversion would be used in this case as well.

Similarly, condition 4 allows the verb-second form of the German sentence (143) to be generated:

(158) (i)   Ich esse gern

       (ii) $[_{\text{C-MAX}}\ [_{\text{N-MAX}}\ \text{Ich}]_i\ [_{\text{C}}\ [_{\text{V}}\ \text{esse}]_j]$
              $[_{\text{I-MAX}}\ [_{\text{N-MAX}}\ \text{t}]_i\ [_{\text{V-MAX}}\ [_{\text{V}}\ [_{\text{ADV}}\ \text{gern}]\ [_{\text{V}}\ \text{t}]_j]]\ [_{\text{I}}\ e]]]$

6.4.4   Case Constraints During Generation

The Case module is very important in the context of generation. In particular, the Case module refines the choices made during lexical selection, and it aids in providing the appropriate argument structure and order during syntactic realization of a phrase.

The lexical selection procedure potentially provides a number of surface forms for a given CLCS token. The Case module provides a filter in certain cases of noun-phrase realization. For example, in the translation shown in figure 6.3, the lexical selection routine picks a number of first-person pronominals as the realization of the $[_{\text{Thing}}\ \text{I}]$ node. During the generation of the Spanish sentence, the pronouns chosen for the $[_{\text{Thing}}\ \text{I}]$ CLCS are *mí*, *yo*, and *mi*, all of which have the features [p1, sg]; however, the Case Filter rules out *yo* (since it has inherent nominative case) and *mi* (since it has inherent possessive case). The pronoun *mí* is the only one that passes the Case Filter since its inherent objective case matches the case assigned by the verb *gustar*.

Similarly, during the generation of the German sentence, the pronouns *mich*, *ich*, and *mir* are chosen as possible subjects of the sentence since they all have the features [p1, sg]. However, only *ich* passes the Case Filter test since its inherent nominative case matches the case assigned by the +*tns* feature associated with the verb *essen*.

The Case module is also important for ruling out illegal clitic-NP combinations. Recall the two invalid structures produced by the generator, (154)(i) and (ii), repeated here as (159)(i) and (ii):

(159) (i)   * María te lo dio el libro

       (ii)   * María te lo dio el libro a tí

As mentioned earlier, these structures have "too much" information: both the noun phrase *el libro* and the more general constituent *lo* are included in the sentence. According to Jaeggli (1981), such sentences are not allowed because of a Case Filter violation. In both of these

sentences, the accusative clitic *lo* absorbs s-government (see section 2.4),
and *el libro* remains ungoverned. Thus, *el libro* does not receive case and
the sentence is ruled out.

Assignment of case is also crucial for determining the appropriate
order of arguments for a given phrase. Throughout our discussion of the
syntactic realization process, we never mentioned the issue of argument
ordering. According to the specification of the $\mathcal{GLR}$ given in (102) of
chapter 4, the arguments are realized in exactly the order that they
occur in the LCS. However, this is not entirely accurate. In fact, the
arguments are left unordered during syntactic realization, and the Case
module provides the appropriate argument ordering after this structure
has been generated. In our example of figure 6.3, the effects of the Case
module are not obvious because *like* only takes one argument in Spanish
(the object of *gustar*), and *eat* is intransitive in German. However, for
double-object verbs such as *give*, the Case module is crucial for providing
the appropriate order. For example, the sentence *I gave to him the
book* is ruled out since the order of the two noun phrases impedes case
assignment to the noun phrase *the book*. On the other hand, the sentence
I gave the book to him is acceptable since *the book* receives case from
give, and *him* receives case from *to*.[21]

This completes the discussion of syntactic constraint application as it
applies to generation. After all the syntactic constraints have applied,
the target-language sentence is produced by reading off the terminal
positions in the syntactic structure: *Me gusta comer (a mí)* (in Spanish)
and *Ich esse gern* (in German).

6.5   Generation Process for Stab-Dar Example

Now that we have looked at how the entire generation process operates,
we will see how it applies to our *stab* translation example repeated here
as (160):

(160) **Conflational divergence:**
   E: I stabbed John
   S: Yo le di puñaladas a Juan
      'I gave knife-wounds to John'

---

[21]See section 2 for a discussion of the dative alternation *I gave him the book*, which
is also a potential surface realization.

We have already discussed the generation of this example to a certain degree in chapter 5. In this section, we will look at the processes of lexical selection and syntactic realization in more detail, and we will see how these operations, coupled with the lexical parameters described in chapter 5, resolve three lexical-semantic divergences: lexical divergence (*i.e.*, the translation of *stab* as the word *dar*); structural divergence (*i.e.*, the translation of the noun phrase *John* as the prepositional phrase *a Juan*); and conflational divergence (*i.e.*, the realization of the conflated effect *knife-wound* as *puñaladas*).

6.5.1   Lexical Selection for Stab-Dar

The English and Spanish RLCS definitions for the *stab* from chapter 5 are repeated here in figure 6.11 (with the modification relevant to the generation of the dative clitic for the variable Z). We will discuss the generation of the Spanish sentence *Yo le di puñaladas a Juan* for this example.

Recall that the lexical selection operation of the **Generate_Phrase** procedure (*i.e.*, step 1) selects a root word whose RLCS fully covers the CLCS. The way this is done is by recursively matching against the RLCS representations from a target-language possibility set. Figure 6.12 illustrates a simplified version of this selection process for a small range of target-language possibilities. The outer ring shows the set of Spanish root words corresponding to the top-level CAUSE node in the CLCS. Of these root word possibilities, a smaller set matches the GO$_{\text{Poss}}$ node at the next level as shown by the middle ring. Note, for example, that the root word *forzar* (the literal translation of *force*) is eliminated as a possibility at this level because its associated LCS does not contain GO$_{\text{Poss}}$. Finally, at the next level (*i.e.*, the TOWARD$_{\text{Poss}}$ level shown in the innermost ring), only the root word *dar* matches.[22] Thus, this root is selected to be the word that will be projected, and the lexical divergence mentioned earlier has been resolved.

Note that lexical selection of this root word involves only three iterations of the matcher in a search space that is reasonably small. Although the compositional nature of the LCS allows for a large set of words to

---

[22]As noted in chapters 2 and 5, there is more than one way to realize the *stab* concept in Spanish. Because a "closest match" scheme is not employed, all possibilities are returned. In the description presented here, we will only talk about one of these possibilities (*i.e.*, *dar*). (Chapter 8 shows other possibilities generated for this sentence.)

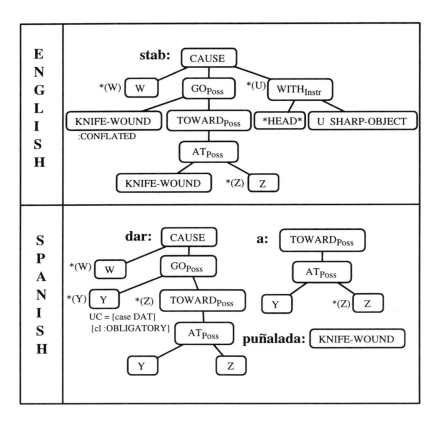

Figure 6.11
The English and Spanish lexical entries for the *stab* event illustrate three divergence types: lexical, structural, and conflational. Note that an extra specification has been provided to allow a dative clitic to be generated for the variable Z.

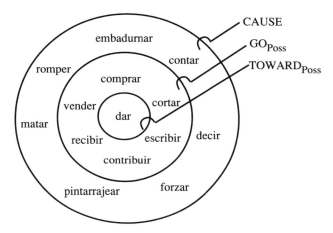

Figure 6.12
The process of lexical selection of the Spanish verb corresponding to *stab*
demonstrates that the target-language possibilities are quickly pared down to a
single verb *dar*.

be defined, the number of primitives to search through at each non-
terminal level during the matching process is bounded by the number
of non-open-ended primitives in the system (currently 33).[23]   This is
because open-ended primitives (*i.e.*, those primitives of type Manner,
Thing, Location, Time, Property, or Purpose) occur only at terminal
nodes; all others (*e.g.*, Events, States, Paths, Positions, and Intensifiers) occur at non-terminal nodes. Thus, the only cause for concern
with respect to the size of the search space is the number of open-ended
primitives. Because these occur only at one level (*i.e.*, the leaf nodes),
the system will take, at most, the same amount of time to search for a
RLCS as it takes to search through all open-ended primitives of a given
type for each word in the sentence. This happens in the worst case,
where all output words are selected from an open-ended class such as
Thing and Property;[24] we know that this doesn't happen in practice
since there is almost always at least one closed-class predicate (*i.e.*, an

---

[23]In general, the maximum number of RLCS levels per word is 4. Thus, the more
precise upper bound on the number of non-open-ended primitives in the search space
for a given word is $4 \times 33 = 132$.

[24]The situation becomes considerably more difficult in cases where some (or all)
of these words are lexically ambiguous.

Event or State) and usually at least one closed-class particle (*i.e.*, a Path
or Place) for each syntactic clause that is generated.

Once the word *dar* is selected in the current example, its associated
argument table is accessed. Given that the lexical entry for *dar* has an
obligatory clitic, the RLCS has an associated argument table analogous
to that of *gustar* given previously in (152). This table looks like the
following:

(161)

Compiled Argument Information: "dar"			
Variable	*Position*	** Marker*	*Restrictions*
W	subject	W	
Y	object	Y	
Z	object	[Path TOWARD_Poss ...]	
Z	clitic	[Position TOWARD_Poss ...]	:OBLIGATORY

In the next section, we will see how this table is used during the syntactic
realization process that produces the target-language structure. This
process will resolve the other two divergence types, conflational and
structural.

6.5.2   Syntactic Realization for Stab-Dar

The general intuition for generating the Spanish syntactic structure for
example (160) was given at the end of chapter 5. In this section, we will
examine this process more closely by walking through the application of
the **Generate_Phrase** function on the CLCS in the current example.
A trace of the entire process is given in figure 6.14. Note that the
sequence of steps taken here are similar in nature to those of figure 4.25;
the **Generate_Phrase** function can be viewed as the reverse processor
of the **Compose_LCS** function. For illustrative purposes, the figure
that shows the generation process is repeated here as figure 6.13 (with a
modification relevant to the generation of the dative clitic for the variable
Z).

The way the syntactic realization process operates for this example
is as follows. The **Generate_Phrase** function is called on the CLCS
and selects a RLCS associated with the word *dar* (step 1) as described
in the last section. This word is projected to the V-MAX level by the
$\mathcal{CSR}$ (step 2.a). Note that this verb is realized as an infinitive and
will later be morphologically synthesized as a past tense verb. The
Generate_Phrase is then entered recursively three times (step 2.b) in

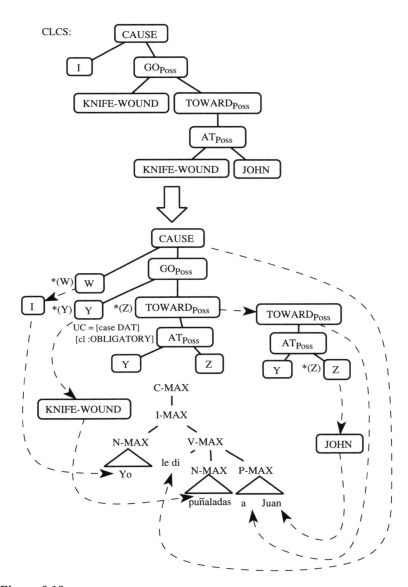

Figure 6.13
The syntactic realization of the Spanish sentence *Yo le di puñaladas a Juan*
involves recursive decomposition of the CLCS into a main verb (*dar*), three
satellites (*Yo, puñaladas,* and *Juan*), and one clitic (*le*).

1. Entering **Generate_Phrase**:
   [$_{\text{Event}}$ CAUSE ([$_{\text{Thing}}$ I],
      [$_{\text{Event}}$ GO$_{\text{Poss}}$ ([$_{\text{Thing}}$ KNIFE-WOUND],
       [$_{\text{Path}}$ TOWARD$_{\text{Poss}}$
        ([$_{\text{Position}}$ AT$_{\text{Poss}}$ ([$_{\text{Thing}}$ KNIFE-WOUND], [$_{\text{Thing}}$ JOHN])])])])]
   RLCS = [$_{\text{Event}}$ CAUSE ([$_{\text{Thing}}$ * W],
      [$_{\text{Event}}$ GO$_{\text{Poss}}$ ([$_{\text{Thing}}$ * Y],
       [$_{\text{Path}}$ * TOWARD$_{\text{Poss}}$
        ([$_{\text{Position}}$ AT$_{\text{Poss}}$ ([$_{\text{Thing}}$ Y], [$_{\text{Thing}}$ Z])])])])] (dar)
   Maximal Projection = $\mathcal{CSR}$(RLCS) → [$_{\text{V-MAX}}$ ... dar ...]

   2. Entering **Generate_Phrase**: [$_{\text{Thing}}$ I]
      RLCS = [$_{\text{Thing}}$ I] (yo, mi, mí)
      Maximal Projection = $\mathcal{CSR}$(RLCS) → [$_{\text{N-MAX}}$ ... {yo, mi, mí} ...]
      Projected Phrase = [$_{\text{N-MAX}}$ {yo, mi, mí}]

   2. Exiting **Generate_Phrase**: [$_{\text{N-MAX}}$ {yo, mi, mí}]

   3. Entering **Generate_Phrase**: [$_{\text{Thing}}$ KNIFE-WOUND]
      RLCS = [$_{\text{Thing}}$ KNIFE-WOUND] (puñalad)
      Maximal Projection = [$_{\text{N-MAX}}$ ... puñalad ...]
      Projected Phrase = [$_{\text{N-MAX}}$ puñalad]

   3. Exiting **Generate_Phrase**: [$_{\text{N-MAX}}$ puñalad]

   4. Entering **Generate_Phrase**:
      [$_{\text{Path}}$ TOWARD$_{\text{Poss}}$
        ([$_{\text{Position}}$ AT$_{\text{Poss}}$ ([$_{\text{Thing}}$ KNIFE-WOUND], [$_{\text{Thing}}$ JOHN])])]
      RLCS = [$_{\text{Path}}$ TOWARD$_{\text{Poss}}$
        ([$_{\text{Position}}$ AT$_{\text{Poss}}$ ([$_{\text{Thing}}$ Y], [$_{\text{Thing}}$ * Z])])] (a)
      Clitic Required: [$_{\text{V-MAX}}$ ... le$_i$ dar ...]
      Maximal Projection = $\mathcal{CSR}$(RLCS) → [$_{\text{P-MAX}}$ ... a ...]

      5. Entering **Generate_Phrase**: [$_{\text{Thing}}$ JOHN]
         RLCS = [$_{\text{Thing}}$ JOHN] (John)
         Maximal Projection = [$_{\text{N-MAX}}$ ... Juan$_i$ ...]
         Projected Phrase = [$_{\text{N-MAX}}$ Juan$_i$]

      5. Entering **Generate_Phrase**: [$_{\text{N-MAX}}$ Juan$_i$]

      Projected Phrase = [$_{\text{P-MAX}}$ a [$_{\text{N-MAX}}$ Juan$_i$]]

   4. Exiting **Generate_Phrase**: [$_{\text{P-MAX}}$ a [$_{\text{N-MAX}}$ Juan$_i$]]

   Projected Phrase = [$_{\text{C-MAX}}$ [$_{\text{I-MAX}}$ [$_{\text{N-MAX}}$ {yo, mi, mí}]
       [$_{\text{V-MAX}}$ le$_i$ dar [$_{\text{N-MAX}}$ puñalad]
        [$_{\text{P-MAX}}$ a [$_{\text{N-MAX}}$ Juan$_i$]]]]]]

1. Exiting **Generate_Phrase**: [$_{\text{C-MAX}}$ [$_{\text{I-MAX}}$ [$_{\text{N-MAX}}$ {yo, mi, mí}]
       [$_{\text{V-MAX}}$ le$_i$ dar [$_{\text{N-MAX}}$ puñalad]
        [$_{\text{P-MAX}}$ a [$_{\text{N-MAX}}$ Juan$_i$]]]]]]

Case Constraints:
Yo le dar puñalad a Juan

Morphological Synthesis:
Yo le di puñaladas a Juan
Yo le di una puñalada a Juan
Yo le daba puñaladas a Juan
Yo le daba una puñalada a Juan

Figure 6.14
The generation process for the Spanish sentence *Yo le di puñaladas a Juan* consists of six entries to the **Generate_Phrase** procedure. Case constraints are then applied, and the sentence is morphologically synthesized. Four possibilities are ultimately returned.

order to syntactically realize the three ∗-marked satellites corresponding to [$_{\text{Thing}}$ I], [$_{\text{Thing}}$ KNIFE-WOUND], and [$_{\text{Path}}$ TOWARD$_{\text{Poss}}$ ...].

On the first recursive call (second invocation of **Generate_Phrase**), three target-language possibilities (*yo*, *mi*, and *mí*) are selected (step 1) since the concept [$_{\text{Thing}}$ I] is associated with the features [p1 sg]. (Note that the case features are not included in the CLCS since these are structurally determined during the generation process.) All three of these are projected up to the N-MAX level by the $\mathcal{CSR}$ (step 2.a); ultimately, only one of these will be selected after the Case constraints of the syntactic component are applied. Since there are no satellites associated with [$_{\text{Thing}}$ I], the projected phrase is then returned (step 3). Note that all three target-language possibilities are carried along throughout the entire process.

On the second recursive call (third invocation of **Generate_Phrase**), only one possibility (*puñalad*) is selected for the concept [$_{\text{Thing}}$ KNIFE-WOUND] (step 1). Note that this word is left in its root form until the full structure is generated, after which the process of morphological synthesis derives the forms *puñalada* and *puñaladas*. The $\mathcal{CSR}$ is then applied (step 2.a) to project this constituent up to the N-MAX level. Since there are no satellites associated with [$_{\text{Thing}}$ KNIFE-WOUND], the projected phrase is then returned (step 3). By realizing this argument overtly on the surface, the generator has resolved the conflational divergence.

On the third recursive call (fourth invocation of **Generate_Phrase**), the word *a* is selected for the concept [$_{\text{Path}}$ TOWARD$_{\text{Poss}}$ ...] (step 1). The generator recognizes that a clitic is required because of the UC specification associated with Z in the RLCS definition for *dar*. Thus, it inserts the clitic into the verb phrase that was previously generated for the main verb *dar*, and it assigns an index i that will eventually be used as a coindex with the overt noun phrase *Juan*. The word *a* is then projected up to the P-MAX level by the $\mathcal{CSR}$ (step 2.a) and the **Generate_Phrase** is called recursively in order to syntactically realize the ∗-marked satellite corresponding to [$_{\text{Thing}}$ JOHN] (step 2.b).

This recursive call constitutes a fifth invocation of **Generate_Phrase**. The word *John* is selected (step 1) and projected up to the N-MAX level by the $\mathcal{CSR}$ (step 2.a). Note that *Juan* receives the index i so that coreference is established between *Juan* and the clitic *le* generated earlier. Because there are no satellites associated with *Juan*, this N-MAX is returned (step 3).

Prior to exiting the fourth invocation of **Generate_Phrase**, the N-MAX phrase containing *Juan* is attached by the $\mathcal{GLR}$ as the internal argument of the P-MAX phrase headed by *a* (step 2.c). This projected phrase is then returned (step 3). Next the P-MAX phrase is attached by the $\mathcal{GLR}$ (step 2.c) as an internal argument of the main verb *dar*. Note that the realization of this argument as a prepositional phrase resolves the structural divergence.

Prior to exiting the outermost invocation of **Generate_Phrase**, the other two satellites, $[_{\text{N-MAX}} \{\text{yo, mi, mí}\}]$ and $[_{\text{N-MAX}} \text{puñalad}]$, are attached by the $\mathcal{GLR}$ (step 2.c) as the external argument and internal argument, respectively. The final result returned by **Generate_Phrase** is the following:

(162) $[_{\text{C-MAX}}$
   $\quad [_{\text{I-MAX}}$
   $\quad\quad [_{\text{N-MAX}} \{\text{yo, mi, mí}\}]$
   $\quad\quad [_{\text{V-MAX}} \text{le}_i \text{ dar } [_{\text{N-MAX}} \text{puñalad}] [_{\text{P-MAX}} a [_{\text{N-MAX}} \text{Juan}_i]]]]]$

Now that all three divergences have been accounted for during the generation of the target-language structure, the syntactic constraints are free to apply to this structure, just as they did to the source-language structure before the CLCS was produced. In particular, the pronoun that is ultimately selected as the subject of the target-language sentence is dependent on case constraints as described above in section 6.4.4. The Case Filter rules out *mi* (since it has inherent possessive case) and *mí* (since it has inherent objective case). The pronoun *yo* is the only one that passes the Case Filter since its inherent nominative case matches the case assigned by the $+tns$ feature associated with the verb *dar*.

The final results are obtained by applying morphological synthesis to the target-language sentence. As described in chapter 3, Spanish has two past tenses, preterit and imperfect, thus, the verb *dar* is realized in both of these tenses. In addition, the root form *puñalad* may be realized in either the singular form or the plural form. Thus, four target-language possibilities are generated:

(163) (i)   Yo le di puñaladas a Juan

       (ii)   Yo le di una puñalada a Juan

       (iii)   Yo le daba puñaladas a Juan

       (iv)   Yo le daba una puñalada a Juan

As it turns out, these four sentences do not have identical interpretations, but have subtle aspectual distinctions pertaining to the duration of the event (*i.e.*, the preterit form *di* implies a punctual activity whereas the imperfect form *daba* implies a prolonged activity) and repetitiveness of the event (*i.e.*, the singular form *puñalada* implies a non-repetitive activity whereas the plural form *puñaladas* implies a repetitive activity). We will address aspectual considerations further in chapter 9.

This chapter has shown how the generator resolves lexical-semantic divergences in a compositional fashion that mirrors that of the LCS composition stage of processing. Now that we have examined the algorithms behind the processing mechanisms and the I/O of these mechanisms, the next chapter will examine a more formal description of the solution to the translation divergences.

7 Formalization of Machine Translation Divergences

This chapter demonstrates one of the fundamental contributions of the current research, namely the formalization of two types of information: (1) the linguistically-grounded classes upon which lexical-semantic divergences are based; and (2) the techniques by which lexical-semantic divergences are resolved. The reason that this contribution is important is that it provides the basis for proving that the lexical-semantic divergence classification proposed in the current framework covers all possible source-language/target-language distinctions based on lexical-semantic properties (*i.e.*, properties associated with entries in the lexicon that are not based on purely syntactic information, idiomatic usage, aspectual knowledge, discourse knowledge, domain knowledge, or world knowledge).

The formalization of these two types of information is advantageous from a computational point of view in that it facilitates the design and implementation of the system: the problem is clearly defined in terms of a small number of divergence categories, and the solution is systematically stated in terms of a uniform translation mapping and a handful of simple lexical-semantic parameters. The formalization is also advantageous from the point of view that it allows one to make an evaluation of the status of the system. For example, given the formal description of the interlingua and target-language root words, one is able to judge whether a particular target-language sentence fully covers the concept that underlies the corresponding source-language sentence. Finally, the formalization of the divergence types and the associated solution allows one to prove certain properties about the system. For example, one might want to determine whether the system is able to handle two or more simultaneous divergences that interact in some way (a problem which has not yet been addressed). With the mechanism of the current approach, one is able to formally prove that such cases are handled in a uniform fashion.

This chapter will focus on the problem of lexical-semantic divergences and will provide support for the view that it is possible to construct a finite cross-linguistic classification of machine translation divergences and to implement a systematic mapping between the interlingua and the surface syntactic structure that accommodates all of the divergences in this classification. The next section discusses the classification of divergences, comparing the current divergence categories to those of other researchers. Section 7.2 formally defines the terms used to classify divergences. Section 7.3 uses this terminology to formalize the divergence classification of the current approach. Section 7.4 defines the solution to the divergence problem in the context of detailed examples (including ones from alternative approaches). Finally, section 7.5 discusses certain issues of relevance to the divergence problem including the resolution of several (recursively) interacting divergence types.

7.1 Classification of Machine Translation Divergences

The divergence problem in machine translation has received increasingly greater attention in recent literature. (See, *e.g.*, Barnett *et al.* (1991a,b), Beaven (1992a,b), Dorr (1990a,b), Kameyama *et al.* (1991), Kinoshita *et al.* (1992), Lindop and Tsujii (1991), Tsujii and Fujita (1991), and Whitelock (1992) and related discussion can be found, for example, in work by Melby (1986) and Nirenburg and Nirenburg (1988).) In particular, Barnett *et al.* (1991a) divide distinctions between the source language and the target language into two categories: translation *divergences*, in which the same information is conveyed in the source and target texts, but the structures of the sentences are different (as in previous work by Dorr (1990a,b)); and translation *mismatches*, in which the information that is conveyed is different in the source and target languages (as in Kameyama *et al.* (1991)).[1] While translation mismatches are a major problem for translation systems which must be addressed, they are outside the scope of the model presented here. (See Barnett *et al.* (1991a,b), Carbonell and Tomita (1987), Meyer *et al.* (1990), Nirenburg *et al.* (1987), Nirenburg and Goodman (1990), Nirenburg and Levin (1989), Wilks (1973), among others, for descriptions of interlingual machine translation approaches that take into account knowledge outside of the domain of lexical semantics.)

Although researchers have only recently begun to systematically classify divergence types, the notion of translation divergences is not a new one in the machine translation community. For example, a number of researchers working on the Eurotra project (mentioned in chapter 1) have

---

[1] An example of the latter situation is the translation of the English word *fish* into Spanish: the translation is *pez* if the fish is still in its natural state, but it is *pescado* if the fish has been caught and is suitable for food. It is now widely accepted that, in such a situation, the machine translation system must be able to derive the required information from discourse context and a model of the domain that is being discussed.

sought to solve divergent source-to-target translations, although the divergences were named differently and were resolved by construction-specific transfer rules. A comprehensive survey of divergence examples is presented by Lindop and Tsujii (1991). The term used in this work is "complex transfer," but as mentioned earlier, these are a class of problems inherent in machine translation itself, not just in the transfer (or interlingual) approaches.

One of the claims made by Lindop and Tsujii (1991) is that the non-Eurotra literature rarely goes into great detail when discussing how divergences are handled. An additional claim is that combinations of divergences and interaction effects between divergent and non-divergent translations are not described in the literature. This chapter seeks to change this perceived state of affairs by providing a detailed description of a solution to all of the (potentially interacting) divergences shown in figure 1.12 (repeated in figure 5.2), not just a subset of them as would typically be found in the description of most translation systems. These divergences are precisely the ones documented by Lindop and Tsujii (1991), although they are classified differently here. The classification of Lindop and Tsujii (1991) misses a variety of generalizations that could be captured if the lexical-semantic requirements of lexical items were considered. Furthermore, it relies on superficial notions such as "1-to-N lexical gaps" rather than on linguistically motivated characterizations of the divergences that are associated with the data. For comparison, a number of examples taken from the survey presented by Lindop and Tsujii (1991) are shown in figure 7.1, reorganized according to the classification proposed here.

The survey of divergence examples by Lindop and Tsujii (1991) constitutes a valuable resource for machine translation researchers because it contains large numbers of complex translation examples taken from a variety of sources and also illustrates precisely the types of problems that make the construction of machine translation systems so difficult. However, the approach taken to resolve these divergences relies on transfer rules that miss out on important cross-linguistic generalizations that could easily be captured at the level of lexical-semantic structure. The framework assumed for the current approach makes use of a linguistically-grounded classification of divergence types that may be formally defined and systematically resolved.

Divergence Classification (Dorr)	Divergence Classification (Lindop and Tsujii)	Example
Thematic	changes in argument structure	E: I like the car G: Mir gefällt der Wagen
	changes in argument structure	E: John misses Mary F: Mary manque à John
	changes in argument structure	E: He lacks something G: Ihm fehlt etwas
Promotional	head switching	D: Hij is toevallig ziek E: He happens to be ill
	head switching	F: Il est probable que Jean viendra E: Jean will probably come
	head switching	E: The baby just fell F: Le bébé vient de tomber
	head switching	E: An attempted murder F: Une tentative de meurte
Demotional	head switching	G: Er liest gern E: He likes reading
Structural	changes in argument structure	E: He aims the gun at him G: Er zielt auf ihn mit dem Gewehr
	changes in argument structure	G: Der Student beantwortet die Frage F: L'étudiant répond à la question
	changes in argument structure	E: He seems ill D: Hij schijnt ziek tu zijn
Conflational	1-to-N lexical gaps	E: Miss P: Sentir a falta
	1-to-N lexical gaps	P: Piscina E: Swimming pool
	N-to-1 lexical gaps	E: Get up early P: madrugar
	N-to-1 lexical gaps	E: John called up Mary F: John a appelé Mary
	N-to-M lexical gaps	E: See again F: Revoir
	N-to-M lexical gaps	F: Ressortir E: Go out again
	default/exception distinctions	E: Know how F: Savoir
	default/exception distinctions	F: Aller en flottant E: Float
	default/exception distinctions	E: Commit a crime F: Commettre un crime
	interpretation	E: Walk across F: Traverser à pied
Categorial	category changes	E: Postwar (adj) G: Nach dem Krieg (pp)
	category changes	D: Hij is in Amsterdam woonachtig (adj) E: He resides in Amsterdam (verb)
	category changes	D: Het is voldoende (adj) E: It suffices (verb)
	category changes	E: Hopefully (adv) F: On espère (ip)
	category changes	E: John is fond (adj) of music F: John aime (verb) la musique
Lexical	N-to-1 lexical gaps	E: Give a cough F: Tousser
	Support verbs	E: Give a cry F: Pousser un cri

Figure 7.1
The divergence examples of Lindop and Tsujii (1991) can be reorganized into the classification of the current framework.

We now turn to a formal description of the terminology used to define the divergence problem.

7.2 Definitions

This section formally defines the representations that have been presented in previous chapters. By now it is clear that the fundamental representation of the system is the interlingua, which is primarily influenced by the representation adopted by Jackendoff (1983, 1990):

Definition 1:
A *Lexical Conceptual Structure* (LCS) is a modified version of the representation proposed by Jackendoff (1983, 1990) that conforms to the following structural form:

$$[_{T(X')} X'$$
$$([_{T(W')} W'],$$
$$[_{T(Z'_1)} Z'_1], \ldots, [_{T(Z'_n)} Z'_n]$$
$$[_{T(Q'_1)} Q'_1], \ldots, [_{T(Q'_m)} Q'_m])]$$

where X' is the *logical head*, W' is the *logical subject*, $Z'_1, \ldots, Z'_n$ are the *logical arguments*, $Q'_1, \ldots, Q'_m$ are the *logical modifiers*, and $T(\phi)$ is the logical *type* (Event, State, Path, Position, *etc.*) corresponding to the *primitive* ϕ (CAUSE, LET, GO, STAY, BE, *etc.*); Primitives are further categorized into *fields* (*e.g.*, Possessional, Identificational, Temporal, Locational, *etc.*).

Example 1:
The LCS representation of *John went happily to school* is:

$$[_{Event} GO_{Loc}$$
$$([_{Thing} JOHN],$$
$$[_{Path} TO_{Loc} ([_{Position} AT_{Loc} ([_{Thing} JOHN], [_{Location} SCHOOL])])]$$
$$[_{Manner} HAPPILY])]$$

where X' corresponds to GO_{Loc}, $T(X')$ corresponds to Event, W' corresponds to JOHN, $T(W')$ corresponds to Thing, Z'_1 corresponds to TO_{Loc}, $T(Z'_1)$ corresponds to Path, Q'_1 corresponds to HAPPILY, and $T(Q'_1)$ corresponds to Manner.

As described in previous chapters, the LCS representation is used both in the lexicon and in the interlingual representation. The former is identified as a *root* LCS (RLCS) and the latter is identified as a *composed* LCS (CLCS):

Definition 2:
A *RLCS* (*i.e.*, a *root* LCS) is an uninstantiated LCS that is associated with
a word definition in the lexicon (*i.e.*, a LCS with unfilled variable positions).

Example 2:
The RLCS associated with the word *go* (from example 1) is:
[Event GO_Loc
    ([Thing X],
    [Path TO_Loc ([Position AT_Loc ([Thing X], [Thing Z])])])]

Definition 3:
A *CLCS* (*i.e.*, a *composed* LCS) is an instantiated LCS that is the result
of combining two or more RLCS's by means of unification (roughly). This
is the *interlingua* or language-independent form that serves as the pivot
between the source and target languages.

Example 3:
If we compose the RLCS for *go* (in example 2) with the RLCS's
for *John* ([Thing JOHN]), *school* ([Location SCHOOL]), and *happily*
([Manner HAPPILY]), we get the CLCS corresponding to *John went happily
to school* (shown in example 1).

Each (content) word in the lexicon is associated with a RLCS, whose
variable positions may have certain restrictions on them such as in-
ternal/external and promotion/demotion information (to be formalized
shortly). The CLCS is a structure that results from combining the lexical items of a source-language sentence into a single underlying pivot
form by means of the LCS composition process described in chapter 4.
We have already seen that the notion of *unification* (as used in definition 3) differs from that of the standard unification frameworks (see,
e.g., Shieber *et al.* (1989, 1990), Kaplan and Bresnan (1982), Kaplan
et al. (1989), Kay (1984), *etc.*) in that it is not directly invertible. That
is, the generation process operates on the CLCS in a unification-like
fashion that roughly mirrors the LCS composition process, but it is not
a direct inverse of this process. The notion of unification used here also
differs from others in that it is a more "relaxed" notion: those words that
are mapped in a "relaxed" way are associated with special lexical information (*i.e.*, the :INT, :EXT, :PROMOTE, :DEMOTE, *, :CAT, and
:CONFLATED parameters, each of which will be formalized shortly).

The four LCS positions given in definition 1 are relevant to the mapping between the interlingual representation and the surface syntactic

representation: (1) *logical head*, (2) *logical subject*, (3) *logical argument*, and (4) *logical modifier*. In example 1, the logical head is GO_{Loc}, the logical subject is [$_{Thing}$ JOHN], the logical argument is [$_{Path}$ TO_{Loc} ...], and the logical modifier is [$_{Manner}$ HAPPILY].

Another fundamental component of the mapping between the interlingual representation and the surface syntactic representation is the syntactic phrase:

Definition 4:
A *syntactic phrase* is a maximal projection which conforms to the following structural form:

[$_{Y\text{-MAX}}$
   $Q\text{-MAX}_{j+1}$ ... $Q\text{-MAX}_k$
   [$_{Y\text{-MAX}}$
     W-MAX
     [$_{X\text{-MAX}}$ [$_X$ $Q\text{-MAX}_1$ ... $Q\text{-MAX}_i$ X $Q\text{-MAX}_{i+1}$ ... $Q\text{-MAX}_j$]
     $Z\text{-MAX}_1$ ... $Z\text{-MAX}_n$]]
   $Q\text{-MAX}_{k+1}$ ... $Q\text{-MAX}_m$]^2

where X is the *syntactic head* (of category V, N, A, P, I, or C), W-MAX is the *external argument*, $Z\text{-MAX}_1$, ..., $Z\text{-MAX}_n$ are the *internal arguments*, and $Q\text{-MAX}_1$, ..., $Q\text{-MAX}_m$ are the *syntactic adjuncts*. In many phrase types, *e.g.*, noun phrases, Y is the same category as X.

Example 4:
The syntactic phrase corresponding to *John went happily to school* is:

[$_{C\text{-MAX}}$ [$_{I\text{-MAX}}$ [$_{N\text{-MAX}}$ John]
      [$_{V\text{-MAX}}$ [$_V$ went] [$_{ADV}$ happily] [$_{P\text{-MAX}}$ to [$_{N\text{-MAX}}$ school]]]]]]

where X-MAX corresponds to V-MAX, X corresponds to [$_V$ went], Y-MAX corresponds to I-MAX (which is further projected up to C-MAX), W-MAX corresponds to [$_{N\text{-MAX}}$ John], Q-MAX corresponds to [$_{ADV}$ happily], and Z-MAX corresponds to [$_{P\text{-MAX}}$ a ...]. Note that this last constituent is itself a phrase that selects a phrase [$_{N\text{-MAX}}$ school] that corresponds to Z-MAX.

The four positions defined in definition 4 are relevant to the mapping between the interlingual representation and the surface syntactic representation: (1) *syntactic head*, (2) *external argument*, (3) *internal*

---

^{2}The reader should bear in mind that the head-initial/spec-initial setting of the constituent order parameter (*i.e.*, the setting for English) is assumed for all of the formal definitions given in this chapter. It should be clear, by now, that the syntactic operations that determine word order are completely independent from the lexical-semantic operations that use these definitions. Thus, the formal definitions can be stated in terms of an arbitrary ordering of constituents, without loss of generality, as long as it is understood that the constituent order is independently determined.

argument, and (4) *syntactic adjunct*. In example 4, the syntactic head is [$_V$ went], the external argument is [$_{N\text{-}MAX}$ John], the internal argument is [$_{P\text{-}MAX}$ a ...], and the syntactic adjunct is [$_{ADV}$ happily].

In addition to the representations involved in the translation mapping, it is also possible to formalize the mapping itself. The two mappings have already been defined in chapter 4. We redefine them formally here:

Definition 5:
The $\mathcal{GLR}$ systematically relates syntactic and lexical-semantic positions as follows:

CLCS: [$_{T(X')}$ X'
          ([$_{T(W')}$ W'],
          [$_{T(Z'_1)}$ Z'$_1$], ..., [$_{T(Z'_n)}$ Z'$_n$],
          [$_{T(Q'_1)}$ Q'$_1$], ..., [$_{T(Q'_m)}$ Q'$_m$])]

Syntax: [$_{Y\text{-}MAX}$
          Q-MAX$_{j+1}$ ... Q-MAX$_k$
          [$_{Y\text{-}MAX}$
              W-MAX
              [$_{X\text{-}MAX}$ [$_X$ Q-MAX$_1$ ... Q-MAX$_i$ X   Q-MAX$_{i+1}$ ... Q-MAX$_j$]
              Z-MAX$_1$ ... Z-MAX$_n$]]
          Q-MAX$_{k+1}$ ... Q-MAX$_m$]

Definition 6:
The $\mathcal{CSR}$ systematically relates a lexical-semantic type $T(\phi')$ to a syntactic category $CAT(\phi)$, where ϕ' is a CLCS constituent related to the syntactic constituent ϕ by the $\mathcal{GLR}$.

Now that we have formally defined the representations and mappings used during translation, we will turn to a classification of divergences that is based on these definitions.

7.3   Formal Classification of Divergences

In general, translation divergences occur when there is an exception to one (or both) of the mappings described by definitions 5 and 6 in one language, but not in the other. This premise allows one to formally define a classification of all possible lexical-semantic divergences that could arise during translation.

Before we define each divergence type, we will first make some revisions to the representations used in definitions 1 and 4 to simplify the presentation. The representation given in definition 1 is revised so that Z' is used to denote a logical argument from the set $\{Z'_1 \dots Z'_n\}$ and Q' is used to denote a logical modifier from the set $\{Q'_1 \dots Q'_m\}$. The resulting representation is considerably simplified:

(164) $[_{T(X')}\ X'\ ([_{T(W')}\ W'],\ [_{T(Z')}\ Z'],\ [_{T(Q')}\ Q'])]$

Similarly, the representation given in definition 4 is revised so that W is used to denote the external argument, Z is used to denote an internal argument from the set $\{Z\text{-}MAX_1 \dots Z\text{-}MAX_n\}$, and Q is used to denote a syntactic adjunct from the set $\{Q\text{-}MAX_1 \dots Q\text{-}MAX_m\}$. The resulting representation has the following simplified form:

(165) $[_{\text{Y-MAX}}\ [_{\text{Y-MAX}}\ W\ [_{\text{X-MAX}}\ X\ Z]]\ Q]^3$

With these simplifications, the $\mathcal{GLR}$ can be conceptualized as the following set of relations:

(166) **Simplified $\mathcal{GLR}$:**
    1. $X' \Leftrightarrow X$
    2. $W' \Leftrightarrow W$
    3. $Z' \Leftrightarrow Z$
    4. $Q' \Leftrightarrow Q$

Figure 7.2 shows the simplified $\mathcal{GLR}$ in terms of tree-like representations.

Before we use this simplified formalization to define the divergence types, the notion of divergence needs further clarification. Throughout this and preceding chapters, the term divergence was defined as a *language-to-language* phenomenon: a sentence in language L_1 translates into a sentence in L_2 in a very different form (*i.e.*, differently shaped parse trees or similarly shaped trees with different basic categories). This definition implies that the divergence exists between the two languages L_1 and L_2, independent of the way the translation is done (*i.e.*, direct, transfer, or interlingua). Within this definition, the following translation example does not exhibit any divergence:

---

[3]For the purposes of this discussion, we will retain the convention that syntactic adjuncts occur on the right at the maximal level. Note that this is not always the case: the setting of the base adjuncts parameter described in chapter 2 determines the side and level at which a particular adjunct will occur.

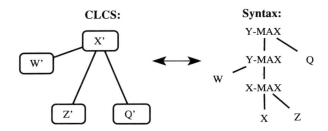

Figure 7.2
The $\mathcal{GLR}$ maps systematically between the CLCS and the syntactic structure.

(167) G: Hans kußt Marie gern ⇔ D: Hans kust Marie graag
       'Hans kisses Mary likingly'
       (Hans likes to kiss Mary)

However, in the following sections, the notion of divergence will be discussed from an *interlingual* point of view, *i.e.*, with respect to an underlying representation (lexical conceptual structure) that has been chosen to describe the source and target language sentences. From this point of view, translations such as (167) are described by means of divergent mappings even though the source- and target-language pairs do not necessarily exhibit any distinctions on the surface. In such cases, there are generally two occurrences of a *language-to-interlingua* divergence (one *from* the surface structure and one *to* the surface structure). By contrast, a *language-to-language* divergence occurs only in the context of a single language-to-interlingua divergence.[4] Thus, for the purposes of this chapter, a divergence is viewed as a consequence of the internal mapping between the surface structure and the interlingual representation (*i.e.*, a *language-to-interlingua* divergence) rather than as an external distinction that shows up on the surface (*i.e.*, a *language-to-language* divergence).

To further illustrate the difference between these two divergence types, consider the thematic divergence example given earlier in (126) of chapter 5. Here the English sentence *I like Mary* is mapped into the interlingual representation without recourse to any divergence mechanisms; the

---

[4]I owe the use of the terms *language-to-interlingua* and *language-to-language* to Clare Voss (personal communication), who very carefully identified this distinction.

Spanish sentence *Me gusta María*, on the other hand, requires a special type of divergence mechanism in order to be realized on the surface.[5] Thus, the divergence is captured by means of access to divergence information that is specified in the Spanish lexical entry, not in the English lexical entry. Put another way, the divergence, in this case, is *caused* by the Spanish because the Spanish lexical entry, without the divergence information, would not coincide with the argument structure chosen for the interlingual representation. In such a case, a language-to-language divergence is reduced to a single language-to-interlingua divergence.

To some extent this approach may be unsettling: the interlingual representation appears to accommodate constructions in one language (without any special information) more readily than it accommodates the corresponding construction in another language. In addition, it seems odd to introduce the notion of a language-to-interlingua divergence for cases that do not exhibit a language-to-language divergence (such as example (167) above). However, it is clearly the case that language-to-language divergences do exist, regardless of the translation approach that is adopted. The appropriate question to ask is whether an approach that addresses the divergence problem from a language-to-interlingua perspective is an improvement over an approach that addresses the problem strictly from a language-to-language point of view. This chapter argues that the language-to-interlingua approach is the correct one given that the alternative would be to handle language-to-language divergences by constructing detailed source-to-target transfer rules for each lexical entry in the source and target language. Thus, although the approach introduces the seemingly unintuitive notion of language-to-interlingua divergences, introducing this notion allows the translation mapping to be defined in terms of a representation that is general enough to carry over to several different language pairs.

We are now prepared to define the divergences on the basis of the simplified formalization presented in (164) and (166) above.

7.3.1   Thematic Divergence

A thematic divergence arises in cases where the $\mathcal{GLR}$ invokes the following sets of relations in place of steps 2 and 3 of (166):

---

[5]This special mechanism will be described in section 7.4.1.

(168) 2.′ W′ ⇔ Z
       3.′ Z′ ⇔ W

Figure 7.3(a) shows the revised mapping.

Thematic divergence is one of three types of possible positioning variations that force the $\mathcal{GLR}$ to be overridden. Two additional positioning variations are promotional and demotional divergences, which will be defined in the next two sections. Whereas thematic divergence involves a repositioning of two satellites relative to the head X, promotional and demotional divergences involve a repositioning of the head X relative to its satellites. Thus, these two divergences, taken together with thematic divergence, account for the entire range of repositioning possibilities. This claim is an important one that will be justified in section 7.5.

7.3.2 Promotional Divergence

Promotional divergence is characterized by the *promotion* (placement into a "higher up" position) of a logical modifier. In such a situation, the logical modifier is associated with the syntactic head position, and the logical head is then associated with an internal argument position. Thus, promotional divergence overrides the $\mathcal{GLR}$, invoking the following sets of relations in place of steps 1 and 4 of (166):

(169) 1.′ X′ ⇔ Z[6]
       4.′ Q′ ⇔ X

Figure 7.3(b) shows the revised mapping.

7.3.3 Demotional Divergence

Demotional divergence is characterized by the *demotion* (placement into a "lower down" position) of a logical head. In such a situation, the logical head is associated with the syntactic adjunct position, and the logical argument is then associated with a syntactic head position. Thus, demotional divergence overrides the $\mathcal{GLR}$, invoking the following sets of relations in place of steps 1 and 3 of (166):

---

[6]This relation does not mean that X replaces Z (if there is a Z), but that X retains the same structural relationship with Z (*i.e.*, Z remains an internal argument of X). To simplify the current description, Z is not shown in the syntactic structure of figure 7.3(b).

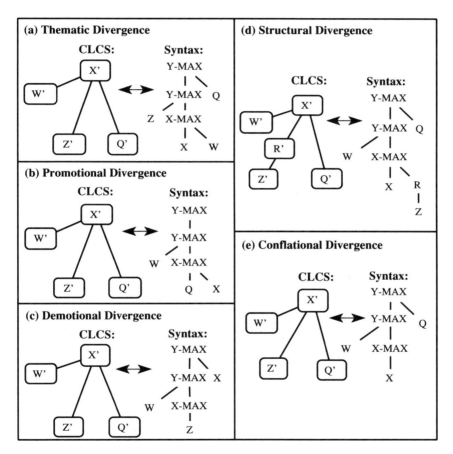

Figure 7.3
The $\mathcal{GLR}$ is overridden in cases where the placement of heads, arguments, and adjuncts does not correspond to the default positions.

(170) 1.′ X′ ⇔ Q^7
        3.′ Z′ ⇔ X

Figure 7.3(c) shows the revised mapping.

The distinction between promotional and demotional divergences may not be intuitively obvious at first glance. In both cases, the translation mapping appears to be associating a main verb with an adverbial satellite, or *vice versa*. However, the distinction between these two *head switching* cases becomes more apparent when we consider the status of the participating lexical tokens more carefully. We will return to this point in section 7.5.

7.3.4 Structural Divergence

Structural divergence differs from the last three divergence types in that it does not alter the positions used in the $\mathcal{GLR}$ mapping, but it changes the nature of the relation between the different positions (*i.e.*, the "⇔" correspondence). Figure 7.3(d) characterizes the alteration that takes place. Note that the mapping of Z′ to the corresponding internal argument position is altered so that it is positioned under the constituent that corresponds to R′.

7.3.5 Conflational Divergence

Conflational divergence is another case in which the ⇔ correspondence is changed. In particular, conflational divergence is characterized by the suppression of a CLCS constituent (or the inverse of this process). The constituent generally occurs in logical argument or logical modifier position; thus, the "⇔" correspondence of either step 3 or step 4 of the $\mathcal{GLR}$ is changed, depending on which position is conflated. Figure 7.3(e) characterizes the alteration that takes place. Note that the Z′ position in the CLCS does not have a corresponding realization in the syntax.

7.3.6 Categorial Divergence

Unlike the previous five divergence types, categorial divergence affects the operation of the $\mathcal{CSR}$, not the $\mathcal{GLR}$. It is characterized by a situation in which $\mathrm{CAT}(\phi)$ is forced to have a different value than would

---

[7]This relation does not mean that X replaces Q (if there is a Q), but that X retains the same structural relationship with Q (*i.e.*, Q remains a syntactic adjunct of X). To simplify the current description, Q is not shown in the syntactic structure of figure 7.3(c).

normally be assigned to $T(\phi')$ by means of the mapping specified in figure 4.18. Thus, categorial divergence is formally described as follows: a lexical-semantic type $T(\phi')$ is related to a syntactic category $\text{CAT}(\phi)$, where $\text{CAT}(\phi) \neq \mathcal{CSR}(T(\phi'))$. In such a case, $\text{CAT}(\phi)$ must be specified through lexical parameterization.

7.3.7 Lexical Divergence

As described in chapter 5, lexical divergence arises only in the context of other divergence types. This is because the choice of lexical items in any language relies crucially on the realization and composition properties of those lexical items. Because the six preceding divergences potentially alter these properties, lexical divergence is viewed as a side effect of other divergences. Thus, the formalization thereof is considered to be some combination of those given above.

We now turn to a formal presentation of the solution to the divergence problem.

7.4 Solution to the Divergence Problem

The solution to the divergence problem relies solely on three types of information: (1) the $\mathcal{GLR}$; (2) the $\mathcal{CSR}$; and (3) a small set of parametric mechanisms. Because the interlingual representation preserves relevant lexical-semantic relations, these three types of information are all that are required for providing a systematic mapping that resolves the divergence types defined in the last section. In particular, the solution given here eliminates the need for transfer rules and relies instead on parameterized mappings that are systematically defined and uniformly applied across all languages. This section formally describes the solution to the divergence problem in the context of detailed examples (including ones from alternative approaches).

As described above, translation divergences occur when there is an exception either to the $\mathcal{GLR}$ or to the $\mathcal{CSR}$ (or to both) in one language, but not in the other. In order to invoke these exceptions, the lexicon includes markers that specify syntactic realization information with lexical items. These markers can be thought of as *parameters* to the LCS component of the system, just as there are parameters associated with the syntactic (GB) component of the system. Note that the $\mathcal{GLR}$ and

$\mathcal{CSR}$ are intended to be language-independent, whereas the parameters
are intended to encode language-specific information about lexical items.
The seven parameters that are used by the system are ones that were
initially introduced in chapter 5, *i.e.*, :INT, :EXT, :PROMOTE, :DE-
MOTE, *, :CAT, and :CONFLATED. In sections 7.4.1–7.4.7, we will
formally define each parameter with respect to the type of divergence
that it is intended to resolve and we will look at how each parametric
solution compares to solutions offered by other approaches.

7.4.1   Parameterization for Thematic Divergence

The first divergence solution to be formalized discussed is the one for
thematic divergence, *i.e.*, the repositioning of arguments with respect to
a given head. Thematic divergence arises only in cases where there is
a logical subject. An example of thematic divergence is the reversal of
the subject with an object as in the thematic divergence example given
earlier in (126) of chapter 5. The syntactic structures are shown here:

(171) [c-max [i-max [n-max I] [v-max [v like] [n-max Mary]]]]
⇕
[c-max [i-max [n-max María] [v-max [v me gusta]]]][8]

Here the object *Mary* has reversed places with the subject *I* in the
Spanish translation. The result is that the object *Mary* turns into the
subject *María*, and the subject *I* turns into the object *me*.

This argument reversal is accounted for by the :INT and :EXT parameters, which determine the positions for the logical subject and logical
argument. The general solution to thematic divergence makes use of
these parameters as follows:

---

[8]For the purposes of this discussion, the Spanish sentence is given in its uninverted
form. As explained in chapter 1 (fn. 3), there are other ways of realizing this sentence.
In particular, a native speaker of Spanish will frequently invert the subject to post-
verbal position:

[c-max [i-max e_i [v-max [v-max [v me gusta]] [n-max María]$_i$]]].

However, this does not affect the internal/external reversal scheme described here
since inversion is a syntactic operation that takes place independently of the process
that handles thematic divergences.

(172) RLCS 1: $[_{T(X')} X' ([_{T(W')} W'], [_{T(Z')} Z'] [_{T(Q')} Q'])]$

RLCS 2: $[_{T(X')} X' ([_{T(W')} :\text{INT } W'], [_{T(Z')} :\text{EXT } Z'] [_{T(Q')} Q'])]$

Translation: $[_{\text{Y-MAX}} [_{\text{Y-MAX}} W [_{\text{X-MAX}} X Z]] Q]$
$$\Updownarrow$$
$[_{T(X')} X' ([_{T(W')} W'], [_{T(Z')} Z'] [_{T(Q')} Q'])]$
$$\Updownarrow$$
$[_{\text{Y-MAX}} [_{\text{Y-MAX}} Z [_{\text{X-MAX}} X W]] Q]$

This assumes that there is only one external argument and zero or more internal arguments. If the situation arises where more than one variable is associated with the :EXT markers, it is assumed that there is an error in the word definition.[9]

Note that the :INT and :EXT markers show up only in the RLCS's. The CLCS does not include any such markers since it is intended to be a language-independent representation for the source- and target-language sentence. In cases where these markers do not show up in the RLCS (e.g., in the English RLCS for *like*), the internal and external arguments are mapped into their default CLCS positions by the $\mathcal{GLR}$.

A number of other translation systems have attempted to accommodate thematic divergences similar to that of example (171). Three examples of such systems were presented in chapter 1: (1) GETA/ARIANE (Vauquois and Boitet (1985), and Boitet (1987)); (2) LMT (McCord (1989)); and (3) METAL (Alonso (1990) and Thurmair (1990)). The rules used by these approaches for resolving thematic divergence were given, respectively, in (19), (21), and (23), repeated here:

(173) plaire(SUBJ(ARG1:GN),OBJ1(ARG2:PREP,GN)) $\Leftrightarrow$
like(SUBJ(ARG2:GN),OBJ1(ARG1:GN))

(174) `gverb(like(dat:*,nom:X),ge+fall,*:X)`

(175) like V $\Rightarrow$ gustar V
NP ([ROLE SUBJ]) $\Rightarrow$ NP ([ROLE IOBJ])
NP ([ROLE DOBJ]) $\Rightarrow$ NP ([ROLE SUBJ])

---

[9]The parameters associated with the RLCS are assumed to be correctly specified for the purposes of this formal description. However, in practice, there might be errors in the lexical entries since they are constructed by hand in the current implementation. Eventually, the intent is to automate the process of lexical entry construction so that these errors can be avoided.

One problem with these approaches is that surface syntactic decisions
are, in a sense, performed off-line by means of lexical entries and transfer rules that specifically encode language-specific syntactic information.
Such a scheme is limited in that it has no potential for relating thematic
divergence to the rest of the space of divergence possibilities. Moreover,
while transfer rules might be deemed suitable for local divergences such
as simple subject-object reversal, it is well known that simple transfer
rules of this type do not readily accommodate more complicated divergences. (See chapter 1 for additional discussion.)

Because the current framework separates syntactic information from
lexical-semantic information, the above divergence types are uniformly
resolved on-line without recourse to language-specific rules. On-line syntactic decisions are made independently of conceptual decisions, and
translation divergences are handled without reference to purely syntactic properties such as word order.

Now that the the solution to thematic divergences has been formalized,
the next two sections formalize the solution to two different positioning divergences, promotional and demotional.[10] These two divergence
types, together with thematic divergences, account for the entire space
of repositioning possibilities. This claim is an important one that will
be justified shortly.

7.4.2 Parameterization for Promotional Divergence

Promotional divergence is characterized by the *promotion* (placement
"higher up") of a logical modifier into a main verb position (or *vice
versa*). This situation arises in the promotional example given earlier
in (129) of chapter 5. The syntactic structures are shown here:

(176) [$_{\text{C-MAX}}$ [$_{\text{I-MAX}}$ [$_{\text{N-MAX}}$ John]
　　　　　[$_{\text{V-MAX}}$ [$_{\text{V}}$ usually [$_{\text{V}}$ goes]] [$_{\text{N-MAX}}$ home]]]]
　　　　　　　　　⇕
　　　[$_{\text{C-MAX}}$ [$_{\text{I-MAX}}$ [$_{\text{N-MAX}}$ Juan]
　　　　　[$_{\text{V-MAX}}$ [$_{\text{V}}$ suele] [$_{\text{V-MAX}}$ [$_{\text{V}}$ ir] [$_{\text{P-MAX}}$ a casa]]]]]

---

[10]The notions of demotion and promotion are not the same as the notions of demotion and advancement in the theory of relational grammar (RG) (see Perlmutter
(1983)). However, it might be possible for the mechanism that is used for RG operations to be used in the LCS scheme as well. (This possibility is addressed below in
section 7.5.)

Here the main verb *go* is modified by an adverbial adjunct *usually* but, in Spanish, *usually* has been placed into a higher position as the main verb *soler*, and the "going home" event has been realized as the complement of this verb.

Promotional divergence is accounted for by the :PROMOTE parameter, which determines the position for the logical head with respect to the logical modifier. The general solution to promotional divergence makes use of this parameter as follows:

(177) RLCS 1: $[_{T(Q')}\ Q']$
       RLCS 2: $[_{T(Q')}$:PROMOTE $Q']$

Translation: $[_{\text{Y-MAX}}\ [_{\text{Y-MAX}}\ W\ [_{\text{X-MAX}}\ X\ Z]]\ Q]$
$$\Updownarrow$$
$[_{T(X')}\ X'\ ([_{T(W')}\ W'],\ [_{T(Z')}\ Z']\ [_{T(Q')}\ Q'])]$
$$\Updownarrow$$
$[_{\text{Y-MAX}}\ [_{\text{Y-MAX}}\ W\ [_{\text{X-MAX}}\ Q\ [\ \ldots\ X\ Z]]]]$

For comparison, we will look at another system that addresses promotional divergences. The LFG-MT system by Kaplan *et al.* (1989) is a system that translates English, French, and German bidirectionally based on *lexical functional grammar* (LFG) by Kaplan and Bresnan (1982). In the LFG formalism, the structure that is the closest to the LCS is the f-structure. For example, the f-structure for the sentence *I gave a doll to Mary* is:[11]

(178)
$$
\begin{bmatrix}
\text{PRED} & \text{'GIVE}\langle(\uparrow \text{SUBJ})(\uparrow \text{OBJ})(\uparrow \text{TO OBJ})\rangle\text{'} \\
\text{SUBJ} & \begin{bmatrix} \text{NUM} & \text{SG} \\ \text{PRED} & \text{'I'} \end{bmatrix} \\
\text{TENSE} & \text{PAST} \\
\text{OBJ} & \begin{bmatrix} \text{SPEC} & \text{A} \\ \text{NUM} & \text{SG} \\ \text{PRED} & \text{'DOLL'} \end{bmatrix} \\
\text{TO} & \begin{bmatrix} \text{PCASE} & \text{TO} \\ \text{OBJ} & [\ \text{PRED} \quad \text{'MARY'}\ ] \end{bmatrix}
\end{bmatrix}
$$

---

[11]The f-structures presented here are taken from Kaplan and Bresnan (1982).

This is analogous to the following LCS:

(179) [Event CAUSE ([Thing I],

    [Event GO_Poss

      ([Thing DOLL],

        [Path TOWARD_Poss

          ([Position AT_Poss ([Thing DOLL], [Thing MARY])])])])]

Ignoring the primitive elements, these two representations are quite similar. The top-level predicate GIVE in the f-structure is analogous to the top-level primitive CAUSE in the LCS. The three f-structure arguments, SUBJ, OBJ, and TO, correspond to the LCS arguments I, DOLL, and TOWARD_Poss, respectively. Moving down one level of recursion, the f-structure argument OBJ under TO corresponds to the LCS argument MARY under [Path TOWARD_Poss ([Position AT_Poss ...])].

As for handling promotional divergences, an example that is addressed by LFG-MT is the following:[12]

(180) **Promotional divergence:**

    E: The baby just fell ⇒ F: Le bébé vient de tomber

                           'The baby just (verb-past) of fall'

Here, the English adverbial *just* is translated as the French main verb *venir* which takes the falling event as its complement *de tomber*. The f-structures that correspond, respectively, to the English and French sentences in this example are the following:

(181) (i)
$$
\left[
\begin{array}{ll}
\text{PRED} & \text{'JUST}\langle(\uparrow \text{ARG})\rangle' \\
\text{ARG} & \left[
\begin{array}{ll}
\text{PRED} & \text{'FALL}\langle(\uparrow \text{SUBJ})\rangle' \\
\text{TENSE} & \text{PAST} \\
\text{SUBJ} & \left[
\begin{array}{ll}
\text{PRED} & \text{'BABY'} \\
\text{NUM} & \text{SG} \\
\text{SPEC} & \left[\begin{array}{ll} \text{DEF} & + \\ \text{PRED} & \text{'THE'} \end{array} \right]
\end{array}
\right]
\end{array}
\right]
\end{array}
\right]
$$

(ii)
$$
\left[
\begin{array}{ll}
\text{PRED} & \text{'VENIR}\langle(\uparrow \text{SUBJ})(\uparrow \text{XCOMP})\rangle' \\
\text{SUBJ} & \left[
\begin{array}{ll}
\text{PRED} & \text{'BÉBÉ'} \\
\text{GENDER} & \text{MASC} \\
\text{NUMB} & \text{SG} \\
\text{SPEC} & \left[\begin{array}{ll} \text{DEF} & + \\ \text{PRED} & \text{'LE'} \end{array} \right]
\end{array}
\right] \\
\text{XCOMP} & \left[
\begin{array}{ll}
\text{PRED} & \text{'TOMBER}\langle(\uparrow \text{SUBJ})\rangle' \\
\text{COMPL} & \text{DE} \\
\text{TENSE} & \text{INF} \\
\text{SUBJ} & [\text{BÉBÉ}]
\end{array}
\right]
\end{array}
\right]
$$

---

[12]The examples presented here and in section 7.4.4 are taken from Kaplan *et al.* (1989).

Because the LFG-MT system is based on construction-specific representations, the mapping operations required in the transfer must be
performed by transfer equations that relate source- and target-language
f-structures. The transfer equations that relate the f-structures (181)(i)
and (ii) are the following:

(182) $(\tau \uparrow \mathrm{PRED} \text{ 'JUST} \langle (\uparrow \mathrm{ARG}) \rangle \text{'}) = \mathrm{VENIR}$
       $(\tau \uparrow \mathrm{XCOMP}) = \tau \, (\uparrow \mathrm{ARG})$

This equation identifies *venir* as the corresponding French predicate,
and it maps the argument of *just* to a complement that is headed by the
prepositional complementizer *de*.

As in UNITRAN, the LFG framework makes an association between
the syntactic structure and the conceptual structure using a set of me-
diating lexical entries. However, a major distinction between these two
frameworks is that the mapping between the syntactic structure and the
conceptual structure is more direct in the LFG framework than in the
LCS framework. The result is that the conceptual representation more
closely reflects the syntactic representation in the former than in the
latter. Thus, if a particular concept can be syntactically expressed in
more than one way, there will be more than one f-structure in the LFG
framework.

A more serious flaw of the LFG-MT system concerns the handling of
divergences in the context of embedded clauses. (For additional discussion, see Sadler and Thompson (1991).) In particular, if the English
sentence in example (180) were realized as an embedded complement
such as *I think that the baby just fell*, it would not be possible to generate the French output. The reason for this is that the LFG-MT system
breaks this sentence down into predicate-argument relations that conform (roughly) to the following logical specification:

(183) think(I,fall(baby))
       just(fall(baby))

The problem is that the logical constituent fall(baby) is predicated of two
logical heads, "think" and "just." The LFG-MT generator is unable to
determine how to compose these concepts and produce an output string.
Because of the compositional nature of the LCS representation and the
full coverage requirement of chapter 6, such complications do not arise in
the current approach. In particular, specific relations are set up between

logical heads and their associated arguments and modifiers so that there could never be any question of how two concepts are composed, even for embedded cases. For the current example, the LCS approach would reduce the logical relations to a single specification for both French and English:

(184) think(I,fall(baby,just))

That is, the "just" component of meaning is a modifier of the "falling" action, regardless of how this constituent is realized on the surface. We will return to the issue of full coverage in section 7.5.

7.4.3 Parameterization for Demotional Divergence

Demotional divergence is characterized by the *demotion* (placement "lower down") of a logical head into an internal argument position (or *vice versa*). This situation arises in the demotional divergence example given earlier in (128) of chapter 5. The syntactic structures are shown here:

(185) [C-MAX [I-MAX [N-MAX I]$_i$ [V-MAX [V like] [C-MAX PRO$_i$ to eat]]]]

$\Updownarrow$

[C-MAX [I-MAX [N-MAX Ich] [V-MAX [V [ADV gern] [V esse]]]]]^{13}

Here the main verb *like* takes the "to eat" event as a complement; but, in German, *like* has been placed into a lower position as the adjunct *gern*, and the "eat" event has been realized as the main verb.

Demotional divergence is accounted for by the :DEMOTE parameter, which determines the position for the logical head with respect to the logical argument. The general solution to promotional divergence makes use of this parameter as follows:

---

[13]The German syntactic structure is shown here in the uninverted base form. In the German surface structure, the verb is moved up into verb-second position and the subject is topicalized:

[C-MAX [N-MAX Ich]$_i$ [V esse]$_j$ [I-MAX [N-MAX t]$_i$ [V-MAX [V [ADV gern] [V t]$_j$]]]].

(186) RLCS 1: $[_{T(X')}$ X' $([_{T(W')}$ W'], $[_{T(Z')}$ Z'] $[_{T(Q')}$ Q'])]

RLCS 2: $[_{T(X')}$ X' $([_{T(W')}$ W'], $[_{T(Z')}$:DEMOTE Z'] $[_{T(Q')}$ Q'])]

Translation: $[_{Y\text{-MAX}}$ $[_{Y\text{-MAX}}$ W $[_{X\text{-MAX}}$ X Z]] Q]
$$\Updownarrow$$
$[_{T(X')}$ X' $([_{T(W')}$ W'], $[_{T(Z')}$ Z'] $[_{T(Q')}$ Q'])]
$$\Updownarrow$$
$[_{Y\text{-MAX}}$ $[_{Y\text{-MAX}}$ W $[_{X\text{-MAX}}$ Z] [... X Q]]]

An example of a system that has addressed demotional divergence was already discussed in chapter 1, namely the MiMo system (Arnold *et al.* (1988), Arnold and Sadler (1990), van Noord *et al.* (1989), van Noord *et al.* (1990), and Sadler *et al.* (1990)). Recall that this system relies on transfer rules to handle such cases:

(187) r!((cat = S).[mod = GERN]) $\Leftrightarrow$ LIKE((cat = S).[r!arg1])

As was mentioned in chapter 1, it is well known that specifying such transfer mappings for all of the lexical items of each source-language/target-language pair is very tedious work. What is more unsettling, however, is the fact that such rules store much of the information that is, or could be, lexically stored. (See chapter 1 for additional discussion.)

Now that the solution to thematic, promotional, and demotional divergences has been presented, we will turn to other divergence types whose solutions pertain not to the repositioning of constituents, but to other types of realization requirements.

7.4.4   Parameterization for Structural Divergence

Structural divergence is characterized by the realization of a logical constituent at compositionally different levels. This situation arises in the structural divergence example given earlier in (125) in chapter 5. The syntactic structures are shown here:

(188) $[_{C\text{-MAX}}$ $[_{I\text{-MAX}}$ $[_{N\text{-MAX}}$ John]
　　　　　　　$[_{V\text{-MAX}}$ $[_V$ entered] $[_{N\text{-MAX}}$ the house]]]]]
$$\Updownarrow$$
$[_{C\text{-MAX}}$ $[_{I\text{-MAX}}$ $[_{N\text{-MAX}}$ Juan]
　　　　　　$[_{V\text{-MAX}}$ $[_V$ entró] $[_{P\text{-MAX}}$ en $[_{N\text{-MAX}}$ la casa]]]]]]

Here the verbal object is realized as a noun phrase (*the house*) in English and as a prepositional phrase (*en la casa*) in Spanish.

Structural divergence is solved by means of the $*$ marker, which is used in a RLCS as a pointer to the position that must be combined with another RLCS in order to arrive at a (portion of a) CLCS. The general solution to structural divergence makes use of this parameter as follows:

(189) RLCS 1: $[_{T(X')} \; X' \; ([_{T(W')} \; W'], \; [_{T(R')} \; R' \; ([_{T(Z')} \; * \; Z'])] \; [_{T(Q')} \; Q'])]$

RLCS 2: $[_{T(X')} \; X' \; ([_{T(W')} \; W'], \; [_{T(R')} \; * \; R' \; ([_{T(Z')} \; Z'])] \; [_{T(Q')} \; Q'])]$

Translation: $[_{Y\text{-}MAX} \; [_{Y\text{-}MAX} \; W \; [_{X\text{-}MAX} \; X \; Z]] \; Q]$
$$\Updownarrow$$
$[_{T(X')} \; X' \; ([_{T(W')} \; W'], \; [_{T(Z')} \; Z'] \; [_{T(Q')} \; Q'])]$
$$\Updownarrow$$
$[_{Y\text{-}MAX} \; [_{Y\text{-}MAX} \; W \; [_{X\text{-}MAX} \; X \; [\ldots R \; Z]]] \; Q]$

Note that the logical argument R' is associated with a $*$ in the RLCS of the target language, but not in the RLCS of the source language. This forces the target language syntactic structure to realize a phrase R that dominates Z; in contrast, no such dominating phrase occurs in the source language structure.

As mentioned in section 7.4.1, GETA/ARIANE handles divergences through the use of transfer rules between source and target dependency-tree structures. As it turns out, rule (173) given above not only addresses a thematic divergence (*i.e.*, subject-object interchange), but it also addresses a structural divergence (*i.e.*, the use of a prepositional phrase for the French object and a noun phrase for the English object). Thus, this rule must simultaneously resolve both divergence types (*i.e.*, it must interchange the subject and object as well as delete the preposition in the English case). The use of such rules not only introduces a severe proliferation of redundancy (as we noted earlier), but it makes the system much more difficult to program, since the designer is forced to think about the interaction effects of different divergence types. Furthermore, such rules will not work for more complex interactions such as the sentence *Leer libros le suele gustar a Juan* ('John usually likes reading books'), which we will discuss in section 7.5.

As we have seen, another machine translation system that is related to UNITRAN in its attempt to map between divergent structures is the LFG-MT system by Kaplan *et al.* (1989). An example of structural divergence that it is designed to handle is the mapping between the German word *beantworten* and the French word *répondre* (both of which mean *to answer*). Consider the following example:

(190) **Structural divergence:**

   G: Der Student beantwortet die Frage ⇒
   F: L'étudiant répond à la question
   'The student answered the question'

Here, the German noun phrase *die Frage* is mapped to a prepositional phrase *à la question* in French. The f-structures that correspond, respectively, to the German and French sentences in this example are the following:

(191) (i)

$$
\begin{bmatrix}
\text{PRED} & \text{'BEANTWORTEN}\langle(\uparrow \text{SUBJ})(\uparrow \text{OBJ})\rangle\text{'} \\
\text{TENSE} & \text{PRESENT} \\
\text{SUBJ} & \begin{bmatrix} \text{PRED} & \text{'STUDENT'} \\ \text{NUM} & \text{SG} \\ \text{GEND} & \text{MASC} \\ \text{SPEC} & \begin{bmatrix} \text{DEF} & + \\ \text{PRED} & \text{'DER'} \end{bmatrix} \end{bmatrix} \\
\text{OBJ} & \begin{bmatrix} \text{PRED} & \text{'FRAGE'} \\ \text{NUM} & \text{SG} \\ \text{GEND} & \text{FEM} \\ \text{SPEC} & \begin{bmatrix} \text{DEF} & + \\ \text{PRED} & \text{'DIE'} \end{bmatrix} \end{bmatrix}
\end{bmatrix}
$$

(ii)

$$
\begin{bmatrix}
\text{PRED} & \text{'RÉPONDRE}\langle(\uparrow \text{SUBJ})(\uparrow \text{AOBJ})\rangle\text{'} \\
\text{TENSE} & \text{PRESENT} \\
\text{SUBJ} & \begin{bmatrix} \text{PRED} & \text{'ÉTUDIANT'} \\ \text{NUM} & \text{SG} \\ \text{GEND} & \text{MASC} \\ \text{SPEC} & \begin{bmatrix} \text{DEF} & + \\ \text{PRED} & \text{'LE'} \end{bmatrix} \end{bmatrix} \\
\text{AOBJ} & \begin{bmatrix} \text{PRED} & \text{'Á}\langle(\uparrow \text{OBJ})\rangle\text{'} \\ \text{PCASE} & \text{AOBJ} \\ \text{OBJ} & \begin{bmatrix} \text{PRED} & \text{'QUESTION'} \\ \text{NUM} & \text{SG} \\ \text{GEND} & \text{FEM} \\ \text{SPEC} & \begin{bmatrix} \text{DEF} & + \\ \text{PRED} & \text{'LA'} \end{bmatrix} \end{bmatrix} \end{bmatrix}
\end{bmatrix}
$$

The transfer equations that relate the f-structures (191)(i) and (ii) are the following:

(192) $(\tau \uparrow \text{PRED 'BEANTWORTEN}\langle(\uparrow \text{SUBJ})(\uparrow \text{OBJ})\rangle\text{'}) = $ répondre

   $(\tau \uparrow \text{SUBJ}) = \tau (\uparrow \text{SUBJ})$

   $(\tau \uparrow \text{AOBJ OBJ}) = \tau (\uparrow \text{OBJ})$

This equation identifies *répondre* as the corresponding French predicate, and it maps the direct object of the verb *beantworten* to object position of a prepositional phrase headed by the word *à*.

This approach suffers from the same proliferation of rules that shows up in the GETA/ARIANE system. The designer is required to make up construction-specific equations for all source-to-target pairs, regardless of whether the source-to-target mapping is divergent. Furthermore, once the target-language f-structure is derived, there is no generalized mapping from this form to the target-language surface structure, even though the mapping appears to be well-defined in the opposite direction (*i.e.*, from the source-language sentence to the corresponding f-structure). The UNITRAN system, on the other hand, attempts to factor out construction-specific information (by means of language-dependent parameter settings), thus allowing the system to operate on the basis of a more general, language-independent mapping between the source and target language.

Recently, the LFG-MT framework has been further developed by Zajac (1990) so that typed feature structures are incorporated into the LFG formalism and the transfer equations are independent of source language analysis rules. Whether this augmented framework offers advantages over the earlier version in terms of handling translation divergences is not clear, since this version is still in the initial stages of development.

7.4.5   Parameterization for Conflational Divergence

Conflational divergence is characterized by the suppression of a CLCS constituent. This situation arises in the conflational divergence example given earlier in (130) of chapter 5. The syntactic structures are shown here:

(193) [c-max [i-max [n-max I]
                    [v-max [v stabbed] [n-max John]]]]
                              ⇕
       [c-max [i-max [n-max Yo]
                    [v-max [v le di] [n-max puñaladas] [p-max a Juan]]]]

Recall that conflation is the incorporation of necessary participants (or arguments) of a given action. Here, English uses the single word *stab* for the two Spanish words *dar* (*give*) and *puñaladas* (*knife-wounds*); this is because the instrument (*i.e.*, the *knife-wound* portion of the lexical token) is incorporated into the main verb in English.

Conflational divergence is resolved by means of the :CONFLATED marker which suppresses the realization of the filler of a particular position.[14] The general solution to structural divergence makes use of this parameter as follows:

(194) RLCS 1: $[_{T(X')}$ X' $([_{T(W')}$ W'], $[_{T(Z')}$ Z'] $[_{T(Q')}$ Q'])]

RLCS 2: $[_{T(X')}$ X' $([_{T(W')}$ W'], $[_{T(Z')}$:CONFLATED Z'] $[_{T(Q')}$ Q'])]

Translation: $[_{Y\text{-}MAX}$ $[_{Y\text{-}MAX}$ W $[_{X\text{-}MAX}$ X Z]] Q]
$$\Updownarrow$$
$[_{T(X')}$ X' $([_{T(W')}$ W'], $[_{T(Z')}$ Z'] $[_{T(Q')}$ Q'])]
$$\Updownarrow$$
$[_{Y\text{-}MAX}$ $[_{Y\text{-}MAX}$ W $[_{X\text{-}MAX}$ X]] Q]

Note that the logical argument Z' is associated with a :CONFLATED marker in the RLCS of the target language, but not in the RLCS of the source language. This forces the target language syntactic structure to suppress the realization of this constituent.

TAUM (English-French, French-English) by Colmerauer *et al.* (1971) is another machine translation system that has attempted to accommodate conflational divergences. The system was defined in close interaction with other research groups such as GETA at the University of Grenoble. (See Isabelle and Bourbeau (1985) and Isabelle (1987) for a summary and substantial achievements of the TAUM project.) At the time of its inception, the TAUM system was an advance over other systems in that the transfer rules were framed in terms of structural correspondences rather than in terms of string-to-string correspondences.

---

[14]Note that the :CONFLATED marker appears to be in complementary distribution with the * marker. In fact, one might consider the use of the :CONFLATED marker to be unnecessary since its presence could be implied by the absence of the * marker. However, the :CONFLATED marker plays an important role in the lexical-semantic representation: it specifies that the "constant" term (*e.g.*, the KNIFE-WOUND of the *stab* RLCS) must obligatorily fill the position, and moreover, that this constant must be a legal LCS primitive of the system. In addition, there is an inherent asymmetry between the :CONFLATED marker and the * marker: whereas the former always occurs in a leaf node position, the latter may occur in *any* position in the RLCS. Because the notion of *conflation* is not meaningful in non-leaf node positions, it would be unreasonable to make the assumption that every non-leaf position without the * marker is conflated. The :CONFLATED marker is used to identify truly conflated positions, not just those positions without the * marker.

The transfer component of TAUM consists of source-to-target tree-transduction mappings between intermediate dependency structures. For various "hard" transfer relations (*i.e.*, translation divergences), the transfer rules make use of lexical transformations in order to establish correspondences between source and target structures. An example of such a case is the following:[15]

(195) **Conflational divergence:**

    E: John swam across the river ⇒

    F: John a traversé la rivière à la nage

    'John crossed the river by swimming'

In this example, the English path component (*across*) is translated as the French main verb (*traverser*), and the English main verb (*swim*) is translated as the French manner component (*à la nage*). The details of how this divergence type might be solved are not discussed by Isabelle (1987). However, given that the TAUM framework uses tree-transduction transfer between intermediate structures, it is likely that such a case is solved by means of a rule of the form:

(196) (X swim (across Y)) ⇔ (X traverser Y (à la nage))

This rule maps the path component (*across*) to the French main verb (*traverser*), and the English main verb (*swim*) to the French adverbial (*à la nage*).

The disadvantage to this approach is that it requires a new transfer rule for every adverbial that might potentially participate in the traverser construction (*e.g.*, *à pied, en courant, en marchant, etc.*). As we have seen, the LCS approach resolves this type of divergence compositionally without recourse to transfer rules.

For comparison, we will briefly examine the current approach operating on this example. The underlying LCS for the two sentences in (195) is the following:

(197) [$_{\text{Event}}$ GO$_{\text{Loc}}$

        ([$_{\text{Thing}}$ JOHN],

        [$_{\text{Path}}$ ACROSS$_{\text{Loc}}$ ([$_{\text{Position}}$ AT$_{\text{Loc}}$ ([$_{\text{Thing}}$ JOHN], [$_{\text{Location}}$ RIVER])])],

        [$_{\text{Manner}}$ SWIMMINGLY])]

---

[15]This example, which is taken from Kittredge *et al.* (1988), is an adapted version of example (10) in Isabelle (1987, p. 256).

The solution to this example relies on the assumption that the divergence type is *conflational i.e.*, that the distinction between the English and French exists by virtue of the fact that the word *swim* includes the manner component *swimmingly*, whereas the word *traverser* does not. Because of this conflational distinction, the manner component is suppressed in English, but is overtly realized (as *à la nage*) in French.[16] This suppression/realization of conceptual components is achieved by the presence/absence of the :CONFLATED marker.

7.4.6 Parameterization for Categorial Divergence

Another divergence type related to the syntactic realization of arguments is categorial divergence. Categorial divergence is characterized by the association of a logical constituent with a syntactic category that is different from the default categorial value. This situation arises in the categorial divergence example given earlier in (127) of chapter 5. The syntactic structures are shown here:

(198) $[_{\text{C-MAX}} [_{\text{I-MAX}} [_{\text{N-MAX}} \text{I}] [_{\text{V-MAX}} [_{\text{V}} \text{am}] [_{\text{A-MAX}} \text{hungry}]]]]$

$\Updownarrow$

$[_{\text{C-MAX}} [_{\text{I-MAX}} [_{\text{N-MAX}} \text{Ich}] [_{\text{V-MAX}} [_{\text{N-MAX}} \text{Hunger}] [_{\text{V}} \text{habe}]]]]^{17}$

Here, the predicate is adjectival (*hungry*) in English but nominal (*Hunger*) in German.

Categorial divergence is distinct from the divergences we have looked at so far in that it does not require the $\mathcal{GLR}$ to be overridden. Instead, a categorial override is required for the $\mathcal{CSR}$ function. This override is achieved by means of the :CAT parameter. The general solution to structural divergence makes use of this parameter as follows:

---

[16]The use of the word *traverser* (*i.e.*, *cross*) instead of *nager* (*i.e.*, *swim*) is independently determined by the fact that the path component ACROSS is present in the conceptual representation (*i.e.*, there would be no way to realize the path component in conjunction with the word *nager*).

[17]The German structure shown here is the base form of the surface syntactic tree. See fn. 6 of chapter 5 for relevant discussion.

(199) RLCS 1: $[_{T(X')}$ X' $([_{T(W')}$ W'], $[_{T(Z')}$:Z'] $[_{T(Q')}$ Q'])]

RLCS 2: $[_{T(X')}$ X' $([_{T(W')}$ W'], $[_{T(Z')}$ (:CAT δ) Z'] $[_{T(Q')}$ Q'])]

Translation: $[_{Y\text{-MAX}}$ $[_{Y\text{-MAX}}$ W $[_{X\text{-MAX}}$ X Z]] Q]

⇕

$[_{T(X')}$ X' $([_{T(W')}$ W'], $[_{T(Z')}$ Z'] $[_{T(Q')}$ Q'])]

⇕

$[_{Y\text{-MAX}}$ $[_{Y\text{-MAX}}$ W $[_{X\text{-MAX}}$ X Z]] Q]

where CAT(Z) = δ-MAX.

Another machine translation system that has attempted to accommodate categorial divergences is the LTAG system (English-French, French-English) by Abeillé *et al.* (1990). The system is a transfer approach that uses synchronous tree-adjoining grammars (as described by Shieber and Schabes (1990)) to map shallow tree-adjoining grammar (TAG) (Joshi (1985)) derivations from one language onto another. The mapping is performed by means of a bilingual lexicon which directly associates source and target trees through links between lexical items and their arguments. Roughly, each bilingual entry contains a mapping between a source-language sentence and a target-language sentence.

This approach handles cases such as the following:

(200) **Categorial divergence:**

E: John is fond of music ⇔ F: John aime la musique
'John loves the music'

Here, the source language concept is realized as the adjectival form *be fond of* in English, whereas the French translation realizes this concept as the verb *aimer*. The transfer rule that accounts for this mapping directly links the adjectival phrase *fond of* in the source-language tree with the verb *aimer* in the target-language tree as shown here:

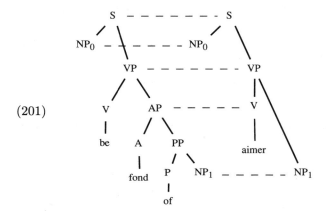

(201)

The transfer correspondence links the AP node in the English tree to
the V node of the French tree.

The advantage of this approach is that it accommodates modifying
phrases in cases such as:

(202) **Categorial divergence:**
E: John is very fond of music ⇔ F: John aime beaucoup la musique
'John loves very much the music'

Here, the English adverb *very* is associated with the predicate *fond of*
(instead of with the main verb) whereas in French, the corresponding
adverbial *beaucoup* is associated with the main verb *aimer*. The mechanism that permits this modification to be appropriately executed is the
linking between the adjectival phrase *fond of* and the verb *aimer*: since
the English main verb *be* has no link associated with it, the modifier
must instead be associated with the adjectival phrase.

While the categorial divergence problem has previously been addressed
in the literature, problems of this more complicated type are not described elsewhere. However, the solution offered by Abeillé *et al.* (1990)
requires *entire* trees to be stored in the transfer dictionary for each
source-to-target pair. This is significantly burdensome as the number
of source and target languages begin to add up. Furthermore, the approach is afflicted with some of the same problems that are inherent
in the MiMo system with respect to representing constructions such as
the *failli finir* combination of example (16). In particular, the use of

transfer rules based on tree mappings results in a severe proliferation of source-to-target mappings because there is a multiplicative effect of all the different combinations of idiom/verb, verb/light-verb, adverb/verb, *etc.* that can arise in any given language.

7.4.7   Parameterization for Lexical Divergence

Unlike the first six divergence types, the final divergence type, lexical divergence, is solved during the process of lexical selection.[18] Thus, there is no specific override marker that is used for this type of divergence. In fact, as mentioned in section 7.3.7, this divergence type arises only in the context of other divergences. For example, in the lexical divergence example (131) of chapter 5, a conflational divergence forces the occurrence of a lexical divergence. The syntactic structures for this example are shown here:

(203) [$_{\text{C-MAX}}$ [$_{\text{I-MAX}}$ [$_{\text{N-MAX}}$ John]
$\qquad\qquad$ [$_{\text{V-MAX}}$ [$_{\text{V}}$ broke] [$_{\text{P-MAX}}$ into [$_{\text{N-MAX}}$ the room]]]]]]
$\qquad\qquad\qquad$ ⇕
$\qquad$ [$_{\text{C-MAX}}$ [$_{\text{I-MAX}}$ [$_{\text{N-MAX}}$ Juan]
$\qquad\qquad$ [$_{\text{V-MAX}}$ [$_{\text{V}}$ forzó] [$_{\text{N-MAX}}$ la entrada] [$_{\text{P-MAX}}$ al cuarto]]]]]

Because the word-particle pair *break into* subsumes two concepts (forceful spatial motion and entry to a location), it is crucial that the word *forzar* (literally, *force*) be selected in conjunction with *entrada* (literally, *entry*) for the underlying break-into concept.

There is also a structural divergence in this example since the prepositional phrase *into the room* must be translated into a noun phrase *entrada al cuarto*. This divergence compounds the lexical divergence problem since it is necessary to choose the target-language word *a* in the absence of a source-language counterpart.

Lexical divergence also shows up in three previously presented examples, (171), (198), and (193), due to the presence of thematic, categorial, and conflational divergences, respectively: in (171), the word *like* is chosen for the word *gustar* (literally, *to please*); in (198); the word *haben*

---

[18]The solution to lexical divergence is trivial for transfer machine translation systems since transfer entries map source-language words directly to their target-language equivalents. (See, *e.g.*, rules (16), (17), (173), (174), (175), (187), (192), (196), and (201).) In general, the lexical selection problem is not addressed by these systems.

(literally, *to have*) is chosen for the word *be*; and in (193) the word *dar* (literally, *to give*) is chosen for the word *stab*.

We now turn to a discussion of certain issues regarding the formalized classification and divergence solution presented above.

7.5   Discussion

We made the claim earlier that the thematic, promotional, and demotional divergences defined above account for the entire range of repositioning possibilities. We will now explore the validity of this claim.

There are two potential types of syntactic relationships that exist between a head and a satellite: the first is complementation (*i.e.*, the internal argument), and the second is adjunction.[19] Given these two types of relationships, there are only a small number of ways syntactic entities may be repositioned. The three CLCS positions that are involved in these relations are X′, Z′, and Q′. If we compute the repositionings combinatorially, there are $3^3 = 27$ configurations (*i.e.*, X′, Z′, and Q′ would map into any of three positions). However, we can eliminate 15 of these (since a CLCS must contain exactly one head), thus leaving only 12 possible configurations. One of these corresponds to the default $\mathcal{GLR}$ mapping (*i.e.*, the logical head, logical argument, and logical modifier map into canonical positions). The remaining 11 configurations can be factored into three cases as follows:

---

[19] We have left out the possibility of an external argument as a participant in the head-satellite relationship. Of course, the external argument *is* a satellite with respect to the head, but it turns out that the external argument, which corresponds to the logical subject in the CLCS, has a special status, and does not have the same repositioning potential that internal arguments and syntactic adjuncts have. In particular, the external argument has the unique property that it never participates as the incorporated argument of a conflational verb. Hale and Keyser (1989) provide evidence that this property holds across all languages. Thus, we take the external argument to have a special status (universally) that exempts it from participating in divergences other than thematic divergence.

1. $X' \Leftrightarrow X$

    1.1 $Q' \Leftrightarrow Z$; $Z' \Leftrightarrow Z$.

    1.2 $Z' \Leftrightarrow Q$; $Q' \Leftrightarrow Q$.

    1.3 $Q' \Leftrightarrow Z$; $Z' \Leftrightarrow Q$.

2. $Q' \Leftrightarrow X$

    2.1 $X' \Leftrightarrow Z$; $Z' \Leftrightarrow Z$.

    2.2 $X' \Leftrightarrow Z$; $Z' \Leftrightarrow Q$.

    2.3 $X' \Leftrightarrow Q$; $Z' \Leftrightarrow Z$.

    2.4 $X' \Leftrightarrow Q$; $Z' \Leftrightarrow Q$.

3. $Z' \Leftrightarrow X$

    3.1 $X' \Leftrightarrow Z$; $Q' \Leftrightarrow Z$.

    3.2 $X' \Leftrightarrow Z$; $Q' \Leftrightarrow Q$.

    3.3 $X' \Leftrightarrow Q$; $Q' \Leftrightarrow Z$.

    3.4 $X' \Leftrightarrow Q$; $Q' \Leftrightarrow Q$.

As it turns out, we are able to rule out cases, 1.3, 2.2, 2.4, 3.1, and 3.3 for the same reasons that rule out cases 1.1 and 1.2 (as we will see shortly), namely that an internal argument Z can never be associated with a logical modifier Q' and that a syntactic adjunct (Q) can never be associated with a logical argument Z'. Thus, we are left with cases 1.1, 1.2, 2.1, 2.3, 3.2, and 3.4. Cases 2.1 and 3.4 correspond to the definitions of promotional and demotional divergences given previously in (169) and (170), respectively. The remaining cases are characterized as shown in figure 7.4. We will now see how each of the remaining cases is ruled out.

It cannot be the case that a logical modifier maps to an internal argument position (case 1.1). A logical modifier is an *optional* participant of a particular action, it need not be "governed" by the lexical item that it modifies. Internal argument positions are reserved for cases in which a government relation must hold; thus, logical modifiers must necessarily be mapped into syntactic adjunct positions.

Similarly, it also cannot be the case that a logical argument maps to a syntactic adjunct position (case 1.2). A logical argument is a *necessary* participant of a particular action and, as such, it must be "governed" by the lexical item that selects it. By contrast, adjunct positions are

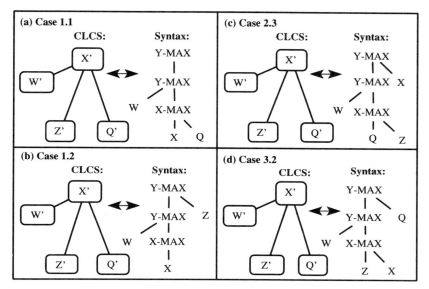

Figure 7.4
Certain repositionings do not occur in natural language. Such cases are not included in the divergence classification and need not be considered by the translation system.

reserved for *optional* modifying participants which do not need to be governed by the lexical item that they are modifying; thus, logical arguments must necessarily be mapped into complement positions.

Another case that is eliminated is the renaming of a logical head as a syntactic adjunct whose head corresponds to a logical modifier (case 2.3). The idea is simply that modification is a one-way relation. If a logical head has a modifier, the head cannot become an adjunct of that modifier because the modifying relation would be reversed (*i.e.*, the logical head would modify the syntactic head rather than the other way around). In contrast, a logical head of a CLCS *can* be mapped to an internal argument position in cases where a logical modifier is mapped to a syntactic head (*i.e.*, the case of promotional divergence presented earlier) since there is no violation of the one-way relation.

A similar argument is used to eliminate the case where a logical head is mapped to an internal argument whose head corresponds to a logical argument (case 3.2). The idea is that heads and arguments participate in a one-way relation. If a logical head has an argument, the head cannot become an internal argument of that argument because the head-argument relation would be reversed (*i.e.*, the logical head would be an argument of the syntactic head rather than the other way around). In contrast, the logical head of a CLCS *can* be mapped to an adjunct (*i.e.*, modifier) position in cases where a logical argument is mapped to a syntactic head (*i.e.*, the case of demotional divergence presented earlier) since there is no violation of the one-way relation.

The argument for the elimination of the last two cases could be viewed as an appeal to a constraint that is analogous to the θ-criterion in syntax. Essentially, this constraint states that all arguments and modifiers must be *licensed* (see Chomsky (1986a) and Abney (1989)) in order to appear either in the syntactic structure or in the conceptual structure. In the context of conceptual structure, a logical modifier may license the realization of a logical head in an internal argument position, but not in an adjunct position since the modifier relationship is already satisfied by virtue of the relationship between the head and the modifier. Similarly, a logical argument may license the realization of a logical head in a syntactic adjunct position, but not in an internal argument position since the head-argument relationship is already satisfied by virtue of the relationship between the head and the argument. Having eliminated the meaningless possibilities, we are left with the promotional and demotional cases presented above.

We will now provide justification for the earlier claim that promotional and demotional divergence should be classified differently, even though they exhibit some of the same properties. It might be argued that these divergences are essentially the same since both cases involve an association of a main verb with an adverbial satellite or *vice versa*. In the examples given earlier, the *promotional* divergence referred to a mapping between the adverbial *usually* and the main verb *soler* and *demotional* divergence referred to a mapping between the adverbial *gern* and the main verb *like*. However, these are taken to be in distinct classes. In the case of *soler-usually*, the main verb *soler* is, in some sense, the token that "triggers" the head switching operation: its presence forces the adverbial satellite *usually* to appear in English, even if we were to substitute some other event for *ir* in Spanish (*e.g.*, *correr a la tienda, leer un libro*, etc.). By contrast, in the case of *like-gern*, the triggering element is not the main verb *like* since we are able to use *like* in other contexts that do not require *gern* (*e.g.*, *I like the car* ⇔ *Mir gefällt der Wagen*); instead, the triggering element is the adverbial satellite *gern*: its presence forces the verb *like* to appear in English even if we were to substitute some other event in place of *essen* in German (*e.g.*, *zum Geschäft laufen, das Buch lesen, etc.*).

Another factor that distinguishes between promotional and demotional divergences is the fact that verbs such as *like* and verbs such as *soler* do not have parallel syntactic distributions, nor do they have analogous logical interpretations. The verb *like* may take a sentential complement that has its own event structure (as in *I like to eat*) or it may take a nominal complement without an event structure (as in *I like the car*). In either case, the verb *like* generally means the same thing (*i.e.*, it describes a state in which an event or a thing is somehow desirable to that person). By contrast, the verb *soler* is a modal verb that contributes an aspectual component of meaning that crucially relies on a verbal complement with an event structure; in a sense, *soler* is analogous to the modal *must* in English in that it cannot be used in isolation but requires the presence of a verbal complement in order for it to be interpretable. In such a configuration, the modal *soler* allows the event to be interpreted as being habitual in nature.

Given these distinctions, it would not be appropriate to consider the "head switching" mapping to be the same for the *soler-usually* and *like-gern* cases. Not only do they have different triggering elements (*i.e.*, the main verb in the former and the adverb in the latter), but they do not have identical syntactic distributions and their logical interpretations are not analogous. Thus, they are taken to be two independent mappings with entirely different syntactic and lexical-semantic ramifications.

As mentioned above (see fn. 10), the notions of demotion and promotion are not the same as the notions of demotion and advancement in the theory of relational grammar (RG) (see Perlmutter (1983)). However, it might be possible for the mechanism that is used for RG operations to be used in the LCS scheme as well. We will now explore this possibility.

The RG framework uses a mechanism for positioning arguments that is similar to the mechanism proposed here. This purely syntactic processing approach uses a graph-theoretic object called a relational network (RN) that represents the grammatical relations (GRs) between the predicate (P), subject (1), direct object (2), and indirect object (3) of a

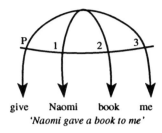

Figure 7.5
The relational network for *Naomi gave a book to me* illustrates the grammatical
relations between the predicate (P), subject (1), direct object (2), and indirect
object (3).

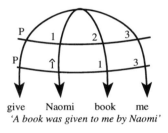

Figure 7.6
The relational network for *A book was given to me by Naomi* illustrates the
application of advancement rules to an RN in order to arrive at the passive form.

clause. For example, the representation for the sentence *Naomi gave a
book to me* is shown in figure 7.5.

   Relational operations can be applied to an RN in order to arrive at
different surface forms. For example, the RN for the passive form of
Naomi gave a book to me is shown in figure 7.6.[20] Such an operation is
called an "advancement" rule in that the *book* argument advances from
a 2-relation to a 1-relation. There are also "demotion" rules, *e.g.*, in
Choctaw, where an initial 1 can become a final 3 as shown in figure 7.7.[21]

---

[20]The î notation is called a 1-chômeur meaning that it bears the 1 relation in the
last stratum before it bears the chômeur relation.
[21]This structure represents the sentence *I dropped the apple*. In Choctaw, the
agent may take on dative morphology in the surface structure; this leaves the subject
position open to be occupied by the theme.

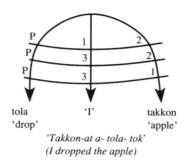

tola   'I'   takkon
'drop'   'apple'

'Takkon-at a- tola- tok'
(I dropped the apple)

Figure 7.7
The relational network for *I dropped the apple* in Choctaw illustrates the operation of demotion rules.

For the most part, modifiers have received little attention in the RG literature. In general, a modifier is given an "Obl" arc in a relation network, but according to Perlmutter and Postal (1983), the limits on the set of oblique grammatical relations (*e.g.*, benefactive, instrumental, temporal, locative, *etc.*) remain obscure. Nevertheless, if the RN notation were set up to include modifiers (however obscure), the RN and its associated relational operations could be used for the advancement and demotion revaluation operations in much the same way that the :PROMOTE and :DEMOTE mechanisms are used in UNITRAN. That is, we could represent the promotion and demotion structures of the current approach in terms of the networks shown in figure 7.8(a) and 7.8(b), respectively.

Note that the first stratum of each of these RN's is essentially the same for both languages (except for a minor deviation in the case of *soler*, where the 2-argument is in the initial stratum of the lower RN rather than that of the higher RN). Perhaps the RN representation could be used for interlingual translation: the initial stratum could be thought of as the *interlingua* common to pairs such as (soler, usually) and (gern, like), and all subsequent strata would then be considered to be language-particular operations.

I will argue that, although the RN representation might be a convenient tool for illustrating the promotion and demotion operations as used in UNITRAN, this representation is not an appropriate vehicle for

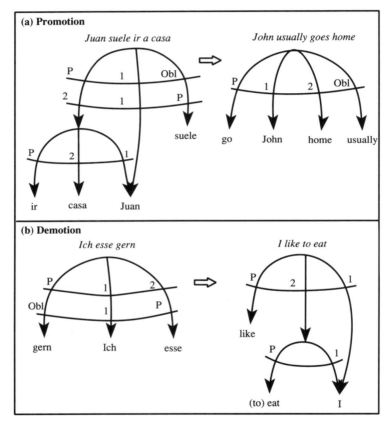

Figure 7.8
The relational network formalism can be used as a tool for representing
promotional and demotional divergences.

interlingual translation for a number of reasons. First, the RN representation is not a "true" interlingual form since, as we have already seen in figure 7.8(b), there are special cases in which not all arguments exist in the initial stratum. Furthermore, the representation does not provide information about argument realization. Thus, the mapping from this representation to the surface form is even more complicated since arguments such as *case* (see figure 7.8(a)) cannot be realized without a preposition. Since there is no representation for prepositions (or *any* functional elements such as determiners, complementizers, and tense elements), it is not clear how this mapping could be achieved even if there *were* some mechanism that accounted for structural divergence.

A related issue is that of lexical representation. The lexicon has received little attention in the RG literature. However, Davies and Dubinsky (1988) have proposed a scheme that allows each lexical entry to specify the "relational valence" (*i.e.*, the set of required GRs for both initial and non-initial strata of a given predicate). The valence set notation could be extended to include predicate demotion and promotion. For example, the entry for *gern* could be specified as:

(204) [P (gern,b) $<c_1>$] $\rightarrow$
$\quad$ {[1 (a,b) $<c_1>$], [2 (c,b) $<c_2>$], [Obl (gern,b) $<c_2>$],
$\quad$ [1 (a,b) $<c_2>$], [P (c,b) $<c_2>$]}

This entry specifies that the RN for clause b is required to have two strata, $<c_1>$ and $<c_2>$, in which the predicate *gern* is demoted into an oblique position (P $\rightarrow$ Obl), the 2-argument c is advanced into predicate position (c $\rightarrow$ P), and the 1-argument is not revalued.

Upon first consideration, it seems that using the RN mechanism to characterize divergences in this way is a reasonable approach. However, Davies and Rosen (1988) argue against the operations shown in (204) stating that there can be exactly one predicate per clause: "it is a general fact ... that P never revalues" (Davies and Rosen (1988, p. 56)). This assertion is based on the premise that the initial GRs do not have a universal correspondence with the thematic roles that are part of semantic structure. In fact, Rosen (1984) has shown conclusively that thematic roles (*i.e.*, argument positions in conceptual structures) cannot be mapped uniformly to any level of GRs, including the initial level, since the strata are intended to reflect syntactic relations that are established *independent of meaning*. In particular, GRs are syntactic positions that are specific to a given language; they do not necessarily correspond to the same set of thematic arguments for two given languages. Rosen provides a large body of evidence (for a number of languages) demonstrating that there can be no universal alignment between semantic roles and initial GRs.

Given these arguments, it appears that while the RN formalism may be useful for illustrating the demotion and promotion operations, it should not (and, most likely, *could* not) be used as an interlingua for machine translation.

The handling of promotional and demotional divergences is a topic that has received recent attention, although it has been labeled differently, depending on how it is manifested. An example of such a case is the *way* construction. This phenomenon has been studied by Jackendoff (1990) in his extended version of the original LCS framework:

(205) Bill belched his way out of the restaurant

In such cases, Jackendoff claims that *belching* is subordinated to a higher predicate like GO, "in effect demoting the meaning of the lexical verb to a subordinate accompaniment or means modifier" (Jackendoff (1990, p. 214)). This characterization is essentially equivalent to that of the *soler-usually* example (*i.e.*, promotional divergence) given earlier.

Jackendoff's approach to handling the *way* construction has been criticized by Marantz (1992) for its use of arbitrary exceptions to the "usual mappings." Marantz takes issue with the characterization of such cases as an idiosyncratic relation between syntax and semantics and proposes, instead, that the conceptual structure looks different from what Jackendoff envisions. Whichever of these proposals is correct, a number of points deserve mention with respect to this topic. First it is clear that neither Jackendoff nor Marantz consider their proposals in the context of interlingual machine translation. Doing so would certainly have made it significantly more difficult to justify either proposal. If the exceptional mappings are indeed arbitrary, then one needs to explain how this affects the handling of different languages. In particular, assuming all languages rely on the same conceptual machinery, the question of how such mappings would be constructed on a a per-language basis needs to be addressed. If, on the other hand, the LCS representation differs from what Jackendoff envisions (*i.e.*, if each language has its own idiosyncratic representation for the *way* construction), this would be problematic for interlingual machine translation because promotionally divergent cases would no longer be based on the same representation.

Another point regarding this issue is that neither Jackendoff nor Marantz mentions the possibility that the exceptional mappings might not be arbitrary. Rather, there might be a fixed number of exceptions, delineated in such a way that only a handful need be considered at any time for any given language. This is why the formal classification of divergences proposed here is a valuable resource: it provides a means for proving that only certain types of exceptions are allowed and that the number of such exceptions is actually quite small.

It is also interesting to note that neither Jackendoff nor Marantz consider the possibility of keeping Jackendoff's version of the LCS intact and using a single parameterized mapping along the lines proposed in the current framework. In fact, the possibility of parameterization is never mentioned. On the other hand, the need for parameterization is not immediately evident if only one language (English) is considered, which is the case for both Jackendoff and Marantz. An unfortunate drawback to considering only one language is that it is easy to overlook natural categories of cases that are related to those under consideration. For example, neither Jackendoff nor Marantz addresses the handling of demotional divergences, which is the analog to the promotional case under consideration.

We now return to the issue of *full coverage* alluded to in section 7.4.2. Recall that this notion was defined in (136) of chapter 6. One of the main advantages to the formalization defined in this chapter is that it allows one to judge whether a target-language concept *fully covers* the concept underlying the source-language sentence, and thus, to make an evaluation of the status of the system. As an illustration of this point, consider the *stab-dar* example of section 7.4.5. The notion of *full coverage* is manifested through the lexical-selection process. The basic idea is that RLCS's are chosen such that they entirely cover the underlying concept. In terms of the mapping from the source-language sentence to the CLCS, this implies that the RLCS's must compose in such a way as to provide a "full cover" (*i.e.*, there must be a path from the root to the leaf nodes that includes all the (content) words of the sentence). In terms of the mapping from the CLCS to the target-language sentence, this implies that the CLCS must be decomposed into (potentially overlapping) RLCS's whose "union" covers the entire CLCS.

From the English sentence in (193), the RLCS's must be chosen for each word in the sentence such that they provide a coherent CLCS. The RLCS for *stab* is:

(206) [$_{\text{Event}}$ CAUSE
    ([$_{\text{Thing}}$ * W],
    [$_{\text{Event}}$ GO$_{\text{Poss}}$
      ([$_{\text{Thing}}$ Y KNIFE-WOUND :CONFLATED],
      [$_{\text{Path}}$ TOWARD$_{\text{Poss}}$
        ([$_{\text{Position}}$ AT$_{\text{Poss}}$ ([$_{\text{Thing}}$ Y KNIFE-WOUND], [$_{\text{Thing}}$ * Z])])])])]

Because Y does not have a * specification, only W and Z need to be filled in. Once these positions are filled in, the resulting CLCS fulfills the full coverage requirement since there is a path from the root to the leaves that covers all of the words of the source-language sentence. The resulting CLCS is:

(207) [$_{\text{Event}}$ CAUSE
    ([$_{\text{Thing}}$ I],
    [$_{\text{Event}}$ GO$_{\text{Poss}}$
      ([$_{\text{Thing}}$ KNIFE-WOUND],
      [$_{\text{Path}}$ TOWARD$_{\text{Poss}}$
        ([$_{\text{Position}}$ AT$_{\text{Poss}}$ ([$_{\text{Thing}}$ KNIFE-WOUND], [$_{\text{Thing}}$ JOHN])])])])]

In order to complete the translation, this CLCS must be decomposed into RLCS's that satisfy the full coverage requirement. The RLCS that is selected as a match for this top-level CLCS is that of the word *dar*:

(208) [$_{\text{Event}}$ CAUSE
    ([$_{\text{Thing}}$ * W],
    [$_{\text{Event}}$ GO$_{\text{Poss}}$
      ([$_{\text{Thing}}$ * Y],
      [$_{\text{Path}}$ * TOWARD$_{\text{Poss}}$
        ([$_{\text{Position}}$ AT$_{\text{Poss}}$ ([$_{\text{Thing}}$ * Y], [$_{\text{Thing}}$ Z])])])])]

Unlike the RLCS for *stab*, the Y position is associated with a * marker; thus, it is necessary to find RLCS's for all three positions W, Y, and Z. Positions W and Y are filled at the leaf level and Z is filled at the TOWARD$_{\text{Poss}}$ level. Once these positions are filled, the combination of the RLCS's for *yo, dar, puñaladas, a,* and *Juan* covers the entire concept. Thus, the full coverage requirement is satisfied.

We now turn to another important issue alluded to in section 7.4.4, namely that of handling interacting divergence types. This issue is one that only recently has received the attention it deserves. In particular, there have been criticisms (see, *e.g.*, Lindop and Tsujii (1991)) of systems that perform transfer on relatively shallow analyses (*e.g.*, early METAL and LTAG) due to the fact that such systems are not likely to be able to handle divergence interactions (although they may be able to handle each divergence type in isolation). The solution adopted in the current approach does not appeal to a shallow analysis (*i.e.*, it does not use a set of already-coded canned "frames" with predetermined argument structure). Rather, the syntactic structures are derived *compositionally* on the basis of two pieces of information: the structure of the CLCS (*i.e.*, the language-independent predicate-argument information), and the lexical entries (*i.e.*, the RLCS's and their associated language-dependent information). It would not be possible to handle interacting divergence types in an approach that maps directly from a set of hard-wired source-language frames to a set of hard-wired target-language frames. This is because an argument that occurs in a divergent phrasal construction might itself be a divergent phrasal construction.

Consider the following example:

(209) **Promotional and Thematic divergence:**
   S: Leer libros le suele gustar a Juan
       'Reading books (him) tends to please (to) John'
   E: John usually likes reading books

This example exhibits a simultaneous occurrence of two types of divergences: the verb *soler* exhibits a promotional divergence with respect to its internal argument *gustar a Juan*, which itself exhibits a thematic divergence. The recursive nature of the $\mathcal{GLR}$ is crucial for handling such cases.

The CLCS for example (209) is the following:

(210) [$_{\text{State}}$ BE$_{\text{Circ}}$

      ([$_{\text{Thing}}$ JOHN],

      [$_{\text{Position}}$ AT$_{\text{Circ}}$

         ([$_{\text{Thing}}$ JOHN], [$_{\text{Event}}$ READ ([$_{\text{Thing}}$ JOHN], [$_{\text{Thing}}$ BOOK])])],

      [$_{\text{Manner}}$ LIKINGLY],

      [$_{\text{Manner}}$ HABITUALLY])][22]

Note that there are two modifiers, LIKINGLY and HABITUALLY. It is the job of the $\mathcal{GLR}$ function to determine the appropriate decomposition of the event on the basis of the language-specific requirements of the RLCS's involved in the mapping. In the current example, the LIKINGLY component is, in a sense, an "inherent" modifier since it appears in the RLCS of both *like* and *gustar*. In contrast, the HABITUALLY modifier is an independent constituent that corresponds to independent RLCS's for *usually* and *soler*.

We will now formally analyze how this example is handled. The two relevant override mappings are specified in (169) and (168), repeated here for convenience:

(211) **Promotional Override:**

    1.′ X′ $\Leftrightarrow$ Z[23]

    4.′ Q′ $\Leftrightarrow$ X

(212) **Thematic Override:**

    1.′ W′ $\Leftrightarrow$ Z

    4.′ Z′ $\Leftrightarrow$ W

In terms of the logical constituents that participate in the divergence mapping, X′ corresponds to [$_{\text{State}}$ BE$_{\text{Circ}}$ ...], W′ corresponds to [$_{\text{Thing}}$ JOHN], Z′ corresponds to [$_{\text{Event}}$ READ ...], and Q′ corresponds to [$_{\text{Manner}}$ HABITUALLY].

Formally, the structure of the English sentence in (209) has the default syntactic representation:

---

[22]For purposes of simplicity, the READ predicate is being used as a shorthand for the following expanded representation:

    [$_{\text{State}}$ BE$_{\text{Perc}}$

      ([$_{\text{Thing}}$ JOHN],

      [$_{\text{Position}}$ AT$_{\text{Perc}}$ ([$_{\text{Thing}}$ JOHN], [$_{\text{Thing}}$ BOOK])],

      [$_{\text{Manner}}$ READINGLY])]

(213) [$_{\text{Y-MAX}}$ [$_{\text{Y-MAX}}$ W [$_{\text{X-MAX}}$ X Z]] Q]

In contrast, the equivalent Spanish sentence has an entirely different syntactic representation:

(214) [$_{\text{Y-MAX}}$ [$_{\text{Y-MAX}}$ Z [$_{\text{X-MAX}}$ Q [... X W]]]]

Note that this structure differs from the default representation in that the external argument is Z, not W, and that the syntactic head is Q, not X. Also, because the promotional mapping forces X into an external argument position, additional structure is created so that X retains its status as a head. This head selects an internal argument which, in this case, is W rather than Z because of the interaction with the thematic divergence.

Suppose we were to generate the Spanish sentence for this example. The RLCS's for the Spanish case conform to the following formal specifications:

(215) *gustar*: [$_{\text{T(X')}}$ X' ([$_{\text{T(W')}}$:INT W'], [$_{\text{T(Z')}}$:EXT Z'])]
    soler: [$_{\text{T(Q')}}$:PROMOTE Q']

When the $\mathcal{GLR}$ is applied to the CLCS of (210), the promotional override (211) is immediately triggered by the :PROMOTE marker in the RLCS for *soler*; this invocation crucially precedes the invocation of the thematic override (168).[24] The promotional override forces Q' (*i.e.*, [$_{\text{Manner}}$ HABITUALLY]) to be realized as the syntactic head *soler*. This head takes an internal argument corresponding to X' ([$_{\text{State}}$ BE$_{\text{Circ}}$ ...]) which is realized as the verb *gustar*. Recall that the structural relation between the subordinated verb and its internal argument is not changed by the promotional mapping (see fn. 6). However, the promotional operation does not retain the relation between the subordinated verb and its external argument; rather, the argument is realized in an external

---

[24]This seems to indicate that there is some notion of prioritization during the resolution of interacting divergence types. In particular, the "head swapping" cases (promotional and demotional) divergences appear to take priority over the "argument swapping" cases (thematic). Although the formal ramifications of this ordering have not yet been established, it should be noted that this prioritization fits in naturally in the current framework given that the syntactic realization process starts by realizing "outer" phrases, but then recursively realizes "inner" phrases before any attachments are made. This is why the algorithm of figure 6.2 makes a recursive call (step 2.b) before attaching the subordinate phrases (step 2.c). The same considerations are necessary during LCS composition, which is why the algorithm of figure 4.21 recursively composes subordinate concepts (step 6.b) before unifying these concepts into the working structure (step 6.c).

position relative to the main verb. Normally, this would mean that the CLCS constituent [$_{\text{Thing}}$ JOHN] would become an external argument of *soler* such as in the non-interacting case: *John suele leer libros*. In the current example, however, the attachment of the external argument is delayed until the recursive application of the $\mathcal{GLR}$ on [$_{\text{State}}$ BE$_{\text{Circ}}$ ...].

At this point, the :INT and :EXT markers trigger the thematic interchange, and the logical subject [$_{\text{Thing}}$ JOHN] is realized as the internal argument *a Juan*. The [$_{\text{Event}}$ READ ...] constituent is then taken to be the external argument of *gustar*, except that this constituent cannot be attached inside of the subordinate phrase due to the promotional divergence. Instead, the current phrase is completed and the external argument is "passed up" to the higher phrase, which then attaches it in an external position relative to the verb *soler*. The final structure is then generated:

(216) [$_{\text{C-MAX}}$
    [$_{\text{I-MAX}}$
        [$_{\text{C-MAX}}$ leer libros]
        [$_{\text{V-MAX}}$ [v le suele]
            [$_{\text{V-MAX}}$ [v gustar] [$_{\text{P-MAX}}$ a Juan]]]]]]

Thus, we have shown how the current framework provides a formal means for demonstrating how interacting divergence types are handled.

To sum up, this chapter has provided a systematic classification of machine translation divergences, and it has shown how this classification may be formally defined, and systematically resolved, through the use of general mapping relations and a small set of cross-linguistic parameters. Because the parameters are used to *factor out* "transfer" information, the current approach obviates the need for transfer rules. We have provided evidence that supports the view that the lexical-semantic divergence classification proposed in the current framework covers all possible source-language/target-language distinctions based on lexical-semantic properties (*i.e.*, properties associated with entries in the lexicon that are not based on purely syntactic information, idiomatic usage, aspectual knowledge, discourse knowledge, domain knowledge, or world knowledge). Given that the characterization of the entire range of potential divergences is manageably small, the task of accommodating divergences is immensely simplified. We have also demonstrated the usefulness of the *full coverage* definition introduced in chapter 6 as an evaluation metric that allows one to judge whether a particular target-language sentence fully covers the concept that underlies the corresponding source-language sentence. Finally, we have shown, formally, that the current model accommodates interacting divergence types.

Having described the framework for the model used in UNITRAN, we turn now to the final area of investigation, *i.e.*, the application of the current model.

III APPLICATION OF THE MODEL

8 Translation Examples

In parts I and II, we discussed the syntactic and lexical-semantic components of the model assumed in UNITRAN. This chapter describes the application of the model to sentences falling in the syntactic and lexical-semantic divergence categories described in previous chapters. The sentences that are handled by the system are shown in figure 8.1. Most of these examples have been discussed previously (see page numbers where applicable). This chapter will focus on the first seven examples, *i.e.*, the cases that correspond to the lexical-semantic divergence examples.

Section 8.1 discusses certain implementational issues concerning the testing of the system on these cases. Section 8.2 examines the results of running the system on each divergence example, isolating some of the problem areas, and addressing the issues underlying these problem areas. Finally, section 8.3 examines a free text example and outlines the limitations of the system with respect to this example.

8.1 Implementational Issues

The next section shows the results of running the system on the lexical-semantic divergences of figure 1.12 (later repeated as figure 5.2).[1] These results include the number of structures and the time it took for each stage of the translation. In addition, these results show the corresponding CLCS's and the target-language sentences that are generated. In cases where an element is associated with an antecedent (either by trace-linking or by binding), a partial phrase structure is shown.

Each translation has an associated screen dump in appendix D; the pointers into this appendix are included (in parentheses) with each target-language result. The screen dumps in appendix D show only one source-language tree, one CLCS, and one target-language tree, even though there may be more than one for each example. (We will see that this is the case as we go through the examples.)

All times shown are in seconds (using the Common Lisp function GET-UNIVERSAL-TIME). The timing is actually a rough calculation since it includes garbage collection, paging, some printing of output, and other machine-dependent operations. The times shown in the screen

---

[1]These results have been automatically converted by a simple program from the actual output printed on the screen into the bracketed format shown here. The system runs on a Symbolics 3600 series machine (with graphics) and also on a Sun Sparc Station (without graphics).

Page	English	Spanish	German
15, 20, 165, 183, 107, 139, 222, 258	I stabbed John	Yo le di puñaladas a Juan (Yo le apuñalé a Juan)	Ich erstach Johann
6, 20, 73, 165, 171, 248	I like Mary	María me gusta a mí (Me gusta María)	Ich habe Marie gern
20, 165, 167, 255	John entered the house	Juan entró en la casa	Johann trat ins Haus hinein
20, 165, 174, 261	I am hungry	Yo tengo hambre	Ich habe Hunger
20, 165, 187, 264	John broke into the room	Juan forzó la entrada al cuarto	Johann brach ins Zimmer ein
20, 165, 254	I like to eat	Me gusta comer	Ich esse gern
20, 165, 180, 250	John usually goes home	Juan suele ir a casa	Johann geht gewöhnlich nach Hause
46, 99	I put the book on the table	Yo puse el libro en la mesa	Ich legte das Buch auf den Tisch
218, 219	Mary gave it to you	María te lo dio	Marie gab es dir
19, 45, 67	*Who did you wonder whether went to school	Quién contemplabas tú que fue a la escuela	*Wer frage ich mich, ob schon nach Hause gegangen ist
—	Who did John seem to like	Quién parece gustar a Juan	Wen scheint Johann gern zu haben
69, 75	John seems to like Mary	María le parece gustar a Juan	Johann scheint Marie gern zu haben
71, 76	We saw Guille	Lo vimos a Guille	Wir sahen Guille
73	I saw the book	Vi el libro	Ich sah das Buch
74	What did John see	Qué vio Juan	Was sah Johann
75	John likes himself	Juan le gusta a sí mismo	Johann hat sich selbst gern
75	There is a man in the room	Hay un hombre en el cuarto	Es ist ein Mann im Zimmer
75	What does John like	Qué le gusta Juan	Was mag Johann
129	Beth bought the doll for Mary	Beth compró la muñeca para María	Beth kaufte die Puppe für Marie
129	John looked for the book	Juan buscó el libro	Johann suchte das Buch
129	John looked at the book	Juan miró el libro	Johann schaute das Buch an
129	The book costs (me) $10.00	El libro me cuesta $10.00	Das Buch kostet (mir) $10.00
129	John believed Mary	Juan creyó a María	Johann glaubte Marie
92	I read the red books	Leí los rojos libros	Ich las die roten Bücher
19, 45, 218	I gave him the book	Yo le di el libro (a él)	Ich gab ihm das Buch
277	John usually likes reading books	Leer libros le suele gustar a Juan	Johann liest gern Bücher
156	John smeared the wall with paint	Juan embadurnó la pared con pintura	Johann beschmierte die Wand mit Farbe
146	John wants to eat breakfast	Juan quiere comer el desayuno	Johann will Frühstück essen
146	John wants Bill to eat breakfast	Juan quiere que Bill coma el desayuno	Johann will daß Bill Frühstück ißt
146	*John believes to eat breakfast	*Juan cree comer el desayuno	Johann glaubt Frühstück zu essen
146	John believes Bill to eat breakfast	Juan cree que Bill come el desayuno	Johann glaubt, daß Bill Frühstück ißt
—	John jogged to school	Juan trotó a la escuela	Johann joggte zur Schule
211, 213	I know that John would have been eating the cake	Yo sé que Juan habría estado comiendo el pastel	Ich weiß, daß Johann den Kuchen gegessen haben würde
137, 159	I stabbed John with a knife	Yo le di puñaladas a Juan con un cuchillo	Ich erstach Johann mit einem Messer
—	I want to eat	Yo quiero comer	Ich will essen
220	Does John like to eat	Le gusta a Juan comer	Ißt Johann gern
220	What does John like to eat	Qué le gusta a Juan comer	Was ißt Johann gern
—	John painted the wall	Juan pintarrajeó la pared	Johann strich die Wand an
—	John knows Mary	Juan conoce a María	Johann kennt Marie
—	John knows German	Juan sabe alemán	Johann kann Deutsch
—	John continues sleeping	Juan continúa durmiendo	Johann schläft weiter

Figure 8.1
A wide range of sentences exhibiting syntactic and lexical-semantic divergences are translated by UNITRAN.

dumps of appendix D are slightly different from the ones shown here (though insignificantly so) because two different timing techniques were used. The screen dump times are shown in parentheses in the examples of the next seven subsections. For parsing and generation, the times are calculated, as shown, by a cumulative sum of the time it takes each GB module to return a result: Total time = time($\overline{\text{X}}$) + time(Bounding) + time(Case)+ time(Binding)+ time(θ).

During the development of UNITRAN, the timing for identical input often changed dramatically (even by orders of magnitude) as different processing modules were added or modified. Adding translation robustness for the general case often significantly lengthened translation times for input that did not directly benefit from the added generality. Note, that we are discussing translation considerations and not the actual efficiency of the implementation of the algorithms. There is considerable opportunity to improve the performance of the system.

Certain sentences resulted in extremely long translation times. Most of these operations did in fact perform very extensive calculations. However, these times also reflect frequent ephemeral garbage collection, the printing of extensive results to an output buffer, and the storage of all the translation results (both good and rejected trees for the parsing, LCS composition, and generation steps) for later retrieval and examination. In general, a fresh system, running with certain output turned off and with little garbage collection, seems to complete translations about twice as fast as the results shown here, which were produced in a single extended run. For example, consider the input of *I am hungry* translated to Spanish and German. In the results, the times shown are 11, 5, 19, and 468 seconds for the parse, LCS composition, Spanish generation, and German generation, respectively. Running the same translations on a fresh machine produced the corresponding times of 3, 1, 9, and 241 seconds, half the duration experienced as part of the extended run. Similarly, for *Johann trat in das Haus hinein*, the times changed from 30 to 14 seconds for the parse, from 12 to 4 seconds for LCS composition, from 93 to 41 seconds for Spanish generation, and from 37 to 21 seconds for English generation.

The durations of the translations are roughly linear with respect to the number of tree structures (both good and rejected) that are produced during the parse, LCS composition, and generation stages. Figure 8.2

Secs	Trees	Trees/Sec	Nodes	Nodes/Sec
18	55	3.1	735	40.8
38	144	3.8	2303	60.6
44	119	2.7	1988	45.2
51	187	3.7	2799	54.9
57	195	3.4	2268	39.8
61	220	3.6	3375	55.3
70	225	3.2	3258	46.5
85	327	3.8	4839	56.9
144	637	4.4	10743	74.6
233	840	3.6	13440	57.7
271	1197	4.4	16894	62.3
277	1009	3.6	10368	37.4

Figure 8.2
The timing results of 12 different translations illustrate that the durations of
translations are roughly linear with respect to the number of structures (both good
and rejected) that are produced during the parse, LCS compositions, and
generation stages.

shows the results for 12 different translations with durations ranging
from 18 to 277 seconds.

It is worth noting that translation in UNITRAN lends itself to parallel processing. That is, a fast initial step (which could perhaps also be
adapted to make use of parallelism) produces a number of parse structures. The first real step of parsing converts each structure into a tree
which is processed by the remaining parse steps. Along the way, many
trees are rejected; at the same time, certain steps may produce additional trees. At the end of parsing, good candidates are sent to the LCS
composition module, which produces CLCS's. Finally, generation steps
process the input from composition, by creating, modifying, and reject-
ing trees as appropriate. Currently, each step processes all candidates
and then passes all survivors to the next step. However, suppose that,
for each step, we had many processors that could perform the operations of that step. Each processor would execute its operation and post
its result. A rejected structure would be tossed into a rejects bin, if
desired, perhaps with justification for the rejection. A (probably modified) structure that survives processing, along with any new structures
produced by a step, would be sent to a queue to await processing by
the next step. The processor that delivered it to the queue would then

check its own queue for another tree to work on. Winning translations could be made available from the processors of the last step as soon as each is produced.

As proof of this concept, a single afternoon was spent implementing an algorithm that takes an individual structure and runs it through each parsing step until it is rejected or finally succeeds. After finishing with a tree, the next tree to process is the one that has already advanced the farthest (i.e., to a step that spawned one or more trees in addition to the one initially passed on). This implementation, while obviously only using a single processor, could still produce a completed parse in a very short time under random, fortuitous conditions. This experiment was not taken any further than the completion of the parsing stage. It involved a simple algorithm that called existing parsing steps. Currently, the LCS composition module analyzes its collected results in order to avoid spawning duplicates and also to find preferred candidates. Some minor rewriting of this code would support LCS composition operating on a single parse tree input. The simplest choice would be to allow duplicates to be introduced to the generation phase and to worry about eliminating them once winning results are produced.

8.2   Divergence Examples

We now turn to a detailed discussion of the translation results for each of the seven lexical-semantic divergence cases.

8.2.1   I Stabbed John

The following example illustrates how conflational divergence is handled:

(217) (i)   E: I stabbed John

      (ii)   S: Yo le di puñaladas a Juan (Yo le apuñalé a Juan)

      (iii)   G: Ich erstach Johann

In particular, the system must select a verb in Spanish that includes the *knife-wound* argument as part of the surface string, whereas English and German use verbs that do not realize this argument on the surface. The translation results are shown in (218)–(220).

(218)

Input:	i stabbed John
Parse:	1 structure; time: $8 + 1 + 1 + 0 + 1 = 11$ seconds (10)

CLCS:	1 structure; time: 4 seconds (5)
	(cause referent
	  (go-poss knife-wound
	   (toward-poss (at-poss knife-wound person))))

Spanish: (D.1.1)	12 structures; time: $337 + 18 + 51 + 1 + 5 = 412$ seconds (414) yo [CL-DAT le]$_i$ apuñalé a [N-MAX juan]$_i$ yo [CL-DAT le]$_i$ apuñalaba a [N-MAX juan]$_i$ yo [CL-DAT se]$_i$ apuñalé a [N-MAX juan]$_i$ yo [CL-DAT se]$_i$ apuñalaba a [N-MAX juan]$_i$ yo [CL-DAT le]$_i$ di puñaladas a [N-MAX juan]$_i$ yo [CL-DAT le]$_i$ di puñalada a [N-MAX juan]$_i$ yo [CL-DAT le]$_i$ daba puñaladas a [N-MAX juan]$_i$ yo [CL-DAT le]$_i$ daba puñalada a [N-MAX juan]$_i$ yo [CL-DAT se]$_i$ di puñaladas a [N-MAX juan]$_i$ yo [CL-DAT se]$_i$ di puñalada a [N-MAX juan]$_i$ yo [CL-DAT se]$_i$ daba puñaladas a [N-MAX juan]$_i$ yo [CL-DAT se]$_i$ daba puñalada a [N-MAX juan]$_i$
German: (D.1.2)	2 structures; time: $74 + 1 + 4 + 0 + 0 = 79$ seconds (82) [N-MAX ich]$_j$ [V erstach]$_i$ [N-MAX t]$_j$ johann [V t]$_i$ [N-MAX johann]$_j$ [V erstach]$_i$ ich [N-MAX t]$_j$ [V t]$_i$

(219)

Input:	yo le di puñaladas a juan
Parse:	16 structures; time: $44 + 6 + 5 + 1 + 71 = 127$ seconds (123)

CLCS:	2 structures preferred (out of 12); time: 57 seconds (60)
	(cause referent (go-poss knife-wound
	  (toward-poss (at-poss knife-wound person))))
	(cause referent
	  (go-poss knife-wound
	   (from-poss (at-poss knife-wound referent))
	   (to-poss (at-poss knife-wound person))))

German: (D.2.1)	2 structures; time: $85 + 2 + 9 + 0 + 0 = 96$ seconds (97) [N-MAX ich]$_j$ [V erstach]$_i$ [N-MAX t]$_j$ johann [V t]$_i$ [N-MAX johann]$_j$ [V erstach]$_i$ ich [N-MAX t]$_j$ [V t]$_i$
English: (D.2.2)	1 structure; time: $16 + 2 + 2 + 0 + 0 = 20$ seconds (21) i stabbed john

(220)

Input:	ich erstach johann
Parse:	1 structure; time: $9 + 0 + 1 + 0 + 1 = 11$ seconds (10)

CLCS:	1 structure; time: 7 seconds (9)
	(cause referent
	  (go-poss knife-wound
	   (toward-poss (at-poss knife-wound person))))

Spanish: (D.3.1)	12 structures; time: $417 + 12 + 65 + 1 + 9 = 504$ seconds (508) yo [CL-DAT le]$_i$ apuñalé a [N-MAX juan]$_i$ yo [CL-DAT le]$_i$ apuñalaba a [N-MAX juan]$_i$ yo [CL-DAT se]$_i$ apuñalé a [N-MAX juan]$_i$ yo [CL-DAT se]$_i$ apuñalaba a [N-MAX juan]$_i$ yo [CL-DAT le]$_i$ di puñaladas a [N-MAX juan]$_i$ yo [CL-DAT le]$_i$ di puñalada a [N-MAX juan]$_i$ yo [CL-DAT le]$_i$ daba puñaladas a [N-MAX juan]$_i$ yo [CL-DAT le]$_i$ daba puñalada a [N-MAX juan]$_i$ yo [CL-DAT se]$_i$ di puñaladas a [N-MAX juan]$_i$ yo [CL-DAT se]$_i$ di puñalada a [N-MAX juan]$_i$ yo [CL-DAT se]$_i$ daba puñaladas a [N-MAX juan]$_i$ yo [CL-DAT se]$_i$ daba puñalada a [N-MAX juan]$_i$
English: (D.3.2)	1 structure; time: $15 + 1 + 2 + 0 + 0 = 18$ seconds (20) i stabbed john

Generating the Spanish sentence (in (218) and (220)) is difficult in this example because there are a potentially large number of output forms that can be produced. In particular, the lexical selection routine determines that there are two possible constructions, *apuñalar* and *dar puñaladas*, both of which are perfectly acceptable. However, the situation is complicated even further due to the two past tenses (preterit and imperfect), and the singular and plural forms of the word *puñalada*. As mentioned in chapter 6, the preterit *di* provides the meaning 'stab at one moment in time,' whereas the imperfect *daba* provides the meaning 'stab over a period of time.' The plural and singular forms of the noun *puñalada* also provides additional meaning: the plural form is the repetitive form of the action (*i.e.*, 'stab repeatedly'), and the singular form is the non-repetitive form (*i.e.*, 'stab once'). These aspectual nuances of meaning are not captured in the translation model presented here, though they could be, eventually (see chapter 10).

The generation of the clitic is problematic in this example, primarily because of the decision to allow *se* to be a non-reflexive dative clitic. In fact, this clitic is only non-reflexive if it occurs in a clitic-doubled construction, *e.g.*, *yo se lo di a Juan* ('I gave it to (him) John'). This problem is easily remedied by making the clitic-realization decision be part of the morphological processing rather than the syntactic processing. In fact, there are already similar decisions that are allotted to the morphological component such as the replacement of the contraction *al* with *a el* prior to parsing. The reverse direction has not yet been implemented, but if it were, it would be easy to replace *le lo* with *se lo* during generation.

Generating from the Spanish to English and German for this example (see (219)) is also difficult because a number of interpretations are assigned during LCS composition. In particular, the word *a* is many-ways ambiguous. It can be composed, as a modifier, into the CLCS as a TO_{Loc}, $TOWARD_{Loc}$, TO_{Loc}, $TOWARD_{Poss}$, AT_{Ident}, AT_{Circ}, or an AT_{Intent}. That is, the prepositional phrase *a Juan* might be considered an adjunct (*e.g.*, *I stabbed him for the benefit of John*, where *him* is someone other than *John*).

We have already seen that UNITRAN does not attempt to apply any sort of disambiguation strategy during generation (*e.g.*, it chooses both *dar* and *apuñalar* as the realization of the *stab* event in Spanish). However, it does execute a preference procedure during LCS composition

as described in chapter 4. This procedure eliminates any CLCS that
incorporates an element as a modifier if there exists another CLCS that
incorporates that same element as an argument. Thus, the modifier
reading of *a Juan* is eliminated. (Note that there are 12 CLCS's, but
only two are "preferred," as shown in parentheses in (219).)

Only the first of the two CLCS's that are ultimately produced is the
correct one. The second CLCS illustrates the more literal meaning of
yo le di puñaladas a Juan, *i.e.*, *I gave knife-wounds to John*. However,
this CLCS is rejected as a possibility during generation due to the fact
that there is no word in either English or German that corresponds to
knife-wounds.

The final point to make about this example is that the free-word
order of German allows for different emphasis distinctions (see (218)
and (219)). Although there is no notion of *focus* in UNITRAN, such a
notion could be accommodated given that discourse-related movement
such as topicalization, passivization, free inversion, *etc.* are freely allowed
if the language permits it.

8.2.2   I Like Mary

The following example illustrates how thematic and conflational divergences are handled:

(221) (i)   E: I like Mary

       (ii)   S: María me gusta a mí (Me gusta María)

       (iii)   G: Ich habe Marie gern

In particular, the *like* concept is realized as the thematically divergent
verbs *gustar* and *gefallen* in Spanish and German, and also as the confla-
tionally divergent construction *gern haben* in German.[2] The translation
results are shown in (222)–(224).

---

[2]The question of whether *gern* and *haben* are actually two separate words is
subject to debate. It has been pointed out to me by Bergler (personal communication)
that the *gern-haben* construction is not analogous to other *gern* constructions (*e.g.*,
the *gern-essen* discussed below in 8.2.6): the former exhibits behavior similar to
separable prefix constructions; the latter does not. Consider the following examples:

(a)   Ich habe Marie gern (I like Mary)
       Ich sollte Marie gern haben (I should like Mary)
     * Ich sollte gern Marie haben (I should like Mary)
(b)   Ich esse Fisch gern (I like to eat fish)
     * Ich sollte Fisch gern essen (I should like to eat fish)
       Ich sollte gern Fisch essen (I should like to eat fish)

	Input:	i like mary
(222)	Parse:	1 structure; time: $10 + 1 + 1 + 0 + 0 = 12$ seconds (10)
	CLCS:	1 structure; time: 2 seconds (3)
		(be-ident referent (at-ident referent person) likingly)
	Spanish: (D.4.1)	1 structure; time: $39 + 1 + 7 + 0 + 1 = 48$ seconds (48) maría [$_{\text{CL-DAT}}$ me]$_i$ gusta a [$_{\text{N-MAX}}$ mí]$_i$
	German: (D.4.2)	7 structures; time: $293 + 5 + 21 + 0 + 1 = 320$ seconds (322) [$_{\text{N-MAX}}$ ich]$_j$ [$_\text{V}$ mag]$_i$ [$_{\text{N-MAX}}$ t]$_j$ marie [$_\text{V}$ t]$_i$ [$_{\text{N-MAX}}$ marie]$_j$ [$_\text{V}$ mag]$_i$ ich [$_{\text{N-MAX}}$ t]$_j$ [$_\text{V}$ t]$_i$ [$_{\text{N-MAX}}$ marie]$_j$ [$_\text{V}$ gefällt]$_i$ [$_{\text{N-MAX}}$ t]$_j$ [$_\text{V}$ t]$_i$ [$_{\text{N-MAX}}$ mir]$_j$ [$_\text{V}$ gefällt]$_i$ marie [$_{\text{N-MAX}}$ t]$_j$ [$_\text{V}$ t]$_i$ [$_{\text{N-MAX}}$ ich]$_j$ [$_\text{V}$ habe]$_i$ [$_{\text{N-MAX}}$ t]$_j$ marie gern [$_\text{V}$ t]$_i$ [$_{\text{N-MAX}}$ marie]$_j$ [$_\text{V}$ habe]$_i$ ich [$_{\text{N-MAX}}$ t]$_j$ gern [$_\text{V}$ t]$_i$ [$_{\text{ADV}}$ gern]$_j$ [$_\text{V}$ habe]$_i$ ich marie [$_{\text{ADV}}$ t]$_j$ [$_\text{V}$ t]$_i$

	Input:	maría me gusta a mí
(223)	Parse:	8 structures; time: $43 + 5 + 14 + 1 + 143 = 206$ seconds (206)
	CLCS:	1 structure preferred (out of 2); time: 12 seconds (15)
		(be-ident referent (at-ident referent person) likingly)
	German: (D.5.1)	7 structures; time: $308 + 6 + 16 + 0 + 2 = 332$ seconds (334) [$_{\text{N-MAX}}$ ich]$_j$ [$_\text{V}$ mag]$_i$ [$_{\text{N-MAX}}$ t]$_j$ marie [$_\text{V}$ t]$_i$ [$_{\text{N-MAX}}$ marie]$_j$ [$_\text{V}$ mag]$_i$ ich [$_{\text{N-MAX}}$ t]$_j$ [$_\text{V}$ t]$_i$ [$_{\text{N-MAX}}$ marie]$_j$ [$_\text{V}$ gefällt]$_i$ [$_{\text{N-MAX}}$ t]$_j$ mir [$_\text{V}$ t]$_i$ [$_{\text{N-MAX}}$ mir]$_j$ [$_\text{V}$ gefällt]$_i$ marie [$_{\text{N-MAX}}$ t]$_j$ [$_\text{V}$ t]$_i$ [$_{\text{N-MAX}}$ ich]$_j$ [$_\text{V}$ habe]$_i$ [$_{\text{N-MAX}}$ t]$_j$ marie gern [$_\text{V}$ t]$_i$ [$_{\text{N-MAX}}$ marie]$_j$ [$_\text{V}$ habe]$_i$ ich [$_{\text{N-MAX}}$ t]$_j$ gern [$_\text{V}$ t]$_i$ [$_{\text{ADV}}$ gern]$_j$ [$_\text{V}$ habe]$_i$ ich marie [$_{\text{ADV}}$ t]$_j$ [$_\text{V}$ t]$_i$
	English: (D.5.2)	1 structure; time: $18 + 0 + 2 + 0 + 1 = 21$ seconds (21) i like mary

	Input:	ich habe marie gern
(224)	Parse:	4 structures; time: $15 + 0 + 3 + 0 + 6 = 24$ seconds (19)
	CLCS:	2 structures preferred (out of 4); time: 10 seconds (12)
		(be-ident referent (at-ident referent person) likingly) (2)
	Spanish: (D.6.1)	2 structures; time: $111 + 2 + 10 + 0 + 0 = 123$ seconds (127) maría [$_{\text{CL-DAT}}$ me]$_i$ guste a [$_{\text{N-MAX}}$ mí]$_i$ maría [$_{\text{CL-DAT}}$ me]$_i$ gusta a [$_{\text{N-MAX}}$ mí]$_i$
	English: (D.6.2)	1 structure; time: $20 + 0 + 1 + 0 + 1 = 22$ seconds (22) i like mary

Because there is no ambiguity resolution during generation, three constructions are generated for German (see (222) and (223)); the equivalent

---

Note that there cannot be any intervening material between *gern* and *haben* in the modal configuration; this is not the case with the *gern-essen* construction. Thus, it might be argued that, in the first case, *gern* is acting as a separable prefix, analogous to prefixes such as *ein* in the word *einbrechen*:

(c)   Johann brach ins Zimmer ein (John broke into the room)
      Johann sollte ins Zimmer einbrechen (John should break into the room)
    * Johann sollte ein ins Zimmer brechen (John should break into the room)

Nevertheless, both *gern* and *haben* clearly have a lexical status beyond the morphemic level (*e.g.*, both are listed independently in standard German dictionaries). Thus, we have adopted an analysis of *gern* and *haben* as independent words that, taken together compositionally, exhibit a pattern of conflation. Those readers who find this characterization unsettling are referred to other (less controversial) examples of conflation in sections 8.2.1 and 8.2.5.

predicates *mögen*, *gefallen*, and *gern haben*, are selected for the *like* concept in German. As in the last example, topicalization allows different tokens to be moved to the front: *ich*, *marie*, *mir*, and *gern*. These are all acceptable translations for *I like Mary*.

The translation from German (see (224)) results in two CLCS's (preferred from four). The reason that there were four to begin with is that there is a modifier ambiguity. That is, the word *gern* can be taken as a modifier, or as an incorporated constituent with respect to *haben*. Again, the preference scheme correctly chooses the appropriate interpretation (*i.e.*, the one in which *gern* is an incorporated argument). As for the two remaining CLCS's, one is associated with indicative mood, and one is associated with subjunctive. Currently, the subjunctive mood is not adequately handled. The system does not yet account for when this mood is, or is not, appropriate. Because the word *habe* may be both in the present indicative form as well as the present subjunctive form, both possibilities are incorporated into the CLCS. Thus, the Spanish sentence *∗María me guste a mí* is generated, even though this is not a grammatical form. We will see in subsequent examples that the indicative form in German is frequently interpreted as the subjunctive form.

Note that the thematic divergence associated with *gustar* and *gefallen* and the conflational divergence of *gern haben* is accounted for in this example.

8.2.3   I Am Hungry

The following example illustrates how categorial divergence is handled:

(225) (i)   E: I am hungry
        (ii)   S: Yo tengo hambre
        (iii)   G: Ich habe Hunger

In German, both forms, *Ich bin hungrig*, and *Ich habe Hunger*, are generated (see (226) and (227)). In contrast, Spanish only allows one construction (analogous to the first of the German constructions): *Yo tengo hambre*. English also allows only one of these constructions (analogous to the second of the German constructions): *I am hungry*. The translation results are shown in (226)–(228).

(226)	Input:	i am hungry
	Parse:	1 structure; time: $9 + 1 + 0 + 0 + 1 = 11$ seconds (10)
	CLCS:	1 structure; time: 5 seconds (6)
		(be-ident referent (at-ident referent hungry))
	Spanish:	1 structure; time: $17 + 1 + 1 + 0 + 0 = 19$ seconds (19)
	(D.7.1)	yo tengo hambre
	German:	5 structures; time: $435 + 6 + 25 + 0 + 2 = 468$ seconds (471)
	(D.7.2)	$[_{\text{N-MAX}}$ ich$]_j$ $[_{\text{V}}$ bin$]_i$ $[_{\text{N-MAX}}$ t$]_j$ hungrig $[_{\text{V}}$ t$]_i$
		$[_{\text{N-MAX}}$ ich$]_j$ $[_{\text{V}}$ habe$]_i$ $[_{\text{N-MAX}}$ t$]_j$ hunger $[_{\text{V}}$ t$]_i$
		$[_{\text{N-MAX}}$ hunger$]_j$ $[_{\text{V}}$ habe$]_i$ ich $[_{\text{N-MAX}}$ t$]_j$ $[_{\text{V}}$ t$]_i$
		$[_{\text{N-MAX}}$ ich$]_j$ $[_{\text{V}}$ habe$]_i$ $[_{\text{N-MAX}}$ t$]_j$ hünger $[_{\text{V}}$ t$]_i$
		$[_{\text{N-MAX}}$ hünger$]_j$ $[_{\text{V}}$ habe$]_i$ ich $[_{\text{N-MAX}}$ t$]_j$ $[_{\text{V}}$ t$]_i$

(227)	Input:	yo tengo hambre
	Parse:	1 structure; time: $13 + 2 + 1 + 1 + 1 = 18$ seconds (15)
	CLCS:	1 structure; time: 3 seconds (4)
		(be-ident referent (at-ident referent hungry))
	German:	3 structures; time: $256 + 1 + 10 + 0 + 0 = 267$ seconds (271)
	(D.8.1)	$[_{\text{N-MAX}}$ ich$]_j$ $[_{\text{V}}$ bin$]_i$ $[_{\text{N-MAX}}$ t$]_j$ hungrig $[_{\text{V}}$ t$]_i$
		$[_{\text{N-MAX}}$ ich$]_j$ $[_{\text{V}}$ habe$]_i$ $[_{\text{N-MAX}}$ t$]_j$ hunger $[_{\text{V}}$ t$]_i$
		$[_{\text{N-MAX}}$ hunger$]_j$ $[_{\text{V}}$ habe$]_i$ ich $[_{\text{N-MAX}}$ t$]_j$ $[_{\text{V}}$ t$]_i$
	English:	1 structure; time: $14 + 0 + 0 + 0 + 0 = 14$ seconds (16)
	(D.8.2)	i am hungry

(228)	Input:	ich habe hunger
	Parse:	2 structures; time: $4 + 0 + 0 + 1 + 1 = 6$ seconds (6)
	CLCS:	2 structures; time: 3 seconds (4)
		(be-ident referent (at-ident referent hungry)) (2)
	Spanish:	2 structures; time: $54 + 1 + 3 + 0 + 0 = 58$ seconds (59)
	(D.9.1)	yo tenga hambre
		yo tengo hambre
	English:	1 structure; time: $15 + 0 + 1 + 0 + 0 = 16$ seconds (16)
	(D.9.2)	i am hungry

An interesting interaction effect shows up in this example. The additional form, *Hünger* (plural of *Hunger*), is generated only in the translation from English to German (not in the translation from English to Spanish). This is due to the fact that the HUNGRY token of the CLCS is not associated with any agreement features since none are available for the word *hungry* in the English input sentence. On the other hand, Spanish *does* provide agreement information: the word *hambre* is a singular form. This information is incorporated into the HUNGRY token of the CLCS during composition, thus ruling out the plural form *Hünger*. Since the plural form is not appropriate, the system would require additional information about the nature of such complements in order to rule out this case. Note that in both cases of German output, the arguments of the main verb are freely permuted.

As in the last example, the subjunctive form *tenga* is generated in Spanish (from the German only) (see (228)) since the verb *habe* can be interpreted as either subjunctive or indicative.

8.2.4   John Entered the House

The following example illustrates how structural divergence is handled:

(229) (i)   E: John entered the house

     (ii)   S: Juan entró en la casa

     (iii)   G: Johann trat ins Haus hinein

In particular, English realizes the location as *the house*, whereas Spanish requires the location to be a prepositional phrase *en la casa*. The German is like Spanish in that it requires a prepositional phrase *in das Haus*, but it also allows the separable prefix *hinein* to be associated with the verb *(hinein)treten*. The translation results are shown in (230)–(232).

(230)

Input:	john entered the house
Parse:	2 structures; time: $14 + 1 + 2 + 1 + 1 = 19$ seconds (20)

CLCS:	2 structures; time: 7 seconds (10)
	(go-loc person
	  (from-loc (in-loc person))
	  (to-loc (in-loc person house))) (2)

Spanish: (D.10.1)	12 structures; time: $75 + 17 + 5 + 0 + 6 = 103$ seconds (104) juan fue a la casa (2) juan fue en la casa (2) juan entraba a la casa (2) juan entró a la casa (2) juan entraba en la casa (2) juan entró en la casa (2)

German:
(D.10.2)
	16 structures; time: $91 + 32 + 9 + 2 + 9 = 143$ seconds (146)
	$[_{\text{N-MAX}}$ johann$]_j$ $[_{\text{V}}$ ging$]_i$ $[_{\text{N-MAX}}$ t$]_j$ in das haus $[_{\text{V}}$ t$]_i$ (2)
	$[_{\text{P-MAX}}$ in das haus$]_j$ $[_{\text{V}}$ ging$]_i$ johann $[_{\text{P-MAX}}$ t$]_j$ $[_{\text{V}}$ t$]_i$ (2)
	$[_{\text{N-MAX}}$ johann$]_j$ $[_{\text{V}}$ ging$]_i$ $[_{\text{N-MAX}}$ t$]_j$ in das heim $[_{\text{V}}$ t$]_i$ (2)
	$[_{\text{P-MAX}}$ in das heim$]_j$ $[_{\text{V}}$ ging$]_i$ johann $[_{\text{P-MAX}}$ t$]_j$ $[_{\text{V}}$ t$]_i$ (2)
	$[_{\text{N-MAX}}$ johann$]_j$ $[_{\text{V}}$ trat$]_i$
	  $[_{\text{N-MAX}}$ t$]_j$ in das haus hinein $[_{\text{V}}$ t$]_i$ (2)
	$[_{\text{P-MAX}}$ in das haus$]_j$ $[_{\text{V}}$ trat$]_i$
	  johann $[_{\text{P-MAX}}$ t$]_j$ hinein $[_{\text{V}}$ t$]_i$ (2)
	$[_{\text{N-MAX}}$ johann$]_j$ $[_{\text{V}}$ trat$]_i$
	  $[_{\text{N-MAX}}$ t$]_j$ in das heim hinein $[_{\text{V}}$ t$]_i$ (2)
	$[_{\text{P-MAX}}$ in das heim$]_j$ $[_{\text{V}}$ trat$]_i$
	  johann $[_{\text{P-MAX}}$ t$]_j$ hinein $[_{\text{V}}$ t$]_i$ (2)

	(231)
Input:	juan entró en la casa
Parse:	4 structures; time: $16 + 1 + 1 + 0 + 18 = 36$ seconds (32)
CLCS:	2 structures; time: 11 seconds (12)
	(go-loc person
	(from-loc (in-loc person))
	(to-loc (in-loc person house))) (2)
German: (D.11.1)	16 structures; time: $121 + 39 + 9 + 1 + 6 = 176$ seconds (177)
	$[_{\text{N-MAX}}$ johann$]_j$ $[_{\text{V}}$ ging$]_i$ $[_{\text{N-MAX}}$ t$]_j$ in das haus $[_{\text{V}}$ t$]_i$ (2)
	$[_{\text{P-MAX}}$ in das haus$]_j$ $[_{\text{V}}$ ging$]_i$ johann $[_{\text{P-MAX}}$ t$]_j$ $[_{\text{V}}$ t$]_i$ (2)
	$[_{\text{N-MAX}}$ johann$]_j$ $[_{\text{V}}$ ging$]_i$ $[_{\text{N-MAX}}$ t$]_j$ in das heim $[_{\text{V}}$ t$]_i$ (2)
	$[_{\text{P-MAX}}$ in das heim$]_j$ $[_{\text{V}}$ ging$]_i$ johann $[_{\text{P-MAX}}$ t$]_j$ $[_{\text{V}}$ t$]_i$ (2)
	$[_{\text{N-MAX}}$ johann$]_j$ $[_{\text{V}}$ trat$]_i$
	$[_{\text{N-MAX}}$ t$]_j$ in das haus hinein $[_{\text{V}}$ t$]_i$ (2)
	$[_{\text{P-MAX}}$ in das haus$]_j$ $[_{\text{V}}$ trat$]_i$
	johann $[_{\text{P-MAX}}$ t$]_j$ hinein $[_{\text{V}}$ t$]_i$ (2)
	$[_{\text{N-MAX}}$ johann$]_j$ $[_{\text{V}}$ trat$]_i$
	$[_{\text{N-MAX}}$ t$]_j$ in das heim hinein $[_{\text{V}}$ t$]_i$ (2)
	$[_{\text{P-MAX}}$ in das heim$]_j$ $[_{\text{V}}$ trat$]_i$
	johann $[_{\text{P-MAX}}$ t$]_j$ hinein $[_{\text{V}}$ t$]_i$ (2)
English: (D.11.2)	8 structures; time: $20 + 4 + 6 + 2 + 4 = 36$ seconds (37)
	john went into the house (2)
	john went into the home (2)
	john entered the home (2)
	john entered the house (2)

	(232)
Input:	johann trat in das haus hinein
Parse:	10 structures; time: $14 + 0 + 6 + 0 + 10 = 30$ seconds (29)
CLCS:	3 structures; time: 12 seconds (13)
	(go-loc person
	(from-loc (in-loc person))
	(to-loc (in-loc person house))) (2)
	(go-loc person (toward-loc (in-loc person house)) within)
Spanish: (D.12.1)	12 structures; time: $73 + 12 + 3 + 1 + 4 = 93$ seconds (95)
	juan fue a la casa (2)
	juan fue en la casa (2)
	juan entraba a la casa (2)
	juan entró a la casa (2)
	juan entraba en la casa (2)
	juan entró en la casa (2)
English: (D.12.2)	8 structures; time: $23 + 4 + 7 + 0 + 3 = 37$ seconds (39)
	john went into the house (2)
	john went into the home (2)
	john entered the home (2)
	john entered the house (2)

There are a number of points to make about this example. First, two similar-looking CLCS's are produced. This is due to the fact that the FROM$_{\text{Loc}}$ path is underspecified (*i.e.*, there is no specification of the place *John* entered *from*, only the place *John* entered *to*). Thus, the place may either be a Thing (as in *car*), or it may be a Location (as in *here*). (The snapshots in appendices D.10.1–D.12.2 show the Location version of the CLCS.) The result is that two syntactic structures are generated for each construction in Spanish, English, and German (this is indicated by a number in parentheses). Currently, this redundant information cannot be eliminated since each word in the output string must be associated with a unique RLCS structure. In order to eliminate the redundancy, a possibility is to allow the underspecified structures (*e.g.*, the unfilled Location and the unfilled Thing) to be considered equivalent; then each syntactic token in the output could be associated with more than one RLCS, as long as the RLCS's are equivalent in some sense.

The second point is that this example illustrates how much of a problem particle selection is. Recall that we discussed this problem with respect to the *enter* example in chapter 5 (fn. 3). During the process of lexical selection, the word *go* is also chosen as a match for the GO_{Loc} portion of the CLCS. Thus, the sentences *Juan fue a la casa, John went into the house*, and *Johann ging in das Haus* are generated as well. The problem arises in choosing the particle for each of these predicates. In Spanish, the word *a* is defined to have the same RLCS as the word *en*. Thus, the selection of *a* is possible in this context, and the system overgenerates: the ungrammatical sentences *∗Juan fue en la casa* and *∗Juan entró a la casa* are produced (see (230) and (232)). Currently there is no way to rule out these sentences, but it appears that some sort of collocation test is required for these cases. (See Nirenburg and Nirenburg (1988) and Pustejovsky and Nirenburg (1987) for an approach to representing certain types of collocations.)

A third point about this example is that the word *home* is also selected for the HOUSE concept. This is slightly awkward in the English and German versions: *John entered the home* and *Johann trat in das Heim hinein*. However, these sentences are grammatical and perfectly understandable. It is expected that the distinction between *house* and *home* would be characterized at some semantic level other than at the level of lexical-conceptual structure.

Finally, the verb *treten* in the German sentences appears with and without the separable prefix *hinein*. The prefix is used mainly for emphasis (it expresses an "inward motion"); the main action, *treten*, can be used either way.

8.2.5   John Broke into the Room

The following example illustrates how lexical divergence is handled:

(233) (i)   E: John broke into the room

  (ii)   S: Juan forzó la entrada al cuarto

(iii) G: Johann brach ins Zimmer ein

In Spanish, this sentence requires a composite construction that includes *forzar* as the main verb. The English and German equivalents of this sentence select is *break into* (*einbrechen*) as the main verb. The translation results are shown in (234)–(236).

(234)

Input:	john broke into the room
Parse:	7 structures; time: $18 + 4 + 4 + 1 + 11 = 38$ seconds (36)

CLCS:	2 structures; time: 16 seconds (18)
	(cause person
	  (go-loc person
	    (from-loc (in-loc person))
	    (to-loc (in-loc person room)))
	  forcefully) (2)

Spanish: (D.13.1)	32 structures; time: $3623 + 247 + 333 + 6 + 44 = 4253$ seconds (4260) juan forzó entrar en el cuarto (2) juan forzaba entrar en el cuarto (2) juan forzó entrar a el cuarto (2) juan forzaba entrar a el cuarto (2) juan forzó ir en el cuarto (2) juan forzaba ir en el cuarto (2) juan forzó ir a el cuarto (2) juan forzaba ir a el cuarto (2) juan forzó entrada en el cuarto (2) juan forzó entradas en el cuarto (2) juan forzaba entrada en el cuarto (2) juan forzaba entradas en el cuarto (2) juan forzó entrada a el cuarto (2) juan forzó entradas a el cuarto (2) juan forzaba entrada a el cuarto (2) juan forzaba entradas a el cuarto (2)
German: (D.13.2)	4 structures; time: $31 + 10 + 1 + 0 + 2 = 44$ seconds (45) [N-MAX johann]$_j$ [V brach]$_i$ [N-MAX t]$_j$ in das zimmer ein [V t]$_i$ (2) [P-MAX in das zimmer]$_j$ [V brach]$_i$ johann [P-MAX t]$_j$ ein [V t]$_i$ (2)

(235)

Input:	juan forzó la entrada a el cuarto
Parse:	56 structures; time: $78 + 15 + 27 + 3 + 283 = 406$ seconds (370)

CLCS:	2 structures preferred (out of 10); time: 103 seconds (102)
	(cause person
	  (go-loc person
	    (from-loc (in-loc person))
	    (to-loc (in-loc person room)))
	  forcefully) (2)

German: (D.14.1)	4 structures; time: $31 + 10 + 2 + 0 + 1 = 44$ seconds (47) [N-MAX johann]$_j$ [V brach]$_i$ [N-MAX t]$_j$ in das zimmer ein [V t]$_i$ (2) [P-MAX in das zimmer]$_j$ [V brach]$_i$ johann [P-MAX t]$_j$ ein [V t]$_i$ (2)
English: (D.14.2)	6 structures; time: $358 + 26 + 350 + 6 + 7 = 747$ seconds (764) john broke into the room (2) [N-MAX john]$_i$ forced [N-MAX himself]$_i$ to enter the room (2) [N-MAX john]$_i$ forced [N-MAX himself]$_i$ to go into the room (2)

Input:	johann brach in das zimmer ein	
Parse:	6 structures; time: $25 + 2 + 14 + 0 + 10 = 51$ seconds (36)	
CLCS:	2 structures; time: 8 seconds (14)	
	(cause person	
	(go-loc person	
	(from-loc (in-loc person))	
	(to-loc (in-loc person room)))	
	forcefully) (2)	
Spanish:	32 structures; time: $9426 + 221 + 932 + 8 + 42 = 10629$ seconds	
(D.15.1)	juan forzó entrar en el cuarto (2) (10634)	
	juan forzaba entrar en el cuarto (2)	
	juan forzó entrar a el cuarto (2)	
	juan forzaba entrar a el cuarto (2)	
	juan forzó ir en el cuarto (2)	
	juan forzaba ir en el cuarto (2)	
	juan forzó ir a el cuarto (2)	
	juan forzaba ir a el cuarto (2)	
	juan forzó entrada en el cuarto (2)	
	juan forzó entradas en el cuarto (2)	
	juan forzaba entrada en el cuarto (2)	
	juan forzaba entradas en el cuarto (2)	
	juan forzó entrada a el cuarto (2)	
	juan forzó entradas a el cuarto (2)	
	juan forzaba entrada a el cuarto (2)	
	juan forzaba entradas a el cuarto (2)	
English:	6 structures; time: $375 + 23 + 349 + 6 + 7 = 760$ seconds (750)	
(D.15.2)	john broke into the room (2)	
	[N-MAX john]$_i$ forced [N-MAX himself]$_i$ to enter the room (2)	
	[N-MAX john]$_i$ forced [N-MAX himself]$_i$ to go into the room (2)	

(236)

Generating the Spanish for this sentence was a highly complex operation (see (236) and (234)) taking 1 hour (for the first run) and 3 hours (for the second run).[3] The primary contribution to the complexity for the Spanish sentence is ambiguity: the system attempts to realize the entering action as *entrar*, *ir*, *entrada*, and *entradas*. Furthermore, there are two past tenses (*forzó* and *forzaba*), and there are two particles (*en* and *a*) for the IN_{Loc} concept (see the discussion about particle selection in the last section). Once these lexical items are selected, the system then attempts to generate all verb-particle combinations. In addition, it attempts to realize the embedded clause both as a tensed clause (*e.g.*, *forzó que entre*) as well as an untensed clause (*e.g.*, *forzó entrar*). With all of these possibilities, it takes an inordinate amount of time to generate the final output forms.

Note that the realization of the *entrada* argument is problematic since the system does not know whether to generate the plural or the singular.

---

[3]Here we can see how inaccurate the timings actually are. Since the Spanish is being generated from the same possibility set (*i.e.*, CLCS's are identical in both of these runs), the time to generate for both runs should be the same. Due to garbage collection, paging, and other operations that are simultaneously executed, these times may be incorrect by as much as a factor of 3 or 4.

(See discussion regarding the analogous problem for *puñaladas* in 8.2.1.) Also the determiner *la* should be included in the output form, but it is not. The reason *entrada* is difficult to realize is that the English and German input do not supply any information regarding number and gender since the *enter* action is a verb in these two languages. (This is similar to the problem that arises in generating *Hunger* in the sentence *Ich habe Hunger*; see section 8.2.3.) The LCS is not the appropriate level at which to represent this type of information since it is concerned primarily with the relationship between predicates and their arguments. It is expected that these missing pieces may be filled in at a different level by a module that is specifically concerned with the analysis of nominal forms. Other than the fact that *entrada* is not correctly realized in this example, all the translations shown are acceptable for the *break-into* concept.

Note that the Spanish input composes into 10 CLCS's, two of which are preferred. This is due to the fact that *a* can be incorporated into the action as a modifier (as it is in *Juan forzó la entrada a tiempo* ('John broke into the room on time'). All modifier readings of *al cuarto* are eliminated since this phrase can also be composed as a locational argument. The two CLCS's that remain are essentially the same except that the place associated with FROM$_{\text{Loc}}$ may either be a Thing (*e.g.*, car), or it may be a location (*e.g.*, here). Because of this ambiguity, two syntactic structures are generated for each construction (in all three languages).

The English forms generated for this sentence are slightly more awkward (see (235) and (236)). The first output form (*John broke into the room*) is the appropriate result. The other two results are *John forced himself to enter the room* and *John forced himself to go into the room*; these are intended to be analogous to *John forced his way into the room*, which would be more acceptable.

The German sentences that are generated are both acceptable. (See (234) and (235).) Note that the *Johann* is emphasized in the first result, whereas *in das Zimmer* is emphasized in the second result. Also, the separable prefix *ein* has been generated in conjunction with *brechen*.

8.2.6   I Like to Eat

The following example illustrates how demotional divergence is handled:

(237) (i)   E: I like to eat

       (ii)   S: Me gusta comer (Comer me gusta a mí)

       (iii)   G: Ich esse gern

In particular, the verb-complement construction *like to eat* is translated
as the verb-adverb construction *esse gern*.[4] The German output is appropriate both in (238), as well as in (239): *Ich esse gern* (and also the
topicalized form where *gern* moves to the front of the sentence). Due
to the presence of the :DEMOTE marker in the lexical entry for *gern*,
the BE_{Circ} portion of the CLCS is mapped to this adverbial form, and
the EAT portion of the action is realized as the main verb in the surface
form. The translation results are shown in (238)–(240).

(238)

Input:	i like to eat
Parse:	1 structure; time: 88 + 20 + 13 + 0 + 2 = 123 seconds (120)
CLCS:	1 structure; time: 6 seconds (8)
	(be-circ referent (at-circ referent (eat referent)) likingly)
Spanish:	1 structure; time: 243 + 3 + 44 + 1 + 2 = 293 seconds (295)
(D.16.1)	comer [$_{CL-DAT}$ me]$_i$ gusta a [$_{N-MAX}$ mí]$_i$
German:	4 structures; time: 226 + 3 + 9 + 0 + 0 = 238 seconds (239)
(D.16.2)	[$_{N-MAX}$ ich]$_j$ [$_V$ esse]$_i$ [$_{N-MAX}$ t]$_j$ gern [$_V$ t]$_i$ (2)
	[$_{ADV}$ gern]$_j$ [$_V$ esse]$_i$ ich [$_{ADV}$ t]$_j$ [$_V$ t]$_i$ (2)

(239)

Input:	me gusta comer
Parse:	5 structures; time: 9 + 1 + 4 + 1 + 5 = 20 seconds (20)
CLCS:	1 structure preferred (out of 2); time: 8 seconds (10)
	(be-circ referent (at-circ referent (eat referent)) likingly)
German:	4 structures; time: 148 + 3 + 10 + 0 + 0 = 161 seconds (162)
(D.17.1)	[$_{N-MAX}$ ich]$_j$ [$_V$ esse]$_i$ [$_{N-MAX}$ t]$_j$ gern [$_V$ t]$_i$ (2)
	[$_{ADV}$ gern]$_j$ [$_V$ esse]$_i$ ich [$_{ADV}$ t]$_j$ [$_V$ t]$_i$ (2)
English:	2 structures; time: 29 + 4 + 3 + 1 + 1 = 38 seconds (38)
(D.17.2)	i like eating
	i like to eat

(240)

Input:	ich esse gern
Parse:	8 structures; time: 10 + 0 + 4 + 0 + 2 = 16 seconds (15)
CLCS:	2 structures preferred (out of 4); time: 7 seconds (9)
	(be-circ referent (at-circ referent (eat referent))
	likingly) (2)
Spanish:	2 structures; time: 301 + 9 + 83 + 2 + 5 = 400 seconds (401)
(D.18.1)	comer [$_{CL-DAT}$ me]$_i$ gusta a [$_{N-MAX}$ mí]$_i$
	comer [$_{CL-DAT}$ me]$_i$ guste a [$_{N-MAX}$ mí]$_i$
English:	2 structures; time: 45 + 6 + 6 + 1 + 1 = 59 seconds (61)
(D.18.2)	i like eating
	i like to eat

---

[4]The CLCS for this example contains an uninstantiated FOOD argument that
does not show up here. However, this argument is displayed (as a variable) in the
screen dumps of appendices D.16.1–D.18.2. Note that the LCS information associated
with this argument (displayed to the left of the CLCS) includes the (FOOD +) feature
specification.

The corresponding Spanish sentence is generated in its uninverted form (although both can be parsed by the system): *Comer me gusta a mí.* (See (238), and (240).) Note that the clitic *me* is linked with the prepositional *a mí*; this object is generated from the *LOWER-SUBJECT* in the lexical entry for *gustar* (see figure 6.1). Thus, even though this token has subject status in the CLCS, it is realized as an object pronoun in the output form (due to the presence of the :INT marker).

The English output takes on two different constructions for this example due to the fact that *like* can take either an infinitival or a progressive complement. Both of these are appropriate.

Note that the demotional divergence associated with *gern* and the thematic divergence associated with *gustar* are accounted for in this example.

8.2.7   John Usually Goes Home

The following example illustrates how promotional divergence is handled:

(241) (i)   E: John usually goes home

      (ii)   S: Juan suele ir a casa

      (iii)   G: Johann geht gewöhnlich nach Hause

The verb-adverb construction *usually go* is translated as the verb-complement construction *suele ir*. The Spanish output is appropriate both in (242) and in (244): *Juan suele ir a casa.* Due to the presence of the :PROMOTE marker in the lexical entry for *soler*, the HABITU-ALLY portion of the CLCS is mapped to the main verb of the sentence, and the GO_{Loc} portion of the action is mapped to the complement of this verb in the surface form. The translation results are shown in (242)–(244).

Input:	john usually goes home
Parse:	2 structures; time: $23 + 3 + 4 + 0 + 2 = 32$ seconds (27)
CLCS:	2 structures; time: 12 seconds (14)
	(go-loc person
	(from-loc (in-loc person))
	(to-loc (in-loc person house))
	habitually) (2)
Spanish:	2 structures; time: $9 + 2 + 2 + 0 + 3 = 16$ seconds (18)
(D.19.1)	juan suele ir a casa (2)
German:	24 structures; time: $41 + 41 + 3 + 1 + 3 = 89$ seconds (90)
(D.19.2)	[N-MAX johann]$_j$ [V geht]$_i$
	[N-MAX t]$_j$ zu hause gewöhnlich [V t]$_i$ (2)
	[P-MAX zu hause]$_j$ [V geht]$_i$
	johann [P-MAX t]$_j$ gewöhnlich [V t]$_i$ (2)
	[ADV gewöhnlich]$_j$ [V geht]$_i$
	johann zu hause [ADV t]$_j$ [V t]$_i$ (2)
	[N-MAX johann]$_j$ [V geht]$_i$
	[N-MAX t]$_j$ zu heim gewöhnlich [V t]$_i$ (2)
	[P-MAX zu heim]$_j$ [V geht]$_i$
	johann [P-MAX t]$_j$ gewöhnlich [V t]$_i$ (2)
	[ADV gewöhnlich]$_j$ [V geht]$_i$
	johann zu heim [ADV t]$_j$ [V t]$_i$ (2)
	[N-MAX johann]$_j$ [V geht]$_i$
	[N-MAX t]$_j$ nach hause gewöhnlich [V t]$_i$ (2)
	[P-MAX nach hause]$_j$ [V geht]$_i$
	johann [P-MAX t]$_j$ gewöhnlich [V t]$_i$ (2)
	[ADV gewöhnlich]$_j$ [V geht]$_i$
	johann nach hause [ADV t]$_j$ [V t]$_i$ (2)
	[N-MAX johann]$_j$ [V geht]$_i$
	[N-MAX t]$_j$ nach heim gewöhnlich [V t]$_i$ (2)
	[P-MAX nach heim]$_j$ [V geht]$_i$
	johann [P-MAX t]$_j$ gewöhnlich [V t]$_i$ (2)
	[ADV gewöhnlich]$_j$ [V geht]$_i$
	johann nach heim [ADV t]$_j$ [V t]$_i$ (2)

(242)

(243)

Input:	juan suele ir a casa
Parse:	60 structures; time: $210 + 78 + 57 + 7 + 841 = 1193$ seconds (1187)

CLCS:	6 structures preferred (out of 12); time: 66 seconds (72)
	(go-loc person (toward-loc (in-loc person house))
	  habitually)
	(go-loc person
	  (from-loc (in-loc person))
	  (to-loc (in-loc person house))
	  habitually) (2)
	(go-loc person
	  (from-loc (at-loc person))
	  (to-loc (at-loc person house))
	  habitually) (2)
	(go-loc person (toward-loc (on-loc person house))
	  habitually)

German:
(D.20.1)
	180 structures;
	time: $366 + 330 + 37 + 6 + 34 = 773$ seconds (778)
	$[_{\text{N-MAX}}$ johann$]_j$ $[_{\text{V}}$ geht$]_i$
	  $[_{\text{N-MAX}}$ t$]_j$ nach hause gewöhnlich $[_{\text{V}}$ t$]_i$ (2)
	$[_{\text{P-MAX}}$ nach hause$]_j$ $[_{\text{V}}$ geht$]_i$
	  johann $[_{\text{P-MAX}}$ t$]_j$ gewöhnlich $[_{\text{V}}$ t$]_i$ (2)
	$[_{\text{ADV}}$ gewöhnlich$]_j$ $[_{\text{V}}$ geht$]_i$
	  johann nach hause $[_{\text{ADV}}$ t$]_j$ $[_{\text{V}}$ t$]_i$ (2)
	$[_{\text{N-MAX}}$ johann$]_j$ $[_{\text{V}}$ gehe$]_i$
	  $[_{\text{N-MAX}}$ t$]_j$ nach hause gewöhnlich $[_{\text{V}}$ t$]_i$ (2)
	$[_{\text{P-MAX}}$ nach hause$]_j$ $[_{\text{V}}$ gehe$]_i$
	  johann $[_{\text{P-MAX}}$ t$]_j$ gewöhnlich $[_{\text{V}}$ t$]_i$ (2)
	$[_{\text{ADV}}$ gewöhnlich$]_j$ $[_{\text{V}}$ gehe$]_i$
	  johann nach hause $[_{\text{ADV}}$ t$]_j$ $[_{\text{V}}$ t$]_i$ (2)
	$[_{\text{N-MAX}}$ johann$]_j$ $[_{\text{V}}$ geht$]_i$
	  $[_{\text{N-MAX}}$ t$]_j$ nach heim gewöhnlich $[_{\text{V}}$ t$]_i$ (2)
	$[_{\text{P-MAX}}$ nach heim$]_j$ $[_{\text{V}}$ geht$]_i$
	  johann $[_{\text{P-MAX}}$ t$]_j$ gewöhnlich $[_{\text{V}}$ t$]_i$ (2)
	$[_{\text{ADV}}$ gewöhnlich$]_j$ $[_{\text{V}}$ geht$]_i$
	  johann nach heim $[_{\text{ADV}}$ t$]_j$ $[_{\text{V}}$ t$]_i$ (2)
	$[_{\text{N-MAX}}$ johann$]_j$ $[_{\text{V}}$ gehe$]_i$
	  $[_{\text{N-MAX}}$ t$]_j$ nach heim gewöhnlich $[_{\text{V}}$ t$]_i$ (2)
	$[_{\text{P-MAX}}$ nach heim$]_j$ $[_{\text{V}}$ gehe$]_i$
	  johann $[_{\text{P-MAX}}$ t$]_j$ gewöhnlich $[_{\text{V}}$ t$]_i$ (2)
	$[_{\text{ADV}}$ gewöhnlich$]_j$ $[_{\text{V}}$ gehe$]_i$
	  johann nach heim $[_{\text{ADV}}$ t$]_j$ $[_{\text{V}}$ t$]_i$ (2)

English: (D.20.2)	34 structures; time: $167 + 41 + 25 + 2 + 9 = 244$ seconds (247) john usually goes in house (3) john usually goes in home (3) john usually goes into house (4) john usually goes into home (4) john usually enters home (2) john usually enters house (2) john usually goes home (2) john usually goes house (2) john usually goes to house (2) john usually goes to home (2) john usually goes onto house (2) john usually goes onto home (2) john usually goes on house (2) john usually goes on home (2)

	Input:	johann geht gewöhnlich nach hause
	Parse:	20 structures; time: $34 + 2 + 22 + 1 + 10 = 69$ seconds (65)
	CLCS:	2 structures; time: 15 seconds (17)
		(go-loc person
		(from-loc (at-loc person))
		(to-loc (at-loc person house))
(244)		habitually) (2)
	Spanish:	2 structures; time: $43 + 3 + 1 + 0 + 3 = 50$ seconds (51)
	(D.21.1)	juan suele ir a casa (2)
	English:	8 structures; time: $39 + 7 + 4 + 1 + 3 = 54$ seconds (56)
	(D.21.2)	john usually goes home (2)
		john usually goes house (2)
		john usually goes to house (2)
		john usually goes to home (2)

By far the most complicated of all the sentences presented thus far is the German output for this example. Again, the problem of particle selection arises with respect to generating the prepositional phrase *nach Hause*. There are 180 output structures in (243), too many to list here. The ones that are not listed include inappropriate particles such as *in*, *bei*, *an*, and *zu*. Only the results containing *nach* are listed in (243). The reason the number of particles generated for this run (from Spanish) is higher than that of (242) (from English) is that the Spanish sentence composes into three types of CLCS representations due to the ambiguity of the word *a*, which can be composed into a TOWARD$_{Loc}$ (IN), a TOWARD$_{Loc}$ (ON), a TO$_{Loc}$ (IN), or a TO$_{Loc}$ (AT). In contrast, the English sentence composes into only one CLCS representation, thus reducing the number of particles that can be generated for this sentence. (Only the particle *zu* is incorrectly generated from the English sentence.)

Even without these additional particles, there are a number of possibilities that are generated. This is because *gehen* ('go') and *treten* ('enter') are both selected for the GO$_{Loc}$ CLCS, and the two forms *heim* and *house* are selected for the HOUSE CLCS. (See discussion in section 8.2.4 regarding *enter* and *house*.)

The other point to make about the German output is that it does not generate *gewöhnlich* ('usually') in the correct position: the sentence *Johann geht nach Hause gewöhnlich* should actually be *Johann geht gewöhnlich nach Hause*.[5] This is because the adjunction parameter. (see figure 2.7) specifies that adverbial adjunction can occur at both the

---

[5]Note that the stressed reading, *Gewöhnlich geht Johann nach Hause*, shows up in the result. This surface form is a reasonable translation. However, the corresponding syntactic structure contains a minimally adjoined adverb trace to the left of the verb trace. Thus, although the surface form is appropriate, the syntactic structure that is generated is not appropriate.

minimal and the maximal levels with respect to a verb in German. In this case, the system has erroneously chosen to realize *gewöhnlich* at the minimal level; once it has found this possibility for adjunction, it does not attempt to find others. This adjunct realization scheme is not general enough to apply to all cases (as in this example). The way that this problem can be remedied is to allow adverbials to lexically specify their allowable adjunction positions, just as lexical heads specify information about their complements. Currently, this is not implemented in UNITRAN.

The English output generated from the Spanish sentence is also unduly complicated (see (243)) for the same reason: particle selection. As for the the English output generated in (244), the result is acceptable (except for the awkwardness of *to home* as discussed in 8.2.4).

It appears that the problem of particle selection is the root of many of the difficulties that arise during generation from lexical conceptual structure. Putting aside the issue of particle selection for now, it is clear from these examples that the LCS approach has solved many of the problems that arise due to lexical-semantic divergences. In the next section, we will look at other examples handled by the system.

8.3 Pushing the Limit

Now that we have looked at the types of sentences that UNITRAN *can* handle, there are still a number of questions that need to be answered:

1. What types of sentences *cannot* UNITRAN currently handle?
2. How much further can the system be pushed?
3. Do the LCS building blocks provide adequate coverage for defining a wide range of words?

We will look at each of these questions in turn.

The answer to question 1 is easy. There are a number of different types of writings, especially poetic and metaphorical writing, that cannot be handled by the UNITRAN system. If we were to pick out a random sentence from a novel, or even a newspaper, it is highly likely that we would run into stylistic idiosyncrasies that would be too difficult to handle. Consider the following sentence taken from a German novel:[6]

---

[6]Ironically enough, this sentence is taken from a German translation of an English science fiction novel by Asimov (1972) called *The Gods Themselves*. Note that the

(245) The Etruscan translations themselves were marvels of dullness.
'Der Text der Übersetzungen war uberaus langweilig.'
(The text of the translations was thoroughly boring.)

The system would not be able to produce this German translation
for the English sentence as the human translator was able to do (for
example, translating 'marvels of dullness' into the German phrase corresponding to 'thoroughly boring'). UNITRAN works best in cases where
compositionality relates source- and target-language phrases. In the
general case, more abstract language is not guaranteed to work and a
more literal translation is likely to be chosen. On the other hand, this
does not come as a surprise since the ability to handle cases that are
this abstract is not necessarily something that most machine translation
experts expect to achieve in the near future.

As it turns out, there are many examples of text that are much more
straightforward, but still contain metaphors that cannot be understood
by the system. For example, in a technical manual describing the com-
mands of the UNIX system, we might come across the instruction:

(246) Use the 'kill' command to kill a process.

The word *kill* is being used here as a synonym for *terminate*; the metaphor comes out of the analogy drawn between a process and a person's
life (*i.e.*, killing a person implies that the person's life is terminated).
Such information is not captured in the LCS representation. Thus, the
translation of (246) into Spanish would result in the selection of the word
matar for *kill*, rather than the more appropriate lexical item *acabar*:

(247) (i)   ?Use el comando 'kill' para matar un proceso.

       (ii)   Use el comando 'kill' para acabar con un proceso.

Because metaphors do not necessarily carry across languages, some
other method must be used to translate metaphorical language. In particular, metaphorical items must be mapped to the conceptual structures underlying their "true" meanings before translation to the target-
language can proceed "normally."

---

sentence is loosely translated in that it does not include the adjective *Etruscan*;
this illustrates the extent to which human translation relies on context to produce a
target-language sentence.

An example of a system that has the capability of providing a metaphor-to-concept mapping is the MIDAS system (Martin (1988)), which represents conventional metaphors and interprets language using these metaphors. For example, the sentence (246) would be interpreted to mean:

(248) Use the 'kill' command to terminate a process.

The way this is done is by making an analogy between a COMPUTER-PROCESS and a LIVING-THING. Since the frame for killing a LIVING-THING includes the implication that the LIVING-THING is terminated, the system is able to understand (246) to be a statement about terminating a process.

Clearly, the problem of metaphor is well outside of the bounds assumed in the design of UNITRAN (and, for that matter, *most* machine translation systems). So the next question to ask is whether the system can be used (at least on a preliminary basis) to translate somewhat more straightforward free text without the ability to process contextual information. That is, how much further can the system be pushed beyond its intended capabilities?

Suppose UNITRAN were given the task of translating the following (more straightforward) newspaper article:[7]

(249) Nachts drangen Diebe in das Büro einer Firma in Nizza ein. Sie hatten dreifaches Pech. Der Geldschrank widerstand ihren Knackversuchen. Um etwas mitzunehmen, stahlen sie einen Büromantel. In diesem Mantel befanden sich die Geldschrankschlüssel, die die Diebe achtlos wegwarfen. Durch die auf den Geldschrankschlüsseln gefundenen Fingerabdrücke konnte der Boss des Diebestrios, der ein alter Kunde der Polizei war, gefaßt werden.

The somewhat literal English (human) translation is:

(250) In the night, thieves broke into the office of a firm in Nice. They had threefold bad luck. The safe resisted their safecracking attempts. In order to take something with them, they stole a lab coat. In this coat was the safekey, which the thieves threw away unmindfully. Through the fingerprints found on the safekey, the boss of the thief-trio, who was an old client of the police, could be apprehended.

---

[7]This article is from Ratych (1970, p. 15).

The questions to ask regarding the translation of this paragraph are:

1. Can we define the words in this text given the LCS building blocks that currently exist?
2. Can the appropriate syntactic and lexical-semantic structure be produced for the sentences once the words have been defined?
3. Can a "reasonable" translation be provided once the syntactic and lexical-semantic structures have been produced?

The answer is 'yes' to all three of these questions for the first five out of the six sentences in the text. All the words can be defined (see figure 8.3(a)–(e)), the appropriate syntactic and semantic structures can be produced (see figures 8.4(a)–(e) and 8.5(a)–(e), respectively), and the translations are "reasonable" in the sense that they convey the meaning of the input even without full understanding of the situational context: [8]

(251) Thieves broke into an office of a firm in Nice at night.

They had three-fold bad luck.

The safe withstood their attempts to be opened.

They stole a lab coat in order to take something with them.

The thieves unmindfully threw away the safekey which was found in the coat.

The boss of the thief-trio, who was an old client of the police, could be apprehended through the fingerprints found on the safekey.

On the other hand, it is harder to answer 'yes' to these questions for the sixth sentence, *Durch die auf den Geldschrankschlüsseln gefundenen Fingerabdrücke konnte der Boss des Diebestrios, der ein alter Kunde der Polizei war, gefaßt werden.* Defining the words is the easy part of the task (see figure 8.6). However, providing a syntactic structure is much more complicated (see figure 8.7). There are a number of reasons that this syntactic structure is difficult to produce. The most notable reason is that there are too many extraction sites for the syntactic component of UNITRAN to handle. This is because there is an implicit assumption in the construction of the phrase-structure templates that a phrase can have at most one head-trace position and one maximal-trace position. (This is an artificial constraint imposed by the algorithm that constructs the phrase-structure templates; it is not a GB constraint.)

---

[8] These results are still preliminary; they have been worked out by hand, but have not yet been machine tested.

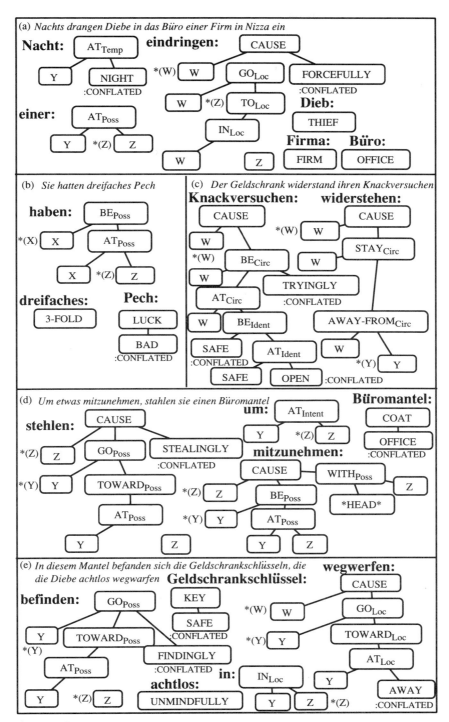

Figure 8.3
All of the words in the first five sentences of (249) are definable in terms of the LCS representation.

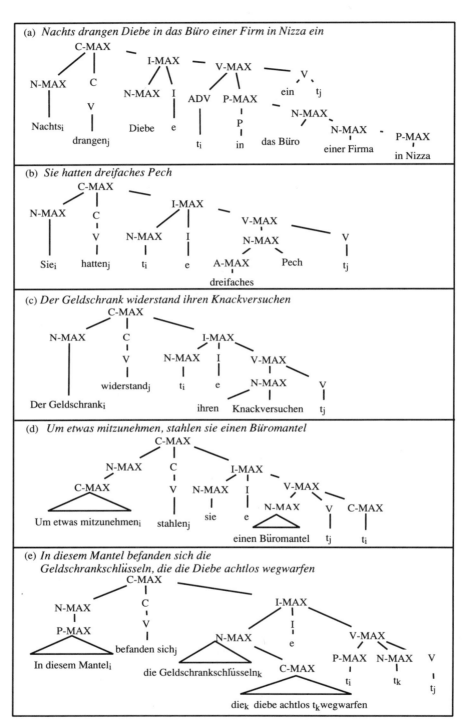

Figure 8.4
The first five sentences of (249) are syntactically analyzable.

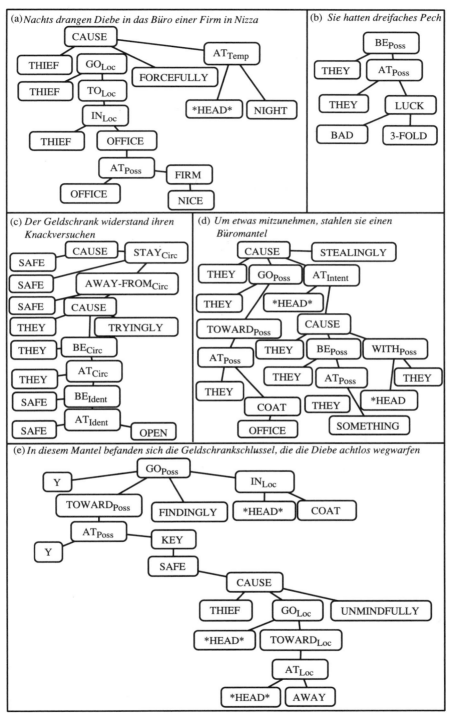

Figure 8.5
The first five sentences of (249) are analyzable in terms of the LCS representation.

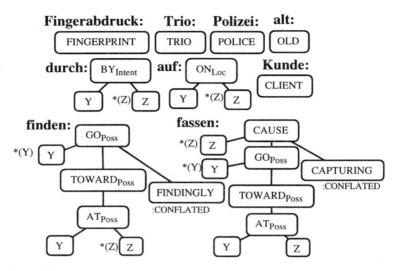

Figure 8.6
All of the words in the sentence *Durch die auf den Geldschrankschlüsseln gefundenen Fingerabdrücke konnte der Boss des Diebestrios, der ein alter Kunde der Polizei war, gefaßt werden* are definable in terms of the LCS representation.

Thus, the verb phrase *gefaßt werden* cannot be analyzed by the syntactic component due to the double maximal extraction (*i.e.*, the noun phrase headed by *Boss* and the prepositional phrase headed by *durch*). Even if this constraint were relaxed so that more than one maximal trace were allowed per phrase, the system would still be bogged down by the sheer complexity of the structure. (In general, a structure that has a large number of traces is analyzed exceedingly slowly due to the fact that empty structures must be predicted in positions for which there are no corresponding input tokens.)

All of these issues aside, the question that remains to be asked is whether we *could* produce the appropriate semantic representation (and translation) if we were somehow magically given the "correct" syntactic structure. The answer is that there is nothing inherent in the LCS component of the system that makes any of this more complicated sentence difficult to process once the appropriate syntactic structure has been produced. The CLCS based on the structure of figure 8.7 is shown in

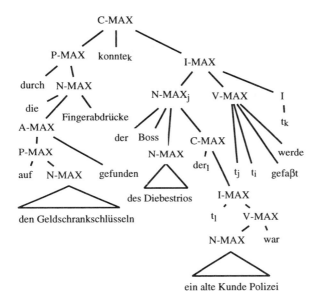

Figure 8.7
The syntactic Structure for *Durch die auf den Geldschrankschlüsseln gefundenen*
Fingerabdrücke konnte der Boss des Diebestrios, der ein alter Kunde der Polizei
war, gefaßt werden is difficult to obtain due to the sheer complexity of the
structure. A factor that contributes to this complexity is the occurrence of multiple
extraction sites.

figure 8.8.

The idea of providing the "correct" structure to the LCS component
of the system is not outside of the realm of possibility. Research by de
Marcken (1990a,b) has resulted in a very fast (usually 0.3 seconds per
sentence; 0.5 seconds for most sentences) large-scale English parser that
uses statistical methods for disambiguation based on the Lancaster-Oslo-
Bergen (LOB) corpus.[9] Such a parser could prove useful for the UNI-
TRAN system since syntactic processing has been abstracted away from
lexical-semantic processing. If the "correct" structure were provided by

---

[9]The fast parser is not the same as the system that is currently being used during
syntactic parsing (*i.e.*, it is not the same as the optimized Earley parser mentioned
in chapter 2). Given that the fast parser is entirely English-specific (and that it relies
on statistical information from an English corpus), the use of this parser on Spanish
and German has remained an area of future investigation.

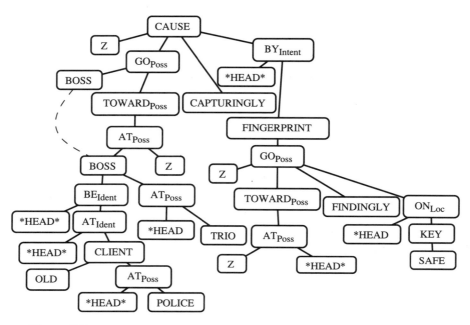

Figure 8.8
It would be possible to construct a CLCS for *Durch die auf den Geldschrankschlüsseln gefundenen Fingerabdrücke konnte der Boss des Diebestrios, der ein alter Kunde der Polizei war, gefaßt werden,* if the appropriate syntactic structure were provided.

the parser, the LCS component could then derive the appropriate underlying representation from which the target-language sentence could be generated. The syntactic structure (before movement has taken place) is the following:

(252) [c-max
        [i-max
          [v-max was captured
            [n-max the boss
              [p-max of the trio]
              [c-max who was an old client of the police]]
            [p-max by means of
              [n-max the fingerprints [a-max found on the safekey]]]]]]

After passive movement has taken place, the result is the following structure:

(253) [$_{\text{C-MAX}}$

    [$_{\text{I-MAX}}$

      [$_{\text{N-MAX}}$ the boss

         [$_{\text{P-MAX}}$ of the trio]

         [$_{\text{C-MAX}}$ who was an old client of the police]]$_i$

      [$_{\text{V-MAX}}$ was captured

         [$_{\text{N-MAX}}$ t]$_i$

         [$_{\text{P-MAX}}$ by means of

            [$_{\text{N-MAX}}$ the fingerprints [$_{\text{A-MAX}}$ found on the safekey]]]]]]]

The surface sentence produced from this structure is the following:

(254) The boss of the trio who was an old client of the police was captured by means of the fingerprints found on the safekey.

Given that UNITRAN does not include a discourse module, the final result would be this non-topicalized translation of the German sentence. If stylistic movement were allowed on the basis of focus information, the prepositional phrase *"by means of ..."* could be moved into specifier position of the clause, thus providing a closer parallel to the German sentence.

Given the difficulties described here, it seems there are still a number of areas for future research regarding the translation of free text. However, as we have seen, it is often possible to provide a reasonable translation for less complicated sentences, without fully understanding the context of the situation.

Now that we have looked at the results obtained through application of the methods described in earlier chapters, the next chapter turns to other areas of current investigation that involve the application of the LCS framework.

9   Current and Future Research: Tense, Aspect, and Lexical Acquisition

This chapter discusses current and future research that is underway with respect to the application of UNITRAN. In particular, it proposes a revised model of translation that integrates tense and aspect with lexical-semantics, thus addressing certain issues concerning temporal/aspectual nuances of meaning that were left open in chapters 3 and 6. The proposed model demonstrates that parameterization is useful for capturing aspectual distinctions across languages, just as it has proven useful for capturing syntactic and lexical-semantic distinctions.

Figure 9.1 places the revised model in the context of work that has already been done. (A preliminary description of this extended model is given by Dorr (1991a, 1992b) and Dorr and Gaasterland (1992).) The model consists of two levels. The first level includes a syntactic module which operates on the basis of the syntactic knowledge described in part I of this book. The extension to the model concerns the second level, which has been renamed the semantic module. This level includes two interacting components, one that operates on the basis of lexical-semantic knowledge (*i.e.*, the type of knowledge described in Part II of this book), and the other that operates on the basis of new knowledge from the temporal/aspectual domain. The interaction between the temporal/aspectual knowledge and the lexical-semantic knowledge will be the focus of this chapter. In addition, the notion of aspectual parameterization will be introduced. Finally, this chapter will discuss how aspectual information may be used as the basis for extraction of information from corpora.

The translation example shown in figure 9.1 illustrates the fact that the English sentence *John went to the store when Mary arrived* may be translated in two ways in Spanish. This example will be discussed throughout the chapter.

9.1   Background

Recently, there has been much discussion in the literature regarding the interaction of tense and aspect with lexical-semantics (see, for example, Appelo (1986), Bennett *et al.* (1990), van Eynde (1990), Herweg (1991), Hinrichs (1988), Maybury (1990), Moens and Steedman (1988), Nakhimovsky (1988), Passonneau (1988), Nirenburg and Pustejovsky (1988), Pustejovsky (1988, 1990, 1991), and Tenny (1987, 1989)). Among those

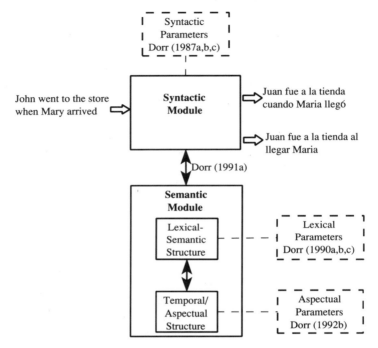

Figure 9.1
The revised model consists of a syntactic module and a semantic module. The
latter module is separated into two interacting components, one that operates on
the basis of lexical-semantic knowledge, and the other that operates on the basis of
temporal/aspectual knowledge.

who have studied the problem of tense, many have taken the work of
Reichenbach (1947) as a starting point (see, for example, Brent (1990)
and Hornstein (1990)), while others have built on the work of Allen
(1983, 1984) (see, for example, Vilain *et al.* (1990) and Williams (1990))
and still others have based their investigation on a combination of Allen
and Reichenbach's work (see, for example, Yip (1985)). Among those
who have studied the problem of aspect, many have built on the work of
Dowty (1979) and Vendler (1967) while others have followed Mourelatos
(1981) and Comrie (1976).

The current research proposes a two-level model that integrates tense
and aspect information, based on theories by both Hornstein (in the

spirit of Reichenbach) and Allen, with lexical-semantic information based on an extended version of Jackendoff's theory that includes a verb classification system proposed by Bennett *et al.* (in the spirit of Dowty and Vendler). The revised model is based on contemporary theories of tense and aspect; the innovation lies in the fact that it examines these theories within the context of machine translation. More recently, Bennett *et al.* (1990) have examined aspect and verb semantics within the context of machine translation. The current approach borrows from, and extends, these ideas by demonstrating how this theoretical framework might be adapted for cross-linguistic applicability.

Figure 9.2 illustrates that, just as divergences occur at the syntactic and lexical-semantic levels, divergences also arise at the aspectual level. The next two sections will focus on this third divergence type and will demonstrate how aspectual distinctions are resolved through parameterization. Section 9.4 then examines an algorithm for the acquisition of aspectual categories from a monolingual corpus. The fundamental assumption behind this algorithm is that the extraction of aspectual information must be based on principles that are well-grounded in linguistic theory. This viewpoint is in direct contrast with a commonly held view that the use of corpora necessarily suggests the use of non-linguistic techniques such as those used in statistical or example-based frameworks.

We will see, throughout this chapter, that the integration of tense and aspect with lexical-semantics is especially critical in machine translation. This is because the lexical selection and temporal/aspectual realization processes are often forced to choose among a large number of lexical and aspectual possibilities during the production of the target-language sentence. Temporal and aspectual information from the source-language sentence constrains the choice of target-language terms. In turn, the target-language terms limit the possibilities for generation of tense and aspect. Thus, there is a two-way communication channel between the two processes.

Syntactic:

(i)   **Null Subject divergence:**
       E: I have seen Mary ⇔ S: He visto a María
                                 (Have seen (to) Mary)

(ii)   **Constituent Order divergence:**
       E: I have seen Mary ⇔ G: Ich habe Marie gesehen
                                 (I have Mary seen)

Lexical-Semantic:

(i)   **Thematic divergence:**
       E: I like Mary ⇔ S: María me gusta a mí (Mary pleases me)

(ii)   **Structural divergence:**
       E: John entered the house ⇔ S: Juan entró en la casa
                                 (John entered in the house)

(iii) **Categorial divergence:**
       S: Yo tengo hambre ⇔ G: Ich habe Hunger (I have hunger)

Aspectual:

(i)   **Iterative Divergence:**
       E: John stabbed Mary ⇔
       S: Juan le dio una puñalada a María
          (John gave a knife-wound to Mary)
       S: Juan le dio puñaladas a María
          (John gave knife-wounds to Mary)

(ii)   **Durative Divergence:**
       E: John met/knew Mary ⇔
       S: Juan conoció a María (John met Mary)
       S: Juan conociá a María (John knew Mary)

Figure 9.2
Aspectual information adds another level of translation divergence.

9.2   Two-Level KR Model: Lexical-Semantic Knowledge and Temporal/Aspectual Knowledge

The hypothesis proposed by Tenny (1987, 1989) is that the mapping between cognitive structure and syntactic structure is governed by aspectual properties. The implication is that lexical-semantic knowledge exists at a level that does not include temporal or aspectual information (though these two levels of knowledge may depend on each other in some way). This hypothesis is consistent with the view adopted here; the current approach assumes that lexical semantic knowledge consists of such notions as predicate-argument structure, well-formedness conditions on predicate-argument structures, and procedures for lexical selection of surface-sentence tokens; all other types of knowledge must be represented at some other level.

In part II of this book, we saw how the LCS representation was used as an interlingua for the system. This level of representation makes use of parameterized information in the lexicon. In the revised processing model, the lexical-semantic level is one of two components of the semantic module. The second level is the temporal/aspectual component. This level is parameterized by means of *selection charts* and *coercion functions*. The notion of *selection charts* will be discussed in section 9.3.1. The notion of *coercion functions* was introduced for English verbs by Bennett *et al.* (1990) (in the spirit of Moens and Steedman (1988)). This work is extended in the current approach by parameterizing the coercion functions and setting the parameters to cover Spanish; this will be discussed in section 9.3.2.

The remainder of this section defines the dividing line between lexical knowledge (*i.e.*, the lexical-semantic structure) and non-lexical knowledge (*i.e.*, tense and aspect), and discusses how these two types of knowledge are combined in the semantic module.

9.2.1   Lexical-Semantic Structure

Lexical-semantic structure exists at a level of knowledge representation that is distinct from that of tense and aspect in that it encodes information about predicates and their arguments, plus the potential realization possibilities in a given language. In terms of the representation proposed by Jackendoff (1983, 1990), the CLCS representations for the two events of figure 9.1 would be the following:

(255) (i)   John went to the store
             [$_{\text{Event}}$ GO$_{\text{Loc}}$
                ([$_{\text{Thing}}$ John],
                [$_{\text{Position}}$ TO$_{\text{Loc}}$ ([$_{\text{Thing}}$ John], [$_{\text{Location}}$ Store])])]

      (ii)   Mary arrived
             [$_{\text{Event}}$ GO$_{\text{Loc}}$
                ([$_{\text{Thing}}$ Mary],
                [$_{\text{Position}}$ TO$_{\text{Loc}}$ ([$_{\text{Thing}}$ Mary], [$_{\text{Location}}$ e])])][1]

Although temporal connectives are not included in Jackendoff's theory, it is assumed that these two structures would be related by means of a lexical-semantic token corresponding to the temporal relation between the two events.

The LCS representation distinguishes between events and states; however, this distinction alone is not sufficient for choosing among similar predicates that occur in different aspectual categories. For example, the lexical entry for the three verbs *ransack, obliterate,* and *destroy,* would contain the following RLCS:

(256) [$_{\text{Event}}$ CAUSE
          ([$_{\text{Thing}}$ * X],
          [$_{\text{Event}}$ GO$_{\text{Loc}}$
             ([$_{\text{Thing}}$ * Y],
             [$_{\text{Position}}$ TO$_{\text{Loc}}$ ([$_{\text{Thing}}$ Y], [$_{\text{Property}}$ DESTROYED])])])]

As it turns out, the only way to distinguish these verbs is by means of aspectual features. In particular, events can be further subdivided into more specific types so that *nonculminative* events such as *ransack* (*i.e.,* events that do not have a definite moment of completion) can be distinguished from *culminative* events such as *obliterate* and *destroy* (*i.e.,* events that have a definite moment of completion). This is a crucial distinction given that these three similar words cannot be used interchangeably in all contexts. Such distinctions are handled by augmenting the lexical-semantic framework so that it has access to aspectual information, which will be described in the next section.

---

[1]The empty location denoted by e corresponds to an unrealized argument of the predicate *arrive*.

9.2.2 Aspectual Structure

The information required for the realization of aspect is considered to be outside of the scope of the lexical-semantic knowledge. This assumption is supported by the fact that a given lexical-semantic representation may correspond to more than one aspectual structure, depending on the context of the linguistic utterance. We will see examples of this shortly.

Following Dowty (1979) and Vendler (1967), aspect is taken to have two components, one comprised of *non-inherent* features (*e.g.*, those features that define the perspective such as simple, progressive, and perfective) and another comprised of *inherent* features (*e.g.*, those features that distinguish between states and events).[2] Non-inherent features are dependent on temporal context; thus, they are not stored with the lexical item and may be controlled during language generation. These are distinguished from inherent features, which are stored with the lexical item and are used for lexical selection. This section discusses the realization of both types of information.

Suppose we are generating a target-language sentence from a lexical-semantic representation that relates the two events from figure 9.1, *John went to the store* and *Mary arrived*. The single lexical-semantic structure corresponding to this combined event may have any number of associated aspectual structures, each of which corresponds to a different surface-sentence utterance:[3]

(257) (i)   John went to the store before Mary arrived
          (simp)   (simp)

    (ii)   John went to the store before Mary had arrived
          (simp)   (perf)

    (iii)   John had gone to the store before Mary arrived
          (perf)   (simp)

    (iv)   John had gone to the store before Mary had arrived
          (perf)   (perf)

The aspectual variations shown here are primarily a function of values of non-inherent features (*i.e.*, perfective *vs.* simple). All of these surface

---

[2]We will see shortly that events are further subdivided into activities, achievements, and accomplishments.

[3]Throughout this chapter, the perfective, progressive, infinitive, and simple aspects are denoted as *perf, prog, inf,* and *simp,* respectively. Note that the term *perfective* refers to either the present or the past (plu) perfective (*i.e.*, it does not specify the tense).

realizations would be perfectly valid if we had the knowledge that the "going to the store" event occurred before the "arriving" event. Thus, the lexical-semantic structure for these two events does not constrain the choice of potential aspectual structures with which it may be associated. Moreover, the aspectual feature values must be determined before the two events can be combined since this information is necessary for selecting the appropriate temporal connectives (*e.g.*, *when*, *before*, *during*, etc.).

Regarding the representation of inherent features, a number of aspectually oriented representations have been proposed that readily accommodate the types of aspectual distinctions that are of concern here. The current work extends these ideas for the augmentation of the interlingual representation. For example, Dowty (1979) and Vendler (1967) have proposed a four-way aspectual classification system for verbs: states, activities, achievements, and accomplishments, each of which has a different degree of telicity (*i.e.*, culminated *vs.* nonculminated), and/or atomicity (*i.e.*, point *vs.* extended).[4] A similar scheme has been suggested by Bach (1986), Nirenburg and Pustejovsky (1988), and Pustejovsky (1988, 1990, 1991) (following Mourelatos (1981) and Comrie (1976)) in which actions are classified into states, processes, and events.

Aspectual information provides fine-grained distinctions that previously were not available in the LCS representation. Thus, the interlingua of the new model is an augmented form of Jackendoff's representation in which events are distinguished from states (as before), but events are further subdivided into activities, achievements, and accomplishments. The subdivision is achieved by means of three features proposed by Bennett *et al.* (1990) following the framework of Moens and Steedman (1988): ±dynamic (*i.e.*, events *vs.* states, as in the Jackendoff framework), ±telic (*i.e.*, culminative events (transitions) *vs.* nonculminative events (activities)), and ±atomic (*i.e.*, point events *vs.* extended events).

The current model imposes this system of features on top of the existing lexical-semantic framework. As an example of how this is done,

---

[4]Dowty's version of this classification collapses achievements and accomplishments into a single event type called a *transition*, which covers both the point and extended versions of the event type. The rationale for this move is that all events have *some* duration, even in the case of so-called punctual events, depending on the granularity of time involved. (See Passonneau (1988) for an adaptation of this scheme as implemented in the PUNDIT system.) For the purposes of this discussion, we will maintain the distinction between achievements and accomplishments.

A	B	C	D	E	Example
State	[-d]	state	state	state(BE)	be, like, know
Act (ext)	[+d, -t, -a]	process	process	event(GO)	ransack, run
Act (pt)	[+d, -t, +a]	process	trans⁵	event(GO)	tap, wink
Ach	[+d, +t, +a]	event	culm trans	event(GO)	obliterate, kill
Acc	[+d, +t, -a]	event	log trans	event(GO)	destroy, arrive

Figure 9.3
A number of different approaches have been proposed for representing aspect. The
common denominator among these schemes is the dependence on dynamicity,
telicity, and atomicity. The encoding of the relevant researchers is as follows: A =
Dowty (1979), Passonneau (1988), Vendler (1967); B= Bennett *et al.* (1990), Moens
and Steedman (1988); C= Bach (1986), Comrie (1976), Mourelatos (1981); D=
Nirenburg and Pustejovsky (1988), Pustejovsky (1988, 1990, 1991); and E=
Jackendoff (1983, 1990).

consider the three verbs, *ransack*, *obliterate*, and *destroy*, whose LCS
representation was given above in (256). These three verbs are distinguished by annotating the LCS representation with the aspectual features [+d,-t,-a] for the verb *ransack*, [+d,+t,-a] for the verb *destroy*,
and [+d,+t,+a] for the verb *obliterate*, thus providing the appropriate
distinction for cases such as the following:

(258) (i)   John ransacked the house { for an hour. / until Jack arrived. }

(ii)   John destroyed the house { for an hour. / until Jack arrived. }

(iii) * John obliterated the house { for an hour. / until Jack arrived. }

This system is essentially equivalent to proposals by Dowty (1979) and
Vendler (1967), but features are used to distinguish the categories more
precisely. Figure 9.3 relates five different characterizations of aspect.

Previous representational frameworks have omitted aspectual distinctions among verbs, and have typically merged events under the single

⁵Nirenburg and Pustejovsky (1988) take point activities one step further than the
proposal by Bennett *et al.* (1990). In particular, "trans" is broken down into simple
transitions (*e.g.*, *give*) and causative transitions (*e.g.*, *send*). Thus, the finest tuning
is actually provided by the Nirenburg and Pustejovsky proposal rather than one by
Bennett *et al.* However, we have chosen the featural representation since it is well-
suited to the specification of coercion functions (as we will see in section 9.3). Note
that we could easily add a new feature (*i.e.*, ±c for the causative/non-causative forms)
to make the current proposal as specific as the one by Nirenburg and Pustejovsky
(1988).

heading of *dynamic* (see, *e.g.*, Yip (1985)). Such frameworks would apply aspectual interpretations uniformly across all verbs that are considered to be dynamic. However, as we have seen with the three verbs *ransack*, *obliterate*, and *destroy*, it cannot be the case that the aspectual interpretations of all dynamic verbs adhere to the same constraints given that their distributions are not identical.

We will discuss the interaction between aspect and lexical semantics in section 9.3, but first we will turn to a brief description of the temporal framework assumed by the current model.

9.2.3   Temporal Structure

Tense is taken to be the external time relationship between a given situation and others. (See, for example, Bennett *et al.* (1990).) Like aspect, tense is considered to be outside of the realm of lexical-semantic knowledge.

In the example of figure 9.1, the source- and target-language sentences consist of two event structures apiece, each of which is associated with its own temporal structure. In the case of *go* (*John went to the store*), the event is associated with the Reichenbachian Basic Tense Structure (BTS) E,R_S, which indicates that the event is in the past.[6] The aspect of this clause is "simple" (as opposed to progressive or perfective). In the case of *arrive* (*Mary arrived*), the event is associated with the same Reichenbachian temporal representation (E,R_S) and aspect (simple), since it too is in the simple past tense.

As for relating these two events, the approach adopted here is based on a neo-Reichenbachian framework proposed by Hornstein (1990) in which the basic tense structures are organized into a Complex Tense Structure

---

[6]It is assumed that the reader is familiar with the Reichenbachian framework, which postulates three theoretical entities: S (the moment of speech), R (a reference point), and E (the moment of the event). The key idea is that certain linear orderings of the three time points get grammaticalized into six basic tenses in English. The corresponding basic tense structures are:

S,R,E	present
E,R_S	past
S_R,E	future
E_S,R	present perfect
E_R_S	past perfect
S_E_R	future perfect

The S, R, and E points may be separated by a line (in which case, the leftmost point is interpreted as temporally earlier than the other) or by a comma (in which case, the points are interpreted as contemporaneous).

(CTS) as follows: the first event (*i.e.*, the main *matrix* clause) is written over the BTS of the second event (*i.e.*, the subordinate *adjunct* clause) and the S and R points are then associated.[7] The entire temporal/aspectual structure for this example would be specified as follows:[8]

$$
(259) \quad
\begin{array}{l}
E_1, R_1 \underline{\quad} S_1 \\
\quad | \quad\;\; | \\
E_2, R_2 \underline{\quad} S_2
\end{array}
\quad
\begin{array}{l}
\text{aspect}_1 = \text{simp} \\
\text{aspect}_2 = \text{simp}
\end{array}
$$

Tense is determined by factors relating not to the particular lexical tokens of the surface sentence, but to the temporal features of the context surrounding the event coupled with certain linguistically motivated constraints on the tense structure of the sentence. In particular, it has been persuasively argued by Hornstein (1990) that all sentences containing a matrix and adjunct clause are subject to a linguistic (syntactic) constraint on tense structure *regardless* of the lexical tokens included in the sentence. For example, Hornstein's linguistic Constraint on Derived Tense Structures (CDTS) requires that the association of S and R points not involve crossover in a complex tense structure:

$$
(260) \quad
\begin{array}{l}
E_1, R_1 \underline{\quad} S_1 \\
\qquad\;\; \diagdown\;\; \downarrow \\
\qquad\quad S_2, R_2, E_2
\end{array}
\quad
\begin{array}{l}
\text{aspect}_1 = \text{simp} \\
\text{aspect}_2 = \text{simp}
\end{array}
$$

Here, the association of R_2 and R_1 violates the CDTS, thus ruling out the sentence.

Note that this linguistic constraint is a syntactic restriction on the manipulation of tense structures, not on the temporal interpretation of tensed sentences. Thus, the constraint holds regardless of the lexical token that is chosen as the connective between the two events:

(261) * John went to the store $\left\{ \begin{array}{l} \text{as} \\ \text{before} \\ \text{after} \\ \text{as soon as} \\ \text{while} \end{array} \right\}$ Mary arrives.

---

[7] In the general case, the association of the S and R points may force the R_2 point to be moved so that it is aligned with the R_1 point. The E_2 point is then placed accordingly.

[8] The aspect of the clauses is included here for the illustrative purposes.

The connecting word that relates the two events must be selected independently of the temporal structure associated with the sentence since the order of E_1 and E_2 in a given CTS does not necessarily correspond to the order imposed by the interpretation of the connective. For example, the CTS for *John went to the store before Mary had arrived* is identical to the CTS for *John went to the store after Mary had arrived*, even though E_1 is placed linearly *after* E_2 in both cases:

$$
(262) \quad
\begin{array}{l}
E_1,R_1 \underline{\quad} S_1 \\
\quad | \qquad | \\
E_2 \underline{\quad} R_2 \underline{\quad} S_2
\end{array}
\qquad
\begin{array}{l}
\text{aspect}_1 = \text{simp} \\
\text{aspect}_2 = \text{perf}
\end{array}
$$

Thus, it is assumed that the knowledge required to determine the temporal structure associated with a sentence exists at a level that is independent from the lexical-semantic knowledge required to select the appropriate lexical items for the surface sentence.

Hornstein's theory of tense assumes that events are points in time. To extend this theory to events that have duration, events are analyzed in terms of Allen's theory of temporal interval relationships (Allen (1983, 1984)). Allen proposes that seven basic relationships and their inverses may exist between two intervals. The interval relationships are *before* ($<$), *after* ($>$) *during* (d), *contains* (di), *overlaps* (o), *overlapped by* (oi), *meets* (m), *met by* (mi), *starts* (s), *started by* (si), *finishes* (f), *finished by* (fi), and *equal* ($=$). The inverse of *equal* is *equal*, so there are a total of 13 different interval relationships. These temporal relations are assumed to be determined from the context in which the source-language sentence is uttered or, perhaps, from some knowledge source such as a database with temporal information (see, for example, Dorr and Gaasterland (1992), Gaasterland (1992) and Gaasterland and Minker (1991)).

For example, if it is determined that the event E_1 *John went to the store* and event E_2 *Mary arrived* have both occurred in the past, then the time of the linguistic utterance S is *after* the two event times.[9] This means that the only possible BTS's (for both E_1 and E_2) are: E,R_S (past), E_S,R (present perfect), and E_R_S (past perfect). In each of these three cases, the event time E and the speech time S are separated

---

[9]It is assumed that the time of the linguistic utterance S refers to the present time.

i.   Past/Past: John went to the store when Mary arrived

$$E_1,R_1 \,\_\, S_1$$

$aspect_1 = simp$
$aspect_2 = simp$

$$E_2,R_2 \,\_\, S_2$$

ii. Past/Pres Perf: *John went to the store when Mary has arrived

$$E_1,R_1 \,\_\, S_1$$

$aspect_1 = simp$
$aspect_2 = perf$

$$E_2 \,\_\, S_2,R_2$$

iii. Past/Past Perf: John went to the store when Mary had arrived

$$E_1,R_1 \,\_\,S_1$$

$aspect_1 = simp$
$aspect_2 = perf$

$$E_2 \,\_\, R_2\,\_S_2$$

iv. Pres Perf/Past: *John has gone to the store when Mary arrived

$$E_1 \,\_\, S_1,R_1$$

$aspect_1 = perf$
$aspect_2 = simp$

$$E_2,R_2 \,\_\, S_2$$

v.   Pres Perf/Pres Perf: John has gone to the store when Mary has arrived

$$E_1 \,\_\, S_1,R_1$$

$aspect_1 = perf$
$aspect_2 = perf$

$$E_2 \,\_\, S_2,R_2$$

vi. Pres Perf/Past Perf: *John has gone to the store when Mary had arrived

$$E_1 \,\_\, S_1,R_1$$

$aspect_1 = perf$
$aspect_2 = perf$

$$E_2 \,\_\, R_2 \,\_\, S_2$$

vii. Past Perf/Past: John had gone to the store when Mary arrived

$$E_1 \,\_\, R_1\,\_S_1$$

$aspect_1 = perf$
$aspect_2 = simp$

$$E_2,R_2 \,\_\, S_2$$

viii. Past Perf/Pres Perf: *John had gone to the store when Mary has arrived

$$E_1 \,\_\, R_1\,\_S_1$$

$aspect_1 = perf$
$aspect_2 = perf$

$$E_2 \,\_\, S_2,R_2$$

ix. Past Perf/Past Perf: John had gone to the store when Mary had arrived

$$E_1 \,\_\, R_1 \,\_S_1$$

$aspect_1 = perf$
$aspect_2 = perf$

$$E_2 \,\_\, R_2 \,\_S_2$$

Figure 9.4
There are nine possible tense/aspect combinations for two events occurring in the past. Four of them are ruled out by the CDTS, which disallows complex tense structures with crossovers.

When				
Temporal	**Matrix**		**Adjunct**	
Relation	**Features**	**Perspective**	**Features**	**Perspective**
$E_1 = E_2$	$[+d,-t,\pm a]$	simp, prog, perf	$[+d,+t,\pm a]$	simp, prog, perf
$E_1 > E_2$	$[+d,+t,\pm a]$	simp	$[+d,+t,\pm a]$	simp
$E_1 < E_2$	$[+d,-t,\pm a]$	perf (past)	$[+d,+t,\pm a]$	simp, perf
E_1 m E_2	$[-d]$	simp	$[+d,+t,\pm a]$	simp
E_1 mi E_2	$[+d,+t,\pm a]$	simp	$[+d,+t,\pm a]$	simp
E_1 di E_2	$[+d,+t,\pm a]$	simp, prog	$[+d,+t,\pm a]$	simp
E_1 fi E_2	$[+d,+t,\pm a]$	prog	$[+d,+t,\pm a]$	simp
E_1 si E_2	$[-d]$	simp	$[+d,+t,\pm a]$	simp

Figure 9.5
Only certain temporal relations are allowed for the *When* connective.

by (at least one) line, thus providing a temporal interpretation in which E occurs before S.

Figure 9.4 illustrates the combination of the two BTS's into nine possible complex tense structures. (One component of the aspectual representation, simple *vs.* perfect, is included as well.) The CDTS rules out four of the nine possibilities leaving the following five cases: [10]

(263) John went to the store when Mary arrived.

(264) John went to the store when Mary had arrived.

(265) John has gone to the store when Mary has arrived.
       [as in: Typically, John has gone ...]

(266) John had gone to the store when Mary arrived.

(267) John had gone to the store when Mary had arrived.

Once the constraint proposed by Hornstein has pared down the possibilities for the tense combinations, the choices of surface sentences are further constrained by selecting the most accurate description of the temporal relation between the two events for the connective *when*. Suppose we have the additional information from the knowledge source that the "going to the store" event occurs before the "arriving" event; in terms of Allen's notation, this would be specified as $E_1 < E_2$. The two sentences that guarantee this relation are (266) and (267). We can ensure that only these two realizations are selected for the *when* connective by using the $E_1 < E_2$ relation as an index into a table (*i.e.*, a *selection*

---

[10] Analogous results would be obtained if we were to switch the matrix and adjunct clauses for this example, although this is not always the case.

chart) that associates the aspectual information of the two events with the *when* connective. A portion of such a table is shown in figure 9.5. [11] Note that, in addition to temporal information, the table also includes the aspectual perspective (*i.e.*, simple, progressive, or perfective) and the aspectual type (*i.e.*, ±dynamic, ±telic, ±atomic); thus, there is a tight coupling of tense and aspect during the realization of the surface form.

From this table we see that there are only two possible realizations for the two GO_{Loc} events in the current example: the first event is associated with the features [+d,-t,-a]; the second event is associated with the features [+d,+t,-a]. There are only five legal tense/aspect combinations from which to choose; thus, the only admissible aspectual realizations are a perfective matrix clause with a simple adjunct clause, or a perfective matrix clause with a perfective adjunct clause. Accordingly, sentences (266) and (267) are selected as legal possibilities for the surface sentence. We will return to additional discussion about the selection of temporal connectives in section 9.3.1.

Note that Hornstein's neo-Reichenbachian theory crucially relies on an asymmetry between the matrix and adjunct clauses. Thus, there is an important distinction between Hornstein (1990), in which the asymmetrical property is fundamental to the theory, and Yip (1985) in which the asymmetrical property is entirely abandoned. Hornstein's intuition is the one adopted here given that we cannot arbitrarily interchange the matrix and adjunct clauses. For example, Yip's theory predicts that we should be able to replace "E_1 after E_2" with "E_2 before E_1," which is not always the case:

(268) (i)   John will go to the store after Mary has arrived.

(ii)   * Mary has arrived before John will go to the store.

(269) (i)   John will go to the store after Mary arrives.

(ii)   * Mary arrives before John will go to the store.

Given this asymmetrical property, it would not be possible to randomly select a matrix/adjunct order and an appropriate temporal connective for a surface sentence solely on the basis of lexical information. What is needed is the temporal relation between the two events and

---

[11] For brevity, only 8 of Allen's 13 relations are shown in this table.

the constraints on their combination before it is possible to derive the matrix/adjunct ordering of the sentence.

In the next section, we will see how the lexical-semantic representation is parametrically combined with the temporal and aspectual representation to provide the framework for generating a target-language surface form.

9.3 Cross-Linguistic Applicability: Parameterization of the Two-Level Model

Although issues concerning lexical-semantics and tense/aspect have been studied extensively, they have not been examined sufficiently in the context of machine translation. In particular, the question of whether theories of aspect by Bennett *et al.*, Dowty, Moens and Steedman, Vendler, and others can be combined with a lexical-semantic model to provide a cross-linguistic account for the selection of lexical items (*e.g.*, in an interlingual translation model) has not been addressed.

Machine translation provides an appropriate testbed for trying out theories of lexical semantics and aspect. The problem of lexical selection during generation of the target language is the most crucial issue in this regard. The featural system outlined above provides a framework that is appropriate not only for the selection of temporal connectives, but also for the selection and aspectual realization of other lexical tokens such as verbal components. The current framework facilitates the selection of temporal connectives and the aspectual realization of verbs. We will discuss each of these, in turn, showing how *selection charts* and *coercion functions* are used as a means of parameterization for these processes.

9.3.1 Selection of Temporal Connectives: Selection Charts

In order to ensure that the framework presented here is cross-linguistically applicable, we must provide a mechanism for handling temporal connective selection in languages other than English. For the purposes of this discussion, we will examine distinctions between English and Spanish only. Consider the following example:

(270) (i)   John went to the store when Mary arrived.

       (ii)   John had gone to the store when Mary arrived.

In section 9.2.3, we discussed the selection of the lexical connective *when* on the basis of the temporal relation between the matrix clause and the adjunct clause. Appendix E shows how temporal information is used to build additional selection charts for English using an analysis by Dorr and Gaasterland (1992). For the remainder of this chapter, we will ignore the temporal component of word selection and will focus instead on how the process of word selection may be parameterized using the aspectual features described in section 9.2.2.

To translate (270)(i) and (ii) into Spanish, we must choose between the lexical tokens *cuando* and *al* in order to generate the equivalent temporal connective for the word *when*. In the case of (270)(i), there are two possible translations, one that uses the connective *cuando*, and one that uses the connective *al*:

(271) (i)   Juan fue a la tienda cuando María llegó.

       (ii)   Juan fue a la tienda al llegar María.

Either one of these sentences is an acceptable translation for (270)(i). However, the same is not true of (270)(ii):[12]

(272) (i)   Juan había ido a la tienda cuando María llegó.

       (ii)   Juan había ido a la tienda al llegar María.

Sentence (272)(i) is an acceptable translation of (270)(ii) but (272)(ii) does not mean the same thing as (270)(ii). This second sentence implies that John has already gone to the store and come back, which is not the preferred reading.

In order to establish an association between these connectives and the aspectual interpretation for the two events (*i.e.*, the matrix and adjunct clause), a table called a *selection chart* is compiled for each language that specifies the contexts in which each connective may be used. Figure 9.6 shows the charts for *when*, *cuando*, and *al*. These charts are an abbreviated form of the actual chart that is being used (*i.e.*, the temporal relation is not shown here.) Specifically, the chart shown in figure 9.6 assumes that the matrix event occurs *after* (>) or *before* (<) the adjunct event (*i.e.*, it corresponds to rows 2 and 3 in figure 9.5).

---

[12]I am indebted to Jorge Lobo (personal communication) for pointing this out to me.

When				
Temporal	Matrix		Adjunct	
Relation	Features	Perspective	Features	Perspective
$E_1 > E_2$	$[+d,+t,\pm a]$	simp	$[+d,+t,\pm a]$	simp
$E_1 < E_2$	$[+d,-t,\pm a]$	perf (past)	$[+d,+t,\pm a]$	simp, perf

Cuando				
$E_1 > E_2$	$[+d,+t,\pm a]$	simp	$[+d,+t,\pm a]$	simp
$E_1 < E_2$	$[+d,-t,\pm a]$	perf (past)	$[+d,+t,\pm a]$	simp, perf

Al				
$E_1 > E_2$	$[+d,+t,\pm a]$	simp	$[+d,+t,\pm a]$	simp
$E_1 < E_2$	$[+d,+t,\pm a]$	perf (past)	$[+d,+t,\pm a]$	simp, perf

Figure 9.6
The selection charts illustrate that *Al* differs from *Cuando* and *When* in that it requires a +telic matrix clause when the matrix event occurs before the adjunct event.

The selection charts can be viewed as inverted dictionary entries in that they map features to words, not words to features.[13] The charts serve as a means of parameterization for the program that generates sentences from the interlingua in that they are allowed to vary from language to language while the procedure for choosing temporal connectives applies cross-linguistically.

The key point to note is that the chart for the Spanish connective *al* is similar to that for the English connective *when* except that, in the *before* ($<$) case, the word *al* requires the matrix event to have the +telic feature (*i.e.*, the matrix action must reach a culmination). This accounts for the distinction between *cuando* and *al* in sentences (272)(i) and (272)(ii) above.[14] That is, the matrix event *había ido* is -telic in (272), thus allowing *cuando*, but not *al*, to be selected when the matrix event precedes the adjunct event. Note that this is not the case with (271): the matrix event *fue* is +telic (*i.e.*, the preterit tense forces (or *coerces*) the verb *fue*

---

[13]Note, however, that the features correspond to the events connected by the words, not to the words themselves.

[14]It has recently been pointed out by Michael Herweg (personal communication) that the telic feature is not traditionally used to indicate a revoked consequence state (*e.g.*, the consequence state that results after returning from the "going to the store" event), but is generally intended to indicate an irrevocable, culminative, consequence state. Thus, it has been suggested that *al* acts more as a complementizer than as a "pure" adverbial connective such as *cuando*; this would explain the realization of the adjunct not as a tensed adverbial clause, but as an infinitival subordinate clause. This possibility is currently under investigation.

to be +telic) and occurs *after* (>) the adjunct event; thus, both *cuando* and *al* are selected.

These tables are used for the selection of temporal connectives during the generation process (for which the relevant index into the tables would be the aspectual features associated with the interlingual representation). The selection of a temporal connective, then, is simply a table look-up procedure based on the aspectual features associated with the events. For example, if we had a [+d,-t,-a] event E_1 (*e.g.*, *run*) and a [+d,+t,-a] event E_2 (*e.g.*, *arrive*), and if we knew that E_1 occurred up until E_2 started, then searching the *when* table would fail, but searching the *until* table (not shown here) would succeed, thus allowing a sentence such as *John ran until Mary arrived* to be generated. The same would be true in the case of Spanish (*i.e.*, *John corrió hasta que llegó María*).

9.3.2   Selection and Aspectual Realization of Verbs: Coercion Functions

Above, we considered the selection of temporal connectives without regard to the selection and aspectual realization of the lexical items that were being connected. Again, to ensure that the framework presented here is cross-linguistically applicable, we must provide a mechanism for handling lexical selection and aspectual realization in languages other than English.

First, we will look more carefully at what is meant by the process of *coercion*. This process induces a change that results in a different set of aspectual features than those that are inherent in the verb. An example of coercion is the use of durative adverbials. Durative adverbials (*e.g.*, *for an hour* and *until*) are viewed as *anti-culminators* (following Bennett *et al.* (1990)) in that they change the main verb from an action that has a definite moment of completion to an action that has been stopped but not necessarily finished. Consider the three verbs given above in (258), repeated here:

(273) (i)   John ransacked the house $\left\{ \begin{array}{l} \text{for an hour.} \\ \text{until Jack arrived.} \end{array} \right\}$

     (ii)   John destroyed the house $\left\{ \begin{array}{l} \text{for an hour.} \\ \text{until Jack arrived.} \end{array} \right\}$

     (iii) * John obliterated the house $\left\{ \begin{array}{l} \text{for an hour.} \\ \text{until Jack arrived.} \end{array} \right\}$

The verb *ransack* is allowed to be modified by a durative adverbial since it is inherently durative; thus, no coercion is necessary in order to use this verb in the durative sense. In contrast, the verb *destroy* is inherently non-durative, but it is *coerced* into a durative action by means of adverbial modification; this accounts for the acceptability of sentence (273)(ii).[15] The verb *obliterate* must necessarily be non-durative (*i.e.*, it is inherently non-durative and non-coercible), thus accounting for the ill-formedness of sentence (273)(iii).

In order to illustrate how coercion functions may be parameterized, consider the translation of the English sentence *John stabbed Mary* into Spanish:[16]

(274) (i)   Juan le dio puñaladas a María

     (ii)   Juan le dio una puñalada a María

Both of these sentences translate literally to "John gave stab wound(s) to Mary." However, the first sentence is the repetitive version of the action (*i.e.*, there were multiple stab wounds), whereas the second sentence is the non-repetitive version of the action (*i.e.*, there was only one stab wound). This distinction is characterized by means of the atomicity feature. In (274)(i), the event is associated with the features [+d,+t,-a], whereas, in (274)(ii) the event is associated with the features [+d,+t,+a].

In order to achieve this distinction, the current approach allows predicates to undergo an atomicity "coercion" in which an inherently non-atomic predicate (such as *dar*) may become atomic under certain conditions. These conditions are language-specific in nature, *i.e.*, they depend on the lexical-semantic structure of the predicate in question. Given the current featural scheme that is imposed on top of the lexical-semantic framework, it is easy to specify *coercion functions* for each language.

A set of coercion functions have been devised for Spanish (see Dorr (1992b)) analogous to those proposed for English by Bennett *et al.* (1990). The way parameterization figures into the coercion is through the specification of different "triggering elements." The triggers for feature coercion of Spanish verbs differ from those of the corresponding

---

[15]Some native speakers consider sentence (273)(ii) to be odd, at best. This is additional evidence for the existence of inherent features and suggests that, in some cases (*i.e.*, for some native speakers), the inherent features are considered to be absolute overrides, even in the presence of modifiers that might potentially change the aspectual features.

[16]As discussed in chapter 5, many other possibilities are available that are not listed here (*e.g.*, *Juan le apuñaló a María*).

English verbs. For example, the atomicity function does not apply under the same conditions for Spanish as it does for English. Example (274) illustrates that a singular NP verbal object triggers the mapping of a [-a] predicate into a [+a] predicate, *i.e.*, a non-atomic event becomes atomic if it is associated with a singular NP object. The parameterized mappings that have been constructed for Spanish in the current model are shown in figure 9.7(a). For the purposes of comparison, the analogous English functions proposed by Bennett *et al.* (1990) are shown in figure 9.7(b).[17]

Using the functions, we are able to apply the notion of feature-based coercion cross-linguistically, while still accounting for parametric distinctions. Thus, feature coercion provides a useful foundation for a model of interlingual machine translation.

A key point about the aspectual features and coercion functions is that they allow for a two-way communication channel between the two processes of lexical selection and aspectual realization.[18] To clarify this point, we return to our example that compares the three English verbs, *ransack, destroy,* and *obliterate* (see example (273) above). Recall that the primary distinguishing feature among these three verbs was the notion of telicity (*i.e.*, culminated *vs.* nonculminated). The lexical-semantic representation for all three verbs is identical, but the telicity feature differs in each case. The verb *ransack* is +telic, *obliterate* is -telic, and *destroy* is inherently -telic, although it may be coerced to +telic through the use of a durative adverbial phrase. Because *destroy* is a "coercible" verb, it is stored in the lexicon as ±telic with a flag that forces -telic to be the inherent (*i.e.*, default) setting. Thus, if we are generating a surface sentence from an interlingual form that matches these three verbs but we know the value of the telic feature from the context of the source-language sentence (*i.e.*, we are able to determine whether the activity reached a definite point of completion), then we will choose *ransack*, if the setting is +telic, or *obliterate* or *destroy*, if the setting is -telic. In this latter case, only the word *destroy* will be

---

[17]Figure 9.7(b) contains a subset of the English functions. The reader is referred to Bennett *et al.* (1990) for additional functions. The abbreviations C and AC stand for culminator, and anti-culminator, respectively.

[18]The details of the algorithms behind the implementation of the two-way communication channel are given in Dorr and Gaasterland (1992). We will illustrate the intuition here by means of example.

(a)

Spanish		
Mapping	*Parameters*	*Examples*
Telicity (C) f(-t)→+t	singular NP complements	Juan le dio una puñalada a María 'John stabbed Mary (once)'
	preterit past	Juan conoció a María 'John met Mary (once)'
Telicity (AC) f(+t)→-t	progressive morpheme	Lee estaba pintando un cuadro 'Lee was painting a picture (for some time)'
	imperfect past	Lee conocía a María 'Lee knew Mary (for some time)'
Atomicity f(+a)→-a	progressive morpheme	Chris está estornudando 'Chris is sneezing (repeatedly)'
	plural NP complements	Juan le dio puñaladas a María 'John stabbed Mary (repeatedly)'

(b)

English		
Mapping	*Parameters*	*Examples*
Telicity (C) f(-t)→+t	singular NP complements	John ran a mile
	culminative duratives	John ran until 6pm
Telicity (AC) f(+t)→-t	progressive morpheme	Lee was painting a picture
	nonculminative duratives	Lee painted the picture for an hour
Atomicity f(+a)→-a	progressive morpheme	Chris is sneezing
	frequency adverbials	Chris ate a sandwich every day

Figure 9.7
The aspectual coercion functions are parameterized for English and Spanish.

selected if the interlingua includes a component that will be realized as a durative adverbial phrase.

Once the aspectual features have guided the lexical selection of the verbs, we are able to use these selections to guide the aspectual realizations that will be used in the surface form. For example, if we have chosen the word *obliterate* we would want to realize the verb in the simple past or present (*e.g.*, *obliterated* or *obliterate*) rather than in the progressive (*e.g.*, *was obliterating* or *is obliterating*). Thus, the aspectual features (and coercion functions) are used to choose lexical items, and the choice of lexical items is used to realize aspectual features.

The coercion functions are crucial for this two-way channel to operate properly. In particular, we must take care not to blindly forbid non-atomic verbs from being realized in the progressive since point activities, which are atomic (*e.g.*, *tap*), are frequently realized in the progressive (*e.g.*, *he was tapping the table*). In such cases the progressive morpheme is being used as an iterator of several identical atomic events as defined in the functions shown in figure 9.7. Thus, we allow "coercible" verbs (*i.e.*, those that have a ±<feature> specification) to be selected and realized with the non-inherent feature setting if coercion is necessary for the aspectual realization of the verb.

9.4 Acquisition of Novel Lexical Entries: Discovering the Link Between LCS and Aspect

In evaluating the aspectual framework proposed here, we will focus on one evaluation metric, namely the ease with which lexical entries may be automatically acquired from on-line resources. While testing the framework against this metric, a number of results have been obtained, including the discovery of a fundamental relationship between aspectual information and lexical-semantic information that provides a link between the primitives of Jackendoff's LCS representations and the features of the aspectual scheme described here. As we will see, this link is crucial for evaluating the framework with respect to ease of lexical acquisition.

9.4.1   Approach

A program has been developed for the automatic acquisition of novel lexical entries for machine translation.[19] We are in the process of building
an English dictionary, and intend to use the same approach for building
dictionaries in other languages, (*e.g.*, Spanish, German, Korean, and
Arabic). The program automatically acquires aspectual representations
from corpora (currently the tagged version of the Lancaster/Oslo-Bergen
(LOB) corpus[20]) by examining the context in which all verbs occur and
then dividing them into four groups: state, activity, accomplishment,
and achievement. As we noted earlier, these four groups correspond to
different combinations of aspectual features (*i.e.*, telic, atomic, and dynamic) that have been imposed on top of the lexical-semantic framework.
Thus, if we are able to isolate these components of verb meaning, we will
have made significant progress toward our ultimate goal of automatically
acquiring full lexical-semantic representations of verb meaning.

The division of verbs into these four groups is based on several syntactic tests that are well-defined in the linguistic literature such as those by
Dowty (1979) shown in figure 9.8.[21] For example, according to Test 1, a
verb that may occur in the progressive (*e.g.*, the verb *hit* in *am hitting*)
is necessarily non-stative (*i.e.*, it must be an activity, accomplishment,
or achievement), whereas a verb that cannot occur in the progressive
(*e.g.*, the verb *know* in *am knowing*) is necessarily a state.

Some tests of verb aspect shown here could not be implemented in
the acquisition program because they require human interpretations.
These tests are marked by asterisks (*). For example, Test 2 requires
human interpretation to determine whether or not a verb has habitual
interpretation in simple present tense. Likewise, Test 5 could not be
implemented because it requires a human interpretation of whether X
for an hour entails X *at all times in the hour*. For similar reasons, Test
6, Test 9, and Test 10 also could not be implemented.

The algorithm for the acquisition program applies Dowty's tests to a
set of sentences corresponding to a particular verb until a unique category has been identified. One complication of this implementation is
that Dowty's tests do not allow the aspectual categories to be uniquely

---

[19]The implementation details of this program are reported in Dorr and Lee (1992).

[20]This corpus was obtained from the Norwegian Computing Center for the
Humanities.

[21]This table is taken from (Bennett *et al.* 1990, p. 250).

	Test	STA [-d]	ACT [+d-t]	ACC [+d+t-a]	ACH [+d+t+a]
1.	X-ing is grammatical	no	yes	yes	yes
* 2.	has habitual inter- pretation in simple present tense	no	yes	yes	yes
3.	spend an hour X-ing, X for an hour	yes	yes	yes	no
4.	take an hour to X, X in an hour	no	no	yes	yes
* 5.	X for an hour entails X at all times in the hour	yes	yes	no	no
* 6.	Y is X-ing entails Y has X-ed	no	yes	no	no
7.	complement of stop	yes	yes	yes	no
8.	complement of finish	no	no	yes	no
* 9.	ambiguity with almost	no	no	yes	no
*10.	Y X-ed in an hour entails Y was X-ing during that hour	no	no	yes	no
11.	occurs with studiously, carefully, etc.	no	yes	yes	no

Figure 9.8
Dowty's eleven tests of verb aspect provide support for a four-way aspectual classification of verbs.

identified in all cases. For example, out of the six tests that have been implemented from Dowty's table, only Test 1 uniquely sets states apart from the other three aspectual categories. That is, Test 1 is the only *implemented* test that has a value in the first column that is different from the other three columns. Note, however, that the value in this column is NO, which poses a problem for the above algorithm. Herein lies one of the major stumbling blocks for the extraction of information from corpora: it is only possible to derive new information in cases where there is a YES value in a given column. By definition, a corpus only provides *positive* evidence; it does not provide *negative* evidence. We cannot say anything about sentences that do *not* appear in the corpus. The fact that a given sentence does not occur in a particular sample of English text does not mean that it can never show up in English. This

Verbs	Jackendoff Primitive	Aspectual Category	Aspectual Features
be	BE	state (STA)	[-d]
like	BE	state (STA)	[-d]
hate	BE	state (STA)	[-d]
go	GO	non-state (ACH)	[+d, +t, +a]
stop	GO	non-state (ACH)	[+d, +t, +a]
start	GO	non-state (ACH)	[+d, +t, +a]
finish	GO	non-state (ACH)	[+d, +t, +a]
avoid	STAY	non-state (ACT)	[+d, -t]
continue	STAY	non-state (ACT)	[+d, -t]
keep	STAY	non-state (ACT)	[+d, -t]

Figure 9.9
Jackendoff's Circumstantial category includes states, achievements, and activities.
These correspond to the primitives BE, GO, and STAY, respectively.

means we are relying solely on the information that *does* appear in the corpus, *i.e.*, we are only able to learn something new about a verb when it corresponds to a YES in one of the rows of figure 9.8.[22]

Given that the identification of stative verbs could not be achieved by Dowty's tests alone, a number of hypotheses were made in order to identify states by other means. A preliminary analysis of the sentences in the corpus reveals that progressive verbs are generally preceded by verbs such as *be, like, hate, go, stop, start, etc.* These verbs fall under a lexical-semantic category identified by Jackendoff (1983, 1990) as the Circumstantial category. Based on this observation, the following hypothesis has been made:

Hypothesis 1: The only types of verbs that are allowed to precede progressive verbs are circumstantial verbs.

Circumstantial verbs subsume stative verbs, but they also include verbs in other categories. In terms of the lexical-semantic primitives proposed by Jackendoff (1983, 1990), the Circumstantial verbs found in a subset of the corpus are categorized as shown in figure 9.9.

An intriguing result of this categorization is that the circumstantial verbs provide a systematic partitioning of Dowty's aspectual categories

---

[22]Note that this is consistent with principles of recent models of language acquisition. For example, the *Subset Principle* proposed by Berwick (1985, p. 37) states that "the learner should hypothesize languages in such a way that positive evidence can refute an incorrect guess."

(*i.e.*, states, activities, and achievements) into primitives of Jackendoff's system (*i.e.*, BE, STAY, and GO). Thus, the analysis of the corpora has provided a crucial link between the primitives of Jackendoff's LCS representation and the features of the aspectual scheme described earlier. If this is the case, then the framework has proven to be well-suited to the task of automatic construction of conceptual structures from corpora.

Assuming this partitioning is correct and complete, Hypothesis 1 can be refined as follows:

Hypothesis 1′: The only types of verbs that are allowed to precede progressive verbs are states, achievements, and activities.

If this hypothesis is valid, the program is in a better position to identify stative verbs because it corresponds to a test that requires positive evidence rather than negative evidence. The hypothesis can be described by adding the following line to figure 9.8:

Test	STA	ACT	ACC	ACH
12. X Y-ing is grammatical	yes	yes	no	yes

Another hypothesis that has been adopted pertains to the distribution of progressives with respect to the verb *go*:

Hypothesis 2: The only types of progressive verbs that are allowed to follow the verb *go* are activities.

This hypothesis was adopted after it was discovered that constructions such as go running, go skiing, go swimming, *etc.* appeared in the corpus, but not constructions such as go eating, go writing, *etc.* The hypothesis can be described by adding the following line to figure 9.8:

Test	STA	ACT	ACC	ACH
13. go X-ing is grammatical	no	yes	no	no

The combination of Dowty's tests and the hypothesized tests allows the four aspectual categories to be more specifically, though not uniquely, identified. The algorithm used to implement these tests is simple. For each verb in the corpus, all sentences containing that verb are put through the aspectual tests until the aspectual category is uniquely identified or until there are no more sentences containing the verb. (See figure 9.10.) Note that these tests are applied in a particular order. The reason for this is that the search tree is pruned faster if the tests that rule out three categories are applied first, then those that rule out

1. Pick out main verbs from all sentences in the corpus and store them in a list called VERBS.

2. For each verb v in VERBS, find all sentences containing v and store them in an array SENTENCES[i] (where i is the position of v in the list VERBS).

3. For each sentence set S_j in SENTENCE[j], loop through each sentence s in S_j:

   (a) Loop through each test $t \in \{13, 8, 4, 11, 3, 7, 1, 12\}$ in order.

   (b) See if test t applies to s; if so, eliminate all aspectual categories with a NO in the row of figure 9.8 corresponding to test t.

   (c) Eliminate possibilities until a unique aspectual category is identified or until all sentences in SENTENCES have been exhausted.

Figure 9.10
The algorithm for determining aspectual categories applies tests to verbs until the aspectual category is uniquely identified.

two, then those that rule out one. The search tree corresponding to the application of Dowty's tests is given in figure 9.11

As shown in the search tree, there are ten possible outcomes. Note, however, that the new tests proposed here still do not guarantee that states will be uniquely identified. In addition to the state category, the achievement category is not uniquely identifiable by the tests. Given that accomplishments and activities are the only categories that are uniquely identified, the following heuristic is used for the remaining cases:

(275) **Aspectual Categorization Heuristic:**
      In cases where a verb cannot be classified into a single unique category, choose the category that is not among those that can be uniquely identified (*i.e.*, choose the category that is either an achievement or a state).

This heuristic provides a second tier of outcomes as shown at the bottom of figure 9.11. For example, the third node from the left corresponds to the case where a verb belongs to one of three categories: activity, accomplishment, or achievement. According to the heuristic in (275), the category that is selected is the achievement category, since the other

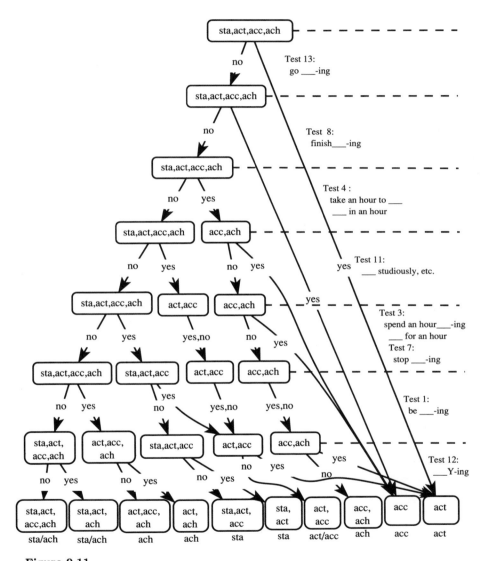

Figure 9.11
The search tree corresponding to the application of Dowty's tests illustrates that accomplishments and activities are uniquely identified, but states and achievements are not.

two (activity and accomplishment) are uniquely identifiable. The logic behind this heuristic is that if we get enough sentences, the verbs from uniquely identifiable categories will already be correctly categorized by the time the last test is applied. That is, if our corpus is big enough, it is highly likely that the uniquely identifiable verbs will occur in enough of the right distributions to be correctly categorized. The cases that are left over, then, are ones that could not be uniquely identified by the proposed tests.

Note that even this heuristic is not enough in some cases. In the worst case, it is possible to arrive at the bottom of the search tree without having been able to uniquely select any of the four categories. This is the case of the left-most node in figure 9.11. In this case, the heuristic would choose either the state or the achievement, since neither of these are uniquely identifiable. A similar situation applies to the second node from the left. Note that it also might be possible to end up with two uniquely identifiable categories and no others (e.g., the fourth node from the right); in this case, the heuristic would have no non-uniquely identifiable categories to choose from. In the current implementation, an arbitrary choice is made in such cases.

9.4.2   Results

Preliminary results have been obtained from running the algorithm of figure 9.10 on 219 sentences of the LOB corpus. Figure 9.12 shows the results.[23] Note that the program was not able to pare down the aspectual category to one in every case. There is likely to be a significant improvement in the classification results once the sample size is increased. Note that there is a slight improvement in results after applying the heuristic in (275). For example, the category chosen for *jailed* is narrowed down to STA after the heuristic is applied.

Presumably more tests would be needed for additional improvements in results. An ultimate objective is to do away with the heuristic and to propose additional tests that would guarantee the unique identification of states and achievements. Such tests are the subject of future research.

In addition, research is currently underway to determine the restrictions (analogous to those shown in figure 9.8) that exist for other languages (e.g., Spanish, German, Korean, and Arabic). Because the pro-

---

[23]For brevity, only a subset of the verbs are shown here.

Verbs	Aspectual Category	
	Before Heuristic	**After Heuristic**
doing	(ACC)	(ACC)
facing	(ACT ACC)	(ACT ACC)
asking	(ACT ACC)	(ACT ACC)
made	(ACC)	(ACC)
drove	(ACT ACC)	(ACT ACC)
welcome	(STA ACT ACC ACH)	(STA ACH)
emphasized	(STA ACT ACC ACH)	(STA ACH)
thanked	(ACT ACC STA)	(STA)
staged	(ACC)	(ACC)
make	(ACC)	(ACC)
continue	(ACT ACC)	(ACT ACC)
writes	(ACC)	(ACC)
building	(ACC)	(ACC)
running	(ACT ACC)	(ACT ACC)
paint	(ACC)	(ACC)
finds	(ACT ACC)	(ACT ACC)
arrives	(ACT ACC)	(ACT ACC)
jailed	(ACT ACC STA)	(STA)
nominating	(ACH ACT ACC)	(ACH)
read	(ACT ACC)	(ACT ACC)
ensure	(STA ACT ACC ACH)	(STA ACH)
act	(ACT ACC)	(ACT ACC)
carry	(ACC)	(ACC)
exercise	(ACC)	(ACC)
impose	(STA ACT ACC ACH)	(STA ACH)
contain	(STA ACT ACC ACH)	(STA ACH)
infuriate	(ACT ACC)	(ACT ACC)

Figure 9.12
Preliminary aspectual classification results have been obtained from running the
acquisition algorithm on 219 sentences of the LOB corpus.

gram is parametrically designed, it is expected to operate uniformly on corpora in other languages as well. Another future area of research is the automatic acquisition of parameter settings for the construction of selection charts and aspectual coercion mappings on a per-language basis.

In summary, this chapter has proposed an extension to the UNITRAN system that integrates temporal/aspectual knowledge into the current lexical-semantic framework. We have examined the question of cross-linguistic applicability and have demonstrated that the integration of aspect with lexical-semantics is especially critical when there are a large number of temporal connectives and verbal selection/realization possibilities that may be generated from a lexical semantic representation. Furthermore, we have illustrated that the selection/realization processes may be parameterized, by means of selection charts and coercion functions, so that the processes may operate uniformly across more than one language. Finally, we have discussed the application of the theoretical foundations to the automatic acquisition of aspectual representations from corpora in order to augment the lexical-semantic representations that have already been created for a large number of verbs.

10 Conclusions

The preceding chapters have presented a solution to machine translation divergences based on an interlingual approach that uses two levels of processing, syntactic and lexical-semantic. The syntactic component consists of parameterized principles (approximately 20 parameters) and the lexical-semantic component currently uses a lexicon based on a parameterized LCS representation (approximately 150 vocabulary items per language). The solution has been implemented in UNITRAN, a bidirectional prototypical system currently operating on Spanish, English, and German, running in Common Lisp. [1]

We have seen that the existence of translation divergences makes the straightforward transfer from source structures into target structures impractical. A central claim of the current approach is that the divergence classification shown in figure 1.12 (repeated in figure 5.2) covers all potential source-language/target-language distinctions based on lexical-semantic properties (*i.e.*, properties associated with entries in the lexicon that are not based on purely syntactic information, idiomatic usage, aspectual knowledge, discourse knowledge, domain knowledge, or world knowledge). Although the machine translation approach described here is interlingual, these divergences are ones that any machine translation system must cope with, not just those that use an interlingual representation.

One of the most important contributions of this work is the formalization of the notion of divergence and the techniques by which divergences are solved. This formalization has provided the foundation for: (1) proving that the lexical-semantic divergence classification proposed in the current framework covers all lexical-semantic distinctions; (2) facilitating the design and implementation of the system by clearly defining a small number of divergence categories; (3) systematically stating the solution to the divergence problem in terms of a uniform translation mapping and handful of simple lexical-semantic parameters; (4) allowing one to judge whether a particular target-language sentence fully covers the concept that underlies the corresponding source-language sentence; and (5) allowing one to prove certain properties about the system such as whether the system is able to handle two or more simultaneous divergences that interact in some way.

---

[1] The system runs on a Symbolics 3600 series machine (with graphics) and also on a Sun Sparc Station (without graphics).

The approach presented here tries to incorporate some of the more promising syntactic and semantic aspects of existing translation systems. Specifically, the model incorporates structural information for realization and positioning of arguments, and it also maintains the ability to select target terms on the basis of compositional properties of conceptual structure. Although most translation systems have some mechanism for processing divergent structures, they do not provide a general procedure that takes advantage of the relationship between lexical-semantic structure and syntactic structure. The current approach is more systematic in that it accounts for language-specific idiosyncrasies that distinguish two languages, while making use of lexical-semantic uniformities that tie the two languages together. This is achieved is through the use of parameters that are set according to the characteristics of the languages involved in the translation. Seven parameters are associated with entries in the lexicon, thus accommodating lexical-semantic divergences from seven categories: thematic, promotional, demotional, structural, categorial, conflational, and lexical. The parameterized approach allows a language-independent conceptual structure to be mapped systematically to the surface syntactic representation by means of routines that are general enough to operate uniformly across different languages.

The application of the model on a wide range of examples has demonstrated that translation divergences are adequately handled by the current approach. However, empirical studies have shown that a number of problems remain, most of which are related to the difficulty of selecting a particle to accompany a verb during the generation process (*e.g.*, distinguishing between the Spanish prepositions *a* and *en* and among the German prepositions *an*, *bei*, *in*, *nach*, and *zu*). In most cases, the particles in question are spatially oriented. Given that the LCS does not contain enough information to distinguish among different spatial nuances of meaning, the system often overgenerates in these cases. Current research is underway (see, *e.g.*, Dorr and Voss (1993) and Voss (forthcoming)) to extend the LCS representation to handle such spatial distinctions.

Surprisingly, empirical studies have also shown that the place the system is most likely to break down is during syntactic processing, not during lexical-semantic processing. In general, once the correct syntactic structure is derived, the lexical-semantic processor is capable of composing an interlingual representation. This is because the mapping between the syntactic structure and the LCS representation is systematically defined such that the syntax of the two representations approaches an isomorphism. Thus, there is nothing inherently complex about the LCS processing component of the system.

The current approach eliminates many of the problems associated with the direct replacement and transfer approaches of previous systems in that it does not make use of syntactic rules that are meticulously tailored to each of the source and target languages, nor does it require detailed source-to-target transfer rules. On the other hand, because UNITRAN is designed (deliberately) to operate on one sentence at a time, it has a number of inherent limitations. For example, the system does not incorporate context or domain knowledge. Therefore, it cannot use discourse, situational expectations, or domain information during the translation process. There has been a great deal of work in this area (*e.g.*, see Barnett *et al.* (1991a,b) Carbonell and Tomita (1987), Meyer *et al.* (1990), Nirenburg *et al.* (1987), Nirenburg (1989), Nirenburg and Goodman (1990), and Wilks (1973)) that might prove useful in the future.

Another area that requires further investigation is the development of a large-scale lexicon for processing within the LCS framework. Automatic lexical acquisition is becoming more critical to the success of machine translation because it is a tedious undertaking to construct dictionary representations by hand for each language.[2] Research is currently underway to investigate the possibility for scaling up the system through automatic means so that a wider range of phenomena and languages may be handled. As we have seen, a preliminary version of an automatic acquisition program is currently being developed by Dorr (1992b) and Dorr and Lee (1992). This program automatically acquires aspectual representations from the tagged version of the LOB corpus by examining the context in which all verbs occur and then dividing them into four groups: state, activity, accomplishment, and achievement. The division of verbs into these four groups is based on several syntactic tests that are well-defined in the linguistic literature such as those by Dowty (1979). This research has led to the discovery of a fundamental link between a subset of Jackendoff's primitives (those in the Circumstan-

---

[2] The lexicon has been shown to be a major bottleneck for the development of UNITRAN: it took more than one person-month to define just 150 words per language.

tial field) and the features of Dowty's aspectual scheme. If the link
turns out to be generalizable to other fields, then the LCS framework
could prove to be well-suited to the task of automatic construction of
conceptual structures from corpora. This possibility is currently under
investigation.

Another possibility that is currently under investigation with respect
to lexical acquisition is the implementation of a procedure that makes
use of a small set of conceptual structures, as a starting point, and then
acquires syntactic and semantic information on the basis of these initial
representations plus machine-readable definitions from the Longman's
Dictionary of Contemporary English (Proctor (1978)). (LDOCE is useful because it includes collocations and sense frequency, thus making
it possible to determine the argument structures for different words.)
This investigation would benefit from the work of several researchers in
the field of automatic lexicon construction, most notably Boguraev and
Briscoe (1989), Boguraev and Pustejovsky (1990), Briscoe and Copestake (1990), Byrd et al. (1987), Farwell et al. (1992), Montemagni and
Vanderwende (1992), Pustejovsky (1987), and Pustejovsky and Bergler
(1987), among others.

This approach would further benefit from an investigation into the
applicability of the scheme to non-European languages. However, unlike the representation used in the Eurotra project, the LCS is expected
to be more than just a "euroversal" representation (see Copeland et al.
(1991)). Several researchers have investigated the use of an LCS for
languages such as Warlpiri (Hale and Laughren (1983)), Urdu (Husain (1989)), Greek (Olsen (1991)), Arabic (Shaban (1991)), and Chinese, Indo-European, and North American Indian (Talmy (1983, 1985)),
among others. These investigations will be useful for future extensions
of UNITRAN to handle other languages.

A Summary of Divergence Examples with Respect to Syntactic Parameters and Principles

This appendix illustrates the effect of the syntactic parameters with respect to the divergence examples given in sections 2.3–2.9.

GB Module	GB Parameter	Divergence Type	Syntactic Divergence Example
$\overline{\text{X}}$	Constituent Order	Constituent Order	E: I have seen him S: Yo le he visto G: Ich habe ihn gesehen
	Base Adjuncts	Adjunct	E: the large book S: el libro grande G: das große Buch
	Affix Removal	Affix	E: John broke into the room S: Juan forzó la entrada al cuarto G: Johann brach ins Zimmer hinein
Gov't	Proper Governors	Preposition Stranding	E: What store did John go to S: * Cuál tienda fue Juan a G: * Welchem Geschäft geht Johann zu
Bounding	Bounding Nodes	Long Distance Movement	E: * Who did you wonder whether went to school S: Quién contemplabas tú que fue a la casa G: * Wer frage ich mich, ob schon nach Hause gegangen ist
Case	Type of Gov't	Clitic	E: * We saw to Guille S: Lo vimos a Guille G: * Wir sahen an Guille
	Case Properties	Case	E: * John believes to be happy S: Juan cree estar contento G: Johann glaubt, glücklich zu sein
Trace	Null Subject	Null Subject	E: * Saw the book S: Vi el libro G: * Sah das Buch
	Chain Conditions	V-Preposing	E: * What saw John S: Qué vio Juan G: Was sah Johann
θ	Clitics	Dative	E: I gave the book to him S: Yo le di el libro a él G: Ich gab ihm das Buch
	Nom-Drop	Pleonastic	E: * I know that was dancing S: Yo sé que había un baile G: Ich weiß daß getanzt wurde

B Morphological Rules

This appendix includes the morphological rules for three languages, English, Spanish, and German. Before describing the morphological rules, we must introduce some notation. The lexical characters are those that occur in the lexicon and the surface characters are those in the surface form of the word to be synthesized or analyzed. A lexical/surface string is represented as $\alpha \Leftrightarrow \beta$, where α is a string of lexical characters, and β is a string of surface characters. A plus marker (+) indicates a suffix appended to a morpheme. The context of the rule application specifies the character occurrences to the left and right of the lexical/surface characters in the rule. (An underscore (___) specifies the position of the lexical/surface characters.) The set notation $\{\ldots,\ldots\}$ indicates that one of the characters in the set must occur. A zero (0) indicates then no characters need to appear in the specified position. A capital letter indicates that any of a set of characters is possible in a specified position.

The English rules are taken from Karttunen and Wittenburg (1983); the notation has been modified slightly. The Spanish and German rules were written by the author. The inspiration for the design of the Spanish automata came from Nassi *et al.* (1965) and Stockwell *et al.* (1965). Several sources provided the inspiration for the design of the German automata including Dollenmayer *et al.* (1984), Kufner (1962), Felshin *et al.* (1989), and Strutz (1986).

B.1 English Morphological Rules

The following sets are used for English:

$$
\begin{aligned}
V &= \text{any vowel} \\
C &= \text{any consonant} \\
C_1 &= \{\text{b, d, f, g, l, m, n, p, r, s, t}\} \\
C_2 &= \text{any consonant except } \mathbf{c} \text{ and } \mathbf{g} \\
Q &= \text{any character except } \mathbf{i} \text{ and } \mathbf{a} \\
S &= \{\text{ch, sh, s, x, z}\} \\
G &= \{\text{g, c}\} \\
E &= \{\text{e, i}\}
\end{aligned}
$$

The morphological rules for English are:

Name	Rule
Epenthesis	+s$\Leftrightarrow$es if S___; else +s$\Leftrightarrow$s
Gemination	C_1+$\Leftrightarrow C_1 C_1$ if CV___V; else C_1+$\Leftrightarrow C_1$
Y-Replacement	y+$\Leftrightarrow$i if C___Q; else y+$\Leftrightarrow$y
Elision	e+$\Leftrightarrow$0 if C_2___V; or CV___e; or G___E; else e+$\Leftrightarrow$e
I-Replacement	ie+$\Leftrightarrow$y if ___i; else ie+$\Leftrightarrow$ie

Some examples that use these morphological rules are:

Rule	Examples
Epenthesis	fox+s$\Leftrightarrow$foxes, church+s$\Leftrightarrow$churches, ski+s$\Leftrightarrow$skis, boy+s$\Leftrightarrow$boys
Gemination	big+er$\Leftrightarrow$bigger, stop+ing$\Leftrightarrow$stopping, cool+er$\Leftrightarrow$cooler, travel+ing$\Leftrightarrow$traveling[1]
Y-Replacement	spy+ed$\Leftrightarrow$spied, happy+ly$\Leftrightarrow$happily, spy+ing$\Leftrightarrow$spying, day+s$\Leftrightarrow$days
Elision	die+ed$\Leftrightarrow$died, move+able$\Leftrightarrow$movable, agree+ed$\Leftrightarrow$agreed, move+s$\Leftrightarrow$moves, race+able$\Leftrightarrow$raceable
I-Replacement	die+ing$\Leftrightarrow$dying, die+ed$\Leftrightarrow$died

---

[1]The reason travel+ing does not trigger gemination is that the gemination rule requires a stressed syllable to precede the affix; this detail is ignored in the above rules, but is taken into account by a special marker in the original implementation (see Karttunen and Wittenburg (1983)). The rule should read: C_1+$\Leftrightarrow C_1 C_1$ if C$\grave{\text{V}}$___V; else C_1+$\Leftrightarrow C_1$, where ` represents phonetic stress.

B.2 Spanish Morphological Rules

The following sets are used for Spanish:

$$
\begin{aligned}
V &= \{a, e, i, o, u, á, é, í, ó, ú, ü\} \\
C &= \text{any consonant} \\
C_1 &= \{n, r\} \\
C_2 &= \text{any consonant except } z \\
B &= \{u, o, a, ú, ü, ó, á\} \\
L &= \{e, o, a, é, ó, á\} \\
L_1 &= \{e, o, é, ó\} \\
H &= \{i, u, í, ú ü\} \\
F &= \{e, i, é í\} \\
M &= \text{any character except } \{e, o, a, é, ó, á\} \\
K &= \text{any character except } g
\end{aligned}
$$

Also, parentheses "()" indicate optionality, and pound sign (#) is used as a morpheme boundary marker.

The morphological rules for Spanish are:

Name	Rule
G-C	<g>+⇔j if ___B; else <g>+⇔g
C-Z	<c>+⇔z if V___B; else <c>+⇔c
C-ZC	<c>+⇔zc if C_1___B; else <c>+⇔c
GU-G	u+⇔0 if g___B; else u+⇔u
N-NG	+⇔g if L_1n___B; else +⇔0
U-Umlaut	<u>+⇔ü if Vg___F; else <u>+⇔u
C-QU	+⇔u if g___VF; else +⇔0
G-GU	c+⇔qu if ___VF; else c+⇔c
ER-Y	+i⇔y if e___L; else +i⇔i
I-Y/II-I[2]	i+(i)⇔y if V___L; else i+(i)⇔i/í
C-Pluralize	C_2+⇔C_2e if ___s#; else C_2+⇔C_2
Z-C	z+⇔c if ___F; else z+⇔z
Z-Pluralize	z+⇔ce if ___s#; else z+⇔z
IAR-Accent	i+⇔í if C___L(C)#; else i+⇔i
UAR-Accent	u+⇔ú if K___L(C)#; else u+⇔u
Remove-Accent	V́C+(V)⇔VC(V)___C#; else V́C+(V)⇔V́C(V)

---

[2]The **else** portion of the I-Y/II-I rule allows i to be accented (´ı) in cases where IAR-Accent requires this lexical/surface string correspondence.

Some examples that use these morphological rules are:

Rule	Examples
G-J	cog+o⇔cojo, lleg+o⇔llego, aflig+o⇔aflijo, pag+an⇔pagan
C-Z	ven\<c\>+o⇔venzo, ejer\<c\>+o⇔ejerzo, atac+a⇔ataca, pare\<c\>+e⇔parece
C-ZC	cono\<c\>+o⇔conozco, pare\<c\>+o⇔parezco
GU-G	distingu+o⇔distingo, distingu+a⇔distinga, distingu+ir⇔distinguir
N-NG	ten+o⇔tengo, ven+o⇔vengo, ven+ir⇔venir
U-Umlaut	averig\<u\>+e⇔averigüe, averig\<u\>+o⇔averiguo, averig\<u\>+ar⇔averiguar, distingu+e⇔distingue
C-QU	atac+é⇔ataqué, atac+ar⇔atacar, atac+en⇔ataquen, parec+er⇔parecer
G-GU	lleg+é⇔llegé, lleg+ar⇔llegar
ER-Y	cre+ió⇔creyó, cre+ó⇔creó, cre+iendo⇔creyendo
I-Y/II-I	contribui+e⇔contribuye, contribui+ir⇔contribuir, hui+o⇔huyo, huir⇔hui+ir,i+iendo⇔yendo
C-Pluralize	ciudad+s⇔ciudades
Z-C	cruz+é⇔crucé, cruz+o⇔cruzo
Z-Pluralize	lapiz+s⇔lápices
IAR-Accent	envi+a⇔envía, envi+amos⇔enviamos
UAR-Accent	continu+e⇔continúe, continu+amos⇔continuamos, fu−+e⇔fue
Remove-Accent	reunión+s⇔reuniones

B.3   German Morphological Rules

The following sets are used for German:

$$V \quad = \quad \{a, e, i, o, u, ä, ö, ü, <a>, <o>, <u>\}$$
$$C \quad = \quad \text{any consonant}$$
$$C_1 \quad = \quad \text{any consonant except l and r}$$
$$N \quad = \quad \text{any non-umlauted letter}$$
$$\text{(entire alphabet except ä, ö, ü,}$$
$$<a>, <o>, \text{and} <u>)$$
$$S \quad = \quad \{s, z, ß\}$$

In addition, special characters are:

:	=	allows consonant doubling
&	=	allows umlauting
–	=	impedes ß-decomposition

Also, parentheses "()" indicate optionality, Kleene star (∗) indicates zero or more occurrences of a character, and α is used as a variable.
The morphological rules for German are:

Name	Rule
E-insertion	+(&)(:)⇔e if C_1___n; else +(&)(:)⇔0
E-deletion	+e⇔0 if V___(&)(:)C; else +e⇔e
S-deletion	+(&)(:)s⇔0 if S___; else +(&)(:)s⇔s
SS-decomposition	ß+(&)(:)⇔ss if V___V; else ß+(&)(:)⇔ß
Maybe-umlaut	<α>⇔ä if ___N∗+&; else <α>⇔ α
Double-n	+(&)(:)⇔n if Cin___en; else +(&)(:)⇔0
Double-s	+(&)(:)⇔s if s___e; else +(&)(:)⇔0

Some examples that use these morphological rules are:

Rule	Examples
E-insertion	schrank+n⇔schranken
E-deletion	sei+en⇔sein, tu+e⇔tue, tue+est⇔tuest
S-deletion	weiß+st⇔weißt, gr<o>-ß+&sten⇔größten
SS-decomposition	heiß+t⇔heißt, eß+en⇔essen, f<u>-ß+&:e⇔füße, k<u>ß+&:e⇔küsse
Maybe-umlaut	w<u>rd+&en⇔würden, w<u>rd+en⇔wurden, <a>pfel+&⇔äpfel, <a>pfel+s⇔apfels
Double-n	Lehrerin+:en⇔Lehrerinnen
Double-s	autobus+:e⇔autobusse

C Linguistic Coverage of Extended Set of Primitives

This appendix gives examples of the types of sentences that are covered by the extended set of primitives presented in chapter 4.

C.1 Position

Primitive	Examples	
STAY$_{Temp}$	Basic:	The meeting remained at noon.
	Causative:	We kept the meeting at noon.
STAY$_{Loc}$	Basic:	The statue remained in the park.
	Causative:	We kept the statue in the park.
BE$_{Temp}$	Basic:	The meeting is at noon.
BE$_{Loc}$	Basic:	The statue is in the park.

C.2 Change of Position

Primitive	Examples	
GO$_{Loc}$	Basic:	The rock fell from the roof to the ground.
	Causative:	John threw the rock from the roof to the ground.
	Permissive:	John dropped the rock from the roof to the ground.
GO$_{Temp}$	Basic:	The meeting changed from 2:00 to 4:00.
	Causative:	We changed the meeting from 2:00 to 4:00.
	Permissive:	We allowed the meeting to change from 2:00 to 4:00.

C.3 Directed Motion

Primitive	Examples	
GO_{Loc}	Basic:	John entered the room.
	Causative:	John broke into the room.
	Permissive:	John let Beth enter the room.
GO_{Poss}	Basic:	Beth received the doll.
	Causative:	John gave the doll to Beth.
	Permissive:	Beth relinquished the doll.

C.4 Manner with Motion

Primitive	Examples	
GO_{Loc}	Basic:	The boat sailed to Cuba.
	Causative	John sailed the boat to Cuba.
	Permissive:	John let the boat sail to Cuba.

C.5 Exchange

Primitive	Examples	
CAUSE-EXCHANGE	Basic:	Beth bought the doll for Mary.

C.6 Physical State

Primitive	Examples	
BE_{Ident}	Basic:	The door is open.
$STAY_{Ident}$	Basic:	The door remained open.
	Causative:	John kept the door open.
	Permissive:	John left the door open.

C.7 Change of Physical State

Primitive	Examples	
GO_{Ident}	Basic:	The door opened.
	Causative:	John opened the door.
	Permissive:	John let the door open.

C.8   Orientation

Primitive	Examples	
ORIENT$_{Loc}$	Basic:	The sign points to Philadelphia.
	Causative:	John pointed the sign to Philadelphia.
	Permissive:	John let the sign point to Philadelphia.

C.9   Existence

Primitive	Examples	
BE$_{Exist}$	Basic:	The house exists on my property.
	Causative:	John built the house on my property.
	Permissive	John allowed the house to exist on my property.
GO$_{Exist}$	Basic:	The house appeared.
	Causative:	The magician made the house disappear.
	Permissive	The magician allowed the house to reappear.
STAY$_{Exist}$	Basic:	The situation persisted.
	Causative:	Bill caused the situation to persist.
	Permissive:	Bill allowed the situation to persist.

C.10   Circumstance

Primitive	Examples	
BE$_{Circ}$	Basic:	John is shipping goods to California.
GO$_{Circ}$	Basic:	John started shipping goods to California.
	Causative:	John forced Beth to ship goods.
	Permissive:	Beth allowed John to start shipping goods.
STAY$_{Circ}$	Basic:	John continued shipping goods.
	Causative:	John kept Beth from shipping goods.
	Permissive:	Beth exempted John from shipping goods.

C.11   Range

Primitive	Examples	
GO-EXT$_{Ident}$	Basic:	Our clients range from psychiatrists to psychopaths.
	Causative:	The sun caused the leaves to range from green to brown.
	Permissive:	Bill allowed the situation to range from bad to worse.
GO-EXT$_{Temp}$	Basic:	The meeting lasted from noon to night.
	Causative:	John made the meeting last from noon to night.
	Permissive:	John allowed the meeting to last from noon to night.
GO-EXT$_{Loc}$	Basic:	The road went from Boston to Albany.
	Causative:	The workers made the road extend from Boston to Albany.

C.12 Intention

Primitive	Examples	
ORIENT$_{Circ}$	Basic:	John intended to ship goods to California.
ORIENT$_{Temp}$	Basic:	John aims to start at 2:00.

C.13 Ownership

Primitive	Examples	
BE$_{Poss}$	Basic:	The doll belongs to Beth.
STAY$_{Poss}$	Basic:	The doll remained in her hands.
	Causative:	Amy kept the doll.

C.14 Ingestion

Primitive	Examples	
EAT	Basic:	John ate breakfast.

C.15 Psychological State

Primitive	Examples	
BE$_{Ident}$	Basic:	Beth liked John.
	Causative:	John pleased Beth.

C.16 Perception and Communication

Primitive	Examples	
HEAR$_{Perc}$	Basic:	John heard Mary.
	Causative:	John listened to Mary.
	Permissive:	Mary told the story to John.
SEE$_{Perc}$	Basic:	John saw Mary.
	Causative:	John watched Mary.
	Permissive:	Mary showed the dress to John.

C.17   Mental Process

Primitive	Examples	
BE_{Perc}	Basic:	Beth knew the lesson.
GO_{Perc}	Basic:	Beth learned the lesson.

C.18   Cost

Primitive	Examples	
$ORIENT_{Ident}$	Basic:	The book costs $10.00.
	Causative:	Beth charged me $10.00 for the book.

C.19   Load/Spray

Primitive	Examples	
GO_{Loc}	Causative:	Bill smeared the wall with paint.

C.20   Contact/Effect

Primitive	Examples	
GO_{Poss}	Basic:	The knife cut Bill.
	Causative:	Mary stabbed Bill with a knife.

D Screen Dumps of Divergence Examples

This appendix contains screen dumps of the examples shown in chapter 8.

D.1   I stabbed John

D.1.1   English to Spanish

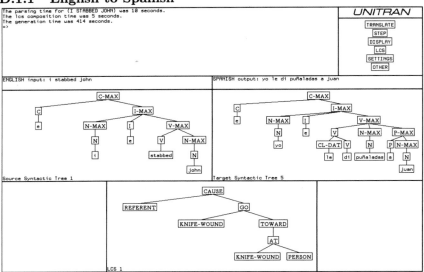

D.1.2   English to German

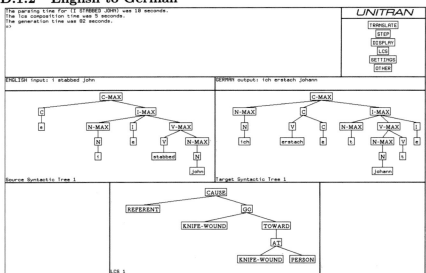

D.2 Yo le di puñaladas a Juan

D.2.1 Spanish to German

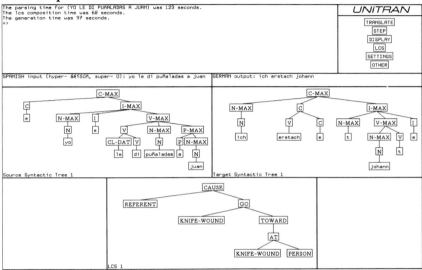

D.2.2 Spanish to English

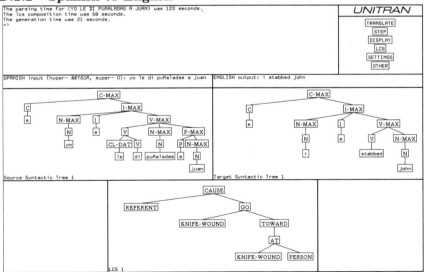

D.3   Ich erstach Johann

D.3.1   German to Spanish

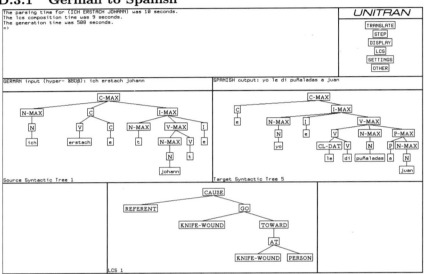

D.3.2   German to English

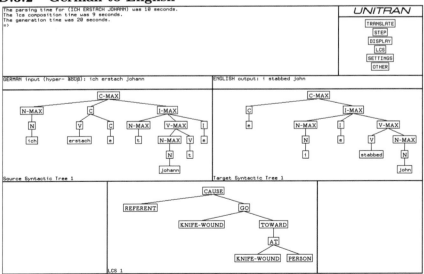

D.4 I like Mary

D.4.1 English to Spanish

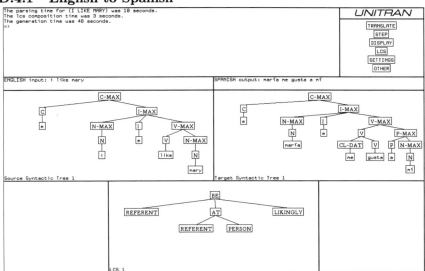

D.4.2 English to German

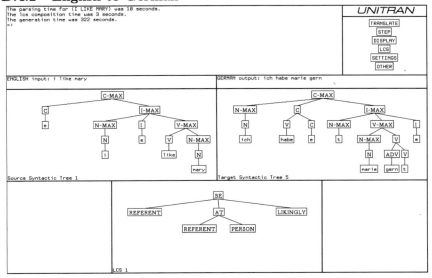

D.5 María me gusta a mí

D.5.1 Spanish to German

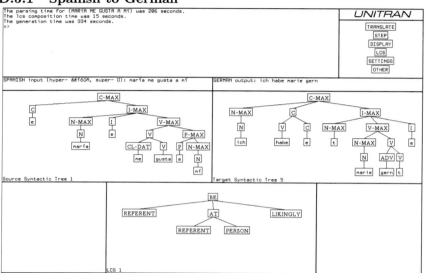

D.5.2 Spanish to English

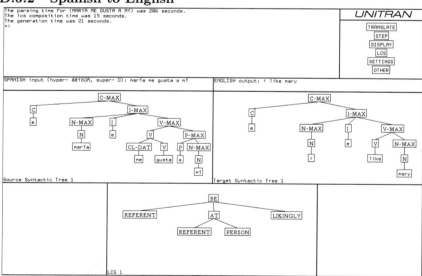

D.6   Ich habe Marie gern

D.6.1   German to Spanish

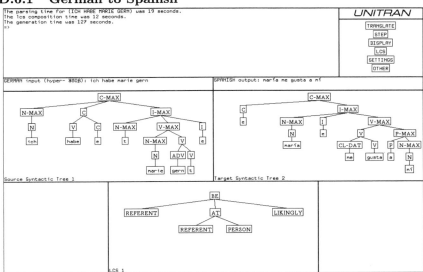

D.6.2   German to English

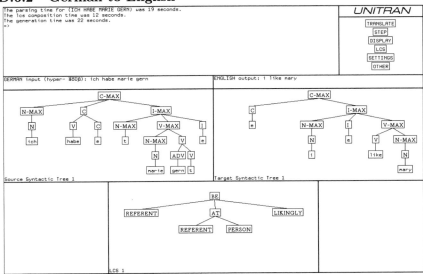

D.7   I am hungry

D.7.1   English to Spanish

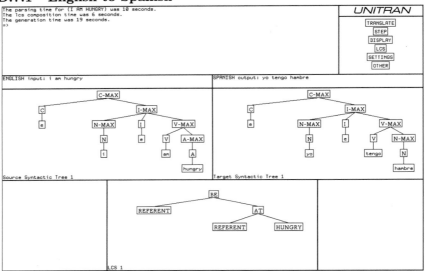

D.7.2   English to German

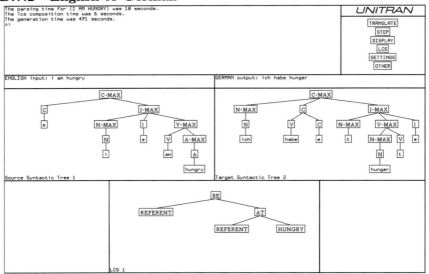

D.8 Yo tengo hambre

D.8.1 Spanish to German

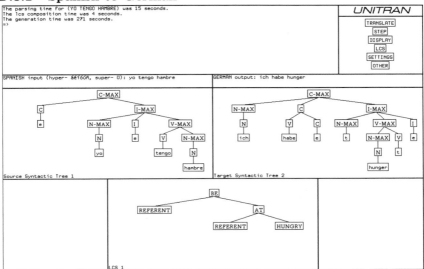

D.8.2 Spanish to English

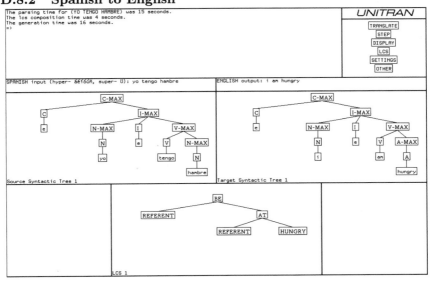

D.9   Ich habe Hunger

D.9.1   German to Spanish

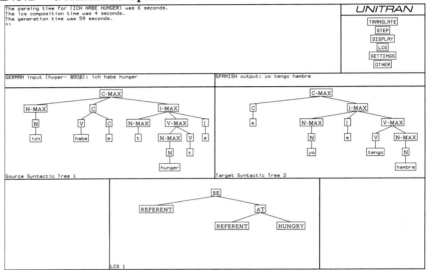

D.9.2   German to English

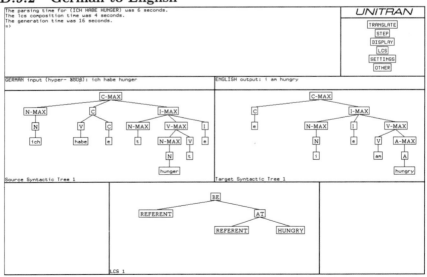

D.10 John entered the house

D.10.1 English to Spanish

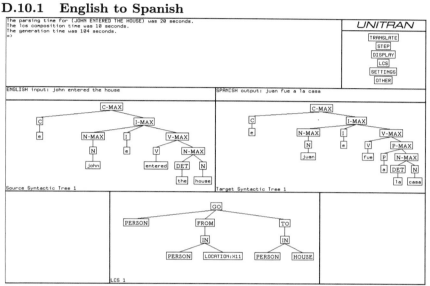

D.10.2 English to German

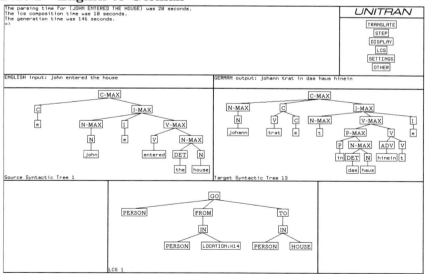

D.11   Juan entró en la casa

D.11.1   Spanish to German

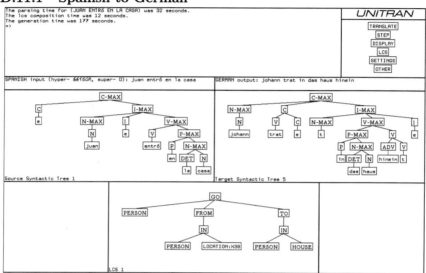

D.11.2   Spanish to English

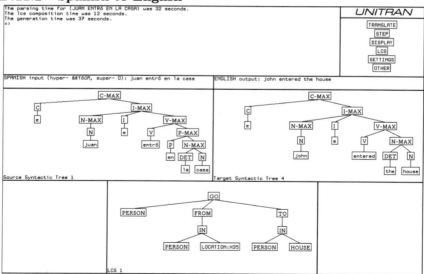

D.12 Johann trat ins Haus hinein

D.12.1 German to Spanish

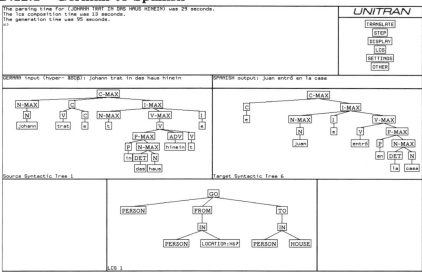

D.12.2 German to English

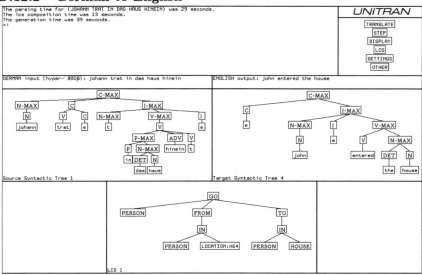

D.13   John broke into the room

D.13.1   English to Spanish

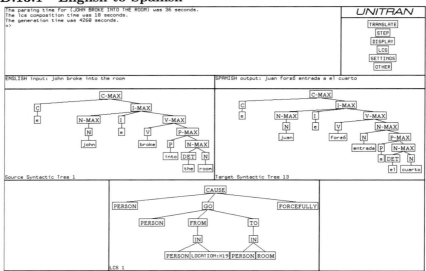

D.13.2   English to German

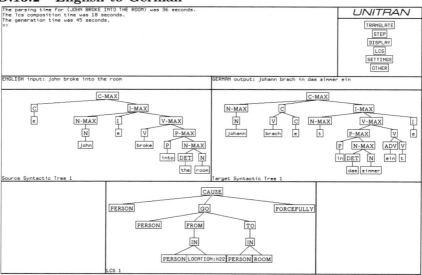

D.14   Juan forzó la entrada al cuarto

D.14.1   Spanish to German

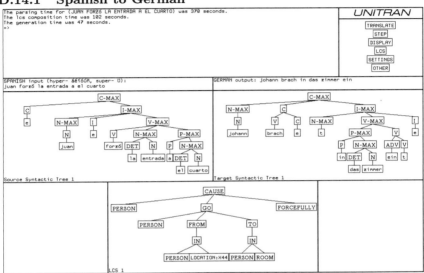

D.14.2   Spanish to English

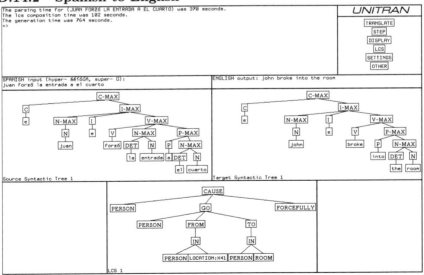

D.15   Johann brach ins Zimmer ein

D.15.1   German to Spanish

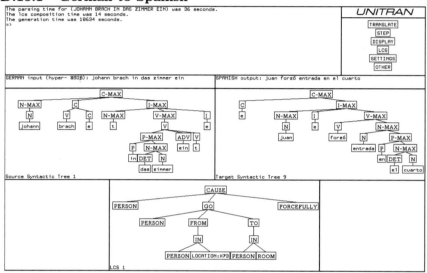

D.15.2   German to English

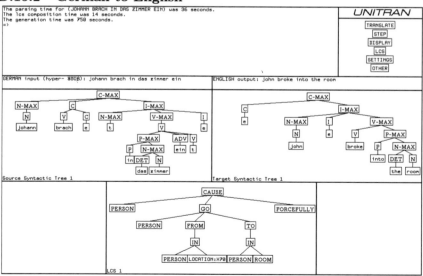

D.16   I like eating

D.16.1   English to Spanish

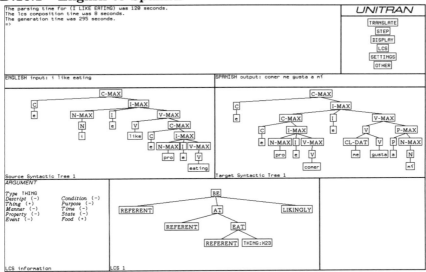

D.16.2   English to German

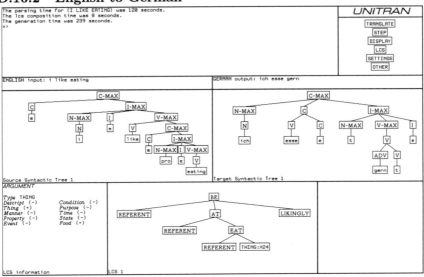

D.17 Comer me gusta a mí

D.17.1 Spanish to German

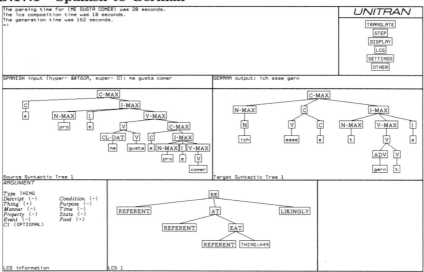

D.17.2 Spanish to English

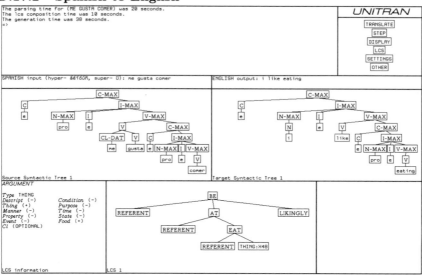

D.18 Ich esse gern

D.18.1 German to Spanish

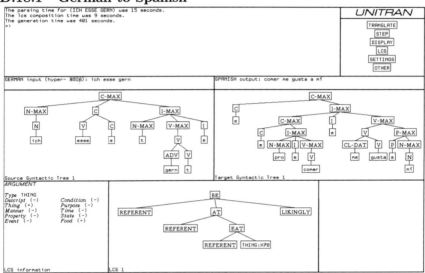

D.18.2 German to English

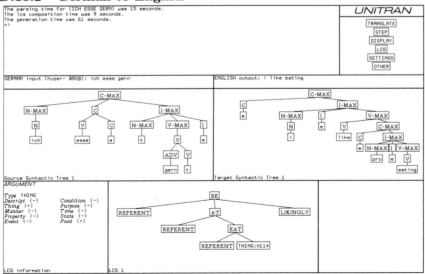

D.19   John usually goes home

D.19.1   English to Spanish

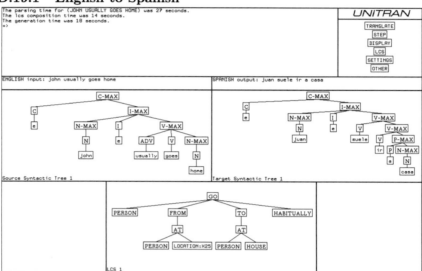

D.19.2   English to German

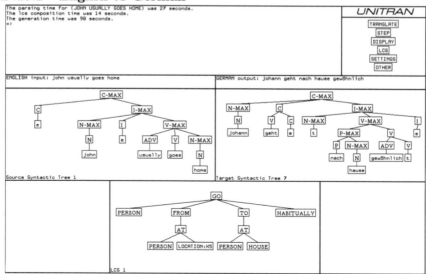

D.20   Juan suele ir a casa

D.20.1   Spanish to German

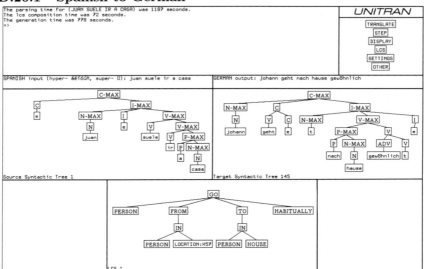

D.20.2   Spanish to English

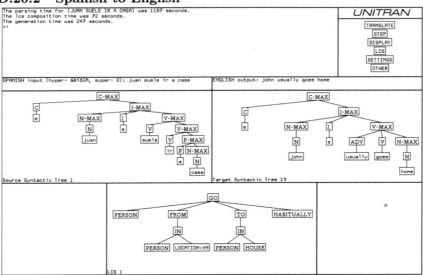

D.21 Johann geht gewöhnlich nach Hause

D.21.1 German to Spanish

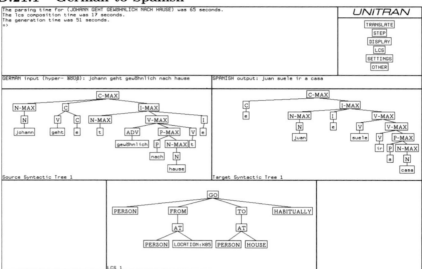

D.21.2 German to English

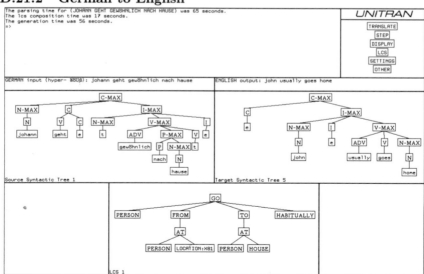

E Selection Charts for When, While, Before, and After

A two-dimensional "selection chart" has been constructed for the temporal connectives *when*, *while*, *before*, and *after* on the basis of an analysis by Dorr and Gaasterland (1992) on a sample of sentences such as the following:

(276) **Progressive / Progressive:**

    (i)   Mary was drawing a circle before John was writing

    (ii)   Mary was drawing a circle before John was laughing

    (iii)   John was laughing before Mary was drawing a circle

    (iv)   John was laughing before Mary was walking to the store

(277) **Progressive / Simple:**

    (i)   Mary was drawing a circle before John wrote a letter

    (ii)   Mary was drawing a circle before John laughed

    (iii)   John was laughing before Mary drew a circle

    (iv)   John was laughing before Mary walked to the store

Figure E.1 shows the charts resulting from an analysis based on two events occurring in the past.[1] One dimension of the charts holds pairs of values for aspectual class and perspective. The other dimension holds the temporal intervals. For each pair of aspectual values and for each temporal interval, if the sample sentences indicate that a word can have that temporal interval meaning for that particular pair of aspectual values, a *yes* is entered in the chart.[2]

For example, in sentence (276)(i) the matrix clause is Dp and the adjunct clause is also Dp. The connecting word *before* can take the meanings <, o, and fi. Thus, a "yes" is entered into the chart for *before* in the coordinates corresponding to (matrix = Dp, adjunct = Dp, interval relationship = <), (matrix = Dp, adjunct = Dp, interval relationship = o), and (matrix = Dp, adjunct = Dp, interval relationship = f).

The charts are used to select one of the four connecting words. Given an interval relation and values for ±dynamic and ±progressive, each

---

[1]For brevity, we shall abbreviate +dynamic/+progressive as Dp; +dynamic/-progressive as Ds (recall, -progressive is simple); -dynamic/-progressive as Ss (recall, -dynamic is state).

[2]Since tense can also have an effect on the meaning of connecting words, a set of charts should be constructed for each allowable matrix/adjunct tense pair. The charts shown here are for sample sentences in which the matrix and adjunct both take the past tense. A question mark in a column means that it is unclear as to whether the word conveys the intended meaning.

WHEN

	=	o	oi	s	si	d	di	m	mi	f	fi	<	>
Dp/Dp	Y	Y	Y	Y	Y	Y	Y			Y	Y		
Dp/Ds							Y	Y	Y		?		
Dp/Ss	Y		Y	Y		Y				Y			
Ds/Dp	Y			Y		Y				Y			
Ds/Ds	Y								Y				Y
Ds/Ss	Y			Y		Y				Y			
Ss/Dp					Y		Y				Y		
Ss/Ds	Y				Y		Y	Y	Y		?		Y
Ss/Ss	Y	Y	Y	Y	Y	Y	Y			Y	Y		

WHILE

	=	o	oi	s	si	d	di	m	mi	f	fi	<	>
Dp/Dp	Y		Y	Y		Y				Y			
Dp/Ds	Y		Y	Y		Y				Y			
Dp/Ss	Y		Y	Y		Y				Y			
Ds/Dp	Y		Y	Y		Y				Y			
Ds/Ds	Y		Y	Y		Y				Y			
Ds/Ss	Y			Y		Y				Y			
Ss/Dp	Y		Y	Y		Y				Y			
Ss/Ds	Y			Y		Y				Y			
Ss/Ss	Y			Y		Y				Y			

BEFORE

	=	o	oi	s	si	d	di	m	mi	f	fi	<	>
Dp/Dp		Y									Y	Y	
Dp/Ds												Y	
Dp/Ss	Y										Y	Y	
Ds/Dp												Y	
Ds/Ds												Y	
Ds/Ss												Y	
Ss/Dp		Y									Y	Y	
Ss/Ds												Y	
Ss/Ss	Y										Y	Y	

AFTER

	=	o	oi	s	si	d	di	m	mi	f	fi	<	>
Dp/Dp			Y							Y			Y
Dp/Ds													Y
Dp/Ss			Y							Y			Y
Ds/Dp			Y							Y			Y
Ds/Ds													Y
Ds/Ss													Y
Ss/Dp			Y							Y			Y
Ss/Ds													Y
Ss/Ss			Y							Y			Y

Figure E.1
The selection charts for *when*, *while*, *before*, and *after* indicate that each connective allows only certain tense/aspect combinations, depending on how the events are temporally related.

chart can be inspected to determine whether its connecting word can be used. The charts are used, in order, from sparsest to densest. A word with a sparse chart has a more specific meaning than one with a dense chart, since it can take fewer meanings. Thus, the word with the sparsest chart that satisfies the given aspectual and temporal interval values will convey the most specific information. For example, given an Ss matrix and an Ss adjunct, and the temporal interval o (overlaps), the connecting word *before* would be selected since the *before* chart contains a *yes* for the coordinates (matrix = Ss, adjunct = Ss, interval relationship = o) and since this chart is sparser than the *when* chart.

In addition to *when, while, before*, and *after*, other temporal connectives that are currently under investigation are: *after, as soon as, at the moment that, before, between, during, since, so long as, until, while, etc.*

Bibliography

Abeillé, Anne, Yves Schabes, and Aravind K. Joshi (1990) "Using Lexicalized Tags for Machine Translation," *Proceedings of Thirteenth International Conference on Computational Linguistics*, Helsinki, Finland, 1–6.

Abney, S. (1989) "A Computational Model of Human Parsing," *Journal of Psycholinguistic Research* 18, 129–144.

Allen, James. F. (1983) "Maintaining Knowledge about Temporal Intervals," *Communications of the ACM* 26:11, 832–843.

Allen, James. F. (1984) "Towards a General Theory of Action and Time," *Artificial Intelligence* 23:2, 123–160.

Alonso, Juan Alberto (1990) "Transfer InterStructure: Designing an 'Interlingua' for Transfer-based MT Systems," *Proceedings of the Third International Conference on Theoretical and Methodological Issues in Machine Translation of Natural Languages*, Linguistics Research Center, The University of Texas, Austin, TX, 189–201.

Appelo, L. (1986) "A Compositional Approach to the Translation of Temporal Expressions in the Rosetta System," *Proceedings of Eleventh International Conference on Computational Linguistics*, Bonn, Germany, 313–318.

Arnold, Doug and Louisa Sadler (1990) "Theoretical Basis of MiMo," *Machine Translation* 5:3, 195–222.

Arnold, Doug, and Louisa Sadler (1992) "Rationalism and the Treatment of Referential Dependencies," *Proceedings of the Fourth International Conference on Theoretical and Methodological Issues in Machine Translation of Natural Languages*, Montreal, Canada, 195–204.

Arnold, Doug and Louis des Tombe (1987) "Basic Theory and Methodology in Eurotra," in *Machine Translation: Theoretical and Methodological Issues*, Sergei Nirenburg (ed.), Cambridge University Press, Cambridge, England, 114–135.

Arnold, Doug, Steven Krauwer, Louis des Tombe, and Louisa Sadler (1988) "Relaxed Compositionality in Machine Translation," *Proceedings of the Second International Conference on Theoretical and Methodological Issues in Machine Translation of Natural Languages*, Carnegie Mellon University, Pittsburgh, PA.

Asimov, Issac (1972) *The Gods Themselves*, Fawcett Publications, Inc., Greenwich, CT.

Bach, E. (1986) "The Algebra of Events," *Linguistics and Philosophy* 9, 5–16.

Bach, E. and R. T. Harms (eds.) (1968) *Universals in Linguistic Theory*, Holt, Rinehart, and Winston, New York, NY.

Barnett, Jim, Inderjeet Mani, Paul Martin, and Elaine Rich (1991a) "Reversible Machine Translation: What to Do When the Languages Don't Line Up," *Proceedings of the Workshop on Reversible Grammars in Natural Language Processing, ACL-91*, University of California, Berkeley, CA, 61–70.

Barnett, Jim, Inderjeet Mani, Elaine Rich, Chinatsu Aone, Kevin Knight, and Juan C. Martinez (1991b) "Capturing Language-Specific Semantic Distinctions in Interlingua-based MT," *Proceedings of Machine Translation Summit*, Washinton, DC, 25–32.

Barton, G. Edward, Jr. (1984) "Toward a Principle-Based Parser," Massachusetts Institute of Technology, Cambridge, MA, AI Memo 788.

Barton, G. Edward, Jr. (1986a) "Constraint Propagation in Kimmo Systems," *Proceedings of the 24th Annual Conference of the Association for Computational Linguistics*, Columbia University, New York, NY, 45–52.

Barton, G. Edward, Jr. (1986b) "Computational Complexity in Two-Level Morphology," *Proceedings of the 24th Annual Conference of the Association for Computational Linguistics*, Columbia University, New York, NY, 53–59.

Barton, G. Edward, Robert C. Berwick, and Eric Sven Ristad (1987) *Computational Complexity and Natural Language*, MIT Press, Cambridge, MA.

Beaven, John (1992a) "Lexicalist Unification-Based Machine Translation," Ph.D. thesis, University of Edinburgh.

Beaven, John (1992b) "Shake and Bake Machine Translation," *Proceedings of Fourteenth International Conference on Computational Linguistics*, Nantes, France, 603–609.

Bennett, P. A., R. L. Johnson, J. McNaught, J M. Pugh, J. C. Sager, H. L. Somers (1986) *Multilingual Aspects of Information Technology*, Gower, Brookfield, VT.

Bennett, Winfield S., Tanya Herlick, Katherine Hoyt, Joseph Liro and Ana Santisteban (1990) "A Computational Model of Aspect and Verb Semantics," *Machine Translation* 4:4, 247–280.

Berwick, Robert C. (1985) *The Acquisition of Syntactic Knowledge*, MIT Press, Cambridge, MA.

Berwick, Robert C. and Sandiway Fong (1990) "Principle-Based Parsing," in *Artificial Intelligence at MIT: Expanding Frontiers*, Patrick H. Winston and Sarah Shellard (eds.), MIT Press, Cambridge, MA, 286–325.

Robert C. Berwick, Steven P. Abney, and Carol Tenny (eds.) (1991) *Principle-based Parsing: Computation and Psycholinguistics*, Kluwer Academic Publishers, Norwell, MA.

Bläser, Brigitte, Ulrike Schwall, and Angelika Storrer (1992) "A Reusable Lexical Database Tool for Machine Translation," *Proceedings of Fourteenth International Conference on Computational Linguistics*, Nantes, France, 510–516.

Boguraev, Branimir and Ted Briscoe (1989) *Computational Lexicography for Natural Language Processing*, Longman, London.

Boguraev, Branimir and James Pustejovsky (1990) "Lexical Ambiguity and the Role of Knowledge Representation in Lexical Design," *Proceedings of Thirteenth International Conference on Computational Linguistics*, Helsinki, Finland, 36–41.

Boitet, Christian (1978) "Where Does GETA Stand at the Beginning of 1977," *CEC*, 88–120.

Boitet, Christian (1987) "Research and Development on MT and Related Techniques at Grenoble University (GETA)," in *Machine Translation: The State of the Art*, Margaret King (ed.), Edinburgh University Press, Edinburgh, 133–153.

Boitet, Christian (1988) "Pros and Cons of the Pivot and Transfer Approaches in Multilingual Machine Translation," in *Recent Developments in Machine Translation*, Dan Maxwell, Klaus Schubert, and Toon Witkam (eds.), Foris, Dordrecht, Holland, 93–107.

Boitet, Christian (1989) "Speech Synthesis and Dialogue Based Machine Translation," *ATR Symposium on Basic Research for Telephone Interpretation*, Kyoto, Japan, 6-5-1-9.

Borer, Hagit, and Kenneth Wexler (1987) "The Maturation of Syntax," in *Parameter Setting*, Thomas Roeper and Edwin Williams (eds.), D. Reidel Publishing Company, Dordrecht, Holland.

Brady, Michael and Robert C. Berwick (eds.) (1983) *Computational Models of Discourse*, MIT Press, Cambridge, MA.

Brent, Michael R. (1988) "Decompositional Semantics and Argument Expression in Natural Language," Master of Science thesis, Department of Electrical Engineering and Computer Science, Massachusetts Institute of Technology.

Brent, Michael R. (1990) "A Simplified Theory of Tense Representations and Constraints on Their Composition," *Proceedings of the 28th Annual Conference of the Association for Computational Linguistics*, University of Pittsburgh, Pittsburgh, PA, 119–126.

Bresnan, Joan (ed.) (1982) *The Mental Representation of Grammatical Relations*, MIT Press, Cambridge, MA.

Brew, Chris (1992) "Letting the Cat out of the Bag: Generation for Shake-and-Bake MT," *Proceedings of Fourteenth International Conference on Computational Linguistics*, Nantes, France, 610–616.

Briscoe, E. J. and A. A. Copestake (1990) "Enjoy the Paper: Lexical Semantics Via Lexicology," *Proceedings of Thirteenth International Conference on Computational Linguistics*, Helsinki, Finland, 42–47.

Brown, Peter F. (1990) "A Statistical Approach to Machine Translation," *Computational Linguistics* 16:2, 79–85.

Brown, Peter F., John Cocke, Stephen A. Della Pietra, Vincent J. Della Pietra, Fredrick Jelinek, Robert L. Mercer, and Paul S. Roossin (1988a) "A Statistical Approach to French/English Translation," *Proceedings of the Second International Conference on Theoretical and Methodological Issues in Machine Translation of Natural Languages*, Carnegie Mellon University, Pittsburgh, PA.

Brown, Peter F., J. Della Pietra, Fredrick Jelinek, Robert L. Mercer, and Paul S. Roossin (1988b) "A Statistical Approach to Language Translation," *Proceedings of Twelveth International Conference on Computational Linguistics*, Budapest, Hungary, 71–76.

Brown, Peter F., Stephen A. Della Pietra, Vincent J. Della Pietra, John D. Lafferty, and Robert L. Mercer (1992) "Analysis, Statistical Transfer, and Synthesis in Machine Translation," *Proceedings of the Fourth International Conference on Theoretical and Methodological Issues in Machine Translation of Natural Languages*, Montreal, Canada, 83–100.

Byrd, Roy J., Nicoletta Calzolari, Martin S. Chodorow, Judith L. Klavans, Mary S. Neff, and Omneya A. Rizk (1987) "Tools and Methods for Computational Linguistics," *Computational Linguistics* 13:3–4, 219–240.

Carbonell, Jaime G. and Masaru Tomita (1987) "Knowledge-based Machine Translation, the CMU Approach," in *Machine Translation: Theoretical and Methodological Issues*, Sergei Nirenburg (ed.), Cambridge University Press, Cambridge, England, 68–89.

Chauché, J. (1975) "Les systemes A.T.E.F. et C.E.T.A.," *Informations* 2, 27–38.

Chomsky, Noam A. (1981) *Lectures on Government and Binding*, Foris Publications, Dordrecht, Holland.

Chomsky, Noam A. (1982) "Some Concepts and Consequences of the Theory of Government and Binding," MIT Press.

Chomsky, Noam A. (1986a) *Knowledge of Language: Its Nature, Origin and Use*, MIT Press, Cambridge, MA.

Chomsky, Noam A. (1986b) *Barriers*, MIT Press, Cambridge, MA.

Chomsky, Noam A. (spring, 1987) "Class Notes, Introduction to Linguistic Theory at an Advanced Level," Massachusetts Institute of Technology, Cambridge, MA, Course 24.957.

Coen, Gary (1991) "Machine Translation on the Competence Model," Ph.D. thesis, University of Texas.

Colmerauer, A. (1971) "Les systèmes-Q ou un formalisme pour analyser et synthétiser des phrases sur ordinateur," *TAUM*, 1–45.

Comrie, Bernard (1976) *Aspect*, Cambridge University Press, Cambridge, England.

Copeland, C., J. Durand, S. Krauwer, and B. Maegaard (1991) "The Eurotra linguistic Specifications," in *Studies in machine Translation and Natural Language Processing, Volume 1*, Erwin Valentini (ed.), Commission of the European Communities, Brussels.

Danlos, Laurence, and Pollet Samvelian (1992) "Translation of the Predicative Element of a Sentence: Category Switching, Aspect, and Diathesis," *Proceedings of the Fourth International Conference on Theoretical and Methodological Issues in Machine Translation of Natural Languages*, Montreal, Canada, 21–34.

Darden, B., C. J. N. Bailey and A. Davison (eds.) (1968) *Papers from the Fourth Regional Meeting of the Chicago Linguistic Society*, University of Chicago, Chicago, IL.

Davies, William and Carol G. Rosen (1988) "Unions as Multi-Predicate Clauses," *Language* 64:1, 52–89.

Davies, William and Stanley Dubinsky (1988) "Grammatical Relations in Lexical Representations," University of Iowa, manuscript.

Derr, M. and K. McKeown (1984) "Using Focus to Generate Complex and Simple Sentences," *Proceedings of Tenth International Conference on Computational Linguistics*, Stanford, CA, 319–326.

Doi, Shinichi and Muraki Kazunori (1992) "Translation Ambiguity Resolution Based on Text Corpora of Source and Target Languages," *Proceedings of Fourteenth International Conference on Computational Linguistics*, Nantes, France, 525–531.

Dollenmayer, David B., Thomas Hansen and Renate Hiller (1984) *Neue Horizonte*, D.C. Heath and Company, Lexington, MA.

Dorr, Bonnie J. (1987a) "UNITRAN: An Interlingual Approach to Machine Translation," *Proceedings of the Sixth Conference of the American Association of Artificial Intelligence*, Seattle, Washington, 534–539.

Dorr, Bonnie J. (1987b) "A Principle-Based Approach to Parsing for Machine Translation," *Proceedings of the Ninth Annual Conference of the Cognitive Science Society*, University of Washington, Seattle, WA, 78–88.

Dorr, Bonnie J. (1987c) "UNITRAN: A Principle-Based Approach to Machine Translation," AI Technical Report 1000, Master of Science thesis, Department of Electrical Engineering and Computer Science, Massachusetts Institute of Technology.

Dorr, Bonnie J. (1988) "UNITRAN: A Principle-Based Parser for Machine Translation," *Proceedings of the MIT Cognitive Science Parsing Seminar*, MIT, Cambridge, MA, 128–150.

Dorr, Bonnie J. (1989) "Lexical Conceptual Structure and Generation in Machine Translation," *Proceedings of the Eleventh Annual Conference of the Cognitive Science Society*, Ann Arbor, Michigan, 74–81.

Dorr, Bonnie J. (1990a) "Solving Thematic Divergences in Machine Translation," *Proceedings of the 28th Annual Conference of the Association for Computational Linguistics*, University of Pittsburgh, Pittsburgh, PA, 127–134.

Dorr, Bonnie J. (1990b) "A Cross-Linguistic Approach to Machine Translation," *Proceedings of the Third International Conference on Theoretical and Methodological Issues in Machine Translation of Natural Languages*, Linguistics Research Center, The University of Texas, Austin,
TX, 13–32.

Dorr, Bonnie J. (1990c) "Lexical Conceptual Structure and Machine
Translation," Ph.D. thesis, Department of Electrical Engineering and
Computer Science, Massachusetts Institute of Technology.

Dorr, Bonnie J. (1990d) "Machine Translation: A Principle-Based Approach," in *Artificial Intelligence at MIT: Expanding Frontiers*, Patrick
H. Winston and Sarah Shellard (eds.), MIT Press, Cambridge, MA,
326–361.

Dorr, Bonnie J. (1991a) "A Two-Level Knowledge Representation for
Machine Translation: Lexical Semantics and Tense/Aspect," *Proceedings of the Lexical Semantics and Knowledge Representation Workshop, ACL-91*, University of California, Berkeley, CA, 250–263.

Dorr, Bonnie J. (1991b) "Principle-Based Parsing for Machine Transla-
tion," in *Principle-based Parsing: Computation and Psycholinguistics*,
Robert C. Berwick, Steven P. Abney, and Carol Tenny (eds.), Kluwer
Academic Publishers, Norwell, MA, 153–183.

Dorr, Bonnie J. (1991c) "Conceptual Basis of the Lexicon in Machine
Translation," in *Using On-Line Resources to Build a Lexicon*, Uri
Zernik (ed.), Lawrence Erlbaum Associates, Hillsdale, NJ, 263–307.

Dorr, Bonnie J. (1992a) "Machine Translation Divergences: A Lexical-
Semantic Perspective," *Proceedings of the Second Seminar on Computational Lexical Semantics*, Toulouse, France, 169–183.

Dorr, Bonnie J. (1992b) "A Parameterized Approach to Integrating Aspect with Lexical-Semantics for Machine Translation," *Proceedings of
30th Annual Conference of the Association of Computational Linguistics*, University of Delaware, Newark DE, 257–264.

Dorr, Bonnie J. (1992c) "Parameterization of the Interlingua in Machine
Translation," *Proceedings of Fourteenth International Conference on
Computational Linguistics*, Nantes, France, 624–630.

Dorr, Bonnie J. (1992d) "A Two-Level Knowledge Representation for
Machine Translation: Lexical Semantics and Tense/Aspect," in *Lexical Semantics and Knowledge Representation, Lecture Notes in Arti-*

ficial Intelligence 627, James Pustejovsky and Sabine Bergler (eds.), Springer Verlag, Berlin, Germany.

Dorr, Bonnie J. (1992e) "Lexical Semantics for Interlingual Machine Translation," *Machine Translation* 7:3.

Dorr, Bonnie J. (1993a) "A Lexical-Semantic Solution to the Divergence Problem in Machine Translation," in *Computational Lexical Semantics*, Patrick Saint-Dizier and Evelyn Viegas (eds.), Cambridge University Press, Cambridge, England.

Dorr, Bonnie J. (1993b) "Interlingual Machine Translation: A Parameterized Approach," *Artificial Intelligence* 63:1&2.

Dorr, Bonnie J. and Terry Gaasterland (1992) "Reflecting Time in Generated Text: Tense, Aspect and Temporal Connecting Words," Department of Computer Science, University of Maryland, College Park, MD, UMIACS TR 92-92, CS TR 2950.

Dorr, Bonnie J., Pam W. Jordan, and John W. Benoit (1993) "A Survey of Current Research Approaches to Machine Translation," manuscript, University of Maryland, College Park, MD.

Dorr, Bonnie J., and Clare Voss (1993) "Constraints on the Space of MT Divergences," *Working Notes for the AAAI Spring Symposium on Building Lexicons for Machine Translation*, Stanford University, CA.

Dorr, Bonnie J. and Ki Lee (1992) "Building a Lexicon for Machine Translation: Use of Corpora for Aspectual Classification of Verbs," Institute for Advanced Computer Studies, University of Maryland, College Park, MD, UMIACS TR 92-41, CS TR 2876.

Dowty, David (1979) *Word Meaning and Montague Grammar*, Reidel, Dordrecht, Netherlands.

Dowty, David (1991) "Thematic Proto-Roles and Argument Selection," *Language* 67:3, 547–619.

Dowty, D., L. Karttunen, and A. Zwicky (eds.) (1985) *Natural Language Processing: Theoretical, Computational, and Psychological Perspectives*, Cambridge University Press, New York.

Dymetman, Marc (1991) "Inherently Reversible Grammars, Logic Programming, and Computability," *Proceedings of the Reversible Grammar in Natural Language Processing Workshop, ACL-91*, University of California, Berkeley, CA, 20–30.

Earley, Jay (1970) "An Efficient Context-Free Parsing Algorithm," *Communications of the ACM* 13:2, 94–102.

Eberle, Kurt, Walter Kasper, and Christian Rohrer (1992) "Contextual Constraints for Machine Translation," *Proceedings of the Fourth International Conference on Theoretical and Methodological Issues in Machine Translation of Natural Languages*, Montreal, Canada, 213–224.

Elithorn, A. and R. Banerji (eds.) (1984) *Artificial and Human Intelligence*, Elsevier Science Publishers, Amsterdam, Holland.

Estival, Dominique (1990) "Generating French with a Reversible Unification Grammar," *Proceedings of Thirteenth International Conference on Computational Linguistics*, Helsinki, Finland, 106-112.

Eynde, Frank van (1990) "The Semantics of Tense and Aspect," in *Natural Language Processing, Lecture Notes in Artificial Intelligence 476*, M. Filgueiras, L. Damas, N. Moreira, A. P. Tomás (eds.), Springer-Verlag, Berlin, Germany, 158–184.

Farwell, David and Yorick Wilks (1991) "ULTRA: A Multi-lingual Machine Translator," *Proceedings of Machine Translation Summit*, Washinton, DC, 19–24.

Farwell, David, Louise Guthrie, and Yorick Wilks (1992) "The Automatic Creation of Lexical Entries for a Multilingual MT System," *Proceedings of Fourteenth International Conference on Computational Linguistics*, Nantes, France, 532–538.

Fass, Dan (1988) "Collative Semantics: A Semantics for Natural Language Processing," Computing Research Laboratory, New Mexico State University, Memorandum in Computer and Cognitive Science, MCCS-88-118.

Felshin, Susan, Dara Foias, Scott Prager, and Peter Schmidt (1989) "Kimmo Rules for German," Massachusetts Institute of Technology, Cambridge, MA, Athena Language Learning Project.

Fillmore, Charles J. (1968) "The Case for Case," in *Universals in Linguistic Theory*, Bach, E., and R. T. Harms (eds.), Holt, Rinehart, and Winston, 1–88.

Fodor, Janet D. (1990) "Parameters and Parameter-Setting in a Phrase Structure Grammar," in *Language Processing and Language Acquisition*, Lyn Frazier and Jill de Villiers (eds.), Kluwer Academic Publishers, Dordrecht, Holland, 225–255.

Fodor, Jerry A. (1970) "Three Reasons for Not Deriving "Kill" from "Cause to Die"," *Linguistic Inquiry* 1:4, 429–438.

Fong, Sandiway (1991) "Computational Properties of Principle-Based Grammatical Theories," Ph.D. thesis, Department of Electrical Engineering and Computer Science, Massachusetts Institute of Technology.

Frank, Robert (1990) "Licensing and Tree Adjoining Grammar in GB Parsing," *Proceedings of the 28th Annual Conference of the Association for Computational Linguistics*, University of Pittsburgh, Pittsburgh, PA, 111–118.

Frazier, Lyn and Jill de Villiers (eds.) (1990) *Language Processing and Language Acquisition*, Kluwer Academic Publishers, Dordrecht, Holland.

Fujii, Y., K. Suzuki, F. Maruyama, and T. Dasai (1990) "Analysis of Long Sentence In Japanese-English Machine Translation System," *Proceedings of Information Processing Society of Japan.*

Furuse, Osamu and Hitoshi Iida (1992) "An Example-Based Method for Transfer-Driven Machine Translation," *Proceedings of the Fourth International Conference on Theoretical and Methodological Issues in Machine Translation of Natural Languages*, Montreal, Canada, 139–150.

Gaasterland, Terry (1992) "Generating Cooperative Answers for Database Queries," Ph.D. thesis, Department of Computer Science, University of Maryland.

Gaasterland, Terry and Jack Minker (1991) "User Needs and Language Generation Issues in a Cooperative Answering System," *Proceedings of the ICLP Workshop on Advanced Logic Programming Tools and Formalisms for Language Processing*, Paris, France, 1–14.

Gazdar, G., E. Klein, G. Pullum, and I. Sag (1985) *Generalized Phrase Structure Grammar*, Basil Blackwell, Oxford, England.

Goldman, Neil M. (1975) "Conceptual Memory and Inference," in *Conceptual Information Processing*, Roger C. Schank (ed.), Elsevier Science Publishers, Amsterdam, Holland, 289–371.

Granville, Robert (1983) "Cohesion in Computer Text Generation: Lexical Substitution," Massachusetts Institute of Technology, Cambridge, MA, LCS Techical Report 310.

Grimshaw, Jane (1990) *Argument Structure*, MIT Press, Cambridge, MA.

Grimshaw, Jane and Armin Mester (1988) "Light Verbs and θ-Marking," *Linguistic Inquiry* 19:2, 205–232.

Grishman, Ralph and Michiko Kosaka (1992) "Combining Rationalist and Empiricist Approaches to Machine Translation," *Proceedings of the Fourth International Conference on Theoretical and Methodological Issues in Machine Translation of Natural Languages*, Montreal, Canada, 263–274.

Gruber, J. S. (1965) "Studies in Lexical Relations," Ph.D. thesis, Department of Information Science, Massachusetts Institute of Technology.

Haegeman, L. (1991) *Introduction to Government and Binding*, Basil Blackwell, Oxford, England.

Hale, Kenneth and S. Jay Keyser (1986a) "Some Transitivity Alternations in English," Center for Cognitive Science, Massachusetts Institute of Technology, Cambridge, MA, Lexicon Project Working Paper 7.

Hale, Kenneth and S. Jay Keyser (1986b) "A View from the Middle," Center for Cognitive Science, Massachusetts Institute of Technology, Cambridge, MA, Lexicon Project Working Paper 10.

Hale, Kenneth and S. Jay Keyser (1989) "On Some Syntactic Rules in the Lexicon," Center for Cognitive Science, Massachusetts Institute of Technology, Cambridge, MA, manuscript.

Hale, Kenneth and Mary Laughren (1983) "Warlpiri Lexicon Project: Warlpiri Dictionary Entries," Massachusetts Institute of Technology, Cambridge, MA, Warlpiri Lexicon Project.

Herweg, Michael (1991) "Aspectual Requirements of Temporal Connectives: Evidence for a Two-level Approach to Semantics," *Proceedings of the Lexical Semantics and Knowledge Representation Workshop, ACL-91*, University of California, Berkeley, CA, 152–164.

Hinrichs, E. W. (1988) "Tense, Quantifiers, and Contexts," *Computational Linguistics* 14:2, 3–14.

Hornstein, Norbert (1990) *As Time Goes By*, MIT Press, Cambridge, MA.

Hovy, Eduard (1988) *Generating Natural Language Under Pragmatic Constraints*, Lawrence Erlbaum Associates, Hillsdale, NJ.

Husain, Saadia (1989) "A Lexical Conceptual Structure Editor," Bachelor of Science thesis, Department of Electrical Engineering and Computer Science, Massachusetts Institute of Technology.

Hutchins, J. W. (1986) *Machine Translation: Past, Present, Future*, Ellis Horwood Limited, Chichester, England.

Hutchins, J. W. and H. L. Somers (1992) *An Introduction to Machine Translation*, Academic Press, London, England.

Hyams, Nina (1987) "The Theory of Parameters and Syntactic Development," in *Parameter Setting*, Thomas Roeper and Edwin Williams (eds.), D. Reidel Publishing Company, Dordrecht, Holland, 1–22.

Isabelle, Pierre (1987) "Machine Translation at the TAUM Group," in *Machine Translation: The State of the Art*, Margaret King (ed.), Edinburgh University Press, Edinburgh, 247–277.

Isabelle, Pierre and Laurent Bourbeau (1985) "TAUM-AVIATION: Its Technical Features and Some Experimental Results," *Computational Linguistics* 11:1, 18–27.

Ishikawa, Masahiko and Ryoichi Sugimura (1992) "Natural Language Analysis Using a Network Model: Modification Deciding Network," *Proceedings of the Fourth International Conference on Theoretical and Methodological Issues in Machine Translation of Natural Languages*, Montreal, Canada, 55–66.

Jackendoff, Ray S. (1983) *Semantics and Cognition*, MIT Press, Cambridge, MA.

Jackendoff, Ray S. (1990) *Semantic Structures*, MIT Press, Cambridge, MA.

Jackendoff, Ray S. (1992) "What is Semantic Structures About?," *Computational Linguistics* 18:2, 240–242.

Jacobs, Paul S. (1985) "PHRED: A Generator for Natural Language Interfaces," *Computational Linguistics* 11:4, 219–242.

Jaeggli, Osvaldo Adolfo (1981) *Topics in Romance Syntax*, Foris Publications, Dordrecht, Holland/Cinnaminson, USA.

Johnson, Mark (1989) "The Use of Knowledge of Language," *Journal of Psycholinguistic Research* 18:1.

Johnson, Rod, Maghi King, and Louis des Tombe (1985) "EUROTRA: A Multilingual System under Development," *Computational Linguistics* 11:2–3, 155–169.

Jones, Dan and Jun-ichi Tsujii (1990) "High Quality Machine-Driven Text Translation," *Proceedings of the Third International Conference on Theoretical and Methodological Issues in Machine Translation of Natural Languages*, Linguistics Research Center, The University of Texas, Austin, TX, 43–46.

Joshi, Aravind K. (1985) "How Much Context-Sensitivity is Necessary for Characterizing Structural Descriptions — Tree Adjoining Grammars," in *Natural Language Processing: Theoretical, Computational, and Psychological Perspectives*, D. Dowty, L. Karttunen, and A. Zwicky (eds.), Cambridge University Press, New York.

Kameyama, Megumi, Ryo Ochitani, Stanley Peters, and Hidetoshi Sirai (1991) "Resolving Translation Mismatches with Information Flow," *Proceedings of the 29th Annual Meeting of the Association for Computational Linguistics*, University of California, Berkeley, CA, 193–200.

Kaplan, Ronald M. and Joan Bresnan (1982) "Lexical-Functional Grammar: A Formal System for Grammatical Representation," in *The Mental Representation of Grammatical Relations*, Joan Bresnan (ed.), MIT Press, Cambridge, MA, 173–281.

Kaplan, Ronald M., Klaus Netter, Jürgen Wedekind, Annie Zaenen (1989) "Translation By Structural Correspondences," *Proceedings of Fourth Conference of the European Chapter of the Association for Computational Linguistics*, Manchester, 272–281.

Karttunen, L., and K. Wittenburg (1983) "A Two-Level Morphological Analysis of English," *Texas Linguistic Form* 22, 163–278.

Karttunen, L., Ronald M. Kaplan, and Annie Zaenen (1992) "Two-Level Morphology with Composition," *Proceedings of Fourteenth International Conference on Computational Linguistics*, Nantes, France, 141–148.

Kashket, Michael B. (1991) "A Parameterized Parser for English and Warlpiri," Ph.D. thesis, Department of Electrical Engineering and Computer Science, Massachusetts Institute of Technology.

Kay, Martin (1984) "Functional Unification Grammar: A Formalism For Machine Translation," *Proceedings of the Tenth International Conference on Computational Linguistics*, Stanford University, Stanford, CA, 75–78.

Kay, Martin (1991) "Monotonicity, Headedness, and Reversible Grammars," *Proceedings of the Reversible Grammar in Natural Language Processing Workshop, ACL-91*, University of California, Berkeley, CA.

King, Margaret (ed.) (1987) *Machine Translation: The State of the Art*, Edinburgh University Press, Edinburgh.

Kinoshita, Satoshi, John Phillips, and Jun-ichi Tsujii (1992) "Interaction Between Structural Changes in Machine Translation," *Proceedings of Fourteenth International Conference on Computational Linguistics*, Nantes, France, 679–685.

Kittredge, Richard I., Lidija Iordanskaja, and Alain Polguère (1988) "Multi-Lingual Text Generation and the Meaning-Text Theory," *Proceedings of the Conference on Theoretical and Methodological Issues in Machine Translation of Natural Languages*, Carnegie Mellon University, Pittsburgh, PA.

Kufner, Herbert L. (1962) *The Grammatical Structures of English and German*, University of Chicago Press, Chicago Illinois and London.

Lakoff, George (1971) "On Generative Semantics," in *Semantics: An Interdisciplinary Reader*, D. Steinberg and L. A. Jakobovits (eds.), Cambridge University Press, New York, 232–296.

Landsbergen, J., J. Odijk, and A. Schenk (1989) "The Power of Compositional Translation," *Literary and Linguistic Computing* 4:3.

Levin, Beth (1985) "Lexical Semantics in Review," Center for Cognitive Science, Massachusetts Institute of Technology, Cambridge, MA, Lexicon Project Working Paper 1.

Levin, Beth (in press) *English Verb Classes and Alternations: A Preliminary Investigation*, University of Chicago Press, Chicago, IL.

Levin, Beth and Malka Rappaport (1986) "The Formation of Adjectival Passives," *Linguistic Inquiry* 17, 623–662.

Lindop, Jeremy and Jun-ichi Tsujii (1991) "Complex Transfer in MT: A Survey of Examples," Center for Computational Linguistics, UMIST, Manchester, CCL/UMIST Report 91/5.

Lytinen, Steven and Roger C. Schank (1982) "Representation and Translation," Department of Computer Science, Yale University, New Haven, CT, Technical Report 234.

Marantz, Alec (1992) "The way-Constructions and the Semantics of Direct Arguments in English: A Reply to Jackendoff," Department of Linguistics and Philosophy, Massachusetts Institute of Technology, Cambridge, MA, manuscript.

Marcken, Carl de (1989) "Optimized Earley Parser Implementation for Context-Free Grammars," Artificial Intelligence Laboratory, Massachusetts Institute of Technology, Cambridge, MA.

Marcken, Carl de (1990a) "A Large-Scale Parser for Unrestricted Text," Bachelor of Science thesis, Department of Electrical Engineering and Computer Science, Massachusetts Institute of Technology.

Marcken, Carl de (1990b) "Parsing the LOB Corpus," *Proceedings of the 28th Annual Conference of the Association for Computational Linguistics*, University of Pittsburgh, Pittsburgh, PA, 243–251.

Marcus, Mitchell (1980) *A Theory of Syntactic Recognition for Natural Language*, MIT Press, Cambridge, MA.

Marrafa, Palmira and Patrick Saint-Dizier (1991) "Reversibility in a Constraint and Type Based Logic Grammar: Application to Secondary Predication," *Proceedings of the Reversible Grammar in Natural Language Processing Workshop, ACL-91*, University of California, Berkeley, CA, 2–11.

Martin, James (1991) "Representing and Acquiring Metaphor-Based Polysemy," in *Using On-Line Resources to Build a Lexicon*, Uri Zernik (ed.), Lawrence Erlbaum Associates, Hillsdale, NJ, 389–415.

Maruyama, Hiroshi and Hideo Watanabe (1992) "Tree Cover Search Algorithm for Example-Based Machine Translation," *Proceedings of the Fourth International Conference on Theoretical and Methodological Issues in Machine Translation of Natural Languages*, Montreal, Canada, 173–184.

Maxwell, Dan, Klaus Schubert, and Toon Witkam (eds.) (1988) *Recent Developments in Machine Translation*, Foris, Dordrecht, Holland.

Maybury, M. T. (1990) "Using Discourse Focus, Temporal Focus, and Spatial Focus to Plan Narrative Text," *Proceedings of the Fifth International Workshop on Natural Language Generation*, Dawson, Pennsylvania, 70–78.

McCawley, James (1968) "Lexical Insertion in a Transformational Grammar without D-Structure," in *Papers from the Fourth Regional Meet-*

ing of the Chicago Linguistic Society, B. Darden, C. J. N. Bailey and A. Davison (eds.), University of Chicago, Chicago, IL, 71–80.

McCord, Michael C. (1989) "Design of LMT: A Prolog-Based Machine Translation System," *Computational Linguistics* 15:1, 33–52.

McDonald, David D. (1983) "Natural Language Generation as a Computational Problem," in *Computational Models of Discourse*, Michael Brady and Robert C. Berwick (eds.), MIT Press, Cambridge, MA, 209–265.

McDonald, David D. (1991) "Reversible NLP by Deriving the Grammars from the Knowledge Base," *Proceedings of the Reversible Grammar in Natural Language Processing Workshop, ACL-91*, University of California, Berkeley, CA, 40–44.

McKeown, Kathleen (1985) *Text Generation: Using Discourse Strategies and Focus Constraints to Generate Natural Language Text*, Cambridge University Press, Cambridge, England.

McLean, Ian J. (1992) "Example-Based Machine Translation Using Connectionist Matching," *Proceedings of the Fourth International Conference on Theoretical and Methodological Issues in Machine Translation of Natural Languages*, Montreal, Canada, 35–43.

Melby, A. K. (1986) "Lexical Transfer: Missing Element in Linguistic Theories," *Proceedings of Eleventh International Conference on Computational Linguistics*, Bonn, Germany.

Mel'čuk, Igor and Alain Polguère (1987) "A Formal Lexicon in Meaning-Text Theory (Or How to Do Lexica with Words)," *Computational Linguistics* 13:3–4, 261–275.

Merlo, Paola (1992) "On Modularity and Compilation in a Government-Binding Parser," Ph.D. thesis, Department of Linguistics, University of Maryland.

Meyer, Ingrid, Boyan Onyshkevych, and Lynn Carlson (1990) "Lexicographic Principles and Design for Knowledge-Based Machine Translation," Carnegie Mellon University, CMU CMT Technical Report 90-118.

Miezitis, Mara (1988) "Generating Lexical Options by Matching in a Knowledge Base," Technical Report CSRI-217, Master of Science thesis, Department of Department of Computer Science, University of Toronto.

Mitamura, T., E. Nyberg, and J. Carbonell (1991) "An Efficient Interlingua Translation System for Multilingual Document Production," *Proceedings of Machine Translation Summit*, Washinton, DC, 55–61.

Moens, Marc and Mark Steedman (1988) "Temporal Ontology and Temporal Reference," *Computational Linguistics* 14:2, 15–28.

Montemagni, Simonetta and Lucy Vanderwende (1992) "Structural Patterns *vs.* String Patterns for Extracting Semantic Information from Dictionaries," *Proceedings of Fourteenth International Conference on Computational Linguistics*, Nantes, France, 546–552.

Mourelatos, Alexander (1981) "Events, Processes and States," in *Tense and Aspect*, P. J. Tedeschi and A. Zaenen (eds.), Academic Press, New York, NY.

Muraki, K. (1987) "PIVOT: A Two-Phase Machine Translation System," *Machine Translation Summit – Manuscripts and Program*, Japan, 81–83.

Nagao, Makoto (1984) "A Framework of a Mechanical Translation Between Japanese and English By Analogy Principle," in *Artificial and Human Intelligence*, A. Elithorn and R. Banerji (eds.), North-Holland.

Nagao, Makoto (1990) "Dependency Analyzer: A Knowledge-Based Approach to Structural Disambiguation," *Proceedings of Thirteenth International Conference on Computational Linguistics*, Helsinki, Finland, 282–287.

Nakhimovsky, A. (1988) "Aspect, Aspectual Class, and the Temporal Structure of Narrative," *Computational Linguistics* 14:2, 29–43.

Nash, David (1980) "Topics in Warlpiri Grammar," Ph.D. thesis, Department of Department of Linguistics and Philosophy, Massachusetts Institute of Technology.

Nassi, Robert J., Bernard Bernstein, and Theodore F. Nuzzi (1965) *Review Text in Spanish Three Years*, Amsco School Publications, New York, NY.

Neumann, Gunter (1991) "Reversibility and Modularity in Natural Language Generation," *Proceedings of the Reversible Grammar in Natural Language Processing Workshop, ACL-91*, University of California, Berkeley, CA, 31–39.

Nirenburg, Sergei (ed.) (1987) "Machine Translation: Theoretical and Methodological Issues," Cambridge University Press.

Nirenburg, Sergei (1989) "Knowledge-Based Machine Translation," *Machine Translation* 4:1, 5–24.

Nirenburg, Sergei, and Kenneth Goodman (1990) "Treatment of Meaning in MT Systems," *Proceedings of the Third International Conference on Theoretical and Methodological Issues in Machine Translation of Natural Languages*, Linguistics Research Center, The University of Texas, Austin, TX, 171–187.

Nirenburg, Sergei, and Lori Levin (1989) "Knowledge Representation Support," *Machine Translation* 4:1, 25–52.

Nirenburg, Sergei and Irene Nirenburg (1988) "A Framework for Lexical Selection in Natural Language Generation," *Proceedings of Twelveth International Conference on Computational Linguistics*, Budapest, Hungary, 471–475.

Nirenburg, Sergei and James Pustejovsky (1988) "Processing Aspectual Semantics," *Proceedings of Tenth Annual Conference of the Cognitive Science Society*, Montreal, Canada, 658–665.

Nirenburg, Sergei, Victor Raskin, and Allen B. Tucker (1987) "The Structure of Interlingua in TRANSLATOR," in *Machine Translation: Theoretical and Methodological Issues*, Sergei Nirenburg (ed.), Cambridge University Press, Cambridge, England, 90–113.

Nirenburg, Sergei, Rita McCardell, Eric Nyberg, Scott Huffman, and Edward Kenschaft (1988) "Lexical Realization in Natural Language Generation," *Proceedings of the Conference on Theoretical and Methodological Issues in Machine Translation of Natural Languages*, Carnegie Mellon University, Pittsburgh, PA.

Nirenburg, Sergei, Jaime Carbonell, Masaru Tomita, and Kenneth Goodman (1992) *Machine Translation: A Knowledge-Based Approach*, Morgan Kaufmann, San Mateo, CA.

Nomiyama, H. (1991) "Lexical Selection Mechanism Using Target language Knowledge and Its Learning Ability," NL86-8, IPSJ-WG.

Nomiyama, H. (1992) "Machine Translation by Case Generalization," *Proceedings of Fourteenth International Conference on Computational Linguistics*, Nantes, France, 714–720.

Noord, Gertjan van (1990) "Reversible Unification-Based Machine Translation," *Proceedings of Thirteenth International Conference on Computational Linguistics*, Helsinki, Finland, 299–304.

Noord, Gertjan van (1991) "Uniform Processing for Constraint-Based Categorial Grammars," *Proceedings of the Reversible Grammar in Natural Language Processing Workshop, ACL-91*, University of California, Berkeley, CA, 12–19.

Noord, Gertjan van, Joke Dorrepaal, Doug Arnold, Steven Krauwer, Lousia Sadler, and Louis des Tombe (1989) "An Approach to Sentence-Level Anaphora in Machine Translation," *Proceedings of Fourth Conference of the European Chapter of the Association for Computational Linguistics*, Manchester, 299–307.

Noord, Gertjan van, Joke Dorrepaal, Pim van der Eijk, Maria Florenza, and Louis des Tombe (1990) "The MiMo2 Research System," *Proceedings of the Third International Conference on Theoretical and Methodological Issues in Machine Translation of Natural Languages*, Linguistics Research Center, The University of Texas, Austin, TX, 213–233.

Okumura, Akitoshi, Kazunori Muraki, and Kiyoshi Yamabana (1992) "A Pattern-Larning Based, Hybrid Model for the Syntactic Analysis of Structural Relationships among Japanese Clauses," *Proceedings of the Fourth International Conference on Theoretical and Methodological Issues in Machine Translation of Natural Languages*, Montreal, Canada, 45–54.

Olsen, Mari Broman (1991) "Lexical Semantics, Machine Translation, and Talmy's Model of Motion Verbs," Northwestern University, Evanston, IL, Linguistics Working Paper, Volume 3.

Ostler, N. D. M. (1979) "Case-Linking: A Theory of Case and Verb Diathesis Applied to Classical Sanskrit," Ph.D. thesis, Department of Department of Linguistics and Philosophy, Massachusetts Institute of Technology.

Palmer, Martha and Alain Polguère (1992) "A Computational Perspective on the Lexical Analysis of Break," *Proceedings of the Second Seminar on Computational Lexical Semantics*, Toulouse, France, 145–146.

Passonneau, Rebecca J. (1988) "A Computational Model of the Semantics of Tense and Aspect," *Computational Linguistics* 14:2, 44–60.

Pereira, F. C. N. and D. H. D. Warren (1980) "Definite Clause Grammars for Language Analysis — A Survey of the Formalism and a Comparison with Transition Networks," *Artificial Intelligence* 13, 231–278.

Perlmutter, David M. (1983) *Studies in Relational Grammar 1*, The University of Chicago Press, Chicago, IL.

Perlmutter, David M., and Paul M. Postal (1983) "Toward a Universal Characterization of Passivization," in *Studies in Relational Grammar 1*, David M. Perlmutter (ed.), The University of Chicago Press, Chicago, IL, 3–29.

Pick, Herbert L. and Linda P. Acredolo (eds.) (1983) *Spatial Orientation: Theory, Research, and Application*, Plenum Press, New York.

Pinker, Steven (1989) *Learnability and Cognition: The Acquisition of Argument Structure*, MIT Press, Cambridge, MA.

Proctor, P. (1978) *Longman Dictionary of Contemporary English*, Longman, London, England.

Pustejovsky, James (1987) "On The Acquisition of Lexical Entries: The Perceptual Origin of Thematic Relations," *Proceedings of the 25th Annual Conference of the Association for Computational Linguistics*, Stanford University, Stanford, California, 172–178.

Pustejovsky, James (1988) "The Geometry of Events," Center for Cognitive Science, Massachusetts Institute of Technology, Cambridge, MA, Lexicon Project Working Paper 24.

Pustejovsky, James (1989) "The Semantic Representation of Lexical Knowledge," *Proceedings of the First International Lexical Acquisition Workshop*, IJCAI-89, Detroit, MI.

Pustejovsky, James (1990) "The Generative Lexicon," *Computational Linguistics* 17:4, 409–441.

Pustejovsky, James (1991) "The Syntax of Event Structure," *Cognition* 41.

Pustejovsky, James, and Sabine Bergler (1987) "The Acquisition of Conceptual Structure for the Lexicon," *Proceedings of the Sixth Conference of the American Association of Artificial Intelligence*, Seattle, Washington, 566–570.

Pustejovsky, James and Sabine Bergler (eds.) (1992) *Lexical Semantics and Knowledge Representation, Lecture Notes in Artificial Intelligence 627*, Springer Verlag, Berlin, Germany.

Pustejovsky, James, and Sergei Nirenburg (1987) "Lexical Selection in the Process of Generation," *Proceedings of the Sixth Conference of the American Association of Artificial Intelligence*, Seattle, Washington, 201–206.

Rappaport, Malka and Beth Levin (1988) "What to Do with Theta-Roles," in *Thematic Relations*, Wendy Wilkins (ed.), Academic Press.

Rappaport, Malka, Mary Laughren, and Beth Levin (1987) "Levels of Lexical Representation," Center for Cognitive Science, Massachusetts Institute of Technology, Cambridge, MA, Lexicon Project Working Paper 20.

Ratych, Joanna M. (1970) "Dreifaches Pech," in *Interessantes aus Deutschen Zeitungen*, Appleton-Century-Crofts, Meredith Corporation, New York, NY.

Reichenbach, H. (1947) *Elements of Symbolic Logic*, Macmillan, London.

Rieger, Charles J. III (1975) "Conceptual Memory and Inference," in *Conceptual Information Processing*, Roger C. Schank (ed.), Elsevier Science Publishers, Amsterdam, Holland, 157–288.

Ristad, Eric S. (1986) "Computational Complexity of Current GPSG Theory," Massachusetts Institute of Technology, Cambridge, MA, AI Memo 894.

Ritchie, Graeme (1992) "Languages Generated by Two-Level Morphological Rules," *Computational Linguistics* 18:1, 41–59.

Roeper, Thomas, and Jürgen Weissenborn (1990) "How to Make Parameters Work: Comments on Valian," in *Language Processing and Language Acquisition*, Lyn Frazier and Jill de Villiers (eds.), Kluwer Academic Publishers, Dordrecht, Holland, 147–162.

Roeper, Thomas and Edwin Williams (eds.) (1987) *Parameter Setting*, D. Reidel Publishing Company, Dordrecht, Holland.

Rosen, Carol G. (1984) "The Interface between Semantic Roles and Initial Grammatical Relations," in *Studies in Relational Grammar 2*, David M. Perlmutter and Carol G. Rosen (eds.), The University of Chicago Press, Chicago, IL, 38–77.

Sadler, Louisa and Doug Arnold (1992) "A Constraint-Based Approach to Translating Anaphoric Dependencies," *Proceedings of Fourteenth International Conference on Computational Linguistics*, Nantes, France, 728–234.

Sadler, Louisa and Henry S. Thompson (1991) "Structural Non-Correspondence in Translation," *Proceedings of Fifth Conference of the European Chapter of the Association for Computational Linguistics*, Berlin, Germany, 293–298.

Sadler, Louisa, Ian Crookston, Doug Arnold, and Andy Way (1990) "LFG and Translation," *Proceedings of the Third International Conference on Theoretical and Methodological Issues in Machine Translation of Natural Languages*, Linguistics Research Center, The University of Texas, Austin, TX, 121–130.

Safir, Ken (1985) "Missing Subjects in German," in *Studies in German Grammar*, Jindřich Toman (ed.), Foris Publications, Dordrecht, Holland/Cinnaminson, USA, 193–229.

Saint-Dizier, Patrick and Evelyn Viegas (eds.) (in press, 1993) *Computational Lexical Semantics*, Cambridge University Press, Cambridge, England.

Saito, Hiroaki and Masaru Tomita (1986) "On Automatic composition of Sterotypic Documents in Foreign Languages," Department of Computer Science, Carnegie Mellon University, CMU-CS-86-107.

Sanfilippo, Antonio, Ted Briscoe, Ann Copestake, Maria Antonia Marti, Mariona Taule, and Antonietta Alonge (1992) "Translation Equivalence and Lexicalization in the ACQUILEX LKB," *Proceedings of the Fourth International Conference on Theoretical and Methodological Issues in Machine Translation of Natural Languages*, Montreal, Canada, 1–11.

Sato, Satoshi, and Makoto Nagao (1990) "Toward Memory-Based Translation," *Proceedings of Thirteenth International Conference on Computational Linguistics*, Helsinki, Finland, 247–252.

Schank, Roger C. (1972) "Conceptual Dependency: A Theory of Natural Language Understanding," *Cognitive Psychology* 3, 552–631.

Schank, Roger C. (1973) "Identification of Conceptualizations Underlying Natural Language," in *Computer Models of Thought and Language*, Roger C. Schank and K. M. Colby (eds.), Freeman, San Francisco, CA, 187–247.

Schank, Roger C. (ed.) (1975) *Conceptual Information Processing*, Elsevier Science Publishers, Amsterdam, Holland.

Schank, Roger C. and Robert Abelson (1977) *Scripts, Plans, Goals, and Understanding*, Lawrence Erlbaum Associates, Inc., Hillsdale, NJ.

Schank, Roger C. and Kenneth M. Colby (eds.) (1973) *Computer Models of Thought and Language*, Freeman, San Francisco, CA.

Schank, Roger C. and Christopher K. Riesbeck (1981) *Inside Computer Understanding: Five Programs Plus Miniatures*, Lawrence Erlbaum Associates, Inc., Hillsdale, NJ.

Shaban, Marwan (1991) "GB Parsing of Arabic," Master of Science thesis, Department of Computer Science Department, Boston University.

Shapiro, S. C. (ed.) (1987) *Encyclopedia of Artificial Intelligence*, John Wiley and Sons, New York, NY.

Shapiro, S. C. (ed.) (1992) *Encyclopedia of Artificial Intelligence*, second edition, John Wiley and Sons, New York, NY.

Sharp, Randall M. (1985) "A Model of Grammar Based on Principles of Government and Binding," Master of Science thesis, Department of Computer Science, University of British Columbia.

Shieber, Stuart M., and Schabes, Yves (1990) "Synchronous Tree Adjoining Grammars," *Proceedings of Thirteenth International Conference on Computational Linguistics*, Helsinki, Finland, 253–258.

Shieber, Stuart M., Gertjan van Noord, Robert C. Moore, and Fernando C. N. Pereira (1989) "A Semantic-Head-Driven Generation Algorithm for Unification-Based Formalisms," *Proceedings of the 27th Annual Conference of the Association for Computational Linguistics*, University of British Columbia, Vancouver, British Columbia, Canada, 7–17.

Shieber, Stuart M., Gertjan van Noord, Robert C. Moore, and Fernando C. N. Pereira (1990) "Semantic-Head-Driven Generation," *Computational Linguistics* 16:1.

Shopen, Timothy (ed.) (1985) *Grammatical Categories and the Lexicon*, University Press, Cambridge, England.

Sigurd, Bengt (1988) "Translating to and from Swedish by SWETRA — a Multilanguage Translation System," in *Recent Developments in Machine Translation*, Dan Maxwell, Klaus Schubert, and Toon Witkam (eds.), Foris, Dordrecht, 205–218.

Sigurd, Bengt and Eeg-Olofsson, Mats (1991) "Prolog Implementations of English and Swedish GB Grammars," Department of Linguistics, Lund University, Working Papers 38, 169–197.

Siskind, Jeffrey Mark (1989) "Decomposition," Massachusetts Institute of Technology, Cambridge, MA, area exam paper.

Siskind, Jeffrey Mark (1992) "Naive Physics, Event Perception, Lexical Semantics, and Language Acquisition," Ph.D. thesis, Department of Electrical Engineering and Computer Science, Massachusetts Institute of Technology.

Slocum, Jonathan (1988) *Machine Translation Systems*, Cambridge University Press, Cambridge.

Somers, Harold (1992) "Interactive Multilingual Text Generation for a Monolingual User," *Proceedings of the Fourth International Conference on Theoretical and Methodological Issues in Machine Translation of Natural Languages*, Montreal, Canada, 151–161.

Somers, Harold, Jun-ichi Tsujii, and Dan Jones (1990) "Machine Translation Without a Source Text," *Proceedings of Thirteenth International Conference on Computational Linguistics*, Helsinki, Finland, 271–276.

Sondheimer, N., S. Cumming and R. Albano (1990) "How to Realize a concept: Lexical Selection and the Conceptual Network in Text Generation," *Machine Translation* 5:1, 57–78.

Sproat, Richard (1985) "Identification of Conceptualizations Underlying Natural Language," in *Lexical Semantics in Review*, Beth Levin, Lexicon Project Working Paper 1, Center for Cognitive Science, Massachusetts Institute of Technology, Cambridge, MA, 115–124.

Steinberg, D. and L. A. Jakobovits (eds.) (1971) *Semantics: An Interdisciplinary Reader*, Cambridge University Press, New York.

Stockwell, Robert P., J. Donald Bowen, and John W. Martin (1965) *The Grammatical Structures of English and Spanish*, University of Chicago Press, Chicago Illinois and London.

Stowell, Timothy A. (1981) "Origins of Phrase Structure," Ph.D. thesis, Department of Linguistics and Philosophy, Massachusetts Institute of Technology.

Strutz, Henry (1986) *1001 Pitfalls in German*, second edition, Barron's Educational Series, Inc., New York, NY.

Strzalkowski, Tomek (1991) "A General Computational Method for Grammar Inversion," *Proceedings of the Reversible Grammar in Natural Language Processing Workshop, ACL-91*, University of California, Berkeley, CA, 91–99.

Su, Keh-Yi and Jig-Shin Chang (1992) "Why Corpus-Based Statistics-Oriented Machine Translation," *Proceedings of the Fourth International Conference on Theoretical and Methodological Issues in Machine Translation of Natural Languages*, Montreal, Canada, 249–262.

Sumita, E., H. Iida and H. Kohyama (1990) "Example-Based Approach in Machine Translation," *Proceedings of InfoJapan*.

Talmy, Leonard (1983) "How Language Structures Space," in *Spatial Orientation: Theory, Research, and Application*, Herbert L. Pick, Jr., and Linda P. Acredolo (eds.), Plenum Press, New York, 225–282.

Talmy, Leonard (1985) "Lexicalization Patterns: Semantic Structure in Lexical Forms," in *Grammatical Categories and the Lexicon*, Timothy Shopen (ed.), University Press, Cambridge, England, 57–149.

Tedeschi, P. J. and A. Zaenen (eds.) (1981) *Tense and Aspect*, Academic Press, New York, NY.

Tenny, Carol (1987) "Grammaticalizing Aspect and Affectedness," Ph.D. thesis, Department of Linguistics and Philosophy, Massachusetts Institute of Technology.

Tenny, Carol (1989) "The Aspectual Interface Hypothesis," Center for Cognitive Science, Massachusetts Institute of Technology, Cambridge, MA, Lexicon Project Working Paper 1.

Thompson, Henry S. (1991) "Generation and Translation — Towards a Formalism-Independent Characterization," *Proceedings of the Reversible Grammar in Natural Language Processing Workshop, ACL-91*, University of California, Berkeley, CA, 53–60.

Thurmair, Gregor (1990) "Complex Lexical Transfer in METAL," *Proceedings of the Third International Conference on Theoretical and Methodological Issues in Machine Translation of Natural Languages*, Linguistics Research Center, The University of Texas, Austin, TX, 91–107.

Toman, Jindřich (ed.) (1985) *Studies in German Grammar*, Foris Publications, Dordrecht, Holland/Cinnaminson, USA, 193–229.

Torrego, Esther (1984) "On Inversion and Some of Its Effects," *Linguistic Inquiry* 15:1, 103–129.

Trujillo, Arturo (1992) "Locations in the Machine Translation of Prepositional Phrases," *Proceedings of the Fourth International Conference on Theoretical and Methodological Issues in Machine Translation of Natural Languages*, Montreal, Canada, 13–20.

Tsujii, Jun-ich and Kimikazu Fujita (1991) "Lexical Transfer Based on Bilingual Signs: Towards Interaction During Transfer," *Proceedings of the European Chapter of the Association for Computational Linguistics*, Berlin, Germany, 275–280.

Tsujii, Jun-ich and Makoto Nagao (1988) "Dialogue Translation *vs.* Text Translation: Interpretation Based Approach," *Proceedings of Twelveth International Conference on Computational Linguistics*, Budapest, Hungary, 688-693.

Uchida, H. (1989) "ATLAS: Fujitsu Machine Translation System," *Machine Translation Summit II – Manuscripts and Program*, Japan, 129–134.

Valentini, Erwin (ed.) (1991) *Studies in machine Translation and Natural Language Processing, Volume 1*, Commission of the European Communities, Brussels.

Vauquois Bernard (1975) *La Traduction Automatique à Grenoble*, Dunod, Paris.

Vauquois Bernard (1977) *L'évolution des Logiciels et des Modèles Linguistiques pour la Traduction Automatisée*, GETA, Grenoble.

Vauquois Bernard, and Christian Boitet (1985) "Automated Translation at Grenoble University," *Computational Linguistics* 11:1, 28–36.

Vendler, Zeno (1967) "Verbs and Times," *Linguistics in Philosophy*, 97–121.

Vilain, M. and H. Kautz and P. van Beek (1990) "Constraint Propagation Algorithms for Temporal Reasoning: A Revised Report," in *Readings in Qualitative Reasoning about Physical Systems*, D. Weld and J. de Kleer (eds.), Morgan Kaufmann, San Mateo, CA, 373–381.

Voss, Clare (forthcoming) "Encoding and Acquiring Lexical Representations for Machine Translation of Locative Expressions," Ph.D. thesis, Department of Computer Science, University of Maryland.

Wehrli, Eric (1992) "The IPS System," *Proceedings of Fourteenth International Conference on Computational Linguistics*, Nantes, France, 870–874.

Weinberg, Amy (1988) "Locality Principles in Syntax and in Parsing," Ph.D. thesis, Department of Department of Linguistics and Philosophy, Massachusetts Institute of Technology, Cambridge, MA.

Werner, P. and S. Nirenburg (1988) "A Specification Language that Supports the Realization of Intersentential Anaphora," *Proceedings of the AAAI Workshop on Natural Language Generation*, Saint Paul, Minnesota.

Wexler, Kenneth, and M. Rita Manzini (1987) "Parameters and Learnability in Binding Theory," in *Parameter Setting*, Thomas Roeper and Edwin Williams (eds.), D. Reidel Publishing Company, Dordrecht, Holland.

White, Michael (1992) "Conceptual Structures and CCG: Linking Theory and Incorporated Argument Adjuncts," *Proceedings of Fourteenth International Conference on Computational Linguistics*, Nantes, France, 246–252.

Whitelock, Pete (1991) "A Lexicalist Unification Grammar of Japanese," Ph.D. thesis, Department of Language and Linguistics, UMIST.

Whitelock, Pete (1992) "Shake-and-Bake Translation," *Proceedings of Fourteenth International Conference on Computational Linguistics*, Nantes, France, 784–791.

Wilkins, Wendy (ed.) (1988) *Thematic Relations*, Academic Press, New York, NY.

Wilks, Yorick (1973) "An Artificial Intelligence Approach to Machine Translation," in *Computer Models of Thought and Language*, Roger C. Schank and K. M. Colby (eds.), Freeman, San Francisco, CA, 114–151.

Wilks, Yorick (1987) "Primitives," in *Encyclopedia of Artificial Intelligence*, S. C. Shapiro (ed.), John Wiley and Sons, New York, NY, 759–761.

Wilks, Yorick (1992) "Book Review: Semantic Structures by Ray Jackendoff," *Computational Linguistics* 18:1, 95–97.

Wilks, Yorick and Dan Fass (1992) "Preference Semantics," in *Encyclopedia of Artificial Intelligence*, S. C. Shapiro (ed.), John Wiley and Sons, New York, NY, 1182–1194.

Wilks, Yorick, Dan Fass, Cheng-Ming Guo, James E. McDonald, Tony Plate, and Brian M. Slator (1990) "Providing Machine Tractable Dictionary Tools," *Machine Translation* 5:2, 99–154.

Williams, Brian (1990) "Doing Time: Putting Qualitative Reasoning on Firmer Ground," in *Readings in Qualitative Reasoning about Physical Systems*, D. Weld and J. de Kleer (eds.), Morgan Kaufmann, San Mateo, CA, 133–177.

Williams, Edwin (1987) "Introduction," in *Parameter Setting*, Thomas Roeper and Edwin Williams (eds.), D. Reidel Publishing Company, Dordrecht, Holland.

Winston, Patrick H. and Sarah Shellard (eds.) (1990) *Artificial Intelligence at MIT: Expanding Frontiers*, MIT Press, Cambridge, MA.

Yip, Kenneth M. (1985) "Tense, Aspect and the Cognitive Representation of Time," *Proceedings of the 23rd Annual Conference of the Association for Computational Linguistics*, Chicago, IL, 18–26.

Zajac, Rémi (1990) "A Relational Approach to Translation," *Proceedings of the Third International Conference on Theoretical and Methodological Issues in Machine Translation of Natural Languages*, Linguistics Research Center, The University of Texas, Austin, TX, 235–254.

Zajac, Rémi (1991) "A Uniform Architecture for Parsing, Generation, and Transfer," *Proceedings of the Reversible Grammar in Natural Language Processing Workshop, ACL-91*, University of California, Berkeley, CA, 71–80.

Zernik, Uri (ed.) (1991) *Using On-Line Resources to Build a Lexicon*, Lawrence Erlbaum Associates, Hillsdale, NJ.

Zubizarreta, Maria Luisa (1982) "On the Relationship of the Lexicon to Syntax," Ph.D. thesis, Department of Department of Linguistics and Philosophy, Massachusetts Institute of Technology.

Zubizarreta, Maria Luisa (1987) *Levels of Representation in the Lexicon and in the Syntax*, Foris Publications, Dordrecht, Holland/Cinnaminson, USA.

Index